THE ULTIMATE
HTML
REFERENCE

BY **IAN LLOYD**

The Ultimate HTML Reference

by Ian Lloyd

Copyright © 2008 SitePoint Pty Ltd

Managing Editor: Simon Mackie

Technical Editor: Toby Somerville

Expert Reviewer: Lachlan Hunt

Expert Reviewer: Tommy Olsson

Printing History:

First Edition: May 2008

Technical Director: Kevin Yank

Editor: Georgina Laidlaw

Cover Design: Simon Celen

Interior Design: Xavier Mathieu

Notice of Rights

Notice of Liability

Trademark Notice

Published by SitePoint Pty Ltd

48 Cambridge Street Collingwood
VIC Australia 3066
Web: www.sitepoint.com
Email: business@sitepoint.com

ISBN 978-0-9802858-8-8
Printed and bound in United States of America

About the Author

Ian Lloyd runs Accessify.com, a web accessibility site that he started in 2002, and has written or co-written a number of books on the topic of web standards and development, including SitePoint's best-selling beginners' title, *Build Your Own Web Site The Right Way using HTML & CSS*. Ian was previously a member of the Web Standards Project and is a regular speaker at web development conferences, including the highly regarded South By Southwest (SXSW) and @media events. He lives in Swindon, UK, with wife Manda and lively terrier Fraggle, and has a bit of a thing for classic Volkswagen camper vans.

About the Expert Reviewers

Lachlan Hunt (http://lachy.id.au/) worked as a front-end web developer, primarily developing with HTML, CSS, and JavaScript, for four years before joining Opera Software in late 2007.

As a developer and advocate of web standards, he has participated in the WHATWG (http://www.whatwg.org/) and various W3C working groups, including Web API, Web Application Formats, and HTML Working Groups, where he actively contributes to the work on HTML5.

Tommy Olsson is a pragmatic evangelist for web standards and accessibility who lives in the outback of central Sweden. Visit his blog at http://www.autisticcuckoo.net/.

About the Technical Editor

Toby Somerville is a serial webologist who caught the programming bug back in 2000. For his sins, he has been a pilot, a blacksmith, a web applications architect, and a freelance web developer. In his spare time he likes to kite buggy and climb stuff.

About the Technical Director

As Technical Director for SitePoint, **Kevin Yank** oversees all of its technical publications—books, articles, newsletters, and blogs. He has written over 50 articles for SitePoint, but is best known for his book, *Build Your Own Database Driven*

Website Using PHP & MySQL. Kevin lives in Melbourne, Australia, and enjoys performing improvised comedy theater and flying light aircraft.

About SitePoint

SitePoint specializes in publishing fun, practical, and easy-to-understand content for web professionals. Visit http://www.sitepoint.com/ to access our books, newsletters, articles, and community forums.

The Online Reference

The online version of this reference is located at http://reference.sitepoint.com/html. The online version contains everything in this book, and is fully hyperlinked and searchable. The site also allows you to add your own notes to the content and to view those added by others. You can use these user-contributed notes to help us keep the reference up to date, to clarify ambiguities, and to correct any errors.

Your Feedback

If you wish to contact us, for whatever reason, please feel free to email us at books@sitepoint.com. We have a well-staffed email support system set up to track your inquiries. Suggestions for improvement are especially welcome.

Reprint Permissions

Do you want to license parts of this book for photocopying, email distribution, intranet or extranet posting, or for inclusion in a coursepack? Please go to Copyright.com and type in this book's name or ISBN to purchase a reproduction license.

Table of Contents

HTML Concepts

Confused about when to use HTML and when to use XHTML? Want to know what the syntax differences are between the two? Do doctypes and DTDs leave you all discombobulated? Or perhaps you'd simply like to understand the basic structure of a web page?

This section deals with the high-level concepts relating to HTML and XHTML, rather than the specific elements or attributes. Even if you think you know HTML really well, there may be one or two surprises in this section (yes, even for you, there, at the back—the hardened HTML hacker who's been doing it for years!).

Basic Structure of a Web Page

While this reference aims to provide a thorough breakdown of the various HTML elements and their respective attributes, you also need to understand how these items fit into the bigger picture. A web page is structured as follows.

The Doctype

The first item to appear in the source code of a web page is the doctype (p. 6) declaration. This provides the web browser (or other user agent) with information about the type of markup language in which the page is written, which may or may not affect the way the browser renders the content. It may look a little scary at first glance, but the good news is that most WYSIWYG web editors will create the doctype for you automatically after you've selected from a dialog the type of document you're creating. If you aren't using a WYSIWYG web editing package, you can refer to the list of doctypes contained in this reference (p. 6) and copy the one you want to use.

The doctype looks like this (as seen in the context of a very simple HTML 4.01 page without any content):

```
<!DOCTYPE html PUBLIC "-//W3C//DTD HTML 4.01//EN"
    "http://www.w3.org/TR/html4/strict.dtd">
<html>
  <head>
    <title>Page title</title>
  </head>
  <body>
  </body>
</html>
```

In the example above, the doctype relates to HTML 4.01 Strict. In this reference, you'll see examples of HTML 4.01 and also XHTML 1.0 and 1.1, identified as such. While many of the elements and attributes may have the same names, there are some distinct syntactic differences between the various versions of HTML and XHTML. You can find out more about this in the sections entitled HTML Versus XHTML (p. 15) and HTML and XHTML Syntax (p. 11).

The Document Tree

A web page could be considered as a document tree that can contain any number of branches. There are rules as to what items each branch can contain (and these are detailed in each element's reference in the "Contains" and "Contained by" sections). To understand the concept of a document tree, it's useful to consider a simple web page with typical content features alongside its tree view, as shown in Figure 1.1.

```
─<html>
 ───<head>
 ──── ─<meta content="text/html;
        charset=UTF-8" http-equiv="Content-Type"/>
       └<title>My lovely web page</title>
     </head>
 ──── <body>
       ─<h1>This is my lovely web page</h1>
       ─<p>
         ─It has lots of lovely content. It has some
         ─<em>emphasized text</em>
         └and look at this, a blockquote:
        </p>
       ─<blockquote>
          └<p>You fools, I will destroy you
           all!</p>
        </blockquote>
       ─<h2>And here's a subheading</h2>
       ─<p>That about covers it, I think</p>
       └<hr/>
      </body>
    </html>
```

This is my lovely web page

It has lots of lovely content. It has some *emphasized text* and look at this, a blockquote:

> You fools, I will destroy you all!

And here's a subheading

That about covers it, I think

Figure 1.1: The document tree of a simple web page

If we look at this comparison, we can see that the `html` element in fact contains two elements: `head` and `body`. `head` has to subbranches—a `meta` element and a `title`. The `body` element contains a number of headings, paragraphs, and a `blockquote`.

Note that there's some symmetry in the way the tags are opened and closed. For example, the paragraph that reads, "It has lots of lovely content …" contains three text nodes, the second of which is wrapped in an `em` element (for emphasis). The paragraph is closed after the content has ended, and before the next element in the tree begins (in this case, it's a `blockquote`); placing the closing `</p>` after the `blockquote` would break the tree's structure.

html

Immediately after the doctype comes the `html` (p. 70) element—this is the root element of the document tree and everything that follows is a descendant of that root element.

If the root element exists within the context of a document that's identified by its doctype as XHTML, then the `html` element also requires an `xmlns` (XML Namespace) attribute (this isn't needed for HTML documents):

```
<html xmlns="http://www.w3.org/1999/xhtml">
```

Here's an example of an XHTML transitional page:

```
<!DOCTYPE html PUBLIC "-//W3C//DTD XHTML 1.0 Transitional//EN"
    "http://www.w3.org/TR/xhtml1/DTD/xhtml1-transitional.dtd">
<html xmlns="http://www.w3.org/1999/xhtml">
  <head>
    <title>Page title</title>
  </head>
  <body>
  </body>
</html>
```

The html element breaks the document in to two main sections: the head (p. 62) and the body (p. 32).

head

The head element contains meta data—information that describes the document itself, or associates it with related resources, such as scripts and style sheets.

The simple example below contains the compulsory title (p. 116) element, which represents the document's title or name—essentially, it identifies what this document is. The content inside the title may be used to provide a heading that appears in the browser's title bar, and when the user saves the page as a favorite. It's also a very important piece of information in terms of providing a meaningful summary of the page for the search engines, which display the title content in the search results. Here's the title in action:

```
<!DOCTYPE html PUBLIC "-//W3C//DTD XHTML 1.0 Transitional//EN"
    "http://www.w3.org/TR/xhtml1/DTD/xhtml1-transitional.dtd">
<html xmlns="http://www.w3.org/1999/xhtml">
  <head>
    <title>Page title</title>
  </head>
  <body>
  </body>
</html>
```

In addition to the title element, the head may also contain:

- `base` (p. 77)

  defines base URLs for links or resources on the page, and target windows in which to open linked content

- `link` (p. 82)

  refers to a resource of some kind, most often to a style sheet that provides instructions about how to style the various elements on the web page

- `meta` (p. 94)

  provides additional information about the page; for example, which character encoding the page uses, a summary of the page's content, instructions to search engines about whether or not to index content, and so on

- `object` (p. 357)

  represents a generic, multipurpose container for a media object

- `script` (p. 102)

  used either to embed or refer to an external script

- `style` (p. 111)

  provides an area for defining embedded (page-specific) CSS styles

All of these elements are optional and can appear in any order within the `head`. Note that none of the elements listed here actually appear on the rendered page, but they are used to affect the content on the page, all of which is defined inside the `body` element.

body

This is where the bulk of the page is contained. Everything that you can see in the browser window (or viewport) is contained inside this element, including paragraphs, lists, links, images, tables, and more. The `body` (p. 32) element has some unique attributes of its own, all of which are now deprecated, but aside from that, there's little to say about this element. How the page looks will depend entirely upon the content that you decide to fill it with; refer to the alphabetical listing of all HTML elements to ascertain what these contents might be.

Doctypes

The doctype declaration, which should be the first item to appear in the source markup of any web page, is an instruction to the web browser (or other user agent) that identifies the version of the markup language in which the page is written. It refers to a known Document Type Definition, or DTD for short. The DTD sets out the rules and grammar for that flavor of markup, enabling the browser to render the content accordingly.

The doctype contains a lot of information, none of which you will be likely to find yourself being tested on in a job interview, so don't worry if it all seems too difficult to remember. Besides, most web authoring packages will insert a syntactically correct doctype for you anyway, so there's little chance of you getting it wrong.

The doctype begins with the string <!DOCTYPE, which should be written in uppercase:

```
<!DOCTYPE html PUBLIC "-//W3C//DTD XHTML 1.0 Transitional//EN"
    "http://www.w3.org/TR/xhtml1/DTD/xhtml1-transitional.dtd">
```

The next part, which reads html (for XHTML) or HTML, refers to the name of the root element for the document. This information is included for validation purposes, since the DTD itself doesn't say which element is the root element in the document tree:

```
<!DOCTYPE html PUBLIC "-//W3C//DTD XHTML 1.0 Transitional//EN"
    "http://www.w3.org/TR/xhtml1/DTD/xhtml1-transitional.dtd">
```

The PUBLIC statement informs the browser that the DTD is a publicly available resource. If you had decided that the various flavors of HTML or XHTML were lacking in some way, and you wanted to extend the language beyond the defined specifications, you could go to the effort of creating a custom DTD. This would allow you to define custom elements, and would enable your documents to validate according to that DTD; in this case, you'd change the PUBLIC value to SYSTEM. That said, I've never actually seen an author do this—most people live within the limitations of the defined HTML/XHTML specifications (or plug the gaps using Microformats[1]). Here's the PUBLIC statement:

```
<!DOCTYPE html PUBLIC "-//W3C//DTD XHTML 1.0 Transitional//EN"
    "http://www.w3.org/TR/xhtml1/DTD/xhtml1-transitional.dtd">
```

The next section is known as the Public Identifier, and provides information about the owner or guardian of the DTD—in this case, the W3C. The Public Identifier, which is shown here, is *not* case sensitive: it also includes the level of the language that the DTD refers to (XHTML 1.0), and identifies the language of the DTD—*not* the content of the web page, it's important to note. This language is defined as English, or EN for short. Authors should not change this EN reference, regardless of the language contained in the web page.

Note that if the doctype contains the keyword SYSTEM, the Public Identifier section is omitted.

All of this information is highlighted in the short fragment below:

```
<!DOCTYPE html PUBLIC "-//W3C//DTD XHTML 1.0 Transitional//EN"
    "http://www.w3.org/TR/xhtml1/DTD/xhtml1-transitional.dtd">
```

Finally, the doctype includes a URL, known as the System Identifier, which refers to the location of the DTD. If you want to really geek out, you can copy and paste the address into your web browser's location bar and download a copy of the DTD, but be warned that it doesn't make for light reading! Here's the System Identifier:

```
<!DOCTYPE html PUBLIC "-//W3C//DTD XHTML 1.0 Transitional//EN"
    "http://www.w3.org/TR/xhtml1/DTD/xhtml1-transitional.dtd">
```

Table 1.1 shows the doctypes available in the WC3 recommendations.

---

[1] http://reference.sitepoint.com/html/microformats/

Table 1.1: Available Doctypes

Doctype	Description

`<!DOCTYPE html PUBLIC "-//W3C//DTD`
`➥ HTML 4.01//EN"`
`"http://www.w3.org/TR/html4/`
`➥strict.dtd">`
	HTML 4.01 Strict allows the inclusion of structural and semantic markup, but not presentational or deprecated elements such as font (p. 190). framesets (p. 494) are not allowed.

`<!DOCTYPE html PUBLIC "-//W3C//DTD`
`➥ HTML 4.01 Transitional//EN"`
`"http://www.w3.org/TR/html4/`
`➥loose.dtd">`
	HTML 4.01 Transitional allows the use of structural and semantic markup *as well as* presentational elements (such as font (p. 190)), which are deprecated in Strict. framesets (p. 494) are not allowed.

`<!DOCTYPE html PUBLIC "-//W3C//DTD`
`➥ HTML 4.01 Frameset//EN"`
`"http://www.w3.org/TR/html4/`
`➥frameset.dtd">`
	HTML 4.01 Frameset applies the same rules as HTML 4.01 Transitional, but allows the use of frameset (p. 494) content.

`<!DOCTYPE html PUBLIC "-//W3C//DTD`
`➥ XHTML 1.0 Strict//EN"`
`"http://www.w3.org/TR/xhtml1/DTD/`
`➥xhtml1-strict.dtd">`
	XHTML 1.0 Strict, like HTML4.01 Strict, allows the use of structural and semantic markup, but not presentational or deprecated elements (such as font (p. 190)); framesets (p. 494) are not allowed. Unlike HTML 4.01, the markup must be written as well-formed XML.

`<!DOCTYPE html PUBLIC "-//W3C//DTD`
`➥ XHTML 1.0 Transitional//EN"`
`"http://www.w3.org/TR/xhtml1/DTD/`
`➥xhtml1-transitional.dtd">`
	XHTML 1.0 Transitional, like HTML4.01 Transitional, allows the use of structural and semantic markup *as well as* presentational elements (such as font (p. 190)), which are deprecated in Strict; framesets (p. 494) are not allowed. Unlike HTML 4.01, the markup must be written as well-formed XML.

`<!DOCTYPE html PUBLIC "-//W3C//DTD`
`➥ XHTML 1.0 Frameset//EN"`
`"http://www.w3.org/TR/xhtml1/DTD/`
`➥xhtml1-frameset.dtd">`
	XHTML 1.0 Frameset applies the same rules as XHTML 1.0 Transitional, but also allows the use of frameset (p. 494) content.

`<!DOCTYPE html PUBLIC "-//W3C//DTD`
`➥ XHTML 1.1//EN"`
`"http://www.w3.org/TR/xhtml11/DTD/`
`➥xhtml11.dtd">`
	XHTML 1.1 is a reformulation of XHTML 1.0 Strict, thus most of the same rules apply. However, 1.1 allows for modularization, which means that you can add modules (for example, to provide Ruby

Doctype	Description
	support for Chinese, Japanese, and Korean characters).
`<!DOCTYPE HTML PUBLIC "-//W3C//DTD HTML 3.2 Final//EN">`	HTML 3.2 is an archaic doctype that's no longer recommended for use (it's included here for information only).
`<!DOCTYPE HTML PUBLIC "-//IETF//DTD HTML 3.0//EN">`	HTML 3.0 is an archaic doctype that's no longer recommended for use (it's included here for information only).
`<!DOCTYPE HTML PUBLIC "-//IETF//DTD HTML 2.0 Level 2//EN">`	HTML 2.0 is an archaic doctype that's no longer recommended for use (it's included here for information only). Note that there are actually 12 variants of this old doctype, all of which can be found in RFC1866[2] (refer to section 9.6).

Doctype Switching or Sniffing

The way in which a web browser renders a page's content is often affected by the doctype that's defined. Browsers use various modes to determine how to render a web page:

■ **Quirks Mode**

In this mode, browsers violate normal web formatting specifications as a way to avoid the poor rendering (or "breaking," to use the vernacular) of pages that have been written using practices that were commonplace in the late 1990s. The quirks differ from browser to browser. In Internet Explorer 6 and 7, the Quirks Mode displays the document as if it were being viewed in IE version 5.5. In other browsers, Quirks Mode contains a selection of deviations that are taken from Almost Standards mode (explained below).

■ **Standards Mode**

---

[2] http://www.ietf.org/rfc/rfc1866.txt

In this mode, browsers attempt to give conforming documents an exact treatment according to the specification (but this is still dependent on the extent to which the standards are implemented in a given browser).

Almost Standards Mode

Firefox, Safari, and Opera (version 7.5 and above) add a third mode, which is known as Almost Standards Mode. This mode implements the vertical sizing of table cells in a traditional fashion—not rigorously, as defined in the CSS2 specification. (Internet Explorer versions 6 and 7 don't need an Almost Standards Mode, because they don't implement the vertical sizing of table cells rigorously, according to the CSS2 specification, in their respective Standards Modes).

Depending on the doctype that's defined, and the level of detail contained inside the doctype (for example, whether it does or doesn't include a Public Identifier), different browsers trigger different modes from the list above. Doctype switching or sniffing refers to the task of swapping one doctype for another, or changing the level of detail in the doctype, in order to coax a browser to render in one of Quirks, Standards, or Almost Standards Modes.

An example of a situation in which doctype sniffing was put to use most frequently was to address rendering differences between Internet Explorer 6 and earlier versions of the browser, which calculated content widths differently when widths, padding, borders, and margins were applied in CSS. (This topic is not something we'll cover in this HTML reference, but you can find out more in The Ultimate CSS reference[3].) In Internet Explorer 6, depending on the doctype defined, a different rendering mode, namely "the correct way," or "the old IE way," would be used to calculate these widths.

As an example, imagine that you specify the doctype as HTML 4.01 Strict, like so:

```
<!DOCTYPE html PUBLIC "-//W3C//DTD HTML 4.01//EN"
    "http://www.w3.org/TR/html4/strict.dtd">
```

---

[3] http://reference.sitepoint.com/css/ie5boxmodel/

In IE6, the doctype above will cause the browser to render in Standards Mode, which includes using the W3C method for box model calculations. However, you see an entirely different result if you use the following doctype:

```
<!DOCTYPE HTML PUBLIC "-//W3C//DTD HTML 4.01 Transitional//EN">
```

In this scenario, IE6 will use its old, incorrect, non-W3C method for making box model calculations.

Note that this is not the *only* difference between Quirks and Standards Mode—it's *just one* example of the differences between the two modes (but one that caused a great deal of problems because of the disastrous effect it could have on page layout).

For a complete reference of how different browsers behave when different doctypes are provided, refer to the chart at the foot of Henri Sivonen's article "Activating Browser Modes with Doctype."[4]

HTML and XHTML Syntax

Writing valid HTML (or XHTML) is not a terribly difficult task once you know what the rules are, although the rules are slightly more stringent in XHTML than in HTML. The list below provides a quick reference to the rules that will ensure your markup is well-formed and valid. Note that there are other differences between HTML and XHTML which go beyond simple syntax requirements; those differences are covered in HTML Versus XHTML (p. 15).

The Document Tree

A web page is, at its heart, little more than a collection of HTML elements—the defining structures that signify a paragraph, a table, a table cell, a quote, and so on. The element is created by writing an opening tag, and completed by writing a closing tag. In the case of a paragraph, you'd create a p (p. 71) element by typing `<p>Content goes here</p>`.

---

[4] http://hsivonen.iki.fi/doctype/

The elements in a web page are contained in a tree structure in which html is the root element that splits into the head and body elements (as explained in Basic Structure of a Web Page (p. 1)). An element *may* contain other nested elements (although this very much depends on what the parent element is; for example, a p element can contain span, em, or strong elements, among others). Where this occurs, the opening and closing tags must be symmetrical. If an opening paragraph tag is followed by the opening em element, the closing tags must appear in the reverse order, like so: <p>Content goes here, and some of it needs emphasis too</p>. If you were to type <p>Content goes here, and some of it needs emphasis too</p>, you'd have created invalid markup.

Case Sensitivity

In HTML, tag names are case *in*sensitive, but in XHTML they're case sensitive. As such, in HTML, you can write the markup in lowercase, mixed case, or uppercase letters. So **<p>**this is a paragraph**</p>**, as is **<P>**this example**</P>**, and even **<P>**this markup would be valid**</p>**. In XHTML, however, you *must* use lowercase for markup: <p>This is a valid paragraph in XHTML</p>.

Opening and Closing Tags

In HTML, it's possible to omit some closing tags (check each element's reference to see whether an HTML closing tag is required), so this is valid markup: <p>This is my first paragraph.<p>This is my second paragraph.<p>And here's the last one..

In XHTML, all elements must be closed. Hence the paragraph example above would need to be changed to: <p>This is my first paragraph.</p><p>This is my second paragraph.</p><p>And here's the last one.</p>

As well as letting you omit some closing tags, HTML allows you to omit *start* tags—but only on the html, head, body, and tbody elements. This is not a recommended practice, but is technically possible.

For empty elements such as img (p. 333), XHTML requires us to use the XML empty element syntax: <elementname attribute="attributevalue"/>.

Readability Considerations

A browser doesn't care whether you use a single space to separate attributes, ten spaces, or even complete line breaks; it doesn't matter, as long as some space is present. As such, all of the examples below are perfectly acceptable (although the more spaces you include, the larger your web page's file size will be—each occurrence of whitespace takes up additional bytes—so the first example is still the most preferable):

```
<img src="/images/burj.jpg" alt="Burj Al Arab, iconic hotel in
Dubai" class="gallery"/>

<img
     src="/images/burj.jpg"
     alt="Burj Al Arab, iconic hotel in Dubai"
     class="gallery"
/>

<img

     src="/images/burj.jpg"

     alt="Burj Al Arab, iconic hotel in Dubai"

     class="gallery"/>
```

In XHTML all attribute values must be quoted, so you'll need to write `class="gallery"` rather than `class=gallery`. It's valid to omit the quotes from your HTML, though it *may* make reading the markup more difficult for developers revisiting old markup (although this really depends on the developer—it's a subjective thing). It's simply easier *always* to add quotes, rather than to have to remember in which scenarios attribute values require quotes in HTML, as the following piece of HTML demonstrates:

```
<a href="http://example.org">  needs to be quoted because it contains a /
<a href=index.html>  acceptable without quotes in HTML
```

Another reason why it's a good idea always to quote your attributes, even if you're using HTML 4.01, is that your HTML editor may be able to provide syntax coloring that makes the code even easier to scan through. Without the quotes, the software may not be able to identify the difference between elements, attributes, and attribute values. This fact is illustrated in Figure 1.2, which shows a comparison between quoted and unquoted syntax coloring in the Mac text editor TextMate.

```
<title>My lovely web page</title>
</head>

<body id=splash-page>
    <div id=main-content>
        <h1>This is my lovely web page</h1>
<p>It has lots of lovely content. It has son
blockquote:</p>
```

```
<title>My lovely web page</title>
</head>

<body id="splash-page">
    <div id="main-content">
        <h1>This is my lovely web page</h1>
<p>It has lots of lovely content. It has son
blockquote:</p>
```

Figure 1.2: TextMate's syntax coloring taking effect to display quoted attributes

Commenting Markup

You may add comments in your HTML, perhaps to make it clear where sections start or end, or to provide a note to remind yourself why you approached the creation of a page in a certain way. What you use comments for isn't important, but the way that you craft a comment *is* important. The HTML comment looks like this: `<!--this is a comment -->`. It's derived from SGML, which starts with an `<!` and ends with an `>`; the actual comment is, in effect, inside the opening `--` and the closing `--` parts. These hyphens tell the browser when to start ignoring text content, and when to start paying attention again. The fact that the `--` characters signify the beginning and end of the comment means that you *should not use them anywhere inside a comment*, even if you believe that your usage of these characters conforms to SGML rules. Note that you can't use hyphens inside XML comments at all, which is an even stronger reason not to get into the habit.

The markup below shows examples of good and bad HTML comments—see the remark associated with each example for more information:

```
<p>Take the next right.<!-- Look out for the
    signpost for 'Castle' --></p>  a valid comment

<p>Take the next right.<!-- Look out for -- Castle --></p>
not a valid comment; the double dashes in the middle could be
misinterpreted as the end of the comment

<p>Take the next right.<!-- Look out for -- -- Castle --></p>
a valid comment; 'Look out for' is one comment, 'Castle' is another

<p>Take the next right.
  <!----------- --------------------
  This is just asking for trouble. Too
  many hyphens! --></p>
a valid comment; don't use hyphens or <> characters to format comment text

<p <!-- class="lively" -->>Wowzers!</p>
It's not possible to comment out attributes inside an HTML element
```

HTML Versus XHTML

The argument about whether to use HTML or XHTML is one that comes up time and time again. Not so long ago, everyone was advising the use of XHTML almost without question, for no other reason than that it's a newer implementation of HTML and therefore the better option. However, many people who once recommended using XHTML have since changed their minds on the topic—including some SitePoint authors who made very strong arguments as to why examples in their books should be presented in HTML 4 rather than XHTML 1.1.[5]

It seems that we need to clarify what HTML and XHTML are, what their differences are, and why one or the other should be used.

The first thing you should realize is that using HTML is not wrong as long as you specify that you're using HTML with the appropriate doctype (p. 6), and the HTML you use is valid for that doctype. If you want to use HTML 4.01, no one can stop you! Ignore anyone who tells you that XHTML is way to go, and that using HTML

---

[5] This is a topic that I've had to address, as my beginners' book on HTML and CSS, Build Your Own Web Site The Right Way Using HTML & CSS [http://www.sitepoint.com/books/html1/], used XHTML, while the SitePoint Forums members argued about which flavor of HTML should be used. This argument prompted more than a few people who bought my book as complete beginners to ask me directly, "Why do you recommend using XHTML while some people say not to use it?"

4.01 is somehow backwards. That said, you should be aware of the differences between HTML and XHTML, as these may affect your choice of markup.

Main Differences Between XHTML and HTML

The following list details the main differences between XHTML and HTML. Most of them are related to syntax differences, although there are some less obvious variations that you may not be aware of:

- XHTML is more choosy than HTML—there are some elements that absolutely must appear in the XHTML markup, but which may be omitted if you're using HTML 4 and earlier versions. These elements include the `html` (p. 70), `head` (p. 62), and `body` (p. 32) elements (although why you'd want to omit any of them is a mystery to me). In addition, every element you use in XHTML must have both an opening and closing tag (for example, you'd write `<p>This is a paragraph</p>` in XHTML, but `<p>This is all you need` in HTML, as no end tag is required).

- For empty elements—those that hold no content but refer to a resource of some kind, such as an `img` (p. 333), `link` (p. 82), or `meta` (p. 94) element—the tag must have a trailing closing slash, like so: `<img src="moo.jpg" alt="moo"/>`. Evidently, this makes XHTML a little more verbose than HTML, but not to the extent that it has an adverse effect on the page weight.

- XHTML allows us to indicate any element as being empty—for example, an empty paragraph can be expressed as `<p/>`—but this isn't valid when the page is served as text/html[7]. To that end, you should restrict your use of this syntax to elements that are defined to be empty in the HTML specifications.

- In XHTML, all tags must be written in lowercase. In HTML, you can use capital letters for elements, lowercase letters for attributes, or whatever convention you like!

- All attributes in XHTML must be contained in quotes (single or double, but usually double), hence `<input type=submit name=cmdGo/>` would be valid in HTML 4.01, but would be invalid in XHTML. To be valid, it would need to be `<input type="submit" name="cmdGo"/>`.

---

[7] http://reference.sitepoint.com/html/mime-types/

- In XHTML, all attributes must be expressed in attribute-name and attribute-value parings with quote marks surrounding the attribute value part, like so: `class="fuzzy"`.

- In HTML, some elements have attributes that do not *appear* to require a value—for example, the `checked` attribute for checkbox `input` elements (p. 269). I stressed the word "appear" because technically it's the attribute *name* that's omitted, not the value. These are known as Boolean attributes, and in HTML you could specify that a checkbox should be checked simply by typing `<input type="checkbox" name="chkNewsletter" `**`checked`**`>`. In XHTML, though, you must supply both an attribute and value, which results in seemingly needless repetition: `<input type="checkbox" name="chkNewsletter" `**`checked="checked"`**`>`.

- In XHTML, the opening `<html>` tag requires an `xmlns` attribute (XML NameSpace) as follows: `<html `**`xmlns="http://www.w3.org/1999/xhtml"`**`>`. However, strangely, if you omit it, the W3C validator doesn't protest as it should.

- XHTML requires certain characters to appear as named entities. For example, you can't use the & character: it must be expressed using an HTML entity "`&amp;`".

- In XHTML, languages in the document must be expressed using the `xml:lang` attribute instead of `lang`.

- A MIME type must be declared appropriately in the HTTP headers as `"application/xhtml+xml"` (this is the best option), `"application/xml"` (acceptable), or `"text/xml"` (which isn't recommended). The MIME type is set as a configuration option on the server, and is usually Apache or IIS.

- DTDs don't support the validation of mixed namespace documents very well.

- If you use XHTML and set the proper MIME type (see the section below called Serving the Correct MIME Type (p. 20)), you'll encounter a small snag: Internet Explorer. At the time of writing, this browser—which still holds the lion's share of the market—is the only one of the browsers tested for this reference that can't handle a document set with a MIME type of `"application/xhtml+xml"`. When IE encounters a page that contains this HTTP header, it doesn't render the page on screen, but instead prompts the user to download or save the document.

- When you're using XHTML, text encoding should be set within the XML declaration, not in the HTTP headers.

In addition to these points, there are a number of differences between the way that an XHTML document handles scripts and the way it handles style sheets, including:

- There are requirements for the way in which comments inside scripts should be handled; Lachlan Hunt covers this topic thoroughly in his blog entry, "HTML Comments in Scripts."[8]
- `document.write()` and `document.writeln()` do not work in XHTML.
- `innerHTML` property is also ignored by some user agents.
- As XHTML is case sensitive, there can be an issue with element and attribute names in DOM methods. For example, `onClick` and `onSubmit` are invalid, while `onclick` and `onsubmit` are valid.

The list above might discourage some newcomers from learning the XHTML syntax—it does certainly appear that, at the very least, XHTML requires more discipline and thought than HTML! However, one advantage of learning XHTML syntax rather than the looser HTML syntax it is that if you stick to the rules I've outlined above, you'll be creating pages that render just as HTML would in the browser, but which also validate as XHTML. The presence of some XHTML-specific attributes—namely the `xmlns` attribute in the root element, and the use of `xml:lang` rather than `lang`—does mean that you can't simply change the doctype (p. 6) of a valid XHTML document back to an HTML doctype and have the page validate, though. It will contain features that are not understood by, or accepted in, the HTML specifications.

So, there's nothing wrong with learning the HTML 4.01 syntax to begin with, and progressing to XHTML when you feel more comfortable doing so. The transition from HTML to XHTML doesn't have to be a massive step, although some of the habits you'll have picked up while you were marking up HTML documents will need to be unlearned to make this a successful transition. Learning HTML 4.0 is not a bad thing, and it doesn't make you a lazy coder—it's just *different* from XHTML.

---

[8] http://lachy.id.au/log/2005/05/script-comments/

Does XHTML Reduce Your Markup Toolset?

You may have heard or read that choosing XHTML means that you can't use certain presentational elements such as `center` (p. 178), `font` (p. 190), `basefont` (p. 174), or `u` (p. 227). But this isn't strictly true. You may use these elements in XHTML Transitional and Frameset just as you could in HTML Transitional and Frameset—the difference is that they're not allowed in the Strict versions of these markup languages. Hopefully that's a myth busted!

If you do opt to use XHTML Strict (or HTML Strict), and you thereby lose these presentational elements, you'll definitely need to rely on CSS to do the work of prettying things up; this approach also places just a little more emphasis on the use of more structurally orientated elements available in HTML and XHTML. But don't be led to believe that XHTML is in some way *more* structural than HTML 4.01. You're not going to be adding new structural features through your use of XHTML—headings, paragraphs, block quotes, and so on were all present in HTML 4.01.

Regardless of the flavor of markup you choose—HTML or XHTML—you can easily mark up your page using a series of `div` (p. 44) and `span` (p. 220) elements, style it entirely in CSS, validate it, and still be left with a document that offers no apparent meaning or structure about the content it contains. In short, the language is only as good as the pair of hands responsible for crafting it, and thus XHTML doesn't guarantee a better end result!

Opting for HTML for Optimized Page Weights

One possible reason for using HTML 4.01 over XHTML (of any kind or level of strictness) might be that page size is a very important consideration. For example, you may be creating a page that needs to be downloaded over a restricted connection, perhaps to a mobile device of some kind. By using HTML 4.01, you're able to reduce the markup by not using quote marks and not using closing tags where the spec indicates that they're optional.

If you're building your own personal web site, or you're building a site for an organization that doesn't have (or expect) huge amounts of traffic, the aim of achieving slightly leaner page weights probably won't be a *strong* case for using

HTML 4.01. However, if we're talking about a site that receives a significant amount of traffic, the savings may well add up, so you might need to get your calculator out! For example, if your use of HTML 4.01 means that you can omit 100 bytes of characters from a given document (without those deletions having an adverse effect on the document's presentation in the browser), and if that document receives one million hits a day, over the course of a month that saving will amount to almost 3GB of bandwidth. Now, this is just a hypothetical scenario, and this is but one page in a web site, but depending on the number of visitors your site attracts, a shaving of markup here, and a corner cut there—all the while ensuring that your page validates as HTML 4.01—really can encourage you to use HTML rather than XHTML.

Serving the Correct MIME Type

If you intend to create a web page that can be treated as XML and parsed accordingly, you'd probably create that page in XHTML. You may also want to take this course of action for the purposes of including another XML-based technology such as MathML or CML (Chemical Markup Language) in your page. If you do find yourself needing to use those technologies, you're almost certainly not a "typical" web page author, and as such, most of what follows won't really concern you too much ...

In order for your page to be interpreted as proper XML, you must serve it with a MIME type of `"application/xhtml+xml"` (normally, web pages are served as `"text/html"`). Once you do so, you'll have to be *very* careful with the coding of your web page. One validation slip-up—for example, an unquoted attribute value, a non-symmetrical opening and closing of tags, or an unclosed tag—and your web page won't render at all. Users will be presented with a fatal server error of some kind, which will tell them that the page couldn't be parsed or understood. It's very unforgiving!

Here's a simple test that you can try for yourself. Create a simple HTML page using the markup below:

```
<!DOCTYPE html PUBLIC "-//W3C//DTD XHTML 1.0 Transitional//EN"
    "http://www.w3.org/TR/xhtml1/DTD/xhtml1-transitional.dtd">
<html xmlns="http://www.w3.org/1999/xhtml">
  <head>
```

```
      <title>Page title</title>
   </head>
   <body>
     <h1>Hello world</h1>
     <p>This is a web page.</p>
   </body>
 </html>
```

Now save this document with the file extension `.xhtml`, rather than `.htm` or `.html`. Next, open the file in Firefox, Opera, or Safari. Is everything looking okay? Now, make a subtle change: amend the closing `</h1>`—and *only* the closing `</h1>`—to use an uppercase H. Refresh the page and see what happens. If everything's gone to plan, you'll now be looking at a broken web page, similar to the one shown in Figure 1.3.

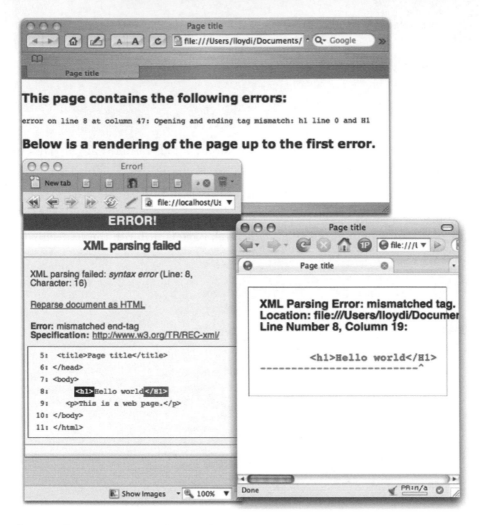

Figure 1.3: A mismatched tag breaking an XHTML document when served as `"application/xhtml+xml"`

What's important about this exercise is that the behavior displayed by these browsers when they open a local file that's not well formed, and has the `.xhtml` extension, is *exactly* the same as the error that they'd present if they encountered a malformed page on the web that was served with the MIME type `"application/xhtml+xml"`. Bear in mind that even if you take the utmost care with your own code, it only takes one poorly formed user comment to do the necessary damage! I'm sure you can see what a tricky problem this can be!

The argument against using XHTML is basically this: if you're not using XHTML for the purposes of creating an XML-based web application of some kind, there's no real reason to use XHTML—you may as well stick to HTML. And if you're intent on creating a web page that validates as XHTML, but it is served with the `"text/html"` MIME type, you won't really reap any kind of benefit either. So if you want to use XHTML, learn it properly and be sure to understand the pitfalls. Otherwise, you may be better off with HTML.

XHTML: Encouraging Good Practices?

I advise people to learn XHTML, not HTML, regardless of whether the web page is going to be treated as an XML web application of some kind or as a simple web page (for more on this thorny topic, see the section entitled Serving the Correct MIME Type (p. 20)). By taking this approach, you're encouraged to nest elements properly, close all your tags properly, and use quotes around all your attributes. This is my preference, but I'm under no illusion as to the fact that if I serve one of these web pages as `"application/xhtml+xml"` and it contains even a slight error, all my good work will end with the fatal error mentioned above. That said, should I later wish to incorporate XML features into my pages, I will have a good starting point to work from.

Given that this is a reference, rather than a guide aimed at total beginners, you likely already know a certain amount about HTML and XHTML; you may feel more comfortable taking the same approach, and using the XHTML syntax. If you're a beginner, however, you may prefer to start with HTML 4.01, but you should still follow the rules for that version of HTML.

HTML/XHTML Accessibility Features

The topic of web accessibility is a detailed and complicated one that can't be explored to the full in this reference. However, many of the HTML elements covered in this reference are designed to improve the accessibility of the content, or have specific attributes that support this goal. Where these elements occur, their accessibility features will be mentioned.

In a nutshell, the concept of accessibility focuses on making your web content easy for a wide range of users to access. This may include people with vision impairments (which can include a wide variety of such impairments, from simple short-sightedness, to complete blindness), people with mobility problems (from a shaky hand resulting from illness, or temporary impairment such as wearing a cast on a broken wrist, to permanent impairments like those experienced by amputees or people suffering paralysis), and those with cognitive issues. While it may seem as if there are a lot of people for whom you may need to make adjustments, the reality is that HTML (or XHTML) is actually a fairly accessible medium to begin with, and is usually made less accessible through the use of harmful techniques. Many of these techniques were introduced many years ago as workarounds to perceived shortcomings in browsers; many developers still use them today, much to the chagrin of more standards-aware web developers.

If you stick to using the right markup for the job—applying headings, lists, paragraphs, and blockquotes as they were intended to be applied—you'll be well on the way to creating accessible content. However, in addition to these basics, a number of HTML elements or attributes that were introduced in HTML 4.01 may be used to enhance the content's accessibility even further. In order to save you time and effort hunting these items down, I've compiled the list below to provide pointers to the most relevant areas.

Tables

- `table` - `summary` attribute (p. 419)

  provides a non-visual summary of the table's content or purpose, which may be useful to people accessing the table using assistive technology

- `th/td` - `scope` attribute (p. 471)

  specifies the direction of the table cells that the header cell relates to

- `th/td` - `headers` attribute (p. 438)

  indicates which table headers are related to a given table data cell, providing context for the data for users of non-visual browsers

Forms

▪ `fieldset` (p. 241) and `legend` (p. 282) elements

logically group related form controls, and provide a title for the grouping via the `legend` element

▪ `label` element (p. 277)

links a form control to the associated descriptive text in a totally unambiguous way—a great aid for users of non-visual browsers, such as those using screen readers to interact with forms

Images

▪ `alt` attribute (p. 337)

provides a text alternative for an important image; can be applied to `img` element or to an `input` of `type` `"image"` (p. 269)

▪ `longdesc` attribute (p. 346)

provides a link to additional information, contained in a separate text file, about the image

General Aids

▪ a well-written document `title` (p. 116)

Although it's not an accessibility feature as such, it's worth noting that the `title` is what will be read out first for screen reader users; hence it provides a golden opportunity for explaining what is to follow.

▪ headings (`h1` (p. 46)-`h6` (p. 60))

Headings provide users of such assistive devices as screen readers with an additional—and quick—method for navigating through a document by skipping from heading to heading.

▪ list items (in `ul` (p. 138) or `ol` (p. 131) elements)

Wrapping navigation items in a list allows users of assistive technology to skip entire blocks of navigation easily, jumping from one navigation level to another.

2

Structural Elements

The elements in this section are used to provide structure in a web page, for instance, indicating sections on a page with a heading, creating a paragraph, and so on. These are the basic building blocks that you'll find yourself using on any web page.

blockquote

```
<blockquote cite="uri">
</blockquote>
```

SPEC		
deprecated	empty	version
NO	NO	HTML 3.2
BROWSER SUPPORT		
IE5.5+ FF1+	Saf1.3+	Op9.2+
PARTIAL PARTIAL	PARTIAL	PARTIAL

Example

The example below is a quote from an as yet unidentified source who despairs about the stupidity of stock photography:

```
<blockquote>
  <p>It's missing alt text, so it's difficult to determine what it's
     supposed to mean. Presumably "oooh, there's been a global
     ecological catastrophe and we've got the last four leaves in the
     world and we've patented the DNA". Or they're rubbing ganja
     leaves together to extract the resin, but are too stupid to
     recognise Marijuana so are trying it with willow or silver
     birch.</p>
</blockquote>
```

The `blockquote` element is a mechanism for marking up a block of text quoted from a person or another document or source. It may be just a few lines, or it may contain several paragraphs (which you'd mark up using nested p (p. 71) elements).

The W3C recommendation states that web page authors should not type quotation marks in the text when they're using `blockquote`—we can leave it to the style sheets to take care of this element of presentation (just as it should be when the q (p. 204) element is used for short, inline quotations). In practice, though, many authors do choose to include quote marks, as browser support for automatically inserting the language-appropriate quotation marks is extremely poor.

By default, most browsers' basic built-in style sheets render `blockquote` content with left and right indentations, as shown in Figure 2.1. As a consequence, many people learned to use `blockquote` to indent the text as a way to draw attention to a paragraph or section of a page. Of course, this is bad practice—it's simply the wrong markup for the job. Only use `blockquote` if you're actually quoting a source; to visually indent a block of text that's *not* a quotation, use CSS (`margin-left`, or any other style property you care to choose).

Note that XHTML allows the `blockquote` element to contain only other block-level elements; in HTML4, the `script` element is also allowed.

> This is a normal paragraph, for comparison's sake. This is a normal paragraph, for comparison's sake. This is a normal paragraph, for comparison's sake. This is a normal paragraph, for comparison's sake. This is a normal paragraph, for comparison's sake. This is a normal paragraph, for comparison's sake.
>
> > It's missing alt text, so it's difficult to determine what it's supposed to mean. Presumably "oooh, there's been a global ecological catastrophe and we've got the last four leaves in the world and we've patented the DNA". Or they're rubbing ganja leaves together to extract the resin, but are too stupid to recognise Marijuana so are trying it with willow or silver birch.
>
> This is a normal paragraph, for comparison's sake. This is a normal paragraph, for comparison's sake. This is a normal paragraph, for comparison's sake. This is a normal paragraph, for comparison's sake. This is a normal paragraph, for comparison's sake. This is a normal paragraph, for comparison's sake.

Figure 2.1: A `blockquote` between two normal paragraphs (note indentation)

Use This For ...

This element is used to mark up one or more paragraphs, which may themselves contain other inline elements (for example `strong` (p. 223), `em` (p. 189) or `a` (p. 146) elements).

Compatibility

Internet Explorer			Firefox			Safari			Opera
5.5	6.0	7.0	1.0	1.5	2.0	1.3	2.0	3.0	9.2
Partial	Partial	Partial	Partial	Partial	Partial	Partial	Partial	Partial	Partial

`blockquote` has been around a long time, but it hasn't aged a day. If you use it in a situation where style sheets aren't applied, and you're relying only on the browser's default (or built-in) set of styles, the `blockquote` renders almost identically across all browsers, just as it did in some of the earliest browsers, none of which rendered the `cite` attribute's value on the page.

The support chart shows as `"partial"` rather than `"full"` because the browsers lack support for indicating the source of the quote through the `cite` (p. 30) attribute.

Other Relevant Stuff

    q (p. 204)

defines an inline quotation

cite *for <blockquote>*

`cite="uri"`

SPEC		
deprecated	required	version
NO	NO	HTML 3.2
BROWSER SUPPORT		
IE7	FF2	Saf3	Op9.2
NONE	NONE	NONE	NONE

Example

This example shows an attribution, created using the `cite` attribute:

```
<blockquote cite="http://www.brucelawson.co.uk/index.php/2005/
➥stupid-stock-photography/">
  <p>It's missing alt text, so it's difficult to determine what it's
     supposed to mean. Presumably "oooh, there's been a global
     ecological catastrophe and we've got the last four leaves in the
     world and we've patented the DNA". Or they're rubbing ganja
     leaves together to extract the resin, but are too stupid to
     recognise Marijuana so are trying it with willow or silver
     birch.</p>
</blockquote>
```

As well as the core (p. 498) and event attributes (p. 509), which are used across all HTML elements, `blockquote` has the `cite` attribute, which is used to identify the online source of the quotation in the form of a URI (for example, `"http://sourcewebsite.doc/document.html"`); the value of the `cite` attribute is not rendered on the screen. As such, browser support for this attribute is marked as none, but because it has other potential uses (for example, in search engine indexing, retrieval of its content via DOM Scripting, and more), and since improved native support for the attribute is anticipated in future browser versions, you should use the `cite` attribute when you use `blockquote`.

Value

The value of `cite` is a URI: the complete path to the source of the quotation (that is, not a relative path from the quoting page).

Compatibility

Internet Explorer			Firefox			Safari			Opera
5.5	6.0	7.0	1.0	1.5	2.0	1.3	2.0	3.0	9.2
None	None	None	None	None	None	None	None	None	None

cite is uniformly ignored by all browsers in a visual sense, although this potentially useful meta data could be extracted and written back into the web page through the magic of DOM Scripting. If DOM Scripting is not the way you want to approach things—perhaps because you have a CMS that's able to reformulate the markup to your needs—a foolproof way to indicate the source of the quotation would be as follows, using a cite (p. 30) *element* rather than the blockquote's cite attribute:

```
<blockquote>
  <p>It's missing alt text, so it's difficult to determine what it's

      supposed to mean. Presumably "oooh, there's been a global
      ecological catastrophe and we've got the last four leaves in
the
      world and we've patented the DNA". Or they're rubbing ganja
      leaves together to extract the resin, but are too stupid to
      recognise Marijuana so are trying it with willow or silver
      birch.</p>
  <p><cite><a href="http://www.brucelawson.co.uk/index.php/2005/
➥stupid-stock-photography/">Bruce Lawson</a></cite></p>
</blockquote>
```

Firefox does at least provide the information to users if they go hunting for it, but it would require them to open a context menu (or right-click on the quote) and select **Properties** in order to display what amounts to very little information, as Figure 2.2 shows.

Figure 2.2: The cite attribute's content revealed in Firefox

Structural Elements

body

```
<body>
</body>
```

SPEC		
deprecated	empty	version
NO	NO	HTML 2
BROWSER SUPPORT			
IE5.5+	FF1+	Saf1.3+	Op9.2+
FULL	FULL	FULL	FULL

Example

The body contains all the content that's to be made visible to the user:

```
<body>
  <h1>101 Ways to make a paper aeroplane</h1>
  <p>Let's start with the basics …</p>
  ⋮
</body>
```

The body element wraps around all of the content that will be displayed on screen (or in other media, such as print), such as headings, paragraphs, images, tables, and so on. It has some unique attributes, including alink (p. 33), link (p. 36), and vlink (p. 38), all of which are now deprecated, as well as a number of other attributes that aren't defined in any standard but are, regrettably, still in common use. These are:

- `marginheight`

    sets the space between the top and bottom of the document content and the viewport (originally defined by Netscape 4)

- `marginwidth`

    sets the space between the left and right of the document content and the viewport (originally defined by Netscape 4)

- `topmargin/bottommargin`

    Internet Explorer's equivalent of `marginheight` (allows us to set top and bottom margins separately)

- `leftmargin/rightmargin`

Internet Explorer's equivalent of `marginwidth` (allows the setting of left and right margins separately)

Note that these attributes are no longer required to achieve the visual effects they were originally intended for—the equivalent CSS for these attributes is the `margin` property (or `margin-top`, `margin-right`, and so on), which is supported by all browsers.

All web pages require a **body** element, with the exception of `frameset` (p. 494)-based web pages, for which the appropriate frameset doctype (p. 6) must be declared.

Use This For ...

Use **body** to hold all the document content that you want to be visible to the reader.

Compatibility

Internet Explorer			Firefox			Safari			Opera
5.5	6.0	7.0	1.0	1.5	2.0	1.3	2.0	3.0	9.2
Full	Full	Full	Full	Full	Full	Full	Full	Full	Full

Every browser listed supports this element type.

alink *for <body>*

```
alink="color"
```

SPEC		
deprecated	required	version
YES	NO	HTML 2
BROWSER SUPPORT		
IE5.5+ FF1+ Saf1.3+ Op9.2+		
FULL FULL FULL FULL		

Example

This markup sets the active links to green:

```
<body alink="green">
  ⋮
</body>
```

When the user clicks on a link (or activates it by tabbing to it and then selecting it with the Return or Enter key), the link color changes briefly to show that the link has been activated; hence `alink` is short for active link. In most cases, this visual effect is displayed so briefly that it isn't even noticed, as the page on which the link was activated is replaced by the page that was requested. However, this active state may be visible in designs that use `frameset` (p. 494)s (where the navigation is located in one `frame` (p. 493) and the content is loaded in another).

Value

This attribute takes as its value a recognized color name (for example, `"blue"` or `"red"`)[1], or a value specified in hexadecimal notation (such as `"#003366"`). Note that it's *not* possible to use shorthand hexadecimal values in HTML as you can in CSS—for example, you can't express `"#cceeff"` as `"#cef"`.

Compatibility

Internet Explorer			Firefox			Safari			Opera
5.5	6.0	7.0	1.0	1.5	2.0	1.3	2.0	3.0	9.2
Full	Full	Full	Full	Full	Full	Full	Full	Full	Full

Every browser listed supports this attribute.

background *for <body>*

```
background="uri"
```

SPEC		
deprecated	required	version
YES	NO	HTML 2
BROWSER SUPPORT		
IE5.5+	FF1+	Saf1.3+	Op9.2+
FULL	FULL	FULL	FULL

Example

This code applies a sandy theme to the page:

```
<body background="sandy.jpg">
  ⋮
</body>
```

The `background` attribute is used to display a background image on the web page. It's not possible to specify how the image is to be displayed (for example, you can't

---

[1] http://reference.sitepoint.com/html/color-names/

specify it to be centered, non-repeating, or aligned to a specific edge of the document); it will simply be repeated along both the x and y axes. Because of this, most web pages to which this technique is applied either display the background as small, repeated images, or use huge images to avoid tiling repetition.

This attribute is now deprecated. Background images should instead be specified using the CSS background or background-image properties. These offer far more flexibility, allowing the author to define whether the image should be repeated on the x or y axis, along both axes, or not at all; it's also possible to position the image relative to any of the document's edges.

Value

This attribute takes as its value the location of the image relative to the referencing document, relative to the server root, or as a complete URI containing the http:// protocol, the server name, and the path to the document on that server.

Compatibility

Internet Explorer			Firefox			Safari			Opera
5.5	6.0	7.0	1.0	1.5	2.0	1.3	2.0	3.0	9.2
Full	Full	Full	Full	Full	Full	Full	Full	Full	Full

Every browser listed supports this attribute.

bgcolor *for <body>*

```
bgcolor="color"
```

SPEC		
deprecated	required	version
YES	NO	HTML 2
BROWSER SUPPORT		
IE5.5+	FF1+	Saf1.3+	Op9.2+
FULL	FULL	FULL	FULL

Example

This markup sets the bgcolor for this document to "yellow":

```
<body bgcolor="yellow">
  ⋮
</body>
```

By default, in the current set of web browsers, a page will have a white background and black text. The `bgcolor` attribute of the `body` element provides a mechanism for changing the default background color, although it should be noted that this attribute is now deprecated and the best method would be to set the background color using Cascading Style Sheets (CSS).

Value

This attribute takes as its value a recognized color name (for example, `"blue"` or `"red"`)[2], or a value specified in hexadecimal notation (such as `"#003366"`). Note that it's *not* possible to use shorthand hexadecimal values in HTML as you can in CSS—for example, you can't express `"#cceeff"` as `"#cef"`.

Compatibility

Internet Explorer			Firefox			Safari			Opera
5.5	6.0	7.0	1.0	1.5	2.0	1.3	2.0	3.0	9.2
Full	Full	Full	Full	Full	Full	Full	Full	Full	Full

Every browser listed supports this attribute.

link *for <body>*

```
link="color"
```

SPEC		
deprecated	required	version
YES	NO	HTML 2
BROWSER SUPPORT		
IE5.5+	FF1+	Saf1.3+	Op9.2+
FULL	FULL	FULL	FULL

Example

This markup sets unvisited links to `"navy"`:

```
<body link="navy">
  ⋮
</body>
```

At some point in the distant past, a decision was made that all hyperlinks on a web page should be underlined and blue, while visited links (p. 38) should be underlined

---

[2]   http://reference.sitepoint.com/html/color-names/

and purple. For people with certain color perception difficulties, it may be very hard to tell the difference between the unvisited and visited links on a page. The link attribute provides one mechanism for overriding that default link color, allowing us to set one that may be more in keeping with the rest of the web page or site design.

This attribute is deprecated, so you should avoid using it. Instead, use CSS to set link colors, using `a, a:link {color:red;}` instead.

Value

This attribute takes as its value a recognized color name (for example, `"blue"` or `"red"`)[3], or a value specified in hexadecimal notation (such as `"#003366"`). Note that it's *not* possible to use shorthand hexadecimal values in HTML as you can in CSS—for example, you can't express `"#cceeff"` as `"#cef"`.

Compatibility

Internet Explorer			Firefox			Safari			Opera
5.5	6.0	7.0	1.0	1.5	2.0	1.3	2.0	3.0	9.2
Full	Full	Full	Full	Full	Full	Full	Full	Full	Full

Every browser listed supports this attribute.

 **text** *for <body>*

`text="color"`

SPEC		
deprecated	required	version
YES	NO	HTML 2
BROWSER SUPPORT		

IE5.5+	FF1+	Saf1.3+	Op9.2+
FULL	FULL	FULL	FULL

Example

The text color is set to lime, contrasting with the black (p. 35):

```
<body bgcolor="black" text="lime">
  <p>This, right here, is retro style.</p>
</body>
```

---

[3] http://reference.sitepoint.com/html/color-names/

The `text` attribute was used in older browsers to change the default body text. The specified settings would apply to any text, be that a heading, a paragraph, or a block quote (link colors were set using their own attributes, `alink` (p. 33), `link` (p. 36), and `vlink` (p. 38), all of which are now deprecated).

This attribute is also deprecated, so you should avoid using it. Instead, use CSS to set the color of body text. The example shown above would translate to the following CSS: `body {background:black;color:lime;}`.

Value

This attribute takes as its value a recognized color name (for example, `"blue"` or `"red"`)[4], or a value specified in hexadecimal notation (such as `"#003366"`). Note that it's *not* possible to use shorthand hexadecimal values in HTML as you can in CSS—for example, you can't express `"#cceeff"` as `"#cef"`.

Compatibility

Internet Explorer			Firefox			Safari			Opera
5.5	6.0	7.0	1.0	1.5	2.0	1.3	2.0	3.0	9.2
Full	Full	Full	Full	Full	Full	Full	Full	Full	Full

Every browser listed supports this attribute.

"..." vlink *for <body>*

```
vlink="color"
```

SPEC		
deprecated	required	version
YES	NO	HTML 2
BROWSER SUPPORT		
IE5.5+	FF1+	Saf1.3+	Op9.2+
FULL	FULL	FULL	FULL

Example

This code sets unvisited links to `"gray"`:

```
<body vlink="gray">
  ⋮
</body>
```

---

[4] http://reference.sitepoint.com/html/color-names/

Visited links will display in purple with an underline, which may not be sufficiently different to the default blue link display for some users (see the section on the (p. 36) attribute for more). The `vlink` attribute allows you to change the color of all links to pages that have previously been visited.

This attribute is deprecated, so you should avoid using it. Instead, use the CSS equivalent to set link colors: `a:visited {color:gray;}`.

Note that the visited state is based on the browser's history. If the user clears the browser's history log, the visited links will once again render as unvisited links.

Value

This attribute takes as its value a recognized color name (for example, `"blue"` or `"red"`)[5], or a value specified in hexadecimal notation (such as `"#003366"`). Note that it's *not* possible to use shorthand hexadecimal values in HTML as you can in CSS—for example, you can't express `"#cceeff"` as `"#cef"`.

Compatibility

Internet Explorer			Firefox			Safari			Opera
5.5	6.0	7.0	1.0	1.5	2.0	1.3	2.0	3.0	9.2
Full	Full	Full	Full	Full	Full	Full	Full	Full	Full

Every browser listed supports this attribute.

---

[5] http://reference.sitepoint.com/html/color-names/

br

`<br/>`

SPEC		
deprecated	empty	version
NO	YES	HTML 3.2
BROWSER SUPPORT		
IE5.5+	FF1+	Saf1.3+	Op9.2+
FULL	FULL	FULL	FULL

Example

This code shows the br in action:

```
<p>If I wanted to create a line break right here,<br/>I
    could use a br element. But I'd feel dirty doing it. There may
    be no good reason for using one.</p>
```

The br element's purpose is very simple: it creates a line break within a block of text, leaving no padding or margins between the two blocks of text created by the line break. While it's still perfectly valid to use this element in XHTML Strict pages (it's not on the list of deprecated elements), you need to take care that you don't misuse it, because:

- It can be used in a presentational manner. For example, you might use a series of br elements in succession to create a new paragraph effect, instead of simply using a (p. 71) or a `blockquote` (p. 28), and applying CSS to set the layout.
- Using br elements becomes a real headache if, later, you want to correct visual inconsistencies and have to sweep through hundreds of files to strip them out.

There are some exceptional cases in which you might be forced to use a br element:

- In poetry, a new line requires just that: a new line. You can't use a p element in this case. (Evidently poetry wasn't high on the list of markup requirements when the HTML recommendations were thrashed out!)
- When you're marking up a postal address, you may need to create single line breaks. However, with the advent of Microformats[6], there's quite a well-established method for dealing with postal (and other) address types that

---

[6] http://reference.sitepoint.com/html/microformats/

avoids the use of the br while offering additional semantic richness. Refer to the section titled http://reference.sitepoint.com/html/hcard/ for more.

This shows the use of br in a poem (well, a poem of sorts):

```
<p>There was an old man from Swindon,<br/>
    A place that rhymed only with 'pinned on,'<br/>
    Okay, well that's fine,<br/>
    Until the fifth line,<br/>
    At which point … well, I'm totally out of luck.</p>
```

Here, we use the br to create line breaks in a postal address:

```
<h3>Postal address:</h3>
<address>
    23 The Ridings,<br/>
    Anywheresville,<br/>
    Hampshire
</address>
```

These examples would render on screen as shown in Figure 2.3.

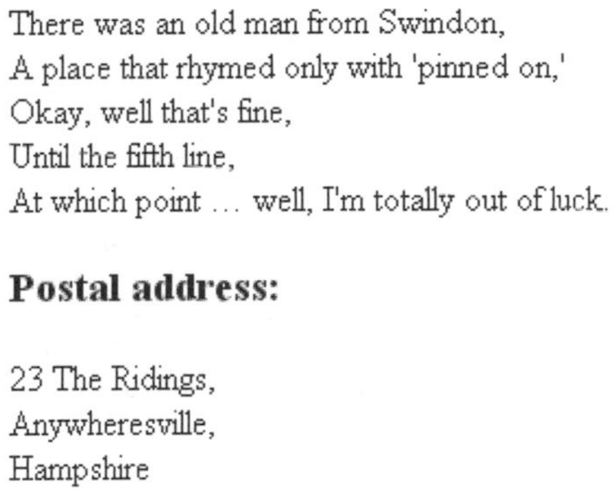

There was an old man from Swindon,
A place that rhymed only with 'pinned on,'
Okay, well that's fine,
Until the fifth line,
At which point … well, I'm totally out of luck.

Postal address:

23 The Ridings,
Anywheresville,
Hampshire

Figure 2.3: An example of the br element in use

Note that the examples shown here use the XHTML syntax for the br element, with a trailing slash to signify that the element is closed:

```
<br/>
```

It's perfectly valid to use the following markup, assuming that you specify an HTML doctype rather than an XHTML doctype:

Structural Elements

```
<br>
```

Use This For ...

The br element is a self-closing element and doesn't contain any content or values.

Compatibility

Internet Explorer			Firefox			Safari			Opera
5.5	6.0	7.0	1.0	1.5	2.0	1.3	2.0	3.0	9.2
Full	Full	Full	Full	Full	Full	Full	Full	Full	Full

Every browser listed supports this element type.

Other Relevant Stuff

  div (p. 44)

divides a page into separate sections

 **clear** *for
*

SPEC		
deprecated	required	version
YES	NO	HTML 3.2
BROWSER SUPPORT		
IE5.5+	FF1+	Saf1.3+	Op9.2+
FULL	FULL	FULL	FULL

```
clear=" { all | left | none | right } "
```

Example

This example shows a br with which a clear attribute is used to take content below a right-aligned image:

```
<p><img src="pool.jpg" alt="sitting by the pool" align="right"/>
    The rest of the day was a lazy one, partly spent by the complex
    pool, partly inside watching British TV, but we couldn't be doing
    this for the rest of the holiday. Already we were missing having
    the car!
  <br clear="all"/>
    I decided to check out what the weather would be doing for the next
    few days, as that would help us make any decisions about future
    excursions.
</p>
```

The `clear` attribute is a deprecated (presentational) attribute that's used to clear any preexisting right or left alignments. It ensures that the content after the `br` element appears beneath the baseline of the previously aligned element; the `br` doesn't just create a line break in the content that's flowing around the right- or left-aligned element.

In the past, this approach would most often have been used to stop content wrapping around a right- or left-aligned image or table.

The correct way of managing alignment issues is to use the CSS `float` property, rather than the HTML `align` attribute. To clear elements, we use the CSS `clear` property like so:

```
<br clear="left"/>  the old-fashioned HTML way

<br style="clear:left;"/>  the CSS way
```

Note that you should avoid inline CSS styles—the inline style above is provided for direct comparison purposes only.

Value

This attribute can take a number of values: `"left"` or `"right"`, to clear previous left or right alignments respectively; `"all"`, to clear both alignments; and `"none"`, to clear nothing.

Compatibility

Internet Explorer			Firefox			Safari			Opera
5.5	6.0	7.0	1.0	1.5	2.0	1.3	2.0	3.0	9.2
Full	Full	Full	Full	Full	Full	Full	Full	Full	Full

Although support for this attribute is good, it's now deprecated, and is highly presentational in its nature. The desired visual effects can all be achieved with CSS and, as such, this attribute shouldn't be used—it's presented here for informational purposes only.

Structural Elements

div

```
<div>
</div>
```

	SPEC		
deprecated	empty		version
NO	NO		HTML 3.2
BROWSER SUPPORT			
IE5.5+	FF1+	Saf1.3+	Op9.2+
FULL	FULL	FULL	FULL

Example

The HTML below shows two `div`s being used in conjunction with `id` attributes to identify different sections of a web page:

```
<div id="main_navigation">
  :
</div>
<div id="body_content">
  <h1>Page heading</h1>
  <p>Body content</p>
</div>
```

The `div` is a generic block-level element. It doesn't convey any meaning about its contents (unlike a `p` element that signifies a paragraph, or an `h1` (p. 46) or `h2` (p. 50) element that would indicate a level 1 or level 2 heading, respectively); as such, it's easy to customize it to your needs. The `div` element is currently the most common method for identifying the structural sections of a document and for laying out a web page using CSS.

Some developers perceive similarities between the `p` and the `div` elements, seeing them as being interchangeable, but this isn't the case. The `p` element offers more semantic information ("this is a paragraph of text, a small collection of thoughts that are grouped together; the next paragraph outlines some different thoughts"), while the `div` element can be used to group almost any elements together. Indeed, it can contain almost any other element, unlike `p`, which can only contain inline elements.

Use This For ...

The `div` is an "anything-goes" element—it can contain any inline or block-level elements you choose, so it has no typical content.

Compatibility

	Internet Explorer			Firefox			Safari		Opera
5.5	6.0	7.0	1.0	1.5	2.0	1.3	2.0	3.0	9.2
Full	Full	Full	Full	Full	Full	Full	Full	Full	Full

This element has no compatibility issues. All the browsers listed support the div element.

Other Relevant Stuff

 p (p. 71)

indicates a paragraph of text

 # align *for <div>*

```
align=" { left | center | right | justify } "
```

SPEC		
deprecated	required	version
YES	NO	HTML 3.2
BROWSER SUPPORT		
IE5.5+	FF1+	Saf1.3+	Op9.2+
FULL	FULL	FULL	FULL

Example

The div below, identified as a "sidebar", will align the content inside the div to the "right" (but as this div is identified with the id attribute, CSS could—and should—be used to set the alignment):

```
<div id="sidebar" align="right">
⋮
</div>
```

The align attribute affects the div's content, aligning it to the "left", "right", or "center", or applying "justify" to justify the content.

This attribute is deprecated. The correct method for aligning a div is to use the CSS text-align attribute.

Value

The accepted values for this element are "left", "right", "center", and "justify".

If "justify" is chosen, text is adjusted so that words stick to both the left and right edges of the containing element, and the final line is left-justified. Some unsightly effects can occur when "justify" is used, as the browsers don't have great rendering engines for this type of effect, and can cause "rivers" in blocks of text (where large gaps appear to flow down through the document).

Compatibility

Internet Explorer			Firefox			Safari			Opera
5.5	6.0	7.0	1.0	1.5	2.0	1.3	2.0	3.0	9.2
Full	Full	Full	Full	Full	Full	Full	Full	Full	Full

Every browser listed supports this attribute.

h1

```
<h1>
</h1>
```

SPEC		
deprecated	empty	version
NO	NO	HTML 3.2

BROWSER SUPPORT			
IE5.5+	FF1+	Saf1.3+	Op9.2+
FULL	FULL	FULL	FULL

Example

This h1 element is used to present a fluffy welcome message:

```
<h1>Welcome to OmniUberMegaCorp's Web Site</h1>
```

The h1 element is used to indicate the most important (or highest-level) heading on the page.

In total, we have six heading levels to choose from—h1 to h6—to add structure to the web page. h1 is the highest heading level (and, by default, the largest in terms of font size) and h6 the lowest (and smallest).

A document's first heading should be an h1, followed by one or more h2 headings; each of these h2 headings can then have a further series of h3 headings below them, and so on, right on down to heading level 6. The HTML 4 spec states that heading levels should not be skipped (that is, you shouldn't have a series of headings in the order h1, h2, h2, h4, which skips the h3 entirely), although it isn't always possible to guarantee such rigidity in the markup, particularly if your pages are generated by a CMS. However, this goal is certainly one for which you should *aim*.

Headings add semantic richness to a document, which can help with search engines' understanding of the makeup of that document, and provide users of assistive devices (such as screen readers) with an additional—and quick—method by which to navigate through a document: they can skip from heading to heading.

Figure 2.4 shows a comparison of the six heading levels in a fictional web site, as rendered by Firefox's default browser style sheet.

Structural Elements

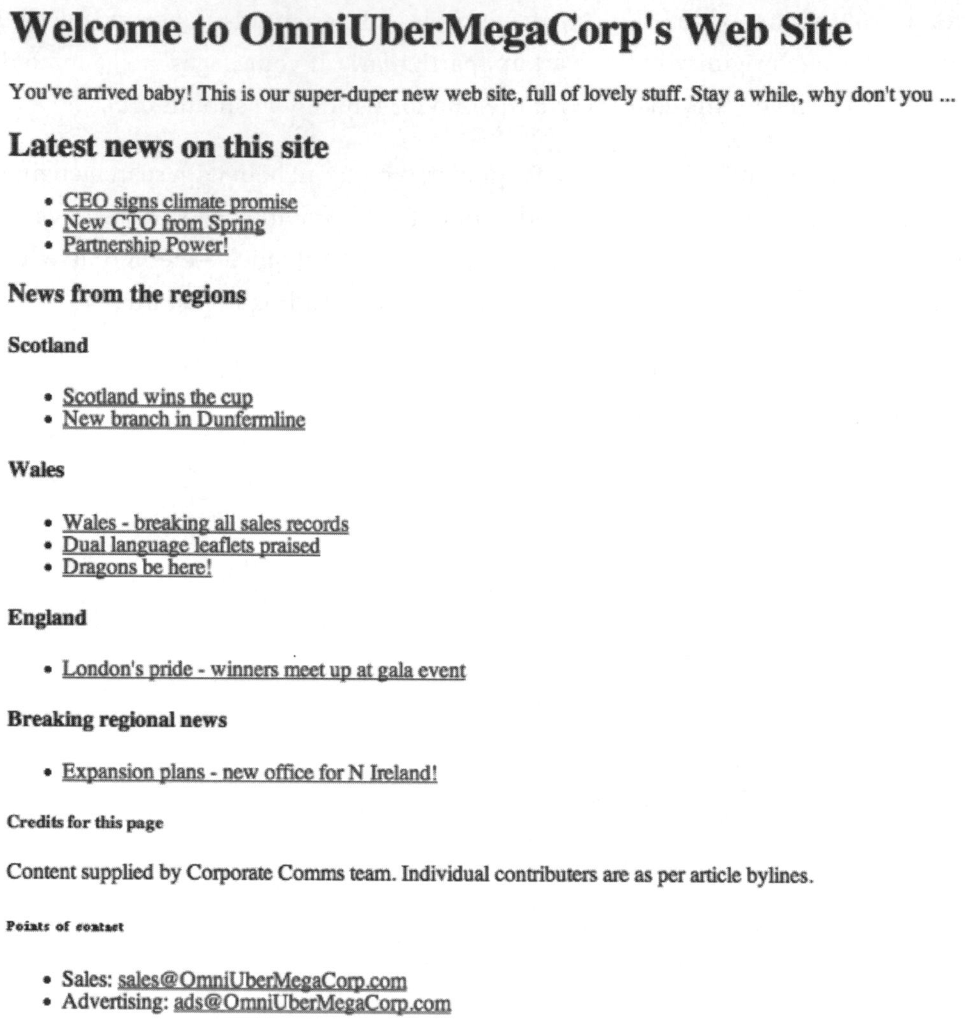

Welcome to OmniUberMegaCorp's Web Site

You've arrived baby! This is our super-duper new web site, full of lovely stuff. Stay a while, why don't you ...

Latest news on this site

- CEO signs climate promise
- New CTO from Spring
- Partnership Power!

News from the regions

Scotland

- Scotland wins the cup
- New branch in Dunfermline

Wales

- Wales - breaking all sales records
- Dual language leaflets praised
- Dragons be here!

England

- London's pride - winners meet up at gala event

Breaking regional news

- Expansion plans - new office for N Ireland!

Credits for this page

Content supplied by Corporate Comms team. Individual contributers are as per article bylines.

Points of contact

- Sales: sales@OmniUberMegaCorp.com
- Advertising: ads@OmniUberMegaCorp.com

Figure 2.4: A comparison of heading sizes in Firefox

The document outline, showing the heading levels, is clear to see using Firefox's Web Developer extension (via that tool's **Information** > **View Document Outline** command), as shown in Figure 2.5.

⟨h1⟩ Welcome to OmniUberMegaCorp's Web Site

⟨h2⟩ Latest news on this site

⟨h3⟩ News from the regions

⟨h4⟩ Scotland

⟨h4⟩ Wales

⟨h4⟩ England

⟨h4⟩ Breaking regional news

⟨h5⟩ Credits for this page

⟨h6⟩ Points of contact

Figure 2.5: Headings/document outline revealed using Firefox's Web Developer Toolbar

Use This For …

This element may contain any text content, but it can't include any block-level elements: only inline or phrase elements can be included.

Compatibility

Internet Explorer			Firefox			Safari			Opera
5.5	6.0	7.0	1.0	1.5	2.0	1.3	2.0	3.0	9.2
Full	Full	Full	Full	Full	Full	Full	Full	Full	Full

There are no compatibility issues with the h1 element—all browsers listed support it.

 # align *for <h1>*

```
align=" { left | center | right | justify } "
```

SPEC		
deprecated	required	version
YES	NO	HTML 3.2
BROWSER SUPPORT		
IE5.5+	FF1+	Saf1.3+	Op9.2+
FULL	FULL	FULL	FULL

Example

The h1 below, identified as a "site-splash-page", will right-align the content inside the h1 (but as it's identified with the id attribute, CSS could—and should—be used to set the alignment):

```
<h1 id="site-splash-page" align="right">Our amazing range
    of services</h1>
```

The `align` attribute affects the text content inside the h1, aligning it to the `"left"`, `"right"`, or `"center"`, or setting it to `"justify"` on the page.

This attribute is deprecated, so the correct method for aligning an h1 is to use the CSS `text-align` property.

Value

The accepted values for h1 are `"left"`, `"right"`, `"center"`, and `"justify"`.

Compatibility

Internet Explorer			Firefox			Safari			Opera
5.5	6.0	7.0	1.0	1.5	2.0	1.3	2.0	3.0	9.2
Full	Full	Full	Full	Full	Full	Full	Full	Full	Full

Every browser listed supports this attribute.

h2

```
<h2>
</h2>
```

SPEC		
deprecated	empty	version
NO	NO	HTML 3.2
BROWSER SUPPORT			
IE5.5+	FF1+	Saf1.3+	Op9.2+
FULL	FULL	FULL	FULL

Example

In this example, an h2 element is used to define a section heading:

```
<h2>Latest news on this site</h2>
```

The h2 element is used to indicate a heading whose level of importance is exceeded only by h1. A document may have several h2 elements, all of which share the same level of importance. The default heading size is shown in Figure 2.6.

Latest news on this site

- CEO signs climate promise
- New CTO from Spring
- Partnership Power!

Figure 2.6: The default level 2 heading

In total, we have six heading levels to choose from—h1 to h6—to add structure to the web page. h1 is the highest heading level (and, by default, the largest in terms of font size) and h6 the lowest (and smallest).

A document's first heading should be an h1, followed by one or more h2 headings; each of these h2 headings can then have a further series of h3 headings below them, and so on, right on down to heading level 6. The HTML 4 spec states that heading levels should not be skipped (that is, you shouldn't have a series of headings in the order h1, h2, h2, h4, which skips the h3 entirely), although it isn't always possible to guarantee such rigidity in the markup, particularly if your pages are generated by a CMS. However, this goal is certainly one for which you should *aim*.

Headings add semantic richness to a document, which can help with search engines' understanding of the makeup of that document, and provide users of assistive devices (such as screen readers) with an additional—and quick—method by which to navigate through a document: they can skip from heading to heading.

Use This For ...

This element may contain any text content, but it can't include any block-level elements: only inline or phrase elements can be included.

Compatibility

Internet Explorer			Firefox			Safari			Opera
5.5	6.0	7.0	1.0	1.5	2.0	1.3	2.0	3.0	9.2
Full	Full	Full	Full	Full	Full	Full	Full	Full	Full

This element has no compatibility issues. All browsers listed support the h2 element.

Structural Elements

align *for <h2>*

`align=" { left | center | right | justify } "`

SPEC		
deprecated	required	version
YES	NO	HTML 3.2
BROWSER SUPPORT			
IE5.5+	FF1+	Saf1.3+	Op9.2+
FULL	FULL	FULL	FULL

Example

The h2 below, identified as a "latest," will align the content inside the h2 to the right (but as it's identified with the id attribute, CSS could—and should—be used to set the alignment):

```
<h2 id="latest" align="right">Latest news on this site</h2>
```

The `align` attribute affects the text content inside the h2, aligning it to the `"left"`, `"right"`, or `"center"`, or setting it to `"justify"` on the page.

This attribute is deprecated. The correct method for aligning an h2 is to use the CSS `text-align` property.

Value

The accepted values for h2 are `"left"`, `"right"`, `"center"`, and `"justify"`.

Compatibility

Internet Explorer			Firefox			Safari			Opera
5.5	6.0	7.0	1.0	1.5	2.0	1.3	2.0	3.0	9.2
Full	Full	Full	Full	Full	Full	Full	Full	Full	Full

Every browser listed supports this attribute.

h3

```
<h3>
</h3>
```

	SPEC	
deprecated	empty	version
NO	NO	HTML 3.2
BROWSER SUPPORT		
IE5.5+	FF1+	Saf1.3+	Op9.2+
FULL	FULL	FULL	FULL

Example

In this example, an h3 element is used to define a section heading:

```
<h3>News from the regions</h3>
```

The h3 element is used to indicate a heading whose level of importance is exceeded by h1 and h2. A document may have several h3 elements, all of which share the same level of importance. The default heading size is shown in Figure 2.7.

News from the regions

Figure 2.7: A level 3 heading

In total, we have six heading levels to choose from—h1 to h6—to add structure to the web page. h1 is the highest heading level (and, by default, the largest in terms of font size) and h6 the lowest (and smallest).

A document's first heading should be an h1, followed by one or more h2 headings; each of these h2 headings can then have a further series of h3 headings below them, and so on, right on down to heading level 6. The HTML 4 spec states that heading levels should not be skipped (that is, you shouldn't have a series of headings in the order h1, h2, h2, h4, which skips the h3 entirely), although it isn't always possible to guarantee such rigidity in the markup, particularly if your pages are generated by a CMS. However, this goal is certainly one for which you should *aim*.

Headings add semantic richness to a document, which can help with search engines' understanding of the makeup of that document, and provide users of assistive devices (such as screen readers) with an additional—and quick—method by which to navigate through a document: they can skip from heading to heading.

Structural Elements

Use This For ...

This element may contain any text content, but it can't include any block-level elements: only inline or phrase elements can be included.

Compatibility

Internet Explorer			Firefox			Safari			Opera
5.5	6.0	7.0	1.0	1.5	2.0	1.3	2.0	3.0	9.2
Full	Full	Full	Full	Full	Full	Full	Full	Full	Full

The h3 element suffers no compatibility issues: all browsers listed support it.

align *for <h3>*

```
align=" { left | center | right | justify } "
```

SPEC		
deprecated	required	version
YES	NO	HTML 3.2
BROWSER SUPPORT		
IE5.5+	FF1+	Saf1.3+	Op9.2+
FULL	FULL	FULL	FULL

Example

The h3 below, identified as "regional," will center the content inside the h3 (but as it is identified with the id attribute, CSS could—and should—be used for setting the alignment):

```
<h3 id="regional" align="center">News from the regions</h3>
```

The align attribute affects the text content inside the h3, aligning it to the "left", "right", or "center", or setting it to "justify".

This attribute is deprecated—the correct method for aligning an h3 is to use the CSS text-align property.

Value

The accepted values for h3 are "left", "right", "center", and "justify".

Compatibility

Internet Explorer			Firefox			Safari			Opera
5.5	6.0	7.0	1.0	1.5	2.0	1.3	2.0	3.0	9.2
Full	Full	Full	Full	Full	Full	Full	Full	Full	Full

Every browser listed supports this attribute.

h4

```
<h4>
</h4>
```

SPEC		
deprecated	empty	version
NO	NO	HTML 3.2
BROWSER SUPPORT		
IE5.5+	FF1+	Saf1.3+	Op9.2+
FULL	FULL	FULL	FULL

Example

In this example, an h4 element is used to define a section heading:

```
<h4>Breaking regional news</h4>
```

The h4 is used to indicate a heading whose level of importance is exceeded by h1, h2, and h3. A document may have several h4 elements, all of which share the same level of importance. The default heading size is shown in Figure 2.8.

Scotland

- Scotland wins the cup
- New branch in Dunfermline

Wales

- Wales - breaking all sales records
- Dual language leaflets praised
- Dragons be here!

England

- London's pride - winners meet up at gala event

Breaking regional news

- Expansion plans - new office for N Ireland!

Figure 2.8: A level 4 heading

In total, we have six heading levels to choose from—h1 to h6—to add structure to the web page. h1 is the highest heading level (and, by default, the largest in terms of font size) and h6 the lowest (and smallest).

A document's first heading should be an h1, followed by one or more h2 headings; each of these h2 headings can then have a further series of h3 headings below them, and so on, right on down to heading level 6. The HTML 4 spec states that heading levels should not be skipped (that is, you shouldn't have a series of headings in the order h1, h2, h2, h4, which skips the h3 entirely), although it isn't always possible to guarantee such rigidity in the markup, particularly if your pages are generated by a CMS. However, this goal is certainly one for which you should *aim*.

Headings add semantic richness to a document, which can help with search engines' understanding of the makeup of that document, and provide users of assistive devices (such as screen readers) with an additional—and quick—method by which to navigate through a document: they can skip from heading to heading.

Use This For ...

This element may contain any text content, but it can't include any block-level elements: only inline or phrase elements can be included.

Compatibility

Internet Explorer			Firefox			Safari			Opera
5.5	6.0	7.0	1.0	1.5	2.0	1.3	2.0	3.0	9.2
Full	Full	Full	Full	Full	Full	Full	Full	Full	Full

The h4 element suffers no compatibility issues: all browsers listed support it.

align *for <h4>*

```
align=" { left | center | right | justify } "
```

SPEC		
deprecated	required	version
YES	NO	HTML 3.2
BROWSER SUPPORT		
IE5.5+ FF1+ Saf1.3+ Op9.2+		
FULL FULL FULL FULL		

Example

The h4 below, identified as "regional-breaking," will align the content inside the h2 to the right (but as it's identified with the id attribute, CSS could—and should—be used to set the alignment):

```
<h4 id="regional-breaking" align="right">Breaking
    regional news</h4>
```

The align attribute affects the text content inside the h4, aligning it to the "left", "right", or "center", or setting it to "justify" on the page.

This attribute is deprecated—the correct method for aligning an h4 is to use the CSS text-align property.

Value

The accepted values for h4 are "left", "right", "center", and "justify".

Compatibility

Internet Explorer			Firefox			Safari			Opera
5.5	6.0	7.0	1.0	1.5	2.0	1.3	2.0	3.0	9.2
Full	Full	Full	Full	Full	Full	Full	Full	Full	Full

Every browser listed supports this attribute.

Structural Elements

h5

```
<h5>
</h5>
```

SPEC		
deprecated	empty	version
NO	NO	HTML 3.2
BROWSER SUPPORT			
IE5.5+	FF1+	Saf1.3+	Op9.2+
FULL	FULL	FULL	FULL

Example

In this example, an h5 element is used to define a section heading:

```
<h5>Credits for this page</h5>
```

The h5 element is used to indicate a heading whose level of importance is exceeded by h1, h2, h3, and h4. A document may have several h5 elements, all of which share the same level of importance. The default heading size is shown in Figure 2.9.

Credits for this page

Content supplied by Corporate Comms team. Individual contributers are as per article bylines.

Figure 2.9: A level 5 heading

In total, we have six heading levels to choose from—h1 to h6—to add structure to the web page. h1 is the highest heading level (and, by default, the largest in terms of font size) and h6 the lowest (and smallest).

A document's first heading should be an h1, followed by one or more h2 headings; each of these h2 headings can then have a further series of h3 headings below them, and so on, right on down to heading level 6. The HTML 4 spec states that heading levels should not be skipped (that is, you shouldn't have a series of headings in the order h1, h2, h2, h4, which skips the h3 entirely), although it isn't always possible to guarantee such rigidity in the markup, particularly if your pages are generated by a CMS. However, this goal is certainly one for which you should *aim*.

Headings add semantic richness to a document, which can help with search engines' understanding of the makeup of that document, and provide users of assistive devices (such as screen readers) with an additional—and quick—method by which to navigate through a document: they can skip from heading to heading.

Use This For ...

This element may contain any text content, but it can't include any block-level elements: only inline or phrase elements can be included.

Compatibility

Internet Explorer			Firefox			Safari			Opera
5.5	6.0	7.0	1.0	1.5	2.0	1.3	2.0	3.0	9.2
Full	Full	Full	Full	Full	Full	Full	Full	Full	Full

The h5 element suffers no compatibility issues: all browsers listed support it.

align *for <h5>*

```
align=" { left | center | right | justify } "
```

SPEC		
deprecated	required	version
YES	NO	HTML 3.2
BROWSER SUPPORT		
IE5.5+	FF1+	Saf1.3+	Op9.2+
FULL	FULL	FULL	FULL

Example

The h5 below, identified as "page-credits," will align the content inside the h5 to the right (but as it is identified with the id attribute, CSS could—and should—be used to set the alignment):

```
<h5 id="page-credits" align="right">Credits for this page</h5>
```

The align attribute affects the text content inside the h5, aligning it to the "left", "right", or "center", or setting it to "justify" on the page.

This attribute is deprecated—the correct method for aligning an h5 is to use the CSS text-align property.

Value

The accepted values for h5 are "left", "right", "center", and "justify".

Compatibility

Internet Explorer			Firefox			Safari			Opera
5.5	6.0	7.0	1.0	1.5	2.0	1.3	2.0	3.0	9.2
Full	Full	Full	Full	Full	Full	Full	Full	Full	Full

Every browser listed supports this attribute.

h6

```
<h6>
</h6>
```

SPEC		
deprecated	empty	version
NO	NO	HTML 3.2
BROWSER SUPPORT		
IE5.5+	FF1+	Saf1.3+	Op9.2+
FULL	FULL	FULL	FULL

Example

In this example, an h6 element is used to define a section heading:

```
<h6>Points of Contact</h6>
```

The h6 element is used to indicate a heading whose level of importance is exceeded by h1, h2, h3, h4, and h5 (or to look at it another way, it has the *lowest* level of importance). A document may have several h6 elements, all of which share the same level of importance. The default heading size is shown in Figure 2.10.

Points of Contact

- Sales: sales@OmniUberMegaCorp.com
- Advertising: ads@OmniUberMegaCorp.com

Figure 2.10: A level 6 heading

In total, we have six heading levels to choose from—h1 to h6—to add structure to the web page. h1 is the highest heading level (and, by default, the largest in terms of font size) and h6 the lowest (and smallest).

A document's first heading should be an h1, followed by one or more h2 headings; each of these h2 headings can then have a further series of h3 headings below them, and so on, right on down to heading level 6. The HTML 4 spec states that heading levels should not be skipped (that is, you shouldn't have a series of headings in the order h1, h2, h2, h4, which skips the h3 entirely), although it isn't always possible to guarantee such rigidity in the markup, particularly if your pages are generated by a CMS. However, this goal is certainly one for which you should *aim*.

Headings add semantic richness to a document, which can help with search engines' understanding of the makeup of that document, and provide users of assistive devices (such as screen readers) with an additional—and quick—method by which to navigate through a document: they can skip from heading to heading.

Use This For ...

This element may contain any text content, but it can't include any block-level elements: only inline or phrase elements can be included.

Compatibility

Internet Explorer			Firefox			Safari			Opera
5.5	6.0	7.0	1.0	1.5	2.0	1.3	2.0	3.0	9.2
Full	Full	Full	Full	Full	Full	Full	Full	Full	Full

The h6 element suffers no compatibility issues: all browsers listed support it.

align *for <h6>*

```
align=" { left | center | right | justify } "
```

SPEC		
deprecated	required	version
YES	NO	HTML 3.2
BROWSER SUPPORT		
IE5.5+ FF1+ Saf1.3+ Op9.2+		
FULL FULL FULL FULL		

Example

The h6 below, identified as "contact-points," will center the content inside the h6 (but as it's identified with the id attribute, CSS could—and should—be used to set the alignment):

```
<h6 id="contact-points" align="center">Points of Contact</h6>
```

The align attribute affects the text content inside the h6, aligning it to the "left", "right", or "center", or setting it to "justify" on the page.

This attribute is deprecated—the correct method for aligning an h6 is to use the CSS text-align property.

Value

The accepted values for h6 are "left", "right", "center", and "justify".

Compatibility

Internet Explorer			Firefox			Safari			Opera
5.5	6.0	7.0	1.0	1.5	2.0	1.3	2.0	3.0	9.2
Full	Full	Full	Full	Full	Full	Full	Full	Full	Full

Every browser listed supports this attribute.

head

```
<head>
</head>
```

SPEC		
deprecated	empty	version
NO	YES	HTML 2
BROWSER SUPPORT		
IE5.5+	FF1+	Saf1.3+	Op9.2+
FULL	FULL	FULL	FULL

Example

This example shows the head, which contains the required title element:

```
<!DOCTYPE html PUBLIC "-//W3C//DTD XHTML 1.0 Transitional//EN"
"http://www.w3.org/TR/xhtml1/DTD/xhtml1-transitional.dtd">
<html xmlns="http://www.w3.org/1999/xhtml">
  <head>
    <title>Page title goes here</title>
  </head>
  <body>
    <!-- content goes here -->
  </body>
</html>
```

The head element is the wrapper for all the head elements that, collectively, instruct the browser where to find style sheets, or define relationships that the document has to others in the web site (link (p. 82)); provide essential meta information (meta (p. 94)); and point to or include scripts that the document will need to apply later on (script (p. 102)).

The head element also includes the title (p. 116) element, which is the only head element that is absolutely required.

Compatibility

Internet Explorer			Firefox			Safari			Opera
5.5	6.0	7.0	1.0	1.5	2.0	1.3	2.0	3.0	9.2
Full	Full	Full	Full	Full	Full	Full	Full	Full	Full

Every browser listed supports this element type.

profile *for <head>*

```
profile="uri"
```

SPEC		
deprecated	required	version
NO	NO	HTML 4
BROWSER SUPPORT		
IE5.5+ FF1+ Saf1.3+ Op9.2+		
FULL FULL FULL FULL		

Example

This example shows a link to a profile XML file in the site's root directory:

```
<head profile="core-defs.xml">
```

The profile attribute is intended to work in conjunction with the meta (p. 94) element (and, in particular, the scheme (p. 101) attribute of that element) to provide a machine-parsable set of rules, most likely in XML format. When presented with a meta element, the user agent can read the contents of the profile referred to in the head to gain a clear understanding of the information contained in the meta's content attribute.

Value

This attribute takes as its value the URI of the profile document.

hr

`<hr/>`

	SPEC		
deprecated	empty		version
NO	YES		HTML 3.2
BROWSER SUPPORT			
IE5.5+	FF1+	Saf1.3+	Op9.2+
FULL	FULL	FULL	FULL

Example

In this example, an hr is used to separate body content from footer information:

```
<p>And with that the actress and the bishop made their
    eventful departure.</p>
<hr/>
<div id="footer">&copy; All content copyright 2007. Even
    the unfunny stuff.</div>
```

The hr element creates in the document a highly visible break that renders as a slim horizontal line running the width of the area to which it's applied. While it's still perfectly valid to use this element in XHTML strict pages, as it's not on the list of deprecated elements, it isn't used a great deal these days, because:

- It's difficult to style consistently across browsers through CSS, or via its own presentational attributes.

- In many cases, it may be better to use a combination of headings and lists to define the document structure, as this will promote ease of navigation for users of assistive technology; the CSS border property can be used to visually style a break in the document.

Use This For ...

The hr element can be used to create a break in a document at a point where there may be a change of thought or meaning, but where it may not necessarily be appropriate to introduce a subheading. A real-world equivalent for this element can be found in books where a divider may appear as three asterisks, or some other collection of characters to indicate a change of scene or momentum.

Compatibility

Internet Explorer			Firefox			Safari			Opera
5.5	6.0	7.0	1.0	1.5	2.0	1.3	2.0	3.0	9.2
Full	Full	Full	Full	Full	Full	Full	Full	Full	Full

Every browser listed supports this element type.

However, the way that the hr element renders differs greatly between browsers, so it doesn't pay to be too precious about design consistency in this case.

color *for <hr>*

```
color="color"
```

SPCC		
deprecated	required	version
YES	NO	N/A
BROWSER SUPPORT		
IE5.5+	FF1+	Saf1.3+	Op9.2
FULL	FULL	FULL	NONE

Example

This code adds a blue horizontal line below the paragraph:

```
<p>And with that the actress and the bishop made a rather
    nice soufflé.</p>
<hr color="blue"/>
<div id="footer">&copy; All content copyright 2007. Even
    the unfunny stuff.</div>
```

The color attribute brightens up the otherwise dull hr element by filling in the hole created by the default beveled appearance.

Value

This attribute takes as its value a recognized color name (for example, "blue" or "red")[8], or a value specified in hexadecimal notation (such as "#003366"). Note that it's *not* possible to use shorthand hexadecimal values in HTML as you can in CSS—for example, you can't express "#cceeff" as "#cef".

---

[8] http://reference.sitepoint.com/html/color-names/

Compatibility

Internet Explorer			Firefox			Safari			Opera
5.5	6.0	7.0	1.0	1.5	2.0	1.3	2.0	3.0	9.2
Full	Full	Full	Full	Full	Full	Full	Full	Full	None

The hr element display varies between browsers, as is support for the color attribute. While most browsers render the horizontal line with a color, when that attribute is combined with the size attribute, the browsers' interpretation of color becomes inconsistent. Some display just a colored outline, others fill the space. However, given that color is a deprecated attribute for this element—in fact it was never in any HTML specification to begin with—it's best to avoid using it altogether, and thereby avoid the potential for validation failure and consistency problems.

"..." noshade *for <hr>*

`noshade="noshade"`

SPEC		
deprecated	required	version
YES	NO	HTML 3.2
BROWSER SUPPORT			
IE5.5+	FF1+	Saf1.3+	Op9.2+
FULL	FULL	FULL	FULL

Example

This code sets an unshaded horizontal line after the paragraph, as depicted in Figure 2.11:

```
<p>And with that the actress and the bishop made their excuses
    and disappeared into the night.</p>
<hr noshade="noshade"/>
<div id="footer">&copy; All content copyright 2007. Even the
    unfunny stuff.</div>
```

Below is a horizontal rule with `noshade="noshade"` attribute:

Figure 2.11: An unshaded horizontal line

By default, most (but not all) browsers display the hr element as a beveled line—an effect that's uniformly recognized as being slightly ugly. noshade is an optional—and deprecated—attribute that switches the bevel effect off, flattening the line.

For XML validation purposes (if noshade is used in XHTML), the attribute must have "noshade" as its associated value:

```
<hr noshade="noshade" />
```

In HTML 3.2 and 4.01, it's perfectly valid to use this format:

```
<hr noshade>
```

Value

The only accepted value for this attribute is "noshade".

Compatibility

Internet Explorer			Firefox			Safari			Opera
5.5	6.0	7.0	1.0	1.5	2.0	1.3	2.0	3.0	9.2
Full	Full	Full	Full	Full	Full	Full	Full	Full	Full

Every browser listed supports this attribute.

Structural Elements

size *for <hr>*

```
size="number"
```

SPEC		
deprecated	required	version
YES	NO	N/A

BROWSER SUPPORT			
IE5.5+	FF1+	Saf1.3+	Op9.2+
FULL	FULL	FULL	FULL

Example

This code places a ten-pixel-high red horizontal rule after the paragraph:

```
<p>And with that the actress and the bishop apologized for being
    a real-life, walking-cliché ending to a non-existent joke.</p>
<hr color="red" size="10"/>
<div id="footer">&copy; All content copyright 2008. Even the
    unfunny stuff.</div>
```

Figure 2.12 shows a rule that's 30 pixels high.

Below is a horizontal rule with `size="30"` attribute:

Figure 2.12: A 30-pixel horizontal line

The `size` attribute determines the `hr` element's height in pixels.

Value

This attribute takes as its value a number wrapped in quotes (which is understood and rendered as pixels on screen—there's no need to specify unit of measurement, as we saw in the example above).

Compatibility

Internet Explorer			Firefox			Safari			Opera
5.5	6.0	7.0	1.0	1.5	2.0	1.3	2.0	3.0	9.2
Full	Full	Full	Full	Full	Full	Full	Full	Full	Full

The `size` attribute is well supported, but as a deprecated (presentational) attribute, it should not be used.

width *for <hr>*

```
width=" { number | percentage } "
```

SPEC		
deprecated	required	version
YES	NO	HTML 3.2
BROWSER SUPPORT		
IE5.5+ FF1+ Saf1.3+ Op9.2+		
FULL FULL FULL FULL		

Example

This code creates a red, ten-pixel-high horizontal line that's 50% of the width of the containing element:

```
<p>And with that the actress explained to the bishop, through a
    series of hand gestures, that she was in fact mute and could not
    possibly have said what she was reported to have done.</p>
<hr color="red" size="10" width="50%"/>
<div id="footer">&copy; All content copyright 2007. Even the
    unfunny stuff.</div>
```

Figure 2.13 shows a horizontal rule set to 50%. The red border is added only to show scale.

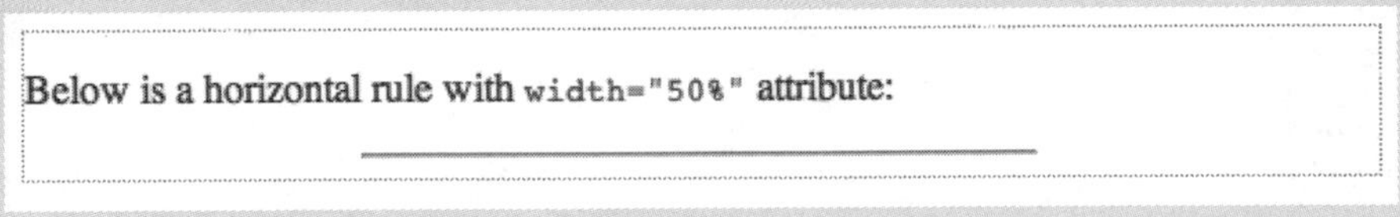

Below is a horizontal rule with `width="50%"` attribute:

Figure 2.13: A horizontal line with a width of 50%

The width attribute determines the hr element's width in pixels (or as a percentage of the containing element, if the % symbol is included); if no width is specified, the hr will take up 100% of its containing element.

Value

This attribute takes as its value a number wrapped in quotes (which is understood and rendered as pixels on screen, so there's no need to specify unit of measurement, as per the example above), or a percentage figure.

Compatibility

Internet Explorer			Firefox			Safari			Opera
5.5	6.0	7.0	1.0	1.5	2.0	1.3	2.0	3.0	9.2
Full	Full	Full	Full	Full	Full	Full	Full	Full	Full

Structural Elements

The width attribute is well supported, but as a deprecated (presentational) attribute, it should not be used.

html

```
<html xmlns="http://www.w3.org/1999/xhtml">
</html>
```

SPEC		
deprecated	empty	version
NO	NO	HTML 2
BROWSER SUPPORT		
IE5.5+	FF1+	Saf1.3+	Op9.2+
FULL	FULL	FULL	FULL

Example

This example shows the html element surrounding all elements in a document:

```
<!DOCTYPE html PUBLIC "-//W3C//DTD XHTML 1.0 Transitional//EN"
"http://www.w3.org/TR/xhtml1/DTD/xhtml1-transitional.dtd">
<html xmlns="http://www.w3.org/1999/xhtml">
  <head>
    <title>Page title goes here</title>
  </head>
  <body>
    <!-- content goes here -->
  </body>
</html>
```

The html element is the outer container for everything that appears in an HTML (or XHTML) document. It can only contain two elements as direct descendants, namely the head (p. 62) element and either a body (p. 32) or frameset (p. 494) element. It can also contain comments. As it is the outermost element in the document, it's also known as the root element.

Although the html element is the outermost element, it does *not* contain the doctype (p. 6)—the doctype must come *before* the html element.

Use This For …

This element will have a place on every single web page you ever create! There's no case in which you would *not* use this element when crafting a web page.

Compatibility

	Internet Explorer		Firefox			Safari			Opera
5.5	6.0	7.0	1.0	1.5	2.0	1.3	2.0	3.0	9.2
Full	Full	Full	Full	Full	Full	Full	Full	Full	Full

Every browser listed supports this element type.

p

```
<p>
</p>
```

SPEC		
deprecated	empty	version
NO	NO	HTML 3.2
BROWSER SUPPORT		
IE5.5+	FF1+	Sat1.3+ Op9.2+
FULL	FULL	FULL FULL

Example

p is used, quite simply, to mark up paragraphs of text:

```
<p>This is a paragraph of text…</p>
<p>…and this is another paragraph.</p>
```

The p element is one of the most commonly used building blocks of HTML. When you use the p element to begin a new paragraph in HTML, it automatically creates some space above and below the content. This space is applied by the browser's built-in style sheets, but you can override it as you see fit using CSS.

In XHTML, it's necessary to wrap the contents of a paragraph in opening <p> and closing </p> tags, while in HTML 4 and earlier versions, it was enough to signify a new paragraph using the opening <p>—no closing tag was needed.

For example, this markup would be perfectly valid in HTML 3.2:

```
<p>So, having failed miserably to manage something as simple as
    "order a breakfast and pay for it," we set about our next task:
    submitting a visa application for our impending visit to
    Thailand. Heaven help us! We're not normally scatty like this,
    so we really must have needed that breakfast!
<p>Thankfully, the rest of the day was nothing like our poor start.
    We got the visa submitted and approved without a hitch, so
    that's one less task for us to do now.
```

Structural Elements

The same markup would not be acceptable in XHTML, but this would:

```
<p>So, having failed miserably to manage something as simple as
    "order a breakfast and pay for it," we set about our next task:
    submitting a visa application for our impending visit to
    Thailand. Heaven help us! We're not normally scatty like this,
    so we really must have needed that breakfast!</p>
<p>Thankfully, the rest of the day was nothing like our poor start.
    We got the visa submitted and approved without a hitch, so
    that's one less task for us to do now.</p>
```

Importantly, while the first example would fail validation as XHTML, the second example will pass, and will *also* pass validation as HTML 3.2.

For the purposes of forwards-compatibility and general good coding practice, it's advisable to use both the opening and closing tags even if you're writing a document that uses an earlier, looser HTML DTD, such as 3.2 or 4.01—this approach supports completeness, rather than shortcuts.

Some developers perceive similarities between the p and the div elements, seeing them as being interchangeable, but this isn't the case. The p element offers more semantic information ("this is a paragraph of text, a small collection of thoughts that are grouped together; the next paragraph outlines some different thoughts"), while the div element can be used to group almost any elements together. Indeed, it can contain almost any other element, unlike p, which can only contain inline elements.

Use This For ...

This element may contain any text content, but it can't include any block-level elements: only inline or phrase elements can be included.

Compatibility

Internet Explorer			Firefox			Safari			Opera
5.5	6.0	7.0	1.0	1.5	2.0	1.3	2.0	3.0	9.2
Full	Full	Full	Full	Full	Full	Full	Full	Full	Full

It causes no compatibility issues, and has excellent support across all tested browsers.

Other Relevant Stuff

 div (p. 44)

divides a page into separate sections

 align *for <p>*

```
align=" { left | center | right | justify } "
```

SPEC		
deprecated	required	version
YES	NO	HTML 3.2
BROWSER SUPPORT		
IE5.5+	FF1+	Saf1.3+	Op9.2+
FULL	FULL	FULL	FULL

Example

The `align` attribute below will center the content inside the two paragraphs (but CSS could—and should—be used to set the alignment):

```
<p align="center">
    Starter: Fruit Salad
</p>
<p align="center">
    Main Course: Roast Duck
</p>
```

The `align` attribute affects the contents of the p, aligning content to the `"left"`, `"right"`, or `"center"`, or setting it to `"justify"` on the page.

This attribute is deprecated—the correct method for aligning a p is to use the CSS `text-align` property.

Figure 2.14 shows the effects of the `align` attribute.

Structural Elements

Left-aligned [align="left"]

This content is left aligned. An align attribute is not specified, so the default behavior—left justification of the content—results. If you used align="left", the result would be exactly the same as this. Compare the ragged right edge of this text with the justified example below. This content is left aligned. An align attribute is not specified, so the default behavior—left justification of the content—results. If you used align="left", the result would be exactly the same as this. Compare the ragged right edge of this text with the justified example below.

Centered Content [align="center"]

Centered content. Centered content.

Right-aligned Content [align="right"]

Right-aligned content. Right-aligned content.

Justified Content[align="justify"]

Jusitifed content—that's what this is. Oh yes, there's no doubt about it. It's very much justified, let me tell you. Jusitifed content—that's what this is. Oh yes, there's no doubt about it. It's very much justified, let me tell you. Jusitifed content—that's what this is. Oh yes, there's no doubt about it. It's very much justified, let me tell you.

Figure 2.14: Left, center, right, and justified alignment

 Mind the Gap

The dotted red border and the gap (margin) between each paragraph have been applied simply to demonstrate alignment more clearly.

Value

The accepted values are "left", "right", "center", and "justify".

If "justify" is chosen, text is adjusted so that words stick to both the left and right edges of the containing element, with the final line left-justified. Some unsightly effects can occur when you're using "justify", as the browsers don't have great rendering engines for this type of effect, and can cause "rivers" in blocks of text (that is, large gaps can appear to flow down through the document).

Compatibility

Internet Explorer			Firefox			Safari			Opera
5.5	6.0	7.0	1.0	1.5	2.0	1.3	2.0	3.0	9.2
Full	Full	Full	Full	Full	Full	Full	Full	Full	Full

Every browser listed supports this attribute.

Head Elements

The elements listed in this section are all contained within the head (p. 62) element, and either provide extra information about the page, or reference other resources that are required for the page to display or behave correctly.

base

```
<base href="uri">
</base>
```

	SPEC	
deprecated	empty	version
NO	YES	HTML 2
BROWSER SUPPORT		
IE5.5+	FF1+	Saf1.3+	Op9.2+
FULL	FULL	FULL	FULL

Example

This markup sets my personal site as the base for all URLs in the document:

```
<base href="http://lloydi.com" target="right"/>
```

The `base` element, which is contained in the head of the document, provides a method for defining the base URL (p. 79) for all links and form submissions on a page. It also provides a common target (p. 81) (in the form of a named window) for all of these links or form submissions.

This element isn't used very often these days, as making links is usually a simple case of creating links to documents relative to the web server root, like so:

```
I've published my <a href="/travel-writing/">holiday diaries</a>,
    including the <a
href="/travel-writing/prague/2006/day2.html">crazy
    bone church at Kutna Hora</a>
```

When the links are accessed, the server will look for the document's reference in the domain root, regardless of the location of the page that contains these links. It doesn't matter one iota whether the referencing page is in the web server's document root folder, or ten directory levels down—the server still looks in the root because the links begin with a "/" character.

Use This For ...

Using the "/" character to signify a link relative to the server's document root is fine, provided you're running the pages from a server. However, there are many scenarios where this isn't going to be the case—documents that are installed and run locally (for example, a set of help files that are installed on a machine) will not work with this technique. The `base` element allows you achieve the effect of smaller link `href` attributes by supplying a domain and even subdirectories.

The `base` element is only going to be useful to you if *all* your relative links or form submissions go to the same location. If your web page contains a mixture of links to different domains or subdirectories on the same server, the `base` element will be a hindrance, not a help.

Compatibility

Internet Explorer			Firefox			Safari			Opera
5.5	6.0	7.0	1.0	1.5	2.0	1.3	2.0	3.0	9.2
Full	Full	Full	Full	Full	Full	Full	Full	Full	Full

It causes no compatibility issues, and has excellent support across all tested browsers.

Other Relevant Stuff

 basefont (p. 174)

sets a basic font size for normal browser text

 ## href *for <base>*

`href="uri"`

	SPEC	
deprecated	required	version
NO	YES	HTML 2
BROWSER SUPPORT		
IE5.5+	FF1+	Saf1.3+	Op9.2+
FULL	FULL	FULL	FULL

Example

The base URL is defined here as a domain:

```
<base href="http://lloydi.com"/>
 ⋮
<p>
  I've published my <a href="/travel-writing/">holiday diaries</a>,
  including the <a href="/travel-writing/prague/2006/day2.html">
  crazy bone church at Kutna Hora</a>.
</p>
```

If all links (a (p. 146)) or form (p. 243) submissions (action (p. 246)) are going to the same location, you may prefer to define the base URL to avoid repeating yourself unnecessarily. The example below illustrates the kind of time saving that this approach can achieve:

```
I've published my
    <a href="http://lloydi.com/travel-writing/">holiday
    diaries</a>, including the <a href="http://lloydi.com/
➡travel-writing/prague/2006/day2.html">crazy bone church at Kutna
    Hora</a>, and our recent trip to <a href="http://lloydi.com/
➡travel-writing/portugal/algarve/day1.html">Portugal</a>.
```

Given that all the links are in the directory "travel-writing" on the domain "lloydi.com", the base href can be used to reduce the markup as follows:

Head Elements

```
<base href="http://lloydi.com/travel-writing/"/>
⋮
I've published my
   <a href="./">holiday diaries</a>,
   including the
   <a href="./prague/2006/day2.html">
   crazy bone church at Kutna Hora</a>, and our recent trip to
   <a href="./portugal/algarve/day1.html">
   Portugal</a>.
```

Note that the syntax dictates that the a (p. 146) element's href values begins with "./".

There's one flaw with using the base element for this purpose, though. Consider a scenario in which you set a base href to be a domain root, like so:

```
<base href="http://example.org/">
```

Then, in the document, you have a link to a fragment identifier called foo: a section within the same page that you'd like the user to be able to jump to:

```
<a href="#foo">Foo</a> links to foo
⋮
<h1 id="foo">Foo</h1> here is the desired destination
```

The problem is that the browser won't jump to that section on the page; instead, it will load the URL http://example.org/#foo.

So while the base element may have its uses, you must be careful to avoid a situation like this. Using a base href value may be akin to using a sledgehammer to knock in a nail.

Value

The value in the base href must be an absolute URI that acts as the base URI for resolving relative URIs, such as "http://www.domain-name.com/".

Compatibility

Internet Explorer			Firefox			Safari			Opera
5.5	6.0	7.0	1.0	1.5	2.0	1.3	2.0	3.0	9.2
Full	Full	Full	Full	Full	Full	Full	Full	Full	Full

It causes no compatibility issues, and has excellent support across all tested browsers.

target *for <base>*

```
target=" { _blank | frame name | _parent | _self |
_top } "
```

SPEC		
deprecated	required	version
NO	NO	HTML 2
BROWSER SUPPORT		
IE6.5+	FF1+	Saf1.3+	Op9.2+
FULL	FULL	FULL	FULL

Example

Here, the base `target` is defined as a frame named `"right"`:

```
<base href="http://lloydi.com" target="right"/>
⋮
<p>
  I've published my <a href="/travel-writing/">holiday diaries</a>,
  including the <a href="/travel-writing/prague/2006/day2.html">
  crazy bone church at Kutna Hora</a>.
</p>
```

The `target` attribute in the `base` element is almost certainly going to be used in the context of a `frameset` (p. 494), where you want all links from a document in one frame (p. 493) to open in another named `frame`. You might also use it in the context of an `iframe` (p. 494), where you wish all links from the "host" document (which contains the `iframe`) to open the destination of the links inside that floating frame (although this is a much less likely scenario than that outlined for `frameset`).

Value

`target` (p. 163) for all the values that can be included in the `target`, and their meanings and uses.

Compatibility

Internet Explorer			Firefox			Safari			Opera
5.5	6.0	7.0	1.0	1.5	2.0	1.3	2.0	3.0	9.2
Full	Full	Full	Full	Full	Full	Full	Full	Full	Full

It causes no compatibility issues, and has excellent support across all tested browsers.

link

SPEC		
deprecated	empty	version
NO	YES	HTML 2
BROWSER SUPPORT		
IE5.5+ FF1+ Saf1.3+ Op9.2+		
PARTIAL PARTIAL PARTIAL PARTIAL		

```
<link href="uri" media="media types"
rel="relationship" rev="relationship" type="content
type"/>
```

Example

In this example, a link element references a style sheet for the current document:

```
<link rel="stylesheet" href="basic.css"/>
```

The link element is used to create links between the referencing document and an external resource; we define the type of this relationship with the use of the rel (p. 88) and rev (p. 91) attributes. The link element is most commonly used for the purpose of linking to one or more style sheets for the document, but may also be used to identify relationships between web pages—for example, which page is the logical next or previous page in a sequence, which page is the contents page for the current page, and so on. Although this use of the link element is well intended, it has few practical uses for the person browsing your site, as the navigation-type link relationships don't provide any clear method of navigating—the user still needs to use whatever controls are visible on the page.

Arguably, it may be better to avoid using the link element for anything *other* than linking to a style sheet if you're hand-coding your web site. If your web site's content is dynamically generated, it may not be difficult to automatically identify the necessary relationships in the link element. On the other hand, if the web site is a roll-your-own affair, it may constitute an unnecessary overhead, and one that's soon neglected.

The link may only appear in the head (p. 62), but there's no limit to the number of individual link elements that you can include (a quick look at the source code of any blog powered by WordPress reveals a whole raft of auto-generated link elements relating to archives).

Use This For ...

This element's used to link to style sheets, and to define relationships between pages—particularly in CMS-generated sites that can automate this process.

Compatibility

Internet Explorer			Firefox			Safari			Opera
5.5	6.0	7.0	1.0	1.5	2.0	1.3	2.0	3.0	9.2
Partial	Partial	Partial	Partial	Partial	Partial	Partial	Partial	Partial	Partial

Excellent browser support is provided for referencing external style sheets, but there's no real support for anything else.

Other Relevant Stuff

 style (p. 111)

contains CSS style information that's embedded into a page

 # charset *for <link>*

charset="*character encoding scheme*"

SPEC		
deprecated	required	version
NO	NO	HTML 4
BROWSER SUPPORT			
IE7	FF2	Saf3	Op9.2
NONE	NONE	NONE	NONE

Example

This example indicates that the referenced document is written in Japanese:

```
<link href="okinawa.html" rel="parent" charset="euc-jp"/>
```

The `charset` attribute is intended to identify the character set used in the document that's referenced within the `link` element.

Value

The value taken by `charset` is a standard character set encoding name[1] (e.g. `"UTF-8"`) defined by IANA.

Compatibility

Internet Explorer			Firefox			Safari			Opera
5.5	6.0	7.0	1.0	1.5	2.0	1.3	2.0	3.0	9.2
None	None	None	None	None	None	None	None	None	None

None of the browsers tested appeared to do anything to notify the user that the referenced document would be presented in any special (or different) character encoding.

In essence, `charset` is a totally useless attribute that fails to do anything practical. Its implementation has been unsuccessful in all browsers, so its use should be avoided entirely.

href *for <link>*

```
href="uri"
```

SPEC		
deprecated	required	version
NO	NO	HTML 2
BROWSER SUPPORT		
IE5.5+	FF1+	Saf1.3+	Op9.2+
FULL	FULL	FULL	FULL

Example

The example below shows a link to a style sheet in the same directory (or folder) as the linking document on the server's file system:

```
<link rel="stylesheet" type="text/css" href="basic.css"/>
```

---

[1] http://www.iana.org/assignments/character-sets

The `href` defines the location of the resource. This may be a style sheet in the same directory (as shown in the example), a page located elsewhere on the same server, or a resource held on another server.

If the referenced resource resided in a directory that was one level higher than the referencing document, the syntax would be as follows:

```
<link rel="stylesheet" type="text/css" href="../basic.css"/>
```

Here, `../` equates to the instruction "move up one directory level in the hierarchy."

You can also reference a document relative to the web site's root (that is, the folder or file after the domain name) like so:

```
<link rel="stylesheet" type="text/css" href="/stylesheets/basic.css"/>
```

This code basically says "refer to the document **basic.css** that can be found in **www.mydomain.com/stylesheets**." This is a very handy way of referencing a document, as you can move the document containing the `link` to any location on the file system without changing the reference.

If you are linking to a resource that's held on some other server, you'd express the `href` using a complete URI, as follows:

```
<link rel="stylesheet" type="text/css"
    href="http://www.somedomainname.com/stylesheets/basic.css"/>
```

Value

This attribute takes as its value the location of the destination document relative to the referencing document, relative to the server root, or as a complete URI containing the `http://` protocol, the server name, and the path to the document on that server.

It's also possible to use as values an `ftp://` location (though it's not common) or data, like so:

```
<link rel="stylesheet" type="text/css"
    href="data:text/css,body%20{%20background%3A%20green%3B%20}"/>
```

Head Elements

We can also use glorious base64 format:

```
<link rel="stylesheet" type="text/css"
    href="data:text/css;base64,Ym9keSB7IGJhY2tncm91bmQ6IGdyZWVuOyB9" />
```

Compatibility

Internet Explorer			Firefox			Safari			Opera
5.5	6.0	7.0	1.0	1.5	2.0	1.3	2.0	3.0	9.2
Full	Full	Full	Full	Full	Full	Full	Full	Full	Full

It causes no compatibility issues, and has excellent support across all tested browsers.

media *for <link>*

```
media=" { all | aural | braille | embossed | handheld
| print | projection | screen | tty | tv } "
```

SPEC		
deprecated	required	version
NO	NO	HTML 4
BROWSER SUPPORT		
IE5.5+	FF1+	Saf1.3+	Op9.2+
FULL	FULL	FULL	FULL

Example

This example shows the application of two different styles for two different media:

```
<link rel="stylesheet" href="basic.css" media="screen"/>
<link rel="stylesheet" href="print.css" media="print"/>
```

If your page is to be viewed on a variety of media, you may want to apply to it a number of separate styles that are specific to each medium.

For example, a typical web page might include a header area, a block of navigation running down the left-hand side, and a sidebar containing related links. None of this content is of any use to users who print the page—after all, you can't click on a printout of related links to access those resources. As such, you might choose to apply certain styles to the page for the screen medium (show navigation areas, and set position, colors, and so on), while applying a different set of rules to the page for the occasions when it's viewed in a printed medium (perhaps hiding the navigation areas entirely).

These subtle changes are made possible by the media attribute. Indeed, in the example HTML, we see that the attribute specifies one style sheet for the screen medium ("basic.css"), and another for the print medium ("print.css").

Value

The acceptable values for media are shown in the syntax section above. You aren't limited to just one media type per link element, though—you can apply multiple media types using a comma-separated list. For example, you may want to apply the main style sheet to "screen" and "projection" (for kiosk, or "full-screen" display), like so:

```
<link rel="stylesheet" href="basic.css"
    media="screen, projection"/>
<link rel="stylesheet" href="print.css" media="print"/>
```

Compatibility

Internet Explorer			Firefox			Safari			Opera
5.5	6.0	7.0	1.0	1.5	2.0	1.3	2.0	3.0	9.2
Full	Full	Full	Full	Full	Full	Full	Full	Full	Full

The browsers tested honor the media types that they are capable of processing—basically the "screen", "print", and "all" values. However, once you step beyond these values, specifying "handheld", "tv", and so on, all bets are off. While it's not the aim of this reference to cover all the different media that might render web content (the handheld part alone, represented by mobile phones, PDAs, and so on, is a minefield of varied support), it would be remiss of me not to warn you that support for the other media types is unreliable. For example, if you specify that a style sheet that you've crafted to look good on your nice, 24-inch, flat-screen monitor should only be for "screen", and you specify a bare, stripped-down version for "handheld", the chances are that many mobile phones will ignore your request and will try to apply your screen style on the handheld device anyway—and they'll probably mangle it in the process.

Opera provides a kiosk (full-screen) mode that makes use of the "projection" media type. When it's operating in full-screen mode, Opera selects the "projection" media type if it's available; otherwise, it uses the "screen" media type.

Head Elements

rel *for <link>*

SPEC		
deprecated	required	version
NO	NO	HTML 2
BROWSER SUPPORT		
IE5.5+	FF1+	Saf1.3+	Op9.2+
PARTIAL	PARTIAL	PARTIAL	PARTIAL

```
rel=" { alternate | bookmark | chapter | contents |
copyright | glossary | help | index | next | prev |
section | start | stylesheet | subsection | icon |
alternate | license | other } "
```

Example

In this example, the `rel` attribute indicates that the referenced document is a style sheet:

```
<link rel="stylesheet" href="basic.css"/>
```

The `rel` attribute defines the relationship that the linked resource has to the document from which it's referenced. In most cases, this resource will simply be `"stylesheet"`, which means, not surprisingly, "the referenced document is a style sheet." Related to this value is `"alternate"`, which is used alongside the `"stylesheet"` value (`rel="alternate stylesheet"`) to indicate that there's another style associated with the page. In fact, you can define several alternative styles, although the main issue with this approach lies in making it clear to the user that an alternative style sheet is available. In Firefox, you can chose **View** > **Page Style** and pick from the available style sheets on offer, but there's no obvious indication in any browser that these alternatives exist—it's usually left to the developer to provide some kind of JavaScript-based style switcher that renders as a control on the page. The following markup shows a page that has one main style sheet and two alternatives:

```
<link rel="stylesheet" href="main.css"
    type="text/css" media="screen"/>
<link rel="alternate stylesheet" title="Higher Contrast"
```

```
    href="contrast.css" type="text/css" media="screen"/>
<link rel="alternate stylesheet" title="Gratuitous CSS"
    href="hot.css" type="text/css" media="screen"/>
```

Note that when you use an alternate style sheet, you should also provide a title attribute that briefly describes the style—this will appear in the browser's page style menu options, as shown in Figure 3.1.

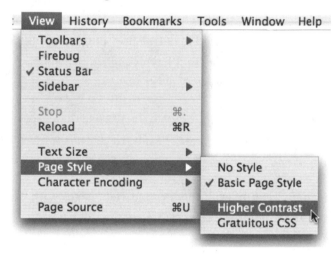

Figure 3.1: The title of the style sheet, as shown in Firefox

Opera also offers us the ability to change the page style from the **View** menu option, but doesn't otherwise draw attention to the alternate style—you have to go hunting for it!

The "`alternate`" attribute value may also be used in the context of XML feeds, namely RSS or Atom, which are indicated with the `type` attribute:

```
<link rel="alternate" type="application/rss+xml"
    href="/rss.xml" title="RSS 2.0">
<link rel="alternate" type="application/atom+xml"
    href="/atom.xml" title="Atom 1.0">
```

If you want to associate a custom icon with your web site (in most browsers, the icon will appear alongside the URL in the address bar, but may also be used when saving a page as a favorite or as a shortcut on the desktop, depending on the browser or operating system), you can use the `rel` attribute as follows:

```
<link rel="shortcut icon" href="/favicon.ico"/>
```

The link refers to an icon that sits in the web server's document root folder, and the convention is to name it favicon.ico (must be a **.ico** file, not a **.gif**, **.jpg** or **.png**). You could place the favorite icon elsewhere on the web server, but you'd have to amend the location specified in the href attribute accordingly.

The relationship aspect of rel really becomes more rich in terms of context and orientation when the attribute is used to define how pages are related to each other. For example, in a sequence of pages that have a logical, linear flow, you can use the rel attribute to define the "next" and "prev" pages in the sequence.

The rel attribute can also be used to indicate the license that applies to the content on the page, using rel="license" href="link-to-license.html". Refer to Microformats' use of rel[2] for more information about this.

You could define many custom relationships between pages with the link element, by moving beyond the predefined values to specify your own.

Value

Refer to the syntax diagram for the acceptable predefined values. Remember, though, that you're not limited to these alone: you can define your own rel attribute value, but it won't be of much use to any web browser (although you might be able to use that information for some other purpose, for example, for querying or accessing the attribute's value using JavaScript and the DOM).

Compatibility

Internet Explorer			Firefox			Safari			Opera
5.5	6.0	7.0	1.0	1.5	2.0	1.3	2.0	3.0	9.2
Partial	Partial	Partial	Partial	Partial	Partial	Partial	Partial	Partial	Partial

The support charts for this element show that partial support is provided by most browsers, as some (Firefox and Opera) are able to provide access to alternate style

---

[2] http://reference.sitepoint.com/html/rel-mf/

sheets when they're encountered, but do not alert the user to the fact that the alternatives are present.

Of those browsers tested, only Opera provides a facility to navigate pages using a toolbar that activates certain options, such as "previous" and "next," when a `link` element with a matching `rel` attribute is found (but even then, this toolbar is hidden by default because it would do nothing for the majority of web sites). Firefox doesn't have this capability by default, but you can install an extension that reveals these navigation features.

With the exceptions of IE 5.5 and IE 6, all the browsers were able to understand and do something useful with a `link` to an XML feed, be that RSS or Atom, usually by indicating the presence of the feed with an icon in the address bar.

The favicon shortcut is well supported, but the way in which it's treated, cached, displayed in your browser's favorites, and so on, differs between browsers and operating systems.

You may get better value from this attribute if you plug in extra functionality using JavaScript and the DOM, or if you use a centralized web service of some kind that's able to make use of the attribute's content (perhaps for analytical purposes, or for refining search results).

rev *for <link>*

```
rev=" { alternate | bookmark | chapter | contents |
copyright | glossary | help | index | next | prev |
section | start | stylesheet | subsection | other } "
```

SPEC		
deprecated	required	version
NO	NO	HTML 2
BROWSER SUPPORT		
IE7	FF2	Saf3	Op9.2
NONE	NONE	NONE	NONE

Example

Here, the `rev` is used to identify the page as the parent for the categories page:

```
<link rel="subsection" rev="parent" href="categories.html"/>
```

Head Elements

While the `rel` attribute (p. 88) defines the relationship of the referenced document or resource to the referencing document, the `rev` attribute is effectively the *reverse* of that: it defines the relationship that the referenced document would classify itself as having with this document. To use a simple example, let's assume that our site has an index page containing references and links to a number of subsection pages. The index page could contain the following code, which identifies that the categories page is a subsection:

```
<link rel="subsection" href="categories.html"/>
```

In the categories page, you could have the following code:

```
<link rel="parent" href="index.html"/>
```

Now, these `link` elements only use the `rel` attribute, and you only see the complete pattern of parent page and subsection when you see both HTML snippets together, although, of course, they're on separate pages. You can use the `rev` attribute to make clear the relationship between pages in both directions. Thus, the two snippets above become:

```
<link rel="subsection" rev="parent" href="categories.html"/>
<link rel="parent" rev="subsection" href="index.html"/>
```

Value

Refer to the syntax diagram for the acceptable predefined values for `rev`. Note, though, that you aren't limited to these values: you can define your own `rev` attribute value, even though it won't be of much use to any web browser. Why would you define your own value? You might be able to use that information for some other purpose—for example, querying or accessing the attribute's value using JavaScript and the DOM.

Compatibility

Internet Explorer			Firefox			Safari			Opera
5.5	6.0	7.0	1.0	1.5	2.0	1.3	2.0	3.0	9.2
None	None	None	None	None	None	None	None	None	None

The support charts indicate no support for this attribute, as none of the browsers do anything useful with it, or change the behavior of anything on the page as a result of it. The real value of adding a `rev` attribute is gained either from plugging in extra functionality to the page using JavaScript and the DOM, or through using a centralized web service of some kind that may be able to make use of the attribute's content.

target *for <link>*

```
target=" { _blank | frame name | _parent | _self |
_top } "
```

SPEC		
deprecated	required	version
YES	NO	HTML 2
BROWSER SUPPORT		
IE7	FF2	Saf3	Op9.2
NONE	NONE	NONE	NONE

Example

The `target` attribute indicates that the referenced document is in a window with the custom name `"subframe"`:

```
<link rel="subsection" rev="parent" target="subframe"
    href="categories.html"/>
```

The `target` attribute is used in the `link` element to identify the window or `frame` (p. 493)—which may be in a `frameset` (p. 494), an `iframe` (p. 494), or even a popup window with a custom window name—that the resource referenced in the `href` (p. 84) attribute applies to.

Value

Refer to the syntax section for the acceptable values for `target`.

Compatibility

Internet Explorer			Firefox			Safari			Opera
5.5	6.0	7.0	1.0	1.5	2.0	1.3	2.0	3.0	9.2
None	None	None	None	None	None	None	None	None	None

The support charts indicate no support for this attribute, as none of the browsers do anything useful with it, or change the behavior of anything on the page as a result of it.

Head Elements

meta

```
<meta content="string"  { http-equiv="http response
header" | name="string" } />
```

SPEC		
deprecated	empty	version
NO	YES	HTML 2
BROWSER SUPPORT		
IE5.5+	FF1+	Saf1.3+	Op9.2+
FULL	FULL	FULL	FULL

Example

Here, a meta element is used to identify character encoding in an HTML document:

```
<meta http-equiv="Content-Type" content="text/html; charset=UTF-8">
```

The meta element provides information about the following document content; that information may be used by the user agent (that is, the browser) to decide how to render content, or it may be meta information that's provided for indexing purposes—for example, to provide keywords that relate to the document for use by search engines or some other form of web service. The meta element can also be used to simulate HTTP response headers (the character encoding snippet provided here is an example of this), or it might simply be used for the purposes of causing a document to reload itself after a set interval.

There's not a standard list of meta properties (although the Dublin Core initiative aims to correct that[3]), so it would be perfectly valid to define the following meta properties:

```
<meta name="department" content="Technology">
<meta name="author" content="John Smith">
```

This definition would also be perfectly valid:

```
<meta name="appearance" content="fluffy">
```

While you can define your own meta information, the question you should ask is whether or not it adds any value. Unless you intend to use this element for the

---

[3] http://dublincore.org/

purposes of indexing, you're advised to stick to a handful of tried-and-tested meta tags:

```
<meta http-equiv="Content-Type" content="text/html; charset=UTF-8">
<!— sets character encoding —>

<meta http-equiv="Refresh" content="5">
<!— refreshes the page content every five seconds —>
```

The following meta tags are the most relevant in terms of search engine indexing and interpretation:[4]

```
<meta name="robots" content="noindex,follow">
<!— instructs search engines not to index this page, but to follow links from the page —>

<meta name="description" content="A brief
    summary/description of the content on the page,
    which may appear in search engine results">

<meta name="keywords" content="reference, SitePoint,
    HTML, XHTML, standards">
<!—comma-separated list of keywords that apply to the page —>
```

The search engines' declining interest in the "description" and "keywords" meta elements may mean that it's preferable for us to drop them entirely. As with all meta elements, there is a danger that, because they are hidden from normal page view, the content can easily go out of date. So unless you know *for a fact* that the content in these types of meta elements is going to be properly maintained *and* that they are in some way beneficial (and this is more likely to be the case when they're used in an intranet where this information may be properly indexed), not using them at all may be the best course of action.

 Optimizing meta Elements? Don't Waste Your Time!

Many search engine optimization (SEO) experts still insist that there's some value in including the "description" and "keywords" meta elements. However, most of these specialists are not party to the ways in which the various search engines

---

[4] Note that the importance of this information has dropped dramatically over the years, as a result of webmasters spamming search engines by stuffing irrelevant content into the "keywords" and "description" meta tags.

> actually work. Their advice is largely based on experience, assumption, reverse engineering, common sense, observed patterns—the list goes on. In short, they can't be *certain* how the likes of Google, Yahoo, Live, Ask, and others handle this content. Certainly, evidence suggests that your efforts are best spent on other aspects of the document whose search ranking you wish to improve.

The syntax of the examples above is appropriate for HTML documents. For XHTML documents, you must remember to include the trailing / character (although it should be noted that there would be little point in adding a Content-Type header as `content="text/html; charset=UTF-8"` if the document is supposed to be XHTML!). This example shows the XHTML syntax:

```
<meta name="robots" content="noindex,follow" />
<!-- the robots meta tag expressed in XHTML syntax -->
```

The `"robots"` meta tag is used to tell robots (that is, search engine crawlers) not to index the content of a page, nor to scan it for links to follow. Different search engines interpret the `"robots"` meta tag differently. For more information about the potential attribute values and their uses, refer to the Search Engine Land article "Meta Robots Tag 101: Blocking Spiders, Cached Pages & More."[5]

Use This For ...

The `meta` element provides information about the document that won't render on the page, but will be machine-parsable.

Compatibility

Internet Explorer			Firefox			Safari			Opera
5.5	6.0	7.0	1.0	1.5	2.0	1.3	2.0	3.0	9.2
Full	Full	Full	Full	Full	Full	Full	Full	Full	Full

Full support is provided for the `meta` element—all browsers expose a document's meta information via the Document Object Model.

---

[5] http://searchengineland.com/070305-204850.php

content *for <meta>*

`content="string"`

SPEC		
deprecated	required	version
NO	YES	HTML 2
BROWSER SUPPORT		
IE5.5+	FF1+	Saf1.3+	Op9.2+
FULL	FULL	FULL	FULL

Example

Here, the content attribute contains a list of categories that the document relates to:

```
<meta name="categories" content="work, projects, current"/>
```

content is a required attribute. It's this part of the meta element that contains the actual meta information, which is defined by the name attribute.

Value

The value of content varies in accordance with the value of the name attribute. It may be a simple summary of the document, a comma-separated list of words or values, a person's name, or any string of characters.

Compatibility

Internet Explorer			Firefox			Safari			Opera
5.5	6.0	7.0	1.0	1.5	2.0	1.3	2.0	3.0	9.2
Full	Full	Full	Full	Full	Full	Full	Full	Full	Full

Full support is provided for the meta element—all browsers expose a document's meta information via the Document Object Model.

Head Elements

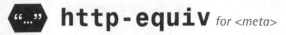 http-equiv *for <meta>*

`http-equiv="http response header"`

SPEC		
deprecated	required	version
NO	NO	HTML 2
BROWSER SUPPORT			
---	---	---	---
IE5.5+	FF1+	Saf1.3+	Op9.2+
FULL	FULL	FULL	FULL

Example

This `http-equiv` attribute defines the character set for the document:

```
<meta http-equiv="Content-Type" content="text/html; charset=UTF-8"/>
```

You can apply many settings to a web server in the form of HTTP response headers—information that's sent back with the response to any request made for a resource on that server. However, not everyone has direct access to their web site's server configuration options; if this is the case, you can use the `meta` element to simulate an HTTP response header. For example, the character encoding may be set at the server, but many web authoring packages include character encoding as a `meta` element just in case this important information is not sent by the server.

Typical uses for the `http-equiv` attribute include managing cache control, page refreshes, and page content safety ratings. If the `http-equiv` attribute is used in the `meta` element, the `name` attribute shouldn't be used.

Note that supplying an HTTP equivalent in a `meta` element is only effective if the server doesn't send the corresponding real header; you can't override an HTTP header with a `meta` element. So using this attribute is only of value when the server doesn't send that particular header, or when there is no server involved—for instance, when you're viewing a document from the local file system.

Value

The value of `http-equiv` varies depending on the way you use it. It may contain any of the following values:

- `"Allow"`
- `"Content-Encoding"`

- "Content-Length"

- "Content-Type"

- "Date"

- "Expires"

- "Last-Modified"

- "Location"

- "Refresh"

- "Set-Cookie"

- "WWW-Authenticate"

Note that "Refresh" is a nonstandard HTTP header extension, the use of which is strongly advised against for accessibility reasons: it takes the control of the page away from the user. This is particularly annoying if the user is having to access the page using a screen reader and the content isn't read out completely before the page refresh kicks in. Using this type of meta attribute value will cause a failure against checkpoints defined in the Web Content Accessibility Guidelines versions 1.0 and 2.0 (still in draft format at time of writing).

Compatibility

Internet Explorer			Firefox			Safari			Opera
5.5	6.0	7.0	1.0	1.5	2.0	1.3	2.0	3.0	9.2
Full	Full	Full	Full	Full	Full	Full	Full	Full	Full

While http-equiv is designed for containing HTTP header information, it doesn't have many applications except with the values of "Content-Type" and "X-UA-Compatible" (introduced in IE8 for handling standards compatibility; a good explanation of this issue can be found in the A List Apart article, "Beyond DOCTYPE: Web Standards, Forward Compatibility, and IE8"[6]).

Head Elements

---

[6] http://www.alistapart.com/articles/beyonddoctype/

name *for <meta>*

`name="string"`

SPEC		
deprecated	required	version
NO	NO	HTML 2
BROWSER SUPPORT		
IE5.5+	FF1+	Saf1.3+	Op9.2+
FULL	FULL	FULL	FULL

Example

This name attribute identifies the content as "categories":

```
<meta name="categories" content="work, projects, current"/>
```

The name attribute is the counterpart to the content attribute, and simply provides a name for the information included in the content attribute. If the name attribute is present, the http-equiv attribute shouldn't be used.

Value

The value of name varies with the value of the content attribute. The name doesn't need to come from a set of standard meta names—you're free to define your own schema for meta information.

Compatibility

Internet Explorer			Firefox			Safari			Opera
5.5	6.0	7.0	1.0	1.5	2.0	1.3	2.0	3.0	9.2
Full	Full	Full	Full	Full	Full	Full	Full	Full	Full

Full support is provided for the meta element—all browsers expose a document's meta information via the Document Object Model.

scheme *for <meta>*

`scheme="uri"`

SPEC		
deprecated	required	version
NO	NO	HTML 4
BROWSER SUPPORT			
IE5.5+	FF1+	Saf1.3+	Op9.2+
FULL	FULL	FULL	FULL

Example

This `scheme` attribute identifies a Dublin Core date scheme:

```
<meta name="DC.date" content="2003-06-08" scheme="DCTERMS.W3CDTF" />
```

The `scheme` attribute provides additional information about the makeup of the `meta` content. It's used in conjunction with the `profile` (p. 63) attribute of the `head` (p. 62) element (this provides a pointer to a set of instructions about the contents of the profile, which relate directly to the meta `name` attribute values).

A `scheme` can be useful for disambiguating some `meta` information that could be interpreted in a number of ways without this extra help—for example, if a date is specified in a `meta` element as `"01-02-07"`, would that mean `"1st February 2007"` or `"2nd January 2002"`?

Value

The value of `scheme` is a URI that specifies the location of the profile information on the server.

Compatibility

Internet Explorer			Firefox			Safari			Opera
5.5	6.0	7.0	1.0	1.5	2.0	1.3	2.0	3.0	9.2
Full	Full	Full	Full	Full	Full	Full	Full	Full	Full

Full support is provided for the `meta` element—all browsers expose a document's meta information via the Document Object Model.

Head Elements

script

```
<script src="uri" type="MIME type">
</script>
```

SPEC		
deprecated	empty	version
NO	NO	HTML 4

BROWSER SUPPORT			
IE5.5+	FF1+	Saf1.3+	Op9.2+
FULL	FULL	FULL	FULL

Example

This script runs after the page has loaded:

```
<script type="text/javascript">
  function doSomethingClever() {
    //clever script goes here
    ⋮
  }
  window.onload = doSomethingClever;
</script>
```

The script element is used to enclose a series of statements in a scripting language that's processed on the client side (that is, it's processed by the user's computer, rather than being processed on the server before being sent to the user's computer). The language that's used may be JavaScript or the Internet Explorer-specific VBScript. These days, however, it's extremely rare to find examples of VBScript used in client-side scripting, except for web pages or applications that are used on intranets whose client base uses Internet Explorer exclusively (and even then, it's not a good idea to do this!).

As well as enclosing scripting statements within the opening `<script>` and closing `</script>` tags, you can use this element to refer to an external script file through the src (p. 108) attribute, usually saved with the **.js** extension, which allows scripts to be shared across an entire site easily.

It's common practice to place all JavaScript functions within script elements inside the head element, from where they're available for use by all the markup on the page that follows. In fact, you can place a script element anywhere on a page, as shown in the following example (whereby a username is dynamically written into the page using an existing JavaScript variable):

```
<p>Well, hello there, <script>writeUserName();</script>,
   how's your day been so far?</p>
```

Note that there are some important differences in the way that HTML 4 and XHTML 1 deal with the content inside scripts.

In HTML 4, the content type is declared as CDATA, which means entity references won't be parsed. The first occurrence of `</` followed by a name start character actually terminates the `script` element, so something like this should fail: `document.write("<p>Hello!</p>")`. In practice, although it's invalid, browsers recover from that error and don't terminate the script until they reach the `</script>` tag. Actually, using the `document.write()` statement is, in itself, a problem in XHTML: `document.write()` can't be used in XHTML documents that are served as XML, due to the way XML is parsed and processed (using it modifies the input stream in a way that isn't compatible with XML parsing requirements).

In an XHTML 1 document that's properly served using the MIME type `"application/xhtml+xml"`, the content type is declared as (#PCDATA), so entities will be parsed and only a `</script>` tag will terminate the element. This means special characters need to be encoded—for example, ampersands will be encoded as `&amp;`, and greater-than symbols will be encoded as `&gt;`—or all content should be wrapped inside `<![CDATA[ … ]]>` sections. To *ensure* that the content inside the opening `<script>` and closing `</script>` tags is parsed correctly when it's included within an XHTML document, use the following comment syntax:

```
<script type="text/javascript"><![CDATA[
  //script goes here
  ⋮
  //]]></script>
```

It's not advisable to use the HTML comment syntax `<!-- -->` to hide script content from older browsers.

Use This For ...

The uses for the `script` element are many and varied; in fact, they're limited only by your imagination, your scripting skills, and your computer's capabilities. Typical uses for JavaScript include image swapping and manipulation, making dynamic changes to content, drag-and-drop functionality, form validation, and so on. This topic really deserves a whole book in its own right.

Compatibility

Internet Explorer			Firefox			Safari			Opera
5.5	6.0	7.0	1.0	1.5	2.0	1.3	2.0	3.0	9.2
Full	Full	Full	Full	Full	Full	Full	Full	Full	Full

Support for embedding the `script` element on the page is not an issue. However, the way that different browsers handle the content—the scripting language itself—can vary massively, depending on the content that's contained. This discussion is well beyond the scope of this reference.

Other Relevant Stuff

 `noscript` (p. 200)

provides alternative content for use when scripts aren't supported or are switched off

 charset *for <script>*

`charset="character encoding scheme"`

SPEC		
deprecated	required	version
NO	NO	HTML 4
BROWSER SUPPORT		
IE5.5+	FF1+	Saf1.3+	Op9.2+
FULL	FULL	FULL	FULL

Example

This example shows a `script` file that's using a slightly different character encoding from the default `"ISO-8859-1"`:

```
<script type="text/javascript" src="/scripts/common.js"
  charset="ISO-8859-15"></script>
```

The `charset` attribute defines the character encoding used in a linked script file (which is referred to by the `src` (p. 108) attribute). You'd use this attribute when the character encoding employed by the external JavaScript file differs from that of the main document. For example, the external script file has the following script:

```
alert("Ευχαριστώ")
```

If the document that links to this eternal file is declared as using `"ISO 8859-1"` encoding, the alert text would be unreadable nonsense. Adding `charset="utf-8"` to the `script` start tag makes it display correctly.

Value

The `charset` attribute takes as its value a space and/or a comma-delimited list of character sets, as set out in RFC 2045 (a fun bit of bedtime reading).[7]

Compatibility

Internet Explorer			Firefox			Safari			Opera
5.5	6.0	7.0	1.0	1.5	2.0	1.3	2.0	3.0	9.2
Full	Full	Full	Full	Full	Full	Full	Full	Full	Full

Every browser listed supports this attribute.

defer _for <script>_

```
defer="defer"
```

SPEC		
deprecated	required	version
NO	NO	HTML 4
BROWSER SUPPORT		
IE5.5+	FF2	Saf3	Op9.2
FULL	NONE	NONE	NONE

Example

This example shows a `script` element with the `defer` attribute set in order to prevent the alert from taking place too early (at which point the button being referred to does not yet exist):

```
<script type="text/javascript" defer>
  alert(document.forms[0].cmdButton.value);
</script>
⋮
<form>
  <input type="submit" name="cmdButton" value="Send it">
</form>
```

---

[7] http://www.ietf.org/rfc/rfc2045.txt

Head Elements

The `defer` attribute is little more than a hint that the browser should—possibly, if it feels like it—defer the execution of a script until later, once it's finished the job of downloading the page's DOM content, as the script isn't going to affect or modify the content of the page in any way, shape, or form.

In the example above, Internet Explorer honors the `defer` attribute and correctly identifies the button's name.

The example shows the attribute expressed in HTML 4.01 syntax. The XHTML syntax would be as follows:

```
<script type="text/javascript" defer="defer">
⋮
</script>
```

However, the only browser that supports this is also the one browser on the list that can't properly handle an XHTML document that's served with the correct MIME type.

Value

The only value that `defer` can take is `"defer"`.

Compatibility

Internet Explorer			Firefox			Safari			Opera
5.5	6.0	7.0	1.0	1.5	2.0	1.3	2.0	3.0	9.2
Full	Full	Full	None	None	None	None	None	None	None

Very poor support is provided for this attribute. Only Internet Explorer honors `defer`; all other browsers ignore its presence. A better option is to use unobtrusive JavaScript techniques that are called using a `window.onload` event handler (or similar scripting).

language *for <script>*

	SPEC	
deprecated	required	version
YES	NO	N/A

language="*string*"

Example

In this example, a `script` is identified as requiring JavaScript 1.2-capable browsers:

```
<script language="JavaScript1.2" src="/scripts/complex.js"></script>
```

The `language` attribute tells the browser which scripting language is to be used inside the `script` block (or in the file referred to by the `src` attribute, as shown in the example). It may be the name of the scripting language, or a version-specific implementation of the language (see the values below).

Note that the `language` attribute is nonstandard, and harks back to the days of what were known as the "browser wars." The appropriate way to identify the contents of the script element is through the `type` (p. 109) attribute (for example, you might specify the content as `"text/javascript"`), and use JavaScript object/feature detection techniques within the script rather than assume that all browsers which support a given version of a scripting language support all of the features of that language—no questions asked.

Value

The values that can be used in this attribute are:

- `"JavaScript"`, `"JavaScript1.1"`, `"JavaScript1.2"`, `"JavaScript1.3"`
- `"JScript"`
- `"VBScript"`
- `"vbs"`

Head Elements

Compatibility

Browser support is generally good, but you can't rely on support for scripting language version numbers alone to decide whether to execute a piece of script or not.

src *for <script>*

```
src="uri"
```

SPEC		
deprecated	required	version
NO	NO	HTML 4
BROWSER SUPPORT			

IE5.5+	FF1+	Saf1.3+	Op9.2+
FULL	FULL	FULL	FULL

Example

In this example, the src attribute refers to a script file named "complex.js":

```
<script type="text/javascript" src="/scripts/complex.js"></script>
```

The power of JavaScript is revealed when common functionality can be shared across a web site, rather than needing to be embedded at the page level over and over again. To achieve this goal, all you need to do is create your JavaScript in a standalone file, save it with the **.js** extension, and then refer to it using the src attribute in the script element. The same rules about locating the resource apply as they do to other external resources (images, links to other pages, and so on). Including "../" in the src indicates that the browser should request the file from a directory one level above the current directory (that is, the directory in which the referring page resides), and "/" indicates that the browser should start looking in the domain document root.

If the src attribute contains a valid URI, the browser should ignore any content that's found inside the opening <script> and closing </script> tags, as illustrated in this code:

```
<script type="text/javascript" src="/scripts/complex.js">
  //the next line should be ignored if /scripts/complex.js exists
  alert("Well howdi ho, pardners!");
</script>
```

When the browser is presented with the above code, the annoying alert should not be displayed to the user; only the contents of **complex.js** should be processed (all the browsers tested honor this markup).

Value

The `src` attribute takes as its value the location of the destination document as:

- relative to the referencing document
- relative reference to the server root
- a complete URI
- the server name, and the path to the document on that server

Compatibility

Internet Explorer			Firefox			Safari			Opera
5.5	6.0	7.0	1.0	1.5	2.0	1.3	2.0	3.0	9.2
Full	Full	Full	Full	Full	Full	Full	Full	Full	Full

It causes no compatibility issues, and has excellent support across all tested browsers.

 type *for <script>*

```
type="MIME type"
```

SPEC		
deprecated	required	version
NO	YES	HTML 4
BROWSER SUPPORT		
IE5.5+ FF1+ Saf1.3+ Op9.2+		
FULL	FULL	FULL FULL

Example

In this example, the `type` attribute identifies the `script` as plain text content comprising JavaScript code:

```
<script type="text/javascript" src="/scripts/complex.js"></script>
```

In HTML 4, the method for identifying the composition of the `script` element's contents was tidied up. The undefined `language` (p. 107) attribute was pushed aside for the `type` attribute, which is a required attribute.

Head Elements

Value

Instead of specifying a scripting language and versions (as does the `language` attribute), the `type` attribute requires a MIME type,[8] which consists of a media type and subtype. In the case of JavaScript, the MIME type would be `"text/javascript"`.

Compatibility

Internet Explorer			Firefox			Safari			Opera
5.5	6.0	7.0	1.0	1.5	2.0	1.3	2.0	3.0	9.2
Full	Full	Full	Full	Full	Full	Full	Full	Full	Full

A small issue surrounds this attribute, or rather the attribute *value* shown in the example above (`"text/javascript"`). According to RFC 4329,[9] the `"text/javascript"` media type is obsolete and should be replaced by `"application/javascript"`. However, the latter isn't supported by Internet Explorer.

xml:space *for <script>*

	SPEC	
deprecated	required	version
NO	NO	XHTML 1.0

`xml:space="preserve"`

Example

This `script` element's whitespace set to `"preserve"` in XHTML 1.0:

```
<script type="text/javascript" src="/scripts/complex.js"
    xml:space="preserve"></script>
```

If the `xml:space` attribute with the value `"preserve"` is applied to the `script` element, the user agent (that is, the browser) must leave all whitespace characters intact, with the exception of leading and trailing whitespace characters, which should be removed. Otherwise, whitespace will be collapsed according to the rules defined in the XHTML modularization guidelines (to provide a much simplified summary, duplicate or unnecessary white spaces are removed). Currently, in XHTML

---

[8] http://reference.sitepoint.com/html/mime-types/
[9] http://www.ietf.org/rfc/rfc4329.txt

1.0, the value is fixed as `"preserve"`, so there's no way not to preserve whitespace in XHTML.

Value

The only value the `xml:space` attribute accepts is `"preserve"`.

 # style

```
<style media="media types" type="MIME type">
</style>
```

SPEC		
deprecated	empty	version
NO	NO	HTML 3.2
BROWSER SUPPORT		
IE5.5+	FF1+	Saf1.3+	Op9.2+
FULL	FULL	FULL	FULL

Example

This page-specific style is embedded using the `style` element:

```
<style type="text/css">
  h2 {color:#000;}
</style>
```

Styles can be applied in CSS at various levels. The first is to link to a style sheet using the `link` (p. 82) element. The next level is to embed a set of style rules at page level by placing them within a `style` element situated inside the `head` (p. 62). (The other methods, to complete the picture, are to create inline styles using the `style` (p. 505) attribute, and user style sheets, which reside on the user's hard drive.)

While this is *not* The Ultimate CSS Reference[10] it's worth noting that as you apply a CSS style at each level in the order stated above, assuming the same selector syntax is used in each case, the more specific or lower-level style will override the style set at the higher level.

It's possible to add comments within the `style` element, but note that the HTML comment syntax `<!-- -->` isn't used—the correct syntax is `/* Comment goes here */`. In an XHTML document that's served as XML (which uses the

Head Elements

---

[10] http://www.sitepoint.com/books/cssref1/

"application/xhtml+xml" MIME type), the contents of the style element should be identified as being character data:

```
<style type="text/css"><![CDATA[
  body {margin:0;}
    ⋮
//]]></style>
```

Refer to the description of script (p. 102) for more information about comment syntax and the parsing of character data.

Use This For ...

You're most likely to use the style element to override the styles set in a linked style sheet, like so:

```
<link rel="stylesheet" href="basic.css"/>
which contains the selector h2 {color:#066;}
    ⋮
<style type="text/css">
  /* override color set in main.css for this page only*/
  h2 {color:#000;}
</style>
```

It wouldn't matter if the style block came first, and was followed by the linked style sheet. Regardless of the order in which the styles are set, the declaration in the style block trumps the identical one inside the linked .css file.

However, you don't have to use style as an override facility alone—some people prefer to embed the style information on each page using a server-side include, as this approach ensures that all the style information is present and correct, and avoids the danger that a link to the style information may break. Note that this approach precludes you from gaining the benefit of having the content cached—a benefit you'd enjoy if the style sheet data were contained in an external style sheet.

Compatibility

Internet Explorer			Firefox			Safari			Opera
5.5	6.0	7.0	1.0	1.5	2.0	1.3	2.0	3.0	9.2
Full	Full	Full	Full	Full	Full	Full	Full	Full	Full

Every browser listed supports this element type.

Other Relevant Stuff

 link (p. 82)

defines the relationship between the current document and other documents or resources

 media *for <style>*

SPEC		
deprecated	required	version
NO	NO	HTML 4
BROWSER SUPPORT		
IE5.5+ FF1+	Saf1.3+	Op9.2+
FULL FULL	FULL	FULL

```
media=" { all | aural | braille | embossed | handheld
| print | projection | screen | tty | tv } "
```

Example

In this example, we have two different media types to which two different styles are applied:

```
<style type="text/css" media="screen">
  #nav {background:#006; padding:2em;}
  ⋮
</script>
<style type="text/css" media="print">
  #nav {display:none}
  ⋮
</script>
```

If your page is to be viewed on a variety of media, you may want to apply to it a number of separate styles that are specific to each medium.

For example, a typical web page might include a header area, a block of navigation running down the left-hand side, and a sidebar containing related links. None of this content is of any use to users who print the page—after all, you can't click on a printout of related links to access those resources. As such, you might choose to apply certain styles to the page for the screen medium (show navigation areas, and set position, colors, and so on), while applying a different set of rules to the page for the occasions when it's viewed in a printed medium (perhaps hiding the navigation areas entirely).

Head Elements

These subtle changes are made possible by the media attribute. Indeed, in the example HTML, we see that the attribute specifies one style sheet for the screen medium ("basic.css"), and another for the print medium ("print.css").

Value

The acceptable values for media are shown in the syntax section. You aren't limited to just one media type per style element—it's possible to apply multiple media types using a comma-separated list. For example, you may wish to apply the main style sheet to "screen" and "projection" (for kiosk, or full-screen displays), like so:

```
<style type="text/css" media="screen, projection">
  #nav {background:#006; padding:2em;}
  ⋮
</script>
<style type="text/css" media="print">
  #nav {display:none}
  ⋮
</script>
```

Compatibility

Internet Explorer			Firefox			Safari			Opera
5.5	6.0	7.0	1.0	1.5	2.0	1.3	2.0	3.0	9.2
Full	Full	Full	Full	Full	Full	Full	Full	Full	Full

The browsers tested honor the media types that they are capable of processing—basically the "screen", "print", and "all" values. However, once you step beyond these values, specifying "handheld", "tv", and so on, all bets are off. While it's not the aim of this reference to cover all the different media that might render web content (the handheld part alone, represented by mobile phones, PDAs, and so on, is a minefield of varied support), it would be remiss of me not to warn you that support for the other media types is unreliable. For example, if you specify that a style sheet that you've crafted to look good on your nice, 24-inch, flat-screen monitor should only be for "screen", and you specify a bare, stripped-down version for "handheld", the chances are that many mobile phones will ignore your request and will try to apply your screen style on the handheld device anyway—and they'll probably mangle it in the process.

type *for <style>*

```
type="MIME type"
```

SPEC		
deprecated	required	version
NO	YES	HTML 4
BROWSER SUPPORT			
IE5.5+	FF1+	Saf1.3+	Op9.2+
FULL	FULL	FULL	FULL

Example

In this example, the MIME type is set to "`text/css`" to indicate that it's standard CSS text:

```
<style type="text/css">
⋮
</script>
```

`type` is a required attribute of the `style` element that identifies the content enclosed between the opening `<style>` and closing `</style>` tags.

Value

A number of MIME types could be applied in the future, but as of now, the only value you need to enter is "`text/css`". (The "`text/css`" media type is defined in RFC 2318.[11])

Compatibility

Internet Explorer			Firefox			Safari			Opera
5.5	6.0	7.0	1.0	1.5	2.0	1.3	2.0	3.0	9.2
Full	Full	Full	Full	Full	Full	Full	Full	Full	Full

Every browser listed supports this attribute.

Head Elements

---

[11] http://www.ietf.org/rfc/rfc2318.txt

xml:space *for <style>*

SPEC		
deprecated	required	version
NO	NO	XHTML 1.0

```
xml:space="preserve"
```

Example

The `script` whitespace is set to "preserve" in XHTML 1.0 using `xml:space` value of "preserve":

```
<style type="text/css" xml:space="preserve">
  #nav      {color:red;}
  #logo     {color:lime;}
  #branding {color:black;}
</style>
```

If the formatting and alignment of your CSS markup is incredibly important to you, you can use the `xml:space` attribute in XHTML 1.0 documents to ensure that whitespace isn't collapsed or removed according to the rules defined in the XHTML modularization guidelines. In XHTML 1.0 recommendation, the value is currently fixed as `"preserve"`, so there's no way not to preserve whitespace in XHTML.

Value

The only value that `xml:space` can take is `"preserve"`.

title

SPEC		
deprecated	empty	version
NO	NO	HTML 2

BROWSER SUPPORT			
IE5.5+	FF1+	Saf1.3+	Op9.2+
FULL	FULL	FULL	FULL

```
<title>
</title>
```

Example

This code shows the `title` in action:

```
<head>
  <title>101 ways to skin a cat - the tutorial!</title>
</head>
```

The `title` element is arguably one of the most important elements in the whole document—and it's a required element for all flavors of HTML/XHTML. The contents of this element are used for all of the following purposes:

- displaying a title in the browser toolbar or in the task bar (on Windows)
- providing for the document a name that's used by the browser when you add the page as a favorite or bookmark
- displaying a title of the page when it appears in search engine results (this is reason enough to take time to ensure that you create a sensible title; otherwise, you risk not being found in search engines for the appropriate search phrase)

For web sites that are hand-coded, and maintained on a page-by-page basis by the web developer, this element can easily fall foul of copy/paste actions (for example, you may all too easily create a new page about products by copying the Press Information page and forgetting to amend the contents of the `title` element to reflect the new content).

Here's one tip regarding the contents of the title element: it's prudent to include your company or organization name in the `title` for all pages; however, avoid front-loading the title with this phrase. For example, if your company is the XYZ Corp, avoid the following:

- XYZ Corp—Our water treatment products
- XYZ Corp—About the company
- XYZ Corp—Contact us

When pages are bookmarked, they'll appear in one alphabetical block. It would be preferable to use the following title content:

- Water treatment products—XYZ Corp
- About XYZ Corp
- Contact us—XYZ Corp

Head Elements

Use This For ...

The `title` is used to summarize the content or purpose of the document. This content represents "elevator pitch" for your document, so be succinct and meaningful, and avoid stuffing keywords into the title for the sake of search results alone.

Compatibility

Internet Explorer			Firefox			Safari			Opera
5.5	6.0	7.0	1.0	1.5	2.0	1.3	2.0	3.0	9.2
Full	Full	Full	Full	Full	Full	Full	Full	Full	Full

Every browser listed supports this element type.

4

List Elements

This section includes all the elements related to lists—ordered lists, unordered lists, and the less-common definition list—as well as the attributes that are unique to these elements.

dl

```
<dl>
</dl>
```

SPEC		
deprecated	empty	version
NO	NO	HTML 2
BROWSER SUPPORT			
IE5.5+	FF1+	Saf1.3+	Op9.2+
FULL	FULL	FULL	FULL

Example

In the example below, a definition list is used to format a number of definitions related to the topic of spam:

```
<dl>
  <dt>Spam</dt>
  <dd>unsolicited email sent in the hope of increasing sales of
      some product, or simply for the purposes of annoying people</dd>
  <dt>Spammer</dt>
  <dd>someone who sends out spam email and therefore deserves to
      develop a nasty incurable disease of some kind</dd>
  <dt>Spam Filter</dt>
  <dd>a tool used in email to 'filter out' likely spam messages,
      usually placing them in a dedicated junk messages folder
      or similar</dd>
</dl>
```

If you want to list a series of items that essentially have a title and a description of some kind (that is, each item has two parts), use the definition list dl element. This element contains a series of definition term (dt (p. 124)) and definition description (dd (p. 123)) pairings.

A definition list would display as illustrated in Figure 4.1.

> Spam
> > unsolicited email sent in the hope of increasing sales of some
> > product, or simply for the purposes of annoying people
> Spammer
> > someone who sends out spam email and therefore deserves to
> > develop a nasty incurable disease of some kind
> Spam Filter
> > a tool used in email to 'filter out' likely spam messages, usually
> > placing them in a dedicated junk messages folder or similar

Figure 4.1: A description list of spam

You can also nest definition lists, as the example below shows:

```
<dl>
 <dt>Spam</dt>
 <dd>unsolicited email sent in the hope of increasing sales of some
     product, or simply for the purposes of annoying people
  <dl>
   <dt>Spammer</dt>
   <dd>someone who sends out spam email and therefore deserves to
       develop a nasty incurable disease of some kind</dd>
   <dt>Spam Filter</dt>
   <dd>a tool used in email to 'filter out' likely spam messages,
       usually placing them in a dedicated junk messages folder
       or similar</dd>
  </dl>
 </dd>
</dl>
```

Without any CSS styles applied, this code would render as shown in Figure 4.2.

Spam

      unsolicited email sent in the hope of increasing sales of some
      product, or simply for the purposes of annoying people
   Spammer

      someone who sends out spam email and therefore
      deserves to develop a nasty incurable disease of some kind
   Spam Filter

      a tool used in email to 'filter out' likely spam messages,
      usually placing them in a dedicated junk messages folder or
      similar

Figure 4.2: A nested definition list

Use This For ...

Typical uses (and hence values) for definition lists include:

- glossaries, such as the example shown above (term: definition)

- event listing (title of event: description of event)

- web site directory (web site name with link: description of web site)

Some people use definition lists for the purposes of marking up dialogues (using dt to denote the speakers, and dd for the words they say). This approach has come straight from the horse's mouth—the W3C HTML recommendation states that

"Another application of dl is for marking up dialogs"—but many people argue that it represents bad practice and is somewhat misguided. You may see definitions lists used in this way, but arguably you shouldn't use them for this purpose, despite what the W3C says, because they're designed to mark up lists of definitions.

Compatibility

Internet Explorer			Firefox			Safari			Opera
5.5	6.0	7.0	1.0	1.5	2.0	1.3	2.0	3.0	9.2
Full	Full	Full	Full	Full	Full	Full	Full	Full	Full

Every browser listed supports this element type.

compact *for <dl>*

```
compact="compact"
```

SPEC		
deprecated	required	version
YES	NO	HTML 2
BROWSER SUPPORT		
IE7	FF2	Saf3	Op9.2
NONE	NONE	NONE	NONE

Example

The compact attribute is applied to a simple definition list in the example below:

```
<dl compact="compact">
  <dt>Spam</dt>
  <dd>unsolicited email sent in the hope of increasing sales of some
      product, or simply for the purposes of annoying people</dd>
  <dt>Spammer</dt>
  <dd>someone who sends out spam email and therefore deserves to
      develop a nasty incurable disease of some kind</dd>
  <dt>Spam Filter</dt>
  <dd>a tool used in email to 'filter out' likely spam messages,
      usually placing them in a dedicated junk messages folder
      or similar</dd>
</dl>
```

The compact attribute's purpose is to instruct the browser to render the definition list into a smaller text block by reducing the spacing between lines and/or reducing the default indentation.

This attribute is now deprecated, and is highly presentational in its nature. The desired visual effects can all be achieved with CSS and, as such, this attribute shouldn't be used—it's presented here for informational purposes only.

Value

The only acceptable value for `compact` is `"compact"`.

Compatibility

Internet Explorer			Firefox			Safari			Opera
5.5	6.0	7.0	1.0	1.5	2.0	1.3	2.0	3.0	9.2
None	None	None	None	None	None	None	None	None	None

Very poor support is provided for this attribute, but given that it's a deprecated attribute whose effects can be achieved using CSS, this shouldn't cause any problems.

dd

```
<dd>
</dd>
```

SPEC		
deprecated	empty	version
NO	NO	HTML 2
BROWSER SUPPORT		
IE5.5+	FF1+	Saf1.3+	Op9.2+
FULL	FULL	FULL	FULL

Example

This example shows the use of two `dd` elements to describe the term "spam:"

```
<dl>
  <dt>Spam</dt>
  <dd>unsolicited email sent in the hope of increasing sales
      of some product</dd>
  <dd>a brand name for tinned meat comprising pork and ham</dd>
</dl>
```

The `dd` is the second part of the `dt` (p. 124) : `dd` pairing that constitutes an item in a definition list (`dl` (p. 120)). While the `dt` contains the term to be defined, the `dd` section of the pairing contains the definition description content.

You can use multiple dt and multiple dd elements to describe the dt elements. The dd element also differs from the dt in that it can contain block-level elements such as example headings and paragraphs.

Use This For ...

The dd element is applied to descriptive text that clearly explains the meaning of the content contained within the preceding dt element. This content can be formatted further using headings (h1 (p. 46), h2 (p. 50), etc.), paragraphs (p (p. 71)) and blockquote (p. 28)s, as well as inline elements.

Compatibility

Internet Explorer			Firefox			Safari			Opera
5.5	6.0	7.0	1.0	1.5	2.0	1.3	2.0	3.0	9.2
Full	Full	Full	Full	Full	Full	Full	Full	Full	Full

Every browser listed supports this element type.

 # dt

SPEC		
deprecated	empty	version
NO	NO	HTML 2

BROWSER SUPPORT			
IE5.5+	FF1+	Saf1.3+	Op9.2+
FULL	FULL	FULL	FULL

```
<dt>
</dt>
```

Example

The example below shows the definition term being used to mark up the word "spam":

```
<dl>
  <dt>Spam</dt>
  <dd>unsolicited email sent in the hope of increasing sales of
      some product, or simply for the purposes of annoying people</dd>
  ⋮
</dl>
```

The dt is the first part of the dt : dd (p. 123) pairing that constitutes an item in a definition list (dl (p. 120)). Note that it can't contain any block-level elements—not even p (p. 71) or heading elements such as h1 (p. 46), h2 (p. 50), and so on. It can only contain text.

You can see the dt in the image below:

Spam
> unsolicited email sent in the hope of increasing sales of some product, or simply for the purposes of annoying people.

Figure 4.3: The example above as viewed in a browser

You can follow multiple dt elements with a single description—for instance, in cases where you have two terms that mean exactly the same thing:

```
<dl>
  <dt>Sofa</dt>
  <dt>Settee</dt>
  <dd>a long upholstered seat with a back and arms, for two or more
      people</dd>
  ⋮
</dl>
```

Use This For ...

The dt element is used to mark up a term of some kind. You can think of a word's entry in a dictionary as a dt, the dd as the explanation of that word, and the book itself as the dl.

Compatibility

Internet Explorer			Firefox			Safari			Opera
5.5	6.0	7.0	1.0	1.5	2.0	1.3	2.0	3.0	9.2
Full	Full	Full	Full	Full	Full	Full	Full	Full	Full

Every browser listed supports this element type.

dir

```
<dir>
</dir>
```

SPEC		
deprecated	empty	version
YES	NO	HTML 2

BROWSER SUPPORT			
IE5.5+	FF1+	Saf1.3+	Op9.2+
FULL	FULL	FULL	FULL

The `dir` element was originally intended to be used specifically to display *directory* lists, rather than to act as a generic list in which any content could be placed. Like the `ol` (p. 131) and `ul` (p. 138) list types, the `dir` element contains a series of `li` (p. 126) items.

Note that although the `li` is a block-level lement, which would normally be able to contain other block-level elements, when it's used in the context of a `dir`, a child `li` element can only contain inline elements.

For more information visit http://reference.sitepoint.com/html/dir/.

li

```
<li>
</li>
```

SPEC		
deprecated	empty	version
NO	NO	HTML 2
BROWSER SUPPORT			
IE5.5+	FF1+	Saf1.3+	Op9.2+
FULL	FULL	FULL	FULL

Example

Here's the `li` element in action, being used within a `ol` element:

```
<ol>
  <li>Remove the outer casing by pushing the plastic rivets
    through.</li>
  <li>Disconnect the main power harness from the inner unit
    (unclip).</li>
  <li>Remove connection to the glow plug.</li>
  <li>Extract unit, keeping upright at all times.</li>
</ol>
```

The `li` element defines an individual list item and can only appear inside the handful of list-related elements detailed above. Each list item is represented by a bullet (for unordered lists, defined by the `ul` (p. 138) element) or a number or letter (in the case of ordered lists, defined by the `ol` (p. 131) element).

The example above shows the `li` as it's used in an ordered list (`ol`), but it could be applied identically inside an unordered list (`ul`):

```
<ul>
  <li>Eggs</li>
  <li>Cheese</li>
  <li>Milk</li>
  <li>Papadums</li>
  <li>Tickle-me Elmo</li>
  <li>Dr Who Remote Control Dalek</li>
</ul>
```

The two types of list items would render as shown in Figure 4.4.

1. Remove the outer casing by pushing the plastic rivets through.
2. Disconnect the main power harness from the inner unit (unclip).
3. Remove connection to the glow plug.
4. Extract unit, keeping upright at all times.

- Eggs
- Cheese
- Milk
- Papadums
- Tickle-me Elmo
- Dr Who Remote Control Dalek

Figure 4.4: An ordered list followed by an unordered list

List items may also appear inside dir (p. 125) and menu (p. 131) elements, although it should be noted that both dir and menu are now deprecated and should no longer be used.

Use This For ...

A list item will usually—but not always—contain text, along with some formatting (phrase) elements. However, an li can contain block-level elements, typically divs (p. 44), nested ul (p. 138) or ol (p. 131) elements, and p (p. 71) elements.

Note that if the li element is contained inside either of the (now deprecated) dir or menu elements, it *cannot* contain block-level elements.

Compatibility

Internet Explorer			Firefox			Safari			Opera
5.5	6.0	7.0	1.0	1.5	2.0	1.3	2.0	3.0	9.2
Full	Full	Full	Full	Full	Full	Full	Full	Full	Full

Every browser listed supports this element type.

type *for <li>*

```
type=" { circle | disc | square | a | A | i | I |
1 } "
```

SPEC		
deprecated	required	version
YES	NO	HTML 2
BROWSER SUPPORT		
IE5.5+ FF1+	Saf1.3+	Op9.2+
PARTIAL FULL	FULL	FULL

Example

The example below shows one item in an unordered list with the **type** set to "circle":

```
<ul>
  <li>Eggs</li>
  <li type="circle">Cheese</li>
  <li>Milk</li>
  <li>Papadums</li>
  <li>Tickle-me Elmo</li>
  <li>Dr Who Remote Control Dalek</li>
</ul>
```

When the **type** attribute is applied to an **li**, it lets the web page author change the style of the glyph for this list item, overriding the style set with the **type** attribute at the parent **ul** or **ol** level, as shown in Figure 4.5.

- Eggs
- Cheese
- Milk
- Papadums
- Tickle-me Elmo
- Dr Who Remote Control Dalek

Figure 4.5: Changing one list item glyph style using the **type** attribute

This attribute is now deprecated, and is highly presentational in its nature. The desired visual effects can all be achieved with CSS and, as such, this attribute shouldn't be used—it's presented here for informational purposes only.

Value

This attribute's value options, and their rendering of the first ten list items, are as follows (provided the li to which the type is applied is inside an ordered list, ol):

- "a": a, b, c, d, e, f, g, h, i, j
- "A": A, B, C, D, E, F, G, H, I, J
- "i": i, ii, iii, iv, v, vi, vii, viii, ix, x
- "I": I, II, III, IV, V, VI, VII, VIII, IX, X
- "1": 1, 2, 3, 4, 5, 6, 7, 8, 9, 10 (default)

If the li in question is inside an unordered list (ul), the options are "disc" (the browser default: a filled circle), "circle" (an outline of a circle, not filled in), and "square" (a filled square, not an outline).

Compatibility

Internet Explorer			Firefox			Safari			Opera
5.5	6.0	7.0	1.0	1.5	2.0	1.3	2.0	3.0	9.2
Partial	Partial	Partial	Full	Full	Full	Full	Full	Full	Full

Good support is provided for the type attribute, but given that it's a deprecated attribute whose effects can be achieved using CSS, you should simply avoid using it.

value *for <li>*

`value="number"`

	SPEC	
deprecated	required	version
YES	NO	HTML 2
BROWSER SUPPORT			
IE5.5+	FF1+	Saf1.3+	Op9.2+
FULL	FULL	FULL	FULL

Example

The example below shows an ordered list item whose `value` is set to `"99"`:

```
<ol>
  <li>Eggs</li>
  <li>Cheese</li>
  <li>Milk</li>
  <li value="99">Papadums</li>
  <li>Tickle-me Elmo</li>
  <li>Dr Who Remote Control Dalek</li>
</ol>
```

When the `value` attribute is applied to an `li`, it sets that list item's number. The `li` elements that follow the one to which `value` is applied increment from that number. Although this attribute takes a numeric value, the value that's actually displayed may be non-numeric (for more on this, see `start` (p. 136)). The browser interpretation of the example code is shown in Figure 4.6.

1. Eggs
2. Cheese
3. Milk
99. Papadums
100. Tickle-me Elmo
101. Dr Who Remote Control Dalek

Figure 4.6: Changing list item numbering using the `value` attribute

Value

This attribute takes a number as its value.

Compatibility

Internet Explorer			Firefox			Safari			Opera
5.5	6.0	7.0	1.0	1.5	2.0	1.3	2.0	3.0	9.2
Full	Full	Full	Full	Full	Full	Full	Full	Full	Full

Good support is provided for the `value` attribute, but given that it's a deprecated attribute, you should simply avoid using it.

menu

```
<menu>
</menu>
```

SPEC		
deprecated	empty	version
YES	NO	HTML 2
BROWSER SUPPORT		
IE5.5+	FF1+	Saf1.3+	Op9.2+
FULL	FULL	FULL	FULL

The `menu` element was originally intended to be used to display lists of menu choices, and is almost identical in its purpose to the `dir` (p. 125) element (except that, unlike `dir`, the `menu` element was *not* intended for multicolumn display).

For more information, visit http://reference.sitepoint.com/html/menu/.

ol

```
<ol>
</ol>
```

SPEC		
deprecated	empty	version
NO	NO	HTML 2
BROWSER SUPPORT		
IE5.5+	FF1+	Saf1.3+	Op9.2+
FULL	FULL	FULL	FULL

Example

The `ol` is used here to mark up a list of maintenance instructions:

```
<ol>
  <li>Remove the outer casing by pushing the plastic rivets
      through.</li>
  <li>Disconnect the main power harness from the inner unit
      (unclip).</li>
  <li>Remove connection to the glow plug.</li>
  <li>Extract unit, keeping upright at all times.</li>
</ol>
```

The `ol` element is similar to the `ul` (p. 138) element in that it's used to group a collection of items together in a list. Each list item is defined by a `li` (p. 126) element, which suggests an order of importance or sequence, as `ol` is an abbreviation of ordered list. The `ol` may be used to mark up a series of steps that someone has to undertake, a table of contents, or a numbered list of references.

There's very little difference between the way browsers render a list that's marked up with a ul and one that's marked up with an ol—with one exception: the bullets in an unordered list are replaced with a series of incrementing numbers, as shown in Figure 4.7.

1. Remove the outer casing by pushing the plastic rivets through.
2. Disconnect the main power harness from the inner unit (unclip).
3. Remove connection to the glow plug.
4. Extract unit, keeping upright at all times.

Figure 4.7: Rendering an ordered list with a series of incrementing numbers

Some level of customization is provided with the ol in terms of the numbering style that's used (you can set this style using the type (p. 135) attribute), but the preferred method for setting the sequence notation is through CSS.

The example above shows a fairly simple set of instructions, but you can also nest one or more lists inside a parent list item, perhaps to expand upon one of the points. If we wanted to expand the "Remove outer casing …" section in the list shown in Figure 4.7, we could start a new unordered list inside that list item. The closing </li> for the first list item doesn't appear until after the nested list is completed (see the notes in the markup below):

```
<ol>
  <li>Remove the outer casing by pushing the plastic rivets through.

  <!-- note that this list item is not closed here -->
    <ul>
      <li>They break easily—be gentle!</li>
      <li>Avoid pushing them through with a sharp edge, in case
          you slip (it may hurt).</li>
    </ul>
  </li>  <!-- the parent for the nested list is actually closed here -->
  <li>Disconnect the main power harness from the inner unit
      (unclip).</li>
  <li>Remove connection to the glow plug.</li>
  <li>Extract unit, keeping upright at all times.</li>
</ol>
```

The result of this nesting can be seen in Figure 4.8.

1. Remove the outer casing by pushing the plastic rivets through.
   ◇ They break easy—be gentle!.
   ◇ Avoid pushing them through with a sharp edge, in case you slip (it may hurt).
2. Disconnect the main power harness from the inner unit (unclip).
3. Remove connection to the glow plug.
4. Extract unit, keeping upright at all times.

Figure 4.8: Nesting an unordered list within an ordered list

Use This For ...

This element can be used with any content that needs to be rendered (and thus possibly referenced elsewhere) with some kind of numerical or alphabetical notation, which could include:

- a chart or ranking table

- how-to guides ("Just follow these simple steps.")

- a running order

- a series of geographical waypoints

Compatibility

Internet Explorer			Firefox			Safari			Opera
5.5	6.0	7.0	1.0	1.5	2.0	1.3	2.0	3.0	9.2
Full	Full	Full	Full	Full	Full	Full	Full	Full	Full

Every browser listed supports this element type.

compact *for <ol>*

`compact="compact"`

	SPEC	
deprecated	required	version
YES	NO	HTML 2

BROWSER SUPPORT			
IE7	FF2	Saf3	Op9.2
NONE	NONE	NONE	NONE

Example

Here's compact applied to the maintenance instructions we saw earlier:

```
<ol compact="compact">
  <li>Remove the outer casing by pushing the plastic rivets
      through.</li>
  <li>Disconnect the main power harness from the inner unit
      (unclip).</li>
  <li>Remove connection to the glow plug.</li>
  <li>Extract unit, keeping upright at all times.</li>

</ol>
```

The compact attribute's purpose is to instruct the browser to render the unordered list into a smaller text block by reducing the spacing between lines and/or reducing the default indentation.

This attribute is now deprecated, and is highly presentational in its nature. The desired visual effects can all be achieved with CSS and, as such, this attribute shouldn't be used—it's presented here for informational purposes only.

Value

The only acceptable value is "compact".

Compatibility

Internet Explorer			Firefox			Safari			Opera
5.5	6.0	7.0	1.0	1.5	2.0	1.3	2.0	3.0	9.2
None	None	None	None	None	None	None	None	None	None

Very poor support is provided for this attribute (that is, not a single browser responded to the compact attribute), but given that it's a deprecated attribute and the desired effects can be achieved using CSS, this shouldn't cause any problems.

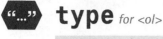

type *for <ol>*

```
type=" { a | A | i | I | 1 } "
```

SPEC		
deprecated	required	version
YES	NO	HTML 2
BROWSER SUPPORT		
IE5.5+	FF1+	Saf1.3+	Op9.2+
FULL	FULL	FULL	FULL

Example

This example shows the type attribute applied to the maintenance steps shown earlier:

```
<ol type="i">
  <li>Remove the outer casing by pushing the plastic rivets
      through.</li>
  <li>Disconnect the main power harness from the inner unit
      (unclip).</li>
  <li>Remove connection to the glow plug.</li>
  <li>Extract unit, keeping upright at all times.</li>

</ol>
```

The type attribute lets the web page author change the style of the numbering (browsers generally begin list numbering at 1, and increase the number by 1 with each new li).

For example, a type of "i" would appear on screen as shown in Figure 4.9.

i. Remove the outer casing by pushing the plastic rivets through.
ii. Disconnect the main power harness from the inner unit (unclip).
iii. Remove connection to the glow plug.
iv. Extract unit, keeping upright at all times.

Figure 4.9: Changing the format of the numbers presented for an ol using the type attribute

This attribute is now deprecated, and is highly presentational in its nature. The desired visual effects can all be achieved with CSS and, as such, this attribute shouldn't be used—it's presented here for informational purposes only.

Value

This attribute's value options, and their rendering of the first ten list items, are as follows:

- "a": a, b, c, d, e, f, g, h, i, j
- "A": A, B, C, D, E, F, G, H, I, J
- "i": i, ii, iii, iv, v, vi, vii, viii, ix, x
- "I": I, II, III, IV, V, VI, VII, VIII, IX, X
- "1": 1, 2, 3, 4, 5, 6, 7, 8, 9, 10 (default)

Compatibility

Internet Explorer			Firefox			Safari			Opera
5.5	6.0	7.0	1.0	1.5	2.0	1.3	2.0	3.0	9.2
Full	Full	Full	Full	Full	Full	Full	Full	Full	Full

Good support is provided for the `type` attribute, but given that it's a deprecated attribute, and the effects can be achieved using CSS, you should simply avoid using it altogether.

start _for <ol>_

```
start="number"
```

SPEC		
deprecated	required	version
YES	NO	HTML 2
BROWSER SUPPORT		
IE5.5+	FF1+	Saf1.3+	Op9.2+
FULL	FULL	FULL	FULL

Example

This example shows the `start` attribute applied to the maintenance steps shown earlier, using a lowercase roman character sequence with a start position of 4:

```
<ol type="i" start="4">
  <li>Remove the outer casing by pushing the plastic rivets
      through.</li>
  <li>Disconnect the main power harness from the inner unit
      (unclip).</li>
  <li>Remove connection to the glow plug.</li>
  <li>Extract unit, keeping upright at all times.</li>

</ol>
```

The start attribute lets the web page author define the start point in the numbering sequence, rather than using the default of "1" (or "a", "A", "i", or "I", depending on the type (p. 135) attribute's value), as demonstrated in Figure 4.10.

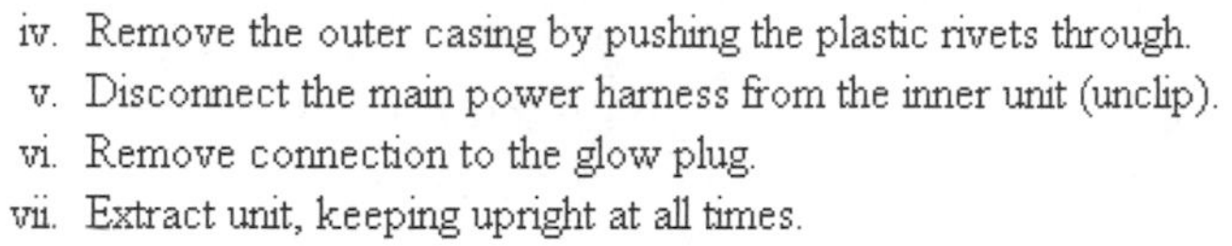

> iv. Remove the outer casing by pushing the plastic rivets through.
> v. Disconnect the main power harness from the inner unit (unclip).
> vi. Remove connection to the glow plug.
> vii. Extract unit, keeping upright at all times.

Figure 4.10: The start attribute lets you set the starting number for an ol

This attribute is now deprecated; however, the fact that it is presentational in nature is a matter of heated debate. The fact that a list continues on from a previous list, for instance, could certainly fall under the heading of semantically meaningful information, worthy of including in the HTML code of the page. Because of this, rumor has it that start will make a reappearance as a fully-endorsed attribute in HTML 5.

Value

The start attribute's value is always expressed as a number, regardless of which type attribute is set. In the examples below, the start points would be "iv", "D", and "4", respectively:

```
<ol type="i" start="4">
```

```
<ol type="A" start="4">
```

```
<ol type="1" start="4">
```

Compatibility

Internet Explorer			Firefox			Safari			Opera
5.5	6.0	7.0	1.0	1.5	2.0	1.3	2.0	3.0	9.2
Full	Full	Full	Full	Full	Full	Full	Full	Full	Full

Good support is provided for the start attribute, but given that it's a deprecated attribute, you should avoid using it if you can.

ul

```
<ul>
</ul>
```

	SPEC	
deprecated	empty	version
NO	NO	HTML 2

BROWSER SUPPORT			
IE5.5+	FF1+	Saf1.3+	Op9.2+
FULL	FULL	FULL	FULL

Example

The ul can be used to mark up a simple shopping list of everyday items, like so:

```
<ul>
    <li>Eggs</li>
    <li>Cheese</li>
    <li>Milk</li>
    <li>Papadums</li>
    <li>Tickle-me Elmo</li>
    <li>Dr Who Remote Control Dalek</li>
</ul>
```

The ul element, the name for which is an abbreviation of unordered list, is used to group a collection of items together in a list, but in a way that doesn't suggest an order of precedence or importance. The ul might be used for anything from a simple shopping list to a collection of links.

Lists have become a very popular mechanism for defining a web site's navigation. This approach constitutes an appropriate use of markup (navigation is, after all, a collection of related items), but was shunned for this purpose for many years, primarily because the default appearance of lists, which sees them rendered as a series of bulleted items, doesn't lend itself to navigation applications. However, with the excellent support provided by current browsers for Cascading Style Sheets (CSS), it's now possible to transform lists to take on almost any appearance.

Using lists for blocks of navigation benefits users who are navigating the Web with assistive technology (such as visually impaired users accessing the web page using a screen reader). By wrapping a site's navigation in a list, we give users the ability to easily skip entire blocks of navigation, jumping from one navigation level to another—a clear advantage over having to move from link to link while trying to get a feel for the web page's structure.

The shopping list example shown above renders as shown in Figure 4.11.

- Eggs
- Cheese
- Milk
- Papadums
- Tickle-me Elmo
- Dr Who Remote Control Dalek

Figure 4.11: Creating a shopping list using ul

Here, the ul is used to mark up a series of links that comprise a web site's main navigation section:

```
<ul>
  <li><a href="/">Home</a></li>
  <li><a href="/about/">About Us</a></li>
  <li><a href="/portfolio/">Portfolio</a></li>
  <li><a href="/clients/">Clients</a></li>
  <li><a href="/contact/">Contact Us </a></li>
</ul>
```

This code would render as shown in Figure 4.12 (without CSS styles applied).

- Home
- About Us
- Portfolio
- Clients
- Contact Us

Figure 4.12: Creating web site navigation using ul

The examples above show fairly simple lists, but you can also nest one or more lists inside a parent list item, to whatever depth is required. If we wanted to expand the About Us section in the navigation list shown, we would start a new unordered list inside the About Us list item. The closing `</li>` for "About Us" doesn't appear until after the nested list is completed (as demonstrated and noted in the markup below):

```
<ul>
  <li><a href="/">Home</a></li>
  <li><a href="/about/">About Us</a>
  <!-- note that this list item is not closed here -->
    <ul>
```

```
      <li><a href="/about/history/">Our history</a></li>
      <li><a href="/aboout/team/">The team</a></li>
      <li><a href="/about/vision/">Our vision</a></li>
    </ul>
  </li>  <!—the parent for the nested list is actually closed here —>
  <li><a href="/portfolio/">Portfolio</a></li>
  <li><a href="/clients/">Clients</a></li>
  <li><a href="/contact/">Contact Us </a></li>
</ul>
```

The result of this nesting can be seen in Figure 4.13.

- Home
- About Us
    - Our history
    - The team
    - Our vision
- Portfolio
- Clients
- Contact Us

Figure 4.13: A nested unordered list

Use This For ...

This element can be used to mark up any piece of content that might conceivably constitute a list, be that:

- the greatest hits of Kevin Federline
- the many reasons why Jar Jar Binks should never have existed
- a birthday gift wish list (that doesn't include socks or shower gel)
- a group of links on a web page
- your top ten favorite cities in the world

Any of the above groups of information could be contained in an unordered list. In fact, the very way that I presented these possibilities would be marked up in HTML using ul and li elements.

Compatibility

Internet Explorer			Firefox			Safari			Opera
5.5	6.0	7.0	1.0	1.5	2.0	1.3	2.0	3.0	9.2
Full	Full	Full	Full	Full	Full	Full	Full	Full	Full

Every browser listed supports this element type.

compact *for <ul>*

```
compact="compact"
```

SPEC		
deprecated	required	version
YES	NO	HTML 2
BROWSER SUPPORT		
IE7	FF2	Saf3	Op9.2
NONE	NONE	NONE	NONE

Example

Here's compact applied to the navigation block we saw earlier:

```
<ul compact="compact">
  <li><a href="/">Home</a></li>
  <li><a href="/about/">About Us</a></li>
  <li><a href="/portfolio/">Portfolio</a></li>
  <li><a href="/clients/">Clients</a></li>
  <li><a href="/contact/">Contact Us</a></li>
</ul>
```

The compact attribute's purpose is to instruct the browser to render the unordered list into a smaller text block by reducing the spacing between lines and/or reducing the default indentation.

This attribute is now deprecated, and is highly presentational in its nature. The desired visual effects can all be achieved with CSS and, as such, this attribute shouldn't be used—it's presented here for informational purposes only.

Value

The only acceptable value for this attribute is "compact".

Compatibility

Internet Explorer			Firefox			Safari			Opera
5.5	6.0	7.0	1.0	1.5	2.0	1.3	2.0	3.0	9.2
None	None	None	None	None	None	None	None	None	None

This attribute has very poor support (that is, not a single browser responded to the `compact` attribute), but given that it's a deprecated attribute and the desired effects can be achieved using CSS, this shouldn't cause any problems.

type *for <ul>*

```
type=" { circle | disc | square } "
```

SPEC		
deprecated	required	version
YES	NO	HTML 2
BROWSER SUPPORT		
IE5.5+	FF1+	Saf1.3+	Op9.2+
FULL	FULL	FULL	FULL

List Elements

Example

This example shows **type** applied to the navigation block we saw earlier:

```
<ul type="circle">
  <li><a href="/">Home</a></li>
  <li><a href="/about/">About Us</a></li>
  <li><a href="/portfolio/">Portfolio</a></li>
  <li><a href="/clients/">Clients</a></li>
  <li><a href="/contact/">Contact Us</a></li>
</ul>
```

This code would render as shown in Figure 4.14.

Figure 4.14: An unordered list with type="circle"

Here's the same list, using a **type** value of "square":

```
<ul type="square">
  <li><a href="/">Home</a></li>
  <li><a href="/about/">About Us</a></li>
  <li><a href="/portfolio/">Portfolio</a></li>
  <li><a href="/clients/">Clients</a></li>
  <li><a href="/contact/">Contact Us</a></li>
</ul>
```

This code would render as shown in Figure 4.15.

Figure 4.15: An unordered list with type="square"

The `type` attribute allows the developer to apply some basic alternative styling to the bullet point that accompanies each list item.

This attribute is now deprecated, and is highly presentational in its nature. The desired visual effects can all be achieved with CSS and, as such, this attribute shouldn't be used—it's presented here for informational purposes only.

Value

The options are `"disc"` (the browser default: a filled circle), `"circle"` (an outline of a circle that's not filled in), and `"square"` (a filled square, not an outline).

Compatibility

Internet Explorer			Firefox			Safari			Opera
5.5	6.0	7.0	1.0	1.5	2.0	1.3	2.0	3.0	9.2
Full	Full	Full	Full	Full	Full	Full	Full	Full	Full

Good support is provided for the `type` attribute. However, given that it's a deprecated attribute whose effects can be achieved—and massively improved upon (for example, you can use background imagery of your choosing, rather than picking from a small selection of basic glyphs)—using CSS, you can avoid using this attribute altogether.

Text Formatting Elements

This is easily the largest section in this reference, in terms of the number of elements that it includes. The text formatting elements listed here range from the extremely useful and oft-used em (p. 189) (emphasis) and strong (p. 223) (strong emphasis), through the peculiar and little-known Ruby markup elements (ruby (p. 216), rb (p. 206), rbc (p. 208), and so on), to the deprecated elements from days long gone, which include marquee (p. 198), tt (p. 226), and big (p. 177)/small (p. 219).

All the elements included here are inline elements elements—they can't be wrapped around any block-level elements (with the exception of del (p. 182) and ins (p. 192), whose properties allow them a special dispensation).

The span (p. 220) element is also listed here. Strictly speaking, it's not a text formatting element, as it doesn't offer any semantic information on its own. That said, the span can't be wrapped around a block element, and is primarily used to surround text content for the purposes of styling or scripting. It is for this reason that it has been included in this index rather than in the Structural Elements (p. 27).

a

```
<a href="uri">
</a>
```

SPEC		
deprecated	empty	version
NO	NO	HTML 2
BROWSER SUPPORT		
IE5.5+ FF1+ Saf1.3+ Op9.2+		
FULL FULL FULL FULL		

Example

The a element is used here to link to a page that lists cakes for sale:

```
<p>You can try our <a href="cakes.html">lovely range of cakes</a>.</p>
```

At one character long, this is one of the smallest elements, but a is the lifeblood of the World Wide Web. It's this element that links the billions of web pages together, allowing you to surf from page to page almost endlessly. To say that it's the most important element of all those presented here would not be an exaggeration.

The a element is usually referred to as a link (not to be confused with the link (p. 82) element, which has a different purpose), or even a hyperlink—although people who refer to hyperlinks probably also talk about "the information superhighway" and think that the film *Tron* is cutting-edge! This element's purpose is simple: it wraps around text, or an image, or both, and refers to another web page, or another section on the same web page; the user can click on the contained text or image, or tab to it and activate with the keyboard's Enter key. The enclosed text will be underlined by default in all browsers, which signifies that it's a clickable link. It's for this reason that you shouldn't use the u (p. 227) element; underlines are best left on links, and links alone. In most browsers, an image that's contained inside an a element will display a border, unless this default is overridden using CSS; the exception is Opera, which doesn't apply a border in this scenario.

The a element has a number of special attributes, which are detailed below, but the one that you'll use most of the time—if it's not the *only* one you'll use—is the href attribute. This attribute indicates the link's destination, be that another web page, a section of the same web page, or some other type of document, such as an image, a spreadsheet, or a PDF document.

If no additional styles are applied using CSS, links will appear as follows:

- An unvisited link appears in blue underlined text.
- A visited link displays in purple underlined text.
- An active link—the link state during the (usually) *very* brief moment between the link's activation and the loading of the next page—appears in red underlined text.

These color codes are replicated in the border of any image that's contained inside an a element (unless it's disabled in CSS). The example code referenced above displays in all browsers, as shown in the image Figure 5.1.

You can try our <u>lovely range of cakes</u>.

Figure 5.1: An example link

Use This For ...

This element is used to contain a—preferably short—link text phrase, or an image (with an appropriate `alt` attribute) that defines the destination of the link.

Compatibility

Internet Explorer			Firefox			Safari			Opera
5.5	6.0	7.0	1.0	1.5	2.0	1.3	2.0	3.0	9.2
Full	Full	Full	Full	Full	Full	Full	Full	Full	Full

It causes no compatibility issues, and has excellent support across all tested browsers.

Text Formatting Elements

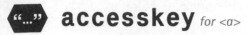

accesskey *for <a>*

`accesskey="key"`

SPEC		
deprecated	required	version
NO	NO	HTML 4
BROWSER SUPPORT			
IE5.5+	FF1+	Saf1.3+	Op9.2+
FULL	FULL	FULL	FULL

Example

In this example, an `accesskey` has been defined on the link to the cake sales page:

```
<a href="cakes.html" accesskey="c">lovely range of cakes</a>
```

The `accesskey` attribute allows the user to activate a control on a page using a keyboard shortcut. This may save time for users who would otherwise need to tab through a series of form controls or move the mouse to get to the desired link. The key combination that activates the link to which the `accesskey` is applied varies depending on the platform and browser combination. For IE/Windows, users press Alt + `accesskey`, while Firefox/Windows users press Alt + Shift + `accesskey`; users of most Mac browsers press Ctrl + `accesskey`; in Opera, pressing Shift + Esc displays a list of links for which `accesskey` attributes are defined, allowing users to choose the key they want to use.

Generally speaking, browsers do not provide any indication to users that an `accesskey` attribute is defined on the link, which is a big issue with the `accesskey`. Most commonly, the `accesskey` value is indicated within a `title` (p. 506) attribute, but this solution still relies on the user mousing over the element to which the accesskey is applied. As such, you may wish to state the `accesskey` value in some other way, for example:

```
<a href="cakes.html" accesskey="c">lovely range of cakes
   [access key = c]</a>
```

Admittedly, this may not be practical or cosmetically pleasing, but without this hint, the user may never realize that an `accesskey` is available.

Value

This attribute takes as its value a single character, which can be numerical, alphabetical, or even a symbol.

Compatibility

Internet Explorer			Firefox			Safari			Opera
5.5	6.0	7.0	1.0	1.5	2.0	1.3	2.0	3.0	9.2
Full	Full	Full	Full	Full	Full	Full	Full	Full	Full

There's some variety in the way that the `accesskey` is activated, but it can work well. The downside of using this attribute is that the keystrokes you define may clash with those defined by other technologies such as screen readers or magnifiers. In addition, different language browsers use different accelerator keys for their own menu options, and these, too, may clash with the accesskeys you've defined. As such, `accesskey` may not work as expected for all users. It may, however, be very useful in controlled environments, such as intranets, where you know exactly which browsers and languages users are running.

charset *for <a>*

SPEC		
deprecated	required	version
NO	NO	HTML 4
BROWSER SUPPORT		
IE7	FF2	Saf3	Op9.2
NONE	NONE	NONE	NONE

```
charset="character encoding scheme"
```

Example

More cakes! Here, a `charset` is defined, as they're special Japanese cakes:

```
<a href="cakes-ja.html" charset="euc-jp">lovely range of
    Japanese cakes (note: this link will take you to a page in Japanese
    language)</a>
```

The `charset` attribute is used to identify the character set used in the document that's being linked to (that is, referenced in the `href` attribute).

Value

This attribute takes a standard character set encoding name (such as "UTF-8").

Compatibility

Internet Explorer			Firefox			Safari			Opera
5.5	6.0	7.0	1.0	1.5	2.0	1.3	2.0	3.0	9.2
None	None	None	None	None	None	None	None	None	None

None of the browsers tested appear to do anything to notify the user that the linked document would be presented in any special (or different) character encoding. As such, this attribute has no real use, and can safely be ignored at this time.

coords _for <a>_

```
coords="coordinates"
```

SPEC		
deprecated	required	version
NO	NO	HTML 3.2
BROWSER SUPPORT		
IE7	FF1+	Saf3	Op9.2+
NONE	FULL	NONE	FULL

Example

This coords attribute defines the top-left and bottom-right coordinates for a rectangular shape:

```
<a href="the-hero.html" shape="rect" coords="132,117,270,185">
    Monday's mustache - 'The Hero'</a>
```

The coords attribute is applied to a link (a (p. 146) element) when the link is contained inside an object (p. 357) element. It's used to position the link over the top of an image. If you think this sounds like an image map, you're right. You can use the coords and shape (p. 161) attributes with an a element to create the same effect you'd achieve using a series of area (p. 320) elements in conjunction with a map (p. 354). Although they do much the same thing, it's useful to compare the two methods. First, let's see the image, which is shown in Figure 5.2.

Figure 5.2: A pack of stylish mustaches; the linked mustaches are clearly outlined

If we used the client-side image map method to achieve this result, the markup would be as follows:

```
<img src="mustaches.png" alt="Mustaches" width="276"
    height="375" border="0" usemap="#Map"/>
<map name="Map" id="Map">
  <area shape="rect" coords="132,117,270,185" href="the-hero.html"
      alt="Monday's mustache - 'The Hero'"/>
  <area shape="poly" coords="136,238,137,301,3,306,3,242"
      href="the-weasel.html" alt="Thursday's mustache -
      'The Weasel'"/>
</map>
```

This example code consists of `area` elements to which `alt`, `coords`, and `shape` attributes are applied. All of these attributes apply to the `map` element.

Now, let's look at the alternative code, in which the `coords` and `shape` attributes are applied to `a` elements instead:

```
<object data="mustaches.png" alt="Mustaches" type="image/png"
    width="276" height="375" border="0" usemap="#Map2">
  <map name="Map2" id="Map2">
```

```
  <ul>
    <li><a href="the-hero.html" shape="rect"
        coords="132,117,270,185">Monday's mustache -
        'The Hero'</a></li>
    <li><a href="the-weasel.html" shape="poly"
        coords="136,238,137,301,3,306,3,242">Thursday's
        mustache - 'The Weasel'</a></li>
  </ul>
 </map>
</object>
```

In the second example, the links have been placed inside a ul (p. 138), and instead of the alt attributes we used for the area in the first example, the text is contained within the link. The idea is that the user will be presented with a list of links in browsers that don't support the object element properly.

Value

The values that can be entered into the coords attribute are as follows:

■ For rectangular shapes ("rect"), the coords attribute will take four values: $x1$, $y1$, $x2$, and $y2$. These values define the top-left corner of the rectangle (how many pixels along and down from the image's top-left corner the boundary will appear), and the bottom-right corner (how many pixels along and up from the image's bottom-right corner the boundary will appear).

■ For circular shapes ("circ"), three values are required: x, y, and r. The x and y coordinates tell the browser where the circle's center point is, while the r value specifies the radius of the circle.

■ Polygonal shapes ("poly"), which are almost always created using a WYSIWYG HTML editor such as Dreamweaver, are defined by a series of x, y coordinates, each of which relates to a point on the polygon's outline.

Compatibility

Internet Explorer			Firefox			Safari			Opera
5.5	6.0	7.0	1.0	1.5	2.0	1.3	2.0	3.0	9.2
None	None	None	Full	Full	Full	None	None	None	Full

This attribute isn't well supported. Safari and Firefox correctly position the links over the image referenced in the object element, but Internet Explorer and Safari don't position the links at all, rendering the technique useless.

The idea behind the technique seems like a good one: you create a list of links for basic browsers, with the `object` element taking over where it's supported, allowing the links to be positioned appropriately (an example of progressive enhancement). However, the reality is that although most browsers support the `object` element reasonably well, not all support the `coords` and `shape` attributes. Therefore, the fallback—a basic list—isn't used, and the positioned links fail to have any effect.

If you wish to achieve this kind of effect, use a series of `area` elements contained within a `map`, and a simple `img` element (a client-side image map). Alternatively, you may consider a technique that uses CSS to position links absolutely over a background image.

href *for <a>*

```
href="uri"
```

SPEC		
deprecated	required	version
NO	NO	HTML 2
BROWSER SUPPORT			
IE5.5+	FF1+	Saf1.3+	Op9.2+
FULL	FULL	FULL	FULL

Example

The example below shows a link between two documents in the same directory on the server's file system:

```
<a href="cakes.html">lovely range of cakes</a>
```

The `href` defines the document to which the link leads. This may be a web page in the same directory, a page somewhere else on the same server, a location within the current page, or a web page—or any another kind of document—stored on another server.

The example shows a link between two documents in the same directory, but if the cake list document was in a directory that's one level higher than the referencing document, the syntax would be as follows:

```
<a href="../cakes.html">lovely range of cakes</a>
```

Here, ../ equates to the instruction, "move up one directory in the hierarchy."

You can also reference a document relative to the web site's root (the file or folder after the domain name):

```
<a href="/cakes.html">lovely range of cakes</a>
```

This link basically instructs the browser to "link to the document **cakes.html** that can be found in **www.mydomain.com/**." This is a very handy way of referencing documents, as you could move the document containing the link to any location on the file system without breaking the link.

If you're linking to a document (of whatever type) that's held on another server, you'd express the href using a complete URI, like so:

```
<a href="http://www.cakebrothers.com/cakes.html">lovely range of
    cakes</a>
```

In a link to another section within the same page, the destination is identified in the href attribute by a hash symbol combined with the id attribute of the destination. This notation is known as a fragment identifier, and is shown below:

```
<!-- Here is the link -->
<p>You can check the facts by reading the
  <a href="#refs">references at the end of this article</a></p>
⋮
<!-- Here is the link's destination -->
<h3><a id="refs" href="#refs">References</a></h3>
```

Note these points from the example above:

■ The href attribute is repeated in the second a element. This isn't a mistake—it's there because *without* it, Internet Explorer users who navigate to the destination would find that, although the document had moved to the correct position on the screen, the focus will not have shifted. If the user were to tab to the next link, the focus would move to the link immediately after the link the user had selected further up the page, rather than the next link after the point in the page at which the references are included.

▓ It's possible to simply apply an `id` attribute to another element—for example, `<h3 id="refs">References</h3>`—and some browsers will allow you to activate a link and jump to that point. However, not all browsers allow this, the notable case being Internet Explorer. That's why we need the seemingly superfluous second `a` element as an anchor, which is wrapped *around* the text inside the `h3`. The syntax for this simplified (but not IE-friendly) markup is shown below:

```
<p>You can check the facts by reading the
  <a href="#refs">references at the end of this article</a></p>
⋮
<h3 id="refs">References</h3>
```

In your own work, you may spot examples that include both a `name` and `id` inside the anchor `a` element. This approach is designed to ensure that the link works in older browsers which may not allow the user to jump from one part of a document to another if the `name` attribute isn't present. However, the last of the common browsers that weren't able to link to a section of a page in this way was Netscape 4, which, thankfully, is now almost completely obsolete. Also, note that in HTML 5 the `name` attribute has been removed, so it's a good idea to break the habit of using `name`.

In addition to links to documents (such as web pages or other document types), the `href` attribute may specify a different protocol, including:

ftp   typed as `<a href="ftp://someftpserver.com/">Browse the FTP server</a>`, which will open a connection to an FTP server

mailto   typed as `<a href="mailto:mrwhatever@somedomain.com">Email me!</a>`, which will trigger an email client to open and create a new message whose To address matches whatever appears after the `mailto:` protocol (in this case, an email to mrwhatever@somedomain.com)

Value

This attribute takes as its value the location of the destination document relative to the referencing document, relative to the server root, or in the form of a complete URI containing the `http://` protocol, the server name, and the path to the document on that server. It may also contain a reference to the `ftp://` or `mailto:` protocols.

Compatibility

Internet Explorer			Firefox			Safari			Opera
5.5	6.0	7.0	1.0	1.5	2.0	1.3	2.0	3.0	9.2
Full	Full	Full	Full	Full	Full	Full	Full	Full	Full

It causes no compatibility issues, and has excellent support across all tested browsers.

hreflang *for <a>*

```
hreflang="ISO language code"
```

SPEC		
deprecated	required	version
NO	NO	HTML 4
BROWSER SUPPORT			
IE7	FF2	Saf3	Op9.2
NONE	NONE	NONE	NONE

Example

A `hreflang` is defined in this link to the cakes list page, as they're special Japanese cakes:

```
<a href="cakes-ja.html" charset="euc-jp" hreflang="ja">lovely range
    of Japanese cakes (note: this link will take you to a page in
    Japanese language)</a>
```

The `hreflang` attribute is used to identify the language of text used in the linked document—the document that's referenced in the `href` attribute. It's *not* used to identify the language of the text contained within the `a` element itself—that would use the `lang` (p. 503) attribute.

Value

This attribute takes a two-letter language code[1] as its value.

---

[1] http://reference.sitepoint.com/html/lang-codes/

Compatibility

Internet Explorer			Firefox			Safari			Opera
5.5	6.0	7.0	1.0	1.5	2.0	1.3	2.0	3.0	9.2
None	None	None	None	None	None	None	None	None	None

None of the browsers tested appear to do anything to notify the user that the linked document would display in any special or different language. However, authors may still be able to use this attribute for their own purposes, as a hook for styling or scripting. For example, you might use CSS to style such links with flag icons to represent the particular language used in the destination file.

name _for <a>_

```
name="string"
```

SPEC		
deprecated	required	version
YES	NO	HTML 3.2
BROWSER SUPPORT		
IE5.5+	FF1+	Saf1.3+	Op9.2+
FULL	FULL	FULL	FULL

Example

The following example shows a link with the name attribute of "mmm-cake":

```
<a href="cakes-ja.html" name="mmm-cake">lovely range
   of Japanese cakes (note: this link will take you to
   a page in Japanese language)</a>
```

The name attribute is used to identify a link destination, or anchor, on a page. It has been superseded by the id (p. 501) attribute, but it's still used for the purposes of backwards compatibility (see the section on the href (p. 153) attribute for more).

Value

This attribute takes a—preferably short—name of the author's choosing. As this attribute will often be paired with a matching id attribute, you should observe the following rules regarding ids.

The id attribute value must begin with a letter in the roman alphabet (a–z or A–Z); this can be followed by any combination of letters (a–z or A–Z), digits (0–9), hyphens (-), underscores (_), colons (:), and periods (.). The id value is case sensitive, thus

`<span id="me">This is me</span>` and `<span id="ME">This is me</a>` would be considered to be separate and uniquely identifiable elements on the same web page.

Compatibility

Internet Explorer			Firefox			Safari			Opera
5.5	6.0	7.0	1.0	1.5	2.0	1.3	2.0	3.0	9.2
Full	Full	Full	Full	Full	Full	Full	Full	Full	Full

The use of the name attribute for the purposes of linking from one part of a page to another is well supported, but if your page is written in XHTML, this attribute's inclusion will cause your page to be invalid.

rel *for <a>*

```
rel="string"
```

SPEC		
deprecated	required	version
NO	NO	HTML 3.2
BROWSER SUPPORT		
IE7	FF2	Saf3	Op9.2
NONE	NONE	NONE	NONE

Example

The following snippet shows a link to a friend's web site, and uses the rel attribute to classify the linked page's relationship to the page on which the link occurs. This example shows an attribute defined in the Microformats XFN[2] pattern:

```
<p>I went over to <a href="http://www.djformat.com/"
    rel="friend">Matt</a>'s house. He was spinning some weird Cuban
    music for a mix he was putting together.</p>
```

The rel attribute is used to provide information about the relationship between the document that's being linked to (as defined in the href (p. 153) attribute) and the referencing document.

---

[2] http://reference.sitepoint.com/html/xfn/

Value

This attribute takes any value—it can even take a series of space-separated values. Some conventions are beginning to form around the use of the `rel` attribute, as detailed in Microformats[3].

Compatibility

Internet Explorer			Firefox			Safari			Opera
5.5	6.0	7.0	1.0	1.5	2.0	1.3	2.0	3.0	9.2
None	None	None	None	None	None	None	None	None	None

The support charts for this element show that no support is provided, as no browser renders the links that use this attribute any differently from normal links, nor does the application of `rel` change the browsers' behavior in any way. The real value of the `rel` attribute is gained either by utilizing it to add functionality via JavaScript and the DOM, or through a centralized web service of some kind that may be able to make use of the attribute's content (perhaps for analytical purposes, or for refining search results).

rev *for <a>*

```
rev="string"
```

SPEC		
deprecated	required	version
NO	NO	HTML 3.2
BROWSER SUPPORT		
IE7	FF2	Saf3	Op9.2
NONE	NONE	NONE	NONE

Example

In the following example, the link to the cakes list is defined so that the `rel`(ationship) shows that the linked document is a page that's classified as a `"product-line"`. Meanwhile, the `rev` attribute indicates that the linked page would treat the referencing page as an index of menus (or `"menu-index"`):

```
<p>You can try our <a href="cakes.html" rel="product-line"
    rev="menu-index">lovely range of cakes</a>.</p>
```

---

[3] http://reference.sitepoint.com/html/microformats/

The rev attribute is essentially the reverse of the rel (p. 158) attribute. The rev defines what *this* document is in relation to the document to which it links (as defined in the href (p. 153) attribute). To put this in colloquial terms (note that these values are not real values!):

- rel = "*This is what I call that fellow over there.*"
- rev = "*This is what that fellow over there thinks I am.*"

Value

This attribute can take any value—even a series of space-separated values. Some conventions are beginning to form around the use of the rel attribute (there's more about this in Microformats[4]).

Compatibility

Internet Explorer			Firefox			Safari			Opera
5.5	6.0	7.0	1.0	1.5	2.0	1.3	2.0	3.0	9.2
None	None	None	None	None	None	None	None	None	None

The support charts for this element show that there's no support, as no browser renders the links that use this attribute any differently from normal links. The real value of adding a rev (or rel) attribute is gained either by utilizing it to add functionality via JavaScript and the DOM, or through a centralized web service of some kind that may be able to make use of the attribute's content (perhaps for analytical purposes, or for refining search results).

---

[4] http://reference.sitepoint.com/html/microformats/

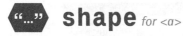

shape *for <a>*

```
shape=" { circle | default | poly | rect } "
```

	SPEC	
deprecated	required	version
NO	NO	HTML 3.2
BROWSER SUPPORT		
IE7	FF1+	Saf3	Op9.2+
NONE	FULL	NONE	FULL

Example

Here, the shape attribute for a hyperlink is set to "poly" (for polygon):

```
<a href="theweasel.html" shape="poly"
    coords="136,238,137,301,3,306,3,242">Thursday's mustache -
    'The Weasel'</a>
```

The shape attribute allows the author to define some simple area hotspots, using "rect" or "default" for rectangles, and "circle" or "poly" for more complex polygonal shapes. It's applied to the a element in the context of an object (p. 357) element. Refer to the Description (p. 150)of the coords attribute for a full rundown of how this attribute works (or rather *doesn't* work) in this context.

Value

This attribute can take values of "circle", "default", "poly", and "rect".

Compatibility

Internet Explorer			Firefox			Safari			Opera
5.5	6.0	7.0	1.0	1.5	2.0	1.3	2.0	3.0	9.2
None	None	None	Full	Full	Full	None	None	None	Full

This attribute isn't well supported. Safari and Firefox correctly position the links over the top of the image referenced in the object element; however, Internet Explorer and Safari don't position the links, and thus render the technique useless.

Refer to the Compatibility (p. 152) section of the coords attribute for more details.

Text Formatting Elements

tabindex *for <a>*

`tabindex="number"`

SPEC		
deprecated	required	version
NO	NO	HTML 3.02
BROWSER SUPPORT		
IE5.5+	FF1+	Saf1.3+ Op9.2+
FULL	FULL	FULL FULL

Example

The `tabindex` is set to "`3`" for the link below:

```
<p>You can try our <a href="cakes.html" tabindex="3">lovely
   range of cakes</a>.</p>
```

The `tabindex` is used to define a sequence that users follow when they use the Tab key to navigate through a page. By default, the natural tabbing order will match the source order in the markup. In certain circumstances it may be necessary to override the default tabbing order, but it's strongly recommended that you craft a page in a logical flow and let the browser work through it in the default order—an approach that negates the need for the `tabindex` attribute.

A `tabindex` can start at 0 and increment in any value. As such, the sequence 1, 2, 3, 4, 5 would be fine, as would 10, 20, 30, 40, 50. If you need to introduce a `tabindex`, it's advisable to use a sequence that contains intervals (like the second example provided), as this will give you the opportunity to inject other controls later if need be (for example, 10, 15, 20) without having to reindex all the `tabindex` values on the page. Should a given `tabindex` value be applied to more than one element in error, the tabbing order of those affected elements will be as per the source markup order.

If a `tabindex` is set anywhere on a page—even if it's the hundredth link or the fiftieth form control—the tab order will start at the element with the lowest `tabindex` value, and work through the increments. Only *then* will the tab order take in the remaining elements for which no `tabindex` has been set. As such, great care must be taken to ensure that adding a `tabindex` doesn't harm the usability of the page as a whole.

If the `disabled` attribute is set on an element which has a `tabindex`, that `tabindex` will be ignored.

Value

This attribute can take any numeric value.

Compatibility

Internet Explorer			Firefox			Safari			Opera
5.5	6.0	7.0	1.0	1.5	2.0	1.3	2.0	3.0	9.2
Full	Full	Full	Full	Full	Full	Full	Full	Full	Full

It causes no compatibility issues, and has excellent support across all tested browsers.

 # target *for <a>*

SPEC		
deprecated	required	version
YES	NO	HTML 2
BROWSER SUPPORT		
IE5.5+	FF1+	Saf1.3+	Op9.2+
FULL	FULL	FULL	FULL

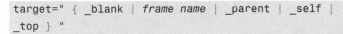

```
target=" { _blank | frame name | _parent | _self |
_top } "
```

Example

Here, the `target` attribute for the a element is set to "_top":

```
<p>You can try our <a href="cakes.html" target="_top">lovely range
   of cakes</a>.</p>
```

The `target` attribute is deprecated and its use as a layout mechanism, like that of the `frameset` (p. 494), is no longer common. However, if you do find yourself having to maintain a frameset-based web site, you may need to open links in frames or windows other than the one in which the source of the link resides.

Value

The attribute can take any of the following values:

- `"_blank"`

  loads content in a completely new window

- `"frame name"`

  loads content in a frame with a custom name

■ "_parent"

loads content in the parent frameset for the current frame

■ "_self"

loads content in the same frame (This attribute isn't normally required, as this is the default behavior unless the base (p. 77)element specifies otherwise. In that case, you'd need to override the specification using "_self"; for example, <base **target="searchresults"**/>.)

■ "_top"

loads content in the top-level frameset (in effect, the whole browser window), no matter how many nested levels down the current frame is located

Compatibility

Internet Explorer			Firefox			Safari			Opera
5.5	6.0	7.0	1.0	1.5	2.0	1.3	2.0	3.0	9.2
Full	Full	Full	Full	Full	Full	Full	Full	Full	Full

It causes no compatibility issues, and has excellent support across all tested browsers.

abbr

```
<abbr title="string">
</abbr>
```

SPEC		
deprecated	empty	version
NO	NO	HTML 4
BROWSER SUPPORT			
IE7+	FF1+	Saf1.3+	Op9.2+
FULL	FULL	FULL	FULL

Example

A simple abbreviation is marked up as follows:

```
<p>The page had the phrase <abbr title="Please Turn Over">PTO</abbr>
    written on it. If only I knew what PTO meant! I turned the page
    to see if that revealed the answer.</p>
```

The abbr element is used to provide a fully expanded alternative to an abbreviated phrase. The intention is that browsers and other assistive technologies will interpret this information and present it to the user in an appropriate format when requested.

Some documents, by their very nature, may include numerous abbreviations or acronyms. Marking up each and every one could cause the document to become very unsightly in some browsers—and would be tedious for the author having to mark each one up! A general convention is to mark up the first instance of any abbreviation or acronym.

Use This For ...

The abbr element contains the text that's part of the abbreviation, and has just one required attribute: the title (p. 167) attribute.

Compatibility

Internet Explorer			Firefox			Safari			Opera
5.5	6.0	7.0	1.0	1.5	2.0	1.3	2.0	3.0	9.2
None	None	Full	Full	Full	Full	Full	Full	Full	Full

Support for abbr is varied. Internet Explorer versions 6 and earlier don't understand the element at all, or make it available in the DOM tree for interrogation.

In all other browsers, the abbr is supported, but in varying visual styles. Firefox and Opera underline a marked-up abbreviation with a light dotted line (this can be styled using CSS); Safari recognizes the abbr content, but doesn't draw attention to it with an underline. Firefox, Opera, and Safari all display the title attribute for the abbreviation as a tooltip (hence, it's available to mouse users, but not keyboard users).

In Firefox, an abbr would display as shown in Figure 5.3 when moused over.

The page had the phrase PTO written on it. If only I knew what PTO meant. So I turned the page to see if that revealed the answer.

Please Turn Over

Figure 5.3: The title attribute of abbr shown in Firefox

In Opera 9.2, the tooltip appears in a similar fashion, but with the text "Title:" appended to it, as shown in Figure 5.4.

Text Formatting Elements

The page had the phrase PTO written on it. If only I knew what PTO meant. So I turned the page to see if that revealed the answer.

Title: Please Turn Over

Figure 5.4: The title attribute of abbr shown in Opera 9.2

As a result of the compatibility issues associated with it, many people prefer not to use this element. Instead, they write it out in full in the document in the first instance, as follows:

```
<p>The page had the phrase PTO (Please Turn Over) written on it. If
    only I knew what PTO meant! So I turned the page to see if that
    revealed the answer.</p>
```

The ways in which browsers deal with the abbr element—presenting it in a tooltip, underlined, italicized, and so on—do little to help users reading the content in printed form. This provides yet another reason to simply write out the abbreviation in the text, as shown in the HTML above. You may consider using generated content in CSS instead, but that approach is hindered by some browser support limitations.

Despite variations in the presentation of abbr content, the support chart shows that full support is provided by all browsers (except for IE 6 and earlier), as there are no guidelines in the W3C specifications to indicate how browsers should treat such content. If the element is exposed in the DOM tree, and if the browser does something with it, that constitutes full support.

Other Relevant Stuff

 acronym (p. 168)

an abbreviation comprising the initial letters of a given phrase

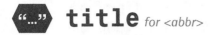

title *for <abbr>*

`title="string"`

SPEC		
deprecated	required	version
NO	NO	HTML 4
BROWSER SUPPORT		
IE7+	FF1+	Saf1.3+	Op9.2+
FULL	FULL	PARTIAL	FULL

Example

The `title` attribute is applied to an abbreviation below:

```
<p>The page had the phrase <abbr title="Please Turn Over">PTO</abbr>
    written on it. If only I knew what PTO meant. So I turned the page
    to see if that revealed the answer.</p>
```

The abbreviation is expanded within the `title` attribute, which, while it's not technically required for the `abbr` element, is advisable at least for the first instance of `abbr`; otherwise, you'd be indicating an abbreviation but not providing any further information about what it's an abbreviation of.

Value

The content of this attribute is the fully expanded version of the abbreviation contained within the element.

Compatibility

Internet Explorer			Firefox			Safari			Opera
5.5	6.0	7.0	1.0	1.5	2.0	1.3	2.0	3.0	9.2
None	None	Full	Full	Full	Full	Partial	Partial	Partial	Full

Browser support is mixed for this attribute in this instance (note that `title` is used for other elements; the compatibility notes here relate *only* to its ability to draw attention to the presence of an abbreviation).

In the chart above, the support levels have been decided on this basis:

- full where the browser displays the abbreviation with an underline and provides tooltip on mouseover

Text Formatting Elements

- partial where the browser provides a tooltip on hover, but doesn't display an underline (though it can be styled with CSS and accessed using JavaScript and the DOM)

- none where no visual rendering is provided, and the attribute isn't recognized in the DOM

acronym

```
<acronym title="string">
</acronym>
```

SPEC		
deprecated	empty	version
NO	NO	HTML 4
BROWSER SUPPORT			
IE6+	FF1+	Saf1.3+	Op9.2+
FULL	FULL	FULL	FULL

Example

An acronym is marked up as follows:

```
<p>He marvelled at how fluid the <acronym title="Graphical User
    Interface">GUI</acronym> was. It truly was a gooey GUI.</p>
```

The acronym element is similar to the abbr (p. 164) element, but takes matters one step further. Whereas the abbr element is used to describe any abbreviated phrase, acronym is used only where the phrase comprises initial letters that make a word. Often, the acronym can be spoken as if it were a word—consider NASA, pronounced "nassa," or GUI, pronounced "gooey." The intention is that browsers and assistive technologies will interpret this information and present it to the user in an appropriate format as and when requested.

The fact that this element is an acronym rather than an abbreviation offers benefits for users of assistive technologies such as screen readers, who may prefer to have the abbreviated phrase announced as a word—"nassa" instead of "enn-ay-ess-ay."

Some documents, by their very nature, may include numerous abbreviations or acronyms. Marking up each and every one could cause the document to become very unsightly in some browsers, and would be tedious for the document's author. A general convention is to mark up the first instance of an acronym.

Use This For ...

The `acronym` element contains only the text that is part of the abbreviation, and has just one attribute: the title (p. 170) attribute.

Compatibility

Internet Explorer			Firefox			Safari			Opera
5.5	6.0	7.0	1.0	1.5	2.0	1.3	2.0	3.0	9.2
None	Full	Full	Full	Full	Full	Full	Full	Full	Full

Support for the `acronym` element is varied, at least in a visual sense. Firefox and Opera underline an abbreviation with a slight dotted line (this can be styled using CSS); Safari recognizes the `acronym` content but doesn't draw attention to it with an underline. Firefox, Opera, and Safari all display the `title` attribute for the abbreviation as a tooltip (so it's available to mouse users, but not keyboard users).

In Firefox, an acronym displays as shown in Figure 5.5.

He marvelled at how fluid the GUI was. It truly was a gooey GUI.

Figure 5.5: The first GUI marked up as an acronym

Because of the compatibility issues, many people prefer not to use this element. Instead, they write it out in full in the document in the first instance, as follows:

```
<p>He marvelled at how fluid the GUI (Graphical User Interface)
    was. It truly was a gooey GUI.</p>
```

The ways in which browsers deal with the `acronym` element—presenting it in a tooltip, underlined, italicized, and so on—do little to help users reading the content in printed form. This provides yet another reason to simply write out the abbreviation in the text, as shown in the HTML above. You might consider using generated content in CSS instead,[5] but that approach is hindered by some browser support limitations.

Despite variations in the presentation of `acronym` content, the support chart shows that full support is provided by all browsers (except for IE 6 and earlier), as there

---

[5] http://reference.sitepoint.com/css/content/

are no guidelines in the W3C specifications to indicate how browsers should treat such content. If the element is exposed in the DOM tree, and if the browser does something with it, that constitutes full support.

Other Relevant Stuff

 abbr (p. 164)

defines an abbreviated form of a longer word or phrase

 ## title *for <acronym>*

```
title="string"
```

SPEC		
deprecated	required	version
NO	NO	HTML 4
BROWSER SUPPORT		
IE6+	FF1+	Saf1.3+	Op9.2+
PARTIAL	FULL	PARTIAL	FULL

Example

The `title` attribute is applied to an acronym below:

```
<p>He marvelled at how fluid the <acronym title="Graphical User
    Interface">GUI</acronym> was. It truly was a gooey GUI.</p>
```

The abbreviation is expanded within the `title` attribute, which, while it's not technically required for the `acronym` element, is advisable at least for the first instance of `acronym`; otherwise, you'd be indicating an abbreviation but not providing any further information about what it's an abbreviation of.

Value

The content of this attribute is the fully expanded version of the content contained between the opening `<acronym>` and closing `</acronym>` tags.

Compatibility

Internet Explorer			Firefox			Safari			Opera
5.5	6.0	7.0	1.0	1.5	2.0	1.3	2.0	3.0	9.2
None	Partial	None	Full	Full	Full	Partial	Partial	Partial	Full

Browser support is mixed for this attribute in this instance (note that `title` is used for other elements—the compatibility notes here relate *only* to its ability to draw attention to the presence of an acronym).

In the chart above, the support levels have been decided on this basis:

- full where the browser displays the acronym with an underline and provides tooltip on mouseover
- partial where the browser provides a tooltip on hover, but doesn't display an underline (though it can be styled with CSS and accessed using JavaScript and the DOM)
- none where no visual rendering is provided, and the attribute isn't recognized in the DOM

address

```
<address>
</address>
```

SPEC		
deprecated	empty	version
NO	NO	HTML 2
BROWSER SUPPORT			
IE5.5+	FF1+	Saf1.3+	Op9.2+
FULL	FULL	FULL	FULL

Example

The contact details of the "Editorial and News Team" are marked up with `address` in this example:

```
<address>Brought to you by the Editorial and News Team:<br/>
  <a href="mailto:news@example.org">Email the news team</a><br/>
  Mail us at PO Box 123, Citysville<br/>
  Tel +1 212 3131
</address>
```

The `address` element isn't used for the purpose that you may expect—that being to mark up a physical location *alone*. Instead, it's used to indicate the contact point for the document in which it appears. This element would usually appear in a header or footer on the page.

An address element *may* contain a geographic location, but it doesn't *have* to; it could also contain a mixture of contact points. In the example shown, the `address` element includes an email point of contact, a mailing location, and a telephone number. For the purposes of marking up a geographic location that may be machine readable, and usable in other services, you should consider marking up the physical location details using the hCard Microformat[6].

Use This For ...

This element is used to mark up contact details for the author or owner of the document, in order that the reader may use these details to contact the document's owner.

Compatibility

Internet Explorer			Firefox			Safari			Opera
5.5	6.0	7.0	1.0	1.5	2.0	1.3	2.0	3.0	9.2
Full	Full	Full	Full	Full	Full	Full	Full	Full	Full

All the browsers tested styled the content inside the `address` element in italics. There's no suggestion in the HTML specification that they should do anything else with this element, and support is stated as full.

Other Relevant Stuff

 The hCard Microformat

---

[6] http://reference.sitepoint.com/html/hcard/

b

```
<b>
</b>
```

SPEC		
deprecated	empty	version
NO	NO	HTML 2
BROWSER SUPPORT		
IE5.5+	FF1+	Saf1.3+	Op9.2+
FULL	FULL	FULL	FULL

Example

A correct usage of the b element is shown below. Here, it's used to show that the text is bold in appearance—it's not signifying importance:

```
<p>The MrBigStuff logo was a mixture of normal and bold
    characters: "Mr <b>Big</b> Stuff"</p>
```

The b (short for bold) element simply styles the text it encloses in a bold typeface—assuming it's not already presented a bold typeface—but offers no semantic meaning about the contained text.

While the b element isn't deprecated—even in XHTML 1.1—its use is declining, as in many cases it's more appropriate to use either an emphasis (em (p. 189)) or strong emphasis (strong (p. 223)) element instead.

The example above would appear as shown in Figure 5.6.

The MrBigStuff logo was a mixture of normal and bold and characters:
"Mr **Big** Stuff"

Figure 5.6: An example of b in action

Use This For ...

This element is used to mark up text which needs to be stylistically offset from the normal prose in a way that doesn't confer any extra importance on that text. The b element should, therefore, be used only as a last resort when no other element is more appropriate. For the examples above, it's preferable to use a b element rather than a span (p. 220) with a bold style applied through CSS.

Text Formatting Elements

Compatibility

Internet Explorer			Firefox			Safari			Opera
5.5	6.0	7.0	1.0	1.5	2.0	1.3	2.0	3.0	9.2
Full	Full	Full	Full	Full	Full	Full	Full	Full	Full

As one of the earliest formatting elements, b has full browser support.

Other Relevant Stuff

 strong (p. 223)

signifies strongly emphasized content

 em (p. 189)

signifies emphasized content

 # basefont

```
<basefont size="number" />
```

SPEC		
deprecated	empty	version
YES	YES	HTML 2
BROWSER SUPPORT		
IE5.5+	FF2	Saf3	Op9.2
FULL	NONE	NONE	NONE

The basefont element was originally devised as a mechanism for re-setting the default size for normal text, using the seven font sizes that were available in early versions of HTML. In most cases, web authors used it once—in the document head (p. 62)—to set a default for the entire document.

For more information visit http://reference.sitepoint.com/html/basefont/

Other Relevant Stuff

 base (p. 77)

specifies a base URL for all relative URLs contained in the document

bdo

```
<bdo dir=" { ltr | rtl } ">
</bdo>
```

	SPEC	
deprecated	empty	version
NO	NO	HTML 4
BROWSER SUPPORT		
IE5.5+	FF1+	Saf3+	Op9.2+
FULL	FULL	FULL	FULL

Example

Here's an example in which the word "Canoe" is reversed:

```
<p>A palindrome is a word, like 'kayak,' that appears
   exactly the same when all the letters are reversed.
   <bdo dir="rtl">Canoe</bdo>, it seems, is not a
   palindrome.</p>
```

The bdo element is used to reverse the direction of text enclosed between the opening
<bdo> and closing </bdo> tags. It will often be used with the lang (p. 503) or xml:lang
(p. 508) attributes, given that a common application of this element is to indicate a
change of language from the rest of the document.

Use This For ...

This element may be used to embed in a page some text that's in a language that
differs from the bulk of the document (for example, embedding a phrase in Hebrew
inside a paragraph of English); it may also be used for purely aesthetic reasons.

Compatibility

Internet Explorer			Firefox			Safari			Opera
5.5	6.0	7.0	1.0	1.5	2.0	1.3	2.0	3.0	9.2
Full	Full	Full	Full	Full	Full	None	None	Full	Full

With the exception of Safari 1.3 and 2, all browsers reverse the text properly.

"…" dir *for <bdo>*

```
dir=" { ltr | rtl } "
```

SPEC		
deprecated	required	version
NO	YES	HTML 4
BROWSER SUPPORT			
IE5.5+	FF1+	Saf3+	Op9.2+
FULL	FULL	FULL	FULL

Example

Here, the direction is set to right-to-left:

```
<p>The sequence was reversed as <bdo dir="rtl">1-2-3-4-5</bdo></p>
```

The bdo element on its own doesn't do an awful lot—it's basically useless without the dir attribute, a required attribute, to set the direction in which text should render, regardless of the order of text in the parent containers.

Value

There are only two possible values for dir: "ltr" or "rtl".

Compatibility

Internet Explorer			Firefox			Safari			Opera
5.5	6.0	7.0	1.0	1.5	2.0	1.3	2.0	3.0	9.2
Full	Full	Full	Full	Full	Full	None	None	Full	Full

With the exception of Safari 1.3 and 2, all browsers reverse the text properly, including nested bdo elements where the outer bdo specifies one direction, and the inner bdo specifies the opposite direction.

big

```
<big>
</big>
```

SPEC		
deprecated	empty	version
NO	NO	HTML 2
BROWSER SUPPORT		
IE5.5+	FF1+	Saf1.3+	Op9.2+
FULL	FULL	FULL	FULL

Example

Here's an example of the big element in use. The tags are nested to show the incremental increase of the text's size:

```
<p>It's <big>bigger, <big>better, and now with <big>20% more
    beetroot goodness!</big></big></big></p>
```

The big element is a text formatting control that increases the enclosed text by one size increment, based on the old HTML font sizes 1 through 7. Each nested big element will further increase the size by one increment.

This element isn't deprecated, but it's used less and less frequently, as there are now better methods for controlling text size (through CSS), and the big element provides no semantic value for any enclosed text— it simply states that the text needs to be bigger.

The example shown in the HTML above would render in the browser as depicted in Figure 5.7.

It's bigger, **better, and now with 20% more beetroot goodness!**

Figure 5.7: Displaying content marked up using the big element

Use This For ...

big is used to affect text content of any kind.

Text Formatting Elements

Compatibility

Internet Explorer			Firefox			Safari			Opera
5.5	6.0	7.0	1.0	1.5	2.0	1.3	2.0	3.0	9.2
Full	Full	Full	Full	Full	Full	Full	Full	Full	Full

As one of the earliest formatting elements, `big` has full browser support.

Other Relevant Stuff

 `small` (p. 219)

sets a reduced font size for the enclosed text

 # blink

```
<blink>
</blink>
```

SPEC		
deprecated	empty	version
YES	NO	N/A
BROWSER SUPPORT			
IE7	FF1+	Saf3	Op9.2+
NONE	FULL	NONE	FULL

The sole purpose of this element is to blink text on and off, and its sole result is the annoyance of all who come across it.

For more information on this element, visit http://reference.sitepoint.com/html/blink/.

 # center

```
<center>
</center>
```

SPEC		
deprecated	empty	version
YES	NO	HTML 3.2
BROWSER SUPPORT			
IE5.5+	FF1+	Saf1.3+	Op9.2+
FULL	FULL	FULL	FULL

The `center` element almost needs no description—the clue to its purpose is right there in its name. `center` centers content. This is a block-level element, so each new `center` element that you create will generate a new block of content.

For more information, visit http://reference.sitepoint.com/html/center/.

cite

```
<cite>
</cite>
```

SPEC		
deprecated	empty	version
NO	NO	HTML 2

BROWSER SUPPORT			
IE5.5+	FF1+	Saf1.3+	Op9.2+
FULL	FULL	FULL	FULL

Example

Selected works of Kurt Vonnegut are marked up in the example below:

```
<p>Kurt Vonnegut, author of such classics as <cite>Slaughterhouse
   5</cite>, <cite>Player Piano</cite>, and <cite>The Sirens of
   Titan</cite>, will be sorely missed by the literary world.</p>
```

The cite element has a very simple purpose: to identify the contained text as a reference to another source, be that a book, a play, a periodical publication, or even another web page or site. If you're referencing a web page, you may also wish to create a link to the reference using the a (p. 146) element.

Most browsers will render cite content in italics, but this style can be overridden using CSS. The example shown above would appear in a browser as depicted in Figure 5.8.

Kurt Vonnegut, author of such classics as *Slaughterhouse 5*, *Player Piano*, and *The Sirens of Titan*, will be sorely missed by the literary world.

Figure 5.8: The cite element in action

Use This For ...

This element is used to affect text content that comprises bibliographic references and references to web pages.

Compatibility

Internet Explorer			Firefox			Safari			Opera
5.5	6.0	7.0	1.0	1.5	2.0	1.3	2.0	3.0	9.2
Full	Full	Full	Full	Full	Full	Full	Full	Full	Full

Text Formatting Elements

The cite element has good browser support. All the major browsers render the affected content in italic type.

code

<code>
</code>

SPEC		
deprecated	empty	version
NO	NO	HTML 2
BROWSER SUPPORT			
IE5.5+	FF1+	Saf1.3+	Op9.2+
FULL	FULL	FULL	FULL

Example

A snippet of HTML on a reference web site, in this case explaining how to use the cite element, would be marked up like this:

```
<p>To indicate a reference to a printed work, you'd use
    the <code>cite</code> attribute as follows: <code>&lt;p&gt;My
    favorite book is &lt;cite&gt;The Two
    Towers&lt;/cite&gt;&lt;/p&gt;</code>.</p>
```

The code element's purpose is to identify computer code—for example, a snippet of HTML or XML, or some other machine-readable code, be that a server-side language such as PERL, or client-side JavaScript. Most browsers will render code content in a fixed-width font, such as Courier, but this style can be overridden using CSS.

The code element is often used in conjunction with the pre (p. 202) element (denoting preformatted text), which is used to preserve in source markup important whitespace and carriage returns that HTML and XHTML would otherwise ignore.

The example shown above would display in the browser as depicted in Figure 5.9.

```
To indicate a reference to a printed work, you'd use the cite attribute
as follows: <p>My favorite book is <cite>The Two
Towers</cite></p>.
```

Figure 5.9: HTML markup displayed using code

Note that because the example is one for which an HTML snippet is rendered on screen—and is marked up with the code element—the opening and closing p tags are written as <p> and </p> respectively. This ensures that the browser displays them on screen, rather than creating a new paragraph within the document that contains them.

Use This For …

This element is used for code, machine-readable processing instructions, HTML, XML, and markup generally.

Compatibility

Internet Explorer			Firefox			Safari			Opera
5.5	6.0	7.0	1.0	1.5	2.0	1.3	2.0	3.0	9.2
Full	Full	Full	Full	Full	Full	Full	Full	Full	Full

The `code` element has good browser support. All the major browsers render it in a fixed-width display, usually Courier.

Other Relevant Stuff

 pre (p. 202)

defines preformatted text in which whitespace and line breaks are preserved

comment

```
<comment data="uri">
</comment>
```

SPEC		
deprecated	empty	version
YES	NO	N/A
BROWSER SUPPORT		
IE5.5+	FF2	Saf3	Op9.2
FULL	NONE	NONE	NONE

The `comment` element is a nonstandard and little-supported element that's used to add comments to markup. Moving forward, it shouldn't be used—use the standard HTML comment syntax of `<!-- comment here -->`.

For more information visit http://reference.sitepoint.com/html/comment/.

Other Relevant Stuff

 Commenting Markup (p. 14)

del

```
<del cite="uri" datetime="datetime">
</del>
```

SPEC		
deprecated	empty	version
NO	NO	HTML 4
BROWSER SUPPORT			
IE5.5+	FF1+	Saf1.3+	Op9.2+
PARTIAL	PARTIAL	PARTIAL	PARTIAL

Example

The following text was hastily revised, yet the author chose to identify what was changed:

```
<p>Bernie enjoyed nothing more than a <del
   datetime="2007-11-05T23:31:05Z">night out on the town at his
   favorite drag queen show</del> <ins
   datetime="2007-11-05T23:33:32Z">quiet night in with a warm cup of
   cocoa.</ins></p>
```

The del element is used to indicate a change that saw the author delete content which appeared in an earlier version of a document.

del can be used to identify any removed content, from a specific word or phrase that's been removed (in which case the del is deemed to be an inline element) to an entire block of content, which could include a number of nested block-level elements (in this case, the del is deemed to be a block-level element).

The del element has a counterpart in the ins (p. 192) element, which is used to identify an insertion of content into a document.

Both elements have optional attributes that provide extra information about the change that has been made to the document, namely the cite (p. 184) and datetime (p. 185) attributes.

The example code above would render on screen as shown in Figure 5.10.

Bernie enjoyed nothing more than a ~~night out on the town at his favorite drag queen show~~ quiet night in with a warm cup of cocoa.

Figure 5.10: The del element in action

Whether a del element is determined to be inline or block level depends on the context in which it's used. If the del is an immediate child of body (p. 32) (with a

Strict doctype (p. 6) declaration), it's a block-level element. If it's a child of a p (p. 71) element, it's deemed to be an inline element.

Note that a del element can't contain block-level child elements when it's used in a context that would make it inline (for example, a del contained in a p can't contain a block-level element).

Use This For ...

This element can be used for inline text content, or blocks of content.

Compatibility

Internet Explorer			Firefox			Safari			Opera
5.5	6.0	7.0	1.0	1.5	2.0	1.3	2.0	3.0	9.2
Partial	Partial	Partial	Partial	Partial	Partial	Partial	Partial	Partial	Partial

The del element has good browser support; all the major browsers render deleted text with a strikethrough.

The browser support charts show partial rather than full support, because of the lack of obvious support for the element-specific attributes (cite and datetime).

Other Relevant Stuff

 ins (p. 192)

identifies inserted content

cite *for <del>*

`cite="uri"`

	SPEC	
deprecated	required	version
NO	NO	HTML 4
BROWSER SUPPORT			
IE7	FF2	Saf3	Op9.2
NONE	NONE	NONE	NONE

Example

The `cite` attribute is used in conjunction with both the `del` and `ins` elements below:

```
<p>Bernie enjoyed nothing more than a <del
   cite="http://berniesworld.com/drag.html"
   datetime="2007-11-05T23:31:05Z">night out on the town at his
   favorite drag queen show</del> <ins
   cite="http://berniesworld.com/drag.html"
   datetime="2007-11-05T23:33:32Z">quiet night in with a warm cup of
   cocoa</ins></p>
```

Perhaps the reason why the `del` element was used to change the page content is explained in an external document. In such cases, you can use the `cite` attribute to point users to that document.

Value

This element takes as its value a reference to another document in the form of a URI.

Compatibility

Internet Explorer			Firefox			Safari			Opera
5.5	6.0	7.0	1.0	1.5	2.0	1.3	2.0	3.0	9.2
None	None	None	None	None	None	None	None	None	None

None of the browsers we tested do anything useful with the `cite` attribute. It would be possible to use DOM scripting to retrieve this information for some purpose, but natively, the most that any of the tested browsers can do with `cite` is shown in the Firefox screenshot in Figure 5.11. To access this information, I had to right-click on the text and select **Properties** from the menu displayed.

Bernie enjoyed nothing more than a ~~night out on the town at his favorite~~ ~~drag queen show~~ <u>quiet night in with a warm cup of cocoa.</u>

Figure 5.11: `cite` properties as found in Firefox

Given that no visual clue is provided to indicate that the `ins` and `del` content has anything extra to reveal, few people would ever discover this information. And even if they did, the URI of the document isn't clickable, nor is the date formatted in a friendly way.

datetime *for <del>*

`datetime="datetime"`

SPEC		
deprecated	required	version
NO	NO	HTML 4
BROWSER SUPPORT			
IE7	FF2	Saf3	Op9.2
NONE	NONE	NONE	NONE

Example

The `datetime` attribute is used below in both the `del` and `ins` elements:

```
<p>Bernie enjoyed nothing more than a <del
    cite="http://berniesworld.com/drag.html"
    datetime="2007-11-05T23:31:05Z">night out on the town at his
    favorite drag queen show</del> <ins
    cite="http://berniesworld.com/drag.html"
    datetime="2007-11-05T23:33:32Z">quiet night in with a warm cup of
    cocoa</ins>
</p>
```

The `datetime` attribute contains the time stamp that reflects the time and date at which the change was made to the content using the `ins` or `del` elements. This attribute must be formatted precisely, right down to the minute and second.

Value

The `datetime` attribute is defined as follows (using the ISO8601 date format[11]):

YYYY-MM-DDThh:mm:ssTZD

Here's what the various components mean:

- YYYY: year (e.g. 2007)
- MM: month (e.g. 11 for November)
- DD: day of the month (e.g. 05)
- T: required character, a separator
- hh: hour (e.g. 23 for 11.00pm)
- mm: minutes (e.g. 31)
- ss: seconds (e.g. 05)
- TZD: Time Zone Designator (Z, which appears in the example HTML above, denotes Zulu, better known as Greenwich Mean Time.)

Compatibility

None of the browsers in the support chart do anything useful with the `datetime` attribute. It would be possible to use DOM scripting to retrieve this information for some purpose, but natively, the most that any of the browsers we tested can do is shown in the Firefox screenshot in Figure 5.12. To access this information, I had to right-click on the text and select **Properties** from the menu that displayed.

---

[11] http://www.w3.org/TR/NOTE-datetime/

Bernie enjoyed nothing more than a ~~night out on the town at his favorite drag queen show~~ <u>quiet night in with a warm cup of cocoa.</u>

Figure 5.12: `datetime` information as discovered in Firefox

Given that no visual clue is provided to indicate that the `ins` and `del` content has anything extra to reveal, few people would ever discover this information. And even if they did, the URI of the document isn't clickable, nor is the date formatted in a friendly way.

dfn

```
<dfn>
</dfn>
```

SPEC		
deprecated	empty	version
NO	NO	HTML 2
BROWSER SUPPORT		
IE5.5+ FF1+	Saf1.3+	Op9.2+
FULL FULL	FULL	FULL

Example

The term "progressive enhancement" is defined in the code below:

```
<p>The concept of <dfn>progressive enhancement</dfn> has been
    about for a few years. You could say that it describes an
    approach to web development from the point of view that 'the
    glass is half full' rather than 'the glass is half empty.'
    Progressive enhancement came to the public's attention when :</p>
```

The `dfn` element is used to identify the defining instance of a term—that is, the point in the document at which a given term (most probably an industry-specific word, or jargon of some kind) is first explained. Some, but not all, browsers will render the content inside the `dfn` element in italics, which is a long-standing typographic convention for presenting the defining instance of a word, particularly in scientific papers. You could use CSS to format the definition content in browsers that don't style the definition in italics.

The example HTML above would render as shown in Figure 5.13.

The concept of *progressive enhancement* has been about for a few years. You could say that it describes an approach to web development from the point of view that 'the glass is half full' rather than 'the glass is half empty'. Progressive enhancement came into the public's attention when ...

Figure 5.13: An example usage of `dfn`

Note that `dfn` is short for defining instance, *not* for definition—you should *not* place the actual definition of the term between the opening `<dfn>` and closing `</dfn>` tags.

Use This For ...

This element is used to hold the text content of the term that is subsequently defined in the text.

Compatibility

Internet Explorer			Firefox			Safari			Opera
5.5	6.0	7.0	1.0	1.5	2.0	1.3	2.0	3.0	9.2
Full	Full	Full	Full	Full	Full	Full	Full	Full	Full

The `dfn` has varied browser support. The major browsers render its content in italic type, but some leave it untouched.

em

```
<em>
</em>
```

SPEC		
deprecated	empty	version
NO	NO	HTML 2

BROWSER SUPPORT			
IE5.5+	FF1+	Saf1.3+	Op9.2+
FULL	FULL	FULL	FULL

Example

This example shows the em element in action:

```
<p>Do you <em>really</em> need to buy those expensive jeans? I mean,
    is it really <em>that</em> important to you to look like some kind
    of circus freak?</p>
```

The em element is used to emphasize text content, and displays in italics in all current browsers. It provides semantic meaning about the text it contains, effectively saying, "this text is slightly more important than other text here." This differentiates em from the i (p. 191) element, which merely sets the font to italics. In most cases, em is the preferred element to use.

The example code above would render as shown in Figure 5.14.

Do you *really* need to buy those expensive jeans? I mean is really *that* important to you to look like some kind of circus freak?

Figure 5.14: Displaying text marked up with em in the browser

The em element shouldn't be used simply to italicize text; the fact that emphasized text is rendered in italics is coincidental. If you have a burning desire to make text italic, but not for the purposes of emphasis, use CSS instead.

Use This For ...

This element is used to mark up text content of any kind that needs moderate emphasis.

Compatibility

Internet Explorer			Firefox			Safari			Opera
5.5	6.0	7.0	1.0	1.5	2.0	1.3	2.0	3.0	9.2
Full	Full	Full	Full	Full	Full	Full	Full	Full	Full

Text Formatting Elements

As one of the earliest formatting elements, em has full browser support.

Other Relevant Stuff

 strong (p. 223)

signifies strongly emphasized content

---

font

```
<font color="color" face="font-family,…"
size="number">
</font>
```

SPEC		
deprecated	empty	version
YES	NO	HTML 3.2
BROWSER SUPPORT			
IE5.5+	FF1+	Saf1.3+	Op9.2+
FULL	FULL	FULL	FULL

The font element is one that inspires a certain amount of loathing in these days of standards-based web design and construction. It was originally introduced as a mechanism for applying arbitrary inline styles, but was basically misused as authors tried to squeeze the most out of their web pages. The problem with font is that it offers no semantic meaning about its contents. A page heading should be marked up using a heading element (for example, h1 (p. 46), h2 (p. 50), and so on), while a quoted block of text should use blockquote (p. 28). The problem with font was that it encouraged page authors to use font to achieve those effects. Hence, we saw markup like <font size="7">Today's news</font>, rather than the more appropriate <h1>Today's news</h1>.

For more information, visit http://reference.sitepoint.com/html/font/.

i

```
<i>
</i>
```

SPEC		
deprecated	empty	version
NO	NO	HTML 2
BROWSER SUPPORT		
IE5.5+ FF1+ Saf1.3+ Op9.2+		
FULL FULL FULL FULL		

Example

The correct usage of the i element is shown below, where it's used to show that the text in a logo uses italics:

```
<p>The logo for the Left-Leaning organization uses italic text on
    the word leaning, as shown here: "left-<i>leaning</i>"</p>
```

The i (short for italic) element styles the text it contains in italics, but offers no semantic meaning about the contained text.

While the i element isn't deprecated—even in XHTML 1.1—its use is declining as, in many cases, it's more appropriate to use either an emphasis (em (p. 189)) or strong emphasis (strong (p. 223)) element instead. However, there are instances where a suitable HTML alternative isn't available, and i must be used.

Use This For ...

This element should be applied to text that needs to be stylistically offset from the normal prose, but in a way that doesn't confer any extra importance on that text. Such applications include:

- the name of a boat
- a technical term
- an idiomatic phrase from another language
- a thought

The i element should, therefore, be used only as a last resort when no other element is more appropriate. For the examples above, it's preferable to use an i element rather than a span (p. 220) to which an italic style is applied via CSS.

Text Formatting Elements

Compatibility

Internet Explorer			Firefox			Safari			Opera
5.5	6.0	7.0	1.0	1.5	2.0	1.3	2.0	3.0	9.2
Full	Full	Full	Full	Full	Full	Full	Full	Full	Full

It causes no compatibility issues, and has excellent support across all tested browsers.

Other Relevant Stuff

 em (p. 189)

signifies emphasized content

ins

```
<ins cite="uri" datetime="datetime">
</ins>
```

SPEC		
deprecated	empty	version
NO	NO	HTML 4

BROWSER SUPPORT			
IE5.5+	FF1+	Saf1.3+	Op9.2+
PARTIAL	PARTIAL	PARTIAL	PARTIAL

Example

The following text was hastily revised, yet the author chose to identify what was changed:

```
<p>Bernie enjoyed nothing more than a <del
   datetime="2007-11-05T23:31:05Z">night out on the town at his
   favorite drag queen show</del> <ins
   datetime="2007-11-05T23:33:32Z">quiet night in with a warm cup of
   cocoa</ins></p>
```

The `ins` element is used to indicate a change to the document that saw the author insert content which wasn't included in an earlier version. If you're familiar with the Track Changes tool in Microsoft Word, you can think of `ins` as HTML's slightly simplified equivalent.

`ins` can be used to identify anything from a specific word or phrase that's been inserted (in which case the `ins` is deemed to be an inline element) to an entire block of content, which could include a number of nested block-level elements (in this case, the `ins` is deemed to be a block-level element).

The ins element has a counterpart in the del (p. 182) element, which is used to identify a deletion from a document.

Both elements have optional attributes that provide extra information about the change to the document, namely the cite (p. 194) and datetime (p. 195) attributes.

The example HTML above would render as shown in Figure 5.15.

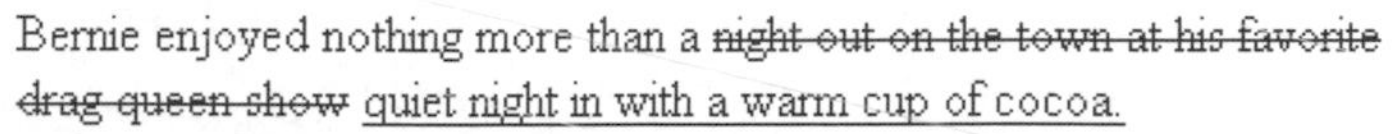

Bernie enjoyed nothing more than a ~~night out on the town at his favorite drag queen show~~ <u>quiet night in with a warm cup of cocoa.</u>

Figure 5.15: A browser interpretation of the ins element

Whether an ins element is determined to be inline or block-level depends on the context in which it's used. If the ins is an immediate child of body (p. 32) (with a Strict doctype (p. 6) declaration), it's a block-level element. If it's a child of a p (p. 71) element, it's deemed to be an inline element.

Note that a ins element can't contain block-level child elements when it's used in a context that would make it inline (for example, an ins contained inside a p can't contain a block-level element).

Use This For ...

This element can be applied to inline text content, or blocks of content.

Compatibility

Internet Explorer			Firefox			Safari			Opera
5.5	6.0	7.0	1.0	1.5	2.0	1.3	2.0	3.0	9.2
Partial	Partial	Partial	Partial	Partial	Partial	Partial	Partial	Partial	Partial

The ins element has good browser support; all the major browsers render inserted text with an underline (although this effect could be restyled using CSS as appropriate).

The browser support charts show partial rather than full support for this element, because of the lack of obvious support for the element-specific attributes (cite and datetime).

Text Formatting Elements

Other Relevant Stuff

 del (p. 182)

identifies deleted content

 cite *for <ins>*

`cite="uri"`

SPEC		
deprecated	required	version
NO	NO	HTML 4
BROWSER SUPPORT		
IE7	FF2	Saf3	Op9.2
NONE	NONE	NONE	NONE

Example

The `cite` attribute is used in conjunction with both the `del` and `ins` elements below:

```
<p>Bernie enjoyed nothing more than a <del
    cite="http://berniesworld.com/drag.html"
    datetime="2007-11-05T23:31:05Z">night out on the town at his
    favorite drag queen show</del> <ins
    cite="http://berniesworld.com/drag.html"
    datetime="2007-11-05T23:33:32Z">quiet night in with a warm cup of
    cocoa</ins></p>
```

Perhaps the reason why the `ins` element was used to change the page content is explained in an external document. In such cases, you can use the `cite` attribute to point users to that document.

Value

This element takes as its value a reference to another document in the form of a URI.

Compatibility

Internet Explorer			Firefox			Safari			Opera
5.5	6.0	7.0	1.0	1.5	2.0	1.3	2.0	3.0	9.2
None	None	None	None	None	None	None	None	None	None

None of the browsers we tested do anything useful with the `cite` attribute. It would be possible to use DOM scripting to retrieve this information for some purpose, but natively, the most that any of the tested browsers can do with `cite` is shown in the Firefox screenshot in Figure 5.16. To access this information, I had to right-click on the text and select Properties from the menu that displayed.

Figure 5.16: The properties of `cite` as discovered in Firefox

Given that no visual clue is provided to indicate that the `ins` and `del` content has anything extra to reveal, few people would ever discover this information. And even if they did, the URI of the document isn't clickable, nor is the date formatted in a friendly way.

"...." **datetime** *for <ins>*

`datetime="datetime"`

SPEC		
deprecated	required	version
NO	NO	HTML 4
BROWSER SUPPORT			
IE7	FF2	Saf3	Op9.2
NONE	NONE	NONE	NONE

Example

The `datetime` attribute is used in both the `del` and `ins` elements below:

```
<p>Bernie enjoyed nothing more than a <del
    cite="http://berniesworld.com/drag.html"
    datetime="2007-11-05T23:31:05Z">night out on the town at his
    favorite drag queen show</del> <ins
    cite="http://berniesworld.com/drag.html"
    datetime="2007-11-05T23:33:32Z">quiet night in with a warm cup of
    cocoa</ins></p>
```

The datetime attribute contains the time stamp that reflects the time and date at which the change was made to the content using the ins or del elements. This attribute must be formatted precisely, right down to the minute and second.

Value

The datetime attribute is defined as follows (using the ISO8601 date format[13]):

YYYY-MM-DDThh:mm:ssTZD

Here's what the various components mean:

- YYYY: year (e.g. 2007)
- MM: month (e.g. 11 for November)
- DD: day of the month (e.g. 05)
- T: required character, a separator
- hh: hour (e.g. 23 for 11.00pm)
- mm: minutes (e.g. 31)
- ss: seconds (e.g. 05)
- TZD: Time Zone Designator (Z, which appears in the example HTML above, denotes Zulu, better known as Greenwich Mean Time.)

Compatibility

None of the browsers in the support chart do anything useful with the datetime attribute. It would be possible to use DOM scripting to retrieve this information for some purpose, but natively, the most that any of the browsers we tested can do is shown in the Firefox screenshot in Figure 5.12. To access this information, I had to right-click on the text and select **Properties** from the menu that displayed.

---

[13] http://www.w3.org/TR/NOTE-datetime

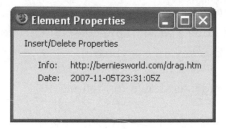

Bernie enjoyed nothing more than a ~~night out on the town at his favorite drag queen show~~ <u>quiet night in with a warm cup of cocoa.</u>

Figure 5.17: How Firefox shows `datetime` information

Given that no visual clue is provided to indicate that the `ins` and `del` content has anything extra to reveal, few people would ever discover this information. And even if they did, the URI of the document isn't clickable, nor is the date formatted in a friendly way.

kbd

```
<kbd>
</kbd>
```

SPEC		
deprecated	empty	version
NO	NO	HTML 2
BROWSER SUPPORT		
IE5.5+	FF1+	Saf1.3+	Op9.2+
FULL	FULL	FULL	FULL

Example

A support site that provides instructions to help Windows users to unfreeze an application might include the following HTML:

```
<p>Hold down <kbd>CTRL</kbd>, <kbd>ALT</kbd>, and <kbd>DELETE</kbd>,
    then select Task Manager</p>
```

The `kbd` element is used to identify keystrokes that the user needs to make on his or her keyboard. These keystrokes could form a string of text, or they could reflect individual key presses that the user must complete (for example, pressing Enter or Backspace). It's most likely to be found in online technical manuals or support sites.

Most browsers will render kbd content in a monospace font, but it's possible to style its display with CSS (for example, setting a background color and a border to make the character appear a little more like a key on a keyboard).

The example HTML above would render as shown in Figure 5.18.

Hold down CTRL, ALT, and DELETE, then select Task Manager

Figure 5.18: The browser displays the kbd element as monospaced

Use This For ...

This element is used to identify individual key presses, complete words that must be typed, or buttons that should be pressed on a keypad.

Compatibility

Internet Explorer			Firefox			Safari			Opera
5.5	6.0	7.0	1.0	1.5	2.0	1.3	2.0	3.0	9.2
Full	Full	Full	Full	Full	Full	Full	Full	Full	Full

The kbd has good browser support; most major browsers render it in a fixed-width font.

marquee

```
<marquee align=" { top | middle | bottom } "
behavior=" { scroll | slide | alternate } "
direction=" { left | right } " loop="number"
bgcolor="color" height=" { number | pecentage } "
width=" { number | pecentage } " hspace="number"
vspace="number" scrollamount="number"
scrolldelay="number">
</marquee>
```

SPEC		
deprecated	empty	version
YES	NO	N/A
BROWSER SUPPORT		
IE5.5+	FF1+ Saf1.3+	Op9.2+
PARTIAL	PARTIAL PARTIAL	PARTIAL

The marquee element provides a way for browsers to render text that moves across the page without having to resort to JavaScript techniques. The marquee is nonstandard but enjoys (or possibly suffers from) good browser support.

For more information, visit http://reference.sitepoint.com/html/marquee/.

nobr

```
<nobr>
</nobr>
```

SPEC		
deprecated	empty	version
YES	NO	N/A
BROWSER SUPPORT			
IE5.5+	FF1+	Saf1.3+	Op9.2+
FULL	FULL	FULL	FULL

nobr is a proprietary element (that is, it wasn't based on any standard). It was used to define sections of text that the browser shouldn't allow to wrap, regardless of what may happen as a consequence of that instruction; for example, when the user reduced the size of the viewport. As it's deprecated—and its effects can be achieved using CSS—you shouldn't use this element; this information is provided for reference purposes only.

For more information, visit http://reference.sitepoint.com/html/nobr/.

Other Relevant Stuff

 pre (p. 202)

defines preformatted text in which whitespace and line breaks are preserved

 wbr (p. 229)

indicates the position in a word at which a break should occur

Text Formatting Elements

noscript

```
<noscript>
</noscript>
```

SPEC		
deprecated	empty	version
NO	NO	HTML 4
BROWSER SUPPORT			
IE5.5+	FF1+	Saf1.3+	Op9.2+
FULL	FULL	FULL	FULL

Example

This example shows a typical application of noscript:

```
<noscript>
  <h1>Houston, we have a problem</h1>
  <p>It appears that your web browser does not support JavaScript,
     or you have temporarily disabled scripting. Either way, this site
     won't work without it. Please take a look at our
     <a href="/support/browsers/">browser support page</a> for more help.
</noscript>
```

The noscript element has but one purpose: to provide content for people accessing the web page with a browser that either doesn't support client-side scripting, or that has had its script support disabled by the user, perhaps for security reasons. Inside noscript you can use the same HTML elements that you'd include the body (p. 32) element; for example, headings, paragraphs, and other elements which are appropriate to the doctype (p. 6) that you specify. However, you can't use noscript inside the head (p. 62) to provide alternatives for JavaScript functions, as that would involve writing content inside the head element.

Note that it's not just humans who might benefit from noscript content. If you have a web page that uses client-side scripting to create navigation, for example, those links will be all but hidden from search engines, which won't parse the scripts contained in the script (p. 102) element. A simplified navigation block within the noscript element can provide a route for search engines to follow when they're indexing your site, regardless of whether the users ever see that content.

There's one gray area that you should be aware of. The content inside the noscript will only appear if scripts aren't supported, or are disabled in the user's browser. There are scenarios in which a script won't be actioned—for example, when security settings on a firewall detect potentially malicious code in an external script file, and block the scripts. This kind of situation may cause a page to render improperly, but `noscript` won't be shown, because in this case scripts *are* supported, it's just that some have been blocked.

The solution? Don't rely on `noscript` completely. It may be better simply to create a message on the page in clear text—for example, in a `div` (p. 44) with an `id` (p. 501) (to uniquely identify the element). Then, use the scripting capability to check that the script's functions, variables, and objects have been successfully loaded and work properly. If all the conditions are met, use scripting to retrospectively remove or update the content of that message. If the part of the script that performs the magic fails to make it through the firewall, so will the ability to remove that warning message.

Use This For ...

This element is used to provide a warning message that scripts aren't supported or have been disabled, to provide a pointer to show users how they can resolve the problem, or alternatively, to provide a simplified version of the content that would have appeared if scripting were enabled (although that approach brings with it the issue of maintaining two versions of your markup).

Compatibility

Internet Explorer			Firefox			Safari			Opera
5.5	6.0	c7.0	1.0	1.5	2.0	1.3	2.0	3.0	9.2
Full	Full	Full	Full	Full	Full	Full	Full	Full	Full

Every browser listed supports this element type.

Other Relevant Stuff

 `script` (p. 102)

contains (or refers to) statements in a scripting language that are to be processed on the client side

plaintext

```
<plaintext>
</plaintext>
```

	SPEC	
deprecated	empty	version
YES	YES	N/A
BROWSER SUPPORT			
IE5.5+	FF1+	Saf1.3+	Op9.2+
PARTIAL	PARTIAL	PARTIAL	PARTIAL

The `plaintext` element was originally intended to instruct the browser to ignore any formatting or HTML markup. As such, `<p>` would appear on screen as `<p>`, rather than actually creating a new paragraph. This element is now deprecated and is probably best forgotten entirely.

For more information, visit http://reference.sitepoint.com/html/plaintext/.

Other Relevant Stuff

 pre (p. 202)

defines preformatted text in which whitespace and line breaks are preserved

pre

```
<pre>
</pre>
```

	SPEC	
deprecated	empty	version
NO	NO	HTML 2
BROWSER SUPPORT			
IE5.5+	FF1+	Saf1.3+	Op9.2+
FULL	FULL	FULL	FULL

Example

A snippet of HTML on a reference web site, in this case using the `pre` and `code` elements to markup some code:

```
<pre><code>//Do a bit of code debugging        ||-- Check Array vals
document.write ("&lt;ul&gt;");
for (i=1;i&lt;array.length;i++)
  {
 str += "&lt;li&gt;Value of array " + i + " is: " +array[i] + "&lt;/li&gt;";

  }
document.write(str);
document.write ("&lt;/ul&gt;");
</code></pre>
```

The pre element is used to preserve important whitespace and carriage returns in source markup that HTML or XHTML would otherwise ignore. By default, only the first space is honored; subsequent spaces—unless specified using the   entity—aren't rendered by browsers. The pre element is most frequently used in conjunction with the code (p. 180) element to render code examples in which the presence of spaces and/or carriage returns may make a crucial difference as to whether the code will work or not when it is copied and pasted elsewhere.

The example presented above would appear on screen as shown in Figure 5.19. Note the spacing before the ||-Check Array vals section, as well as the fact that each line is output on a new line without the need for a br (p. 40) element.

```
//Do a bit of code debugging              ||-- Check Array vals
document.write ("<ul>");
for (i=1;i<array.length;i++)
  {
  str += "<li>Value of array " + i + " is: " +array[i] + "</li>";
  }
document.write(str);
document.write ("</ul>");
```

Figure 5.19: Displaying some code using pre

In this example, JavaScript is being used to write out HTML, which is then rendered on screen. Thus, in the source code, the opening and closing ul and li tags are written as <ul> … </ul>, and <li> … </li> respectively, so that the browser displays them on screen rather than attempting to interpret them and create new list items.

Use This For ...

Use pre for content whose whitespace has semantic meaning. If you want to retain whitespace for visual purposes, but those spaces don't actually have any semantic meaning, use the "white-space" CSS property instead.

Compatibility

Internet Explorer			Firefox			Safari			Opera
5.5	6.0	7.0	1.0	1.5	2.0	1.3	2.0	3.0	9.2
Full	Full	Full	Full	Full	Full	Full	Full	Full	Full

The pre element enjoys good browser support, with all the major browsers rendering it in a fixed-width font—usually Courier.

Other Relevant Stuff

 code (p. 180)

identifies text as computer or machine-readable code

q

```
<q cite="uri">
</q>
```

SPEC		
deprecated	empty	version
NO	NO	HTML 4
BROWSER SUPPORT		
IE7	FF1+ Saf1.3+	Op9.2+
NONE	PARTIAL PARTIAL	PARTIAL

Example

Here's an example of the q element in use:

```
<p>Heck, even Bill Gates is quoted as saying <q>We need
    Microformats,</q> which can only be a good thing for the cause.</p>
```

The q element is little brother (or sister) to the `blockquote` (p. 28) element. Where `blockquote` creates a distinct block of quoted text, the more svelte q element is used for inline quotations. It's intended that the browser should insert the necessary quotation marks, the style of which should depend on the language of the document or that section of the document, rather than the author adding quotation marks, which can cause double quotation marks to appear.

The example code above would render as shown in Figure 5.20.

Heck, even Bill Gates is quoted as saying "We need Microformats", which can only be a good thing for the cause.

Figure 5.20: q in action

Use This For ...

This element is used to mark up a quotation, possibly with attribution in the form of a `cite` attribute, although this is optional.

Compatibility

	Internet Explorer		Firefox			Safari			Opera
5.5	6.0	7.0	1.0	1.5	2.0	1.3	2.0	3.0	9.2
None	None	None	Partial	Partial	Partial	Partial	Partial	Partial	Partial

The q element doesn't cause any discernible change in the style of text in any browser tested, but it does add the necessary quotation marks in all the browsers that were tested (with the exception of Internet Explorer). The support tables show partial rather than full support because of the browsers' failure to reveal the information contained in the cite (p. 205) attribute.

Other Relevant Stuff

 blockquote (p. 28)

used to indicate a block of quoted text, with an attribution that identifies who said or wrote it

 cite *for <q>*

`cite="uri"`

SPEC		
deprecated	required	version
NO	NO	HTML 4
BROWSER SUPPORT		
IE7	FF2	Saf3	Op9.2
NONE	NONE	NONE	NONE

Example

This example shows a quote with the correct attribution in the form of the cite attribute:

```
<p>Heck, even Bill Gates is quoted as saying <q
    cite="http://microformats.org/blog/2006/03/20/
➥bill-gates-at-mix06-we-need-microformats/">We
    need Microformats,</q> which can only be a
    good thing for the cause.</p>
```

Apart from the core (p. 498) and event attributes (p. 509) that are used across all HTML elements, q has the cite attribute, which is used to identify the online source of the quotation in the form of a URI (for example, `"http://sourcewebsite.doc/document.html"`). The value of the cite attribute isn't rendered on screen (although this potentially useful meta data could be extracted and written back into the web page through the magic of DOM Scripting). As such, browser support for this attribute is marked as none, but because it has other potential uses (for search engine indexing, retrieval via DOM Scripting, and more) and there is the likelihood of improved native support being provided for the attribute in future browser versions, you should use the `cite` attribute when you use `q`.

Value

This attribute takes as its value a URI—the complete path (not a relative path from the quoting page) to the source of the quotation.

Compatibility

Internet Explorer			Firefox			Safari			Opera
5.5	6.0	7.0	1.0	1.5	2.0	1.3	2.0	3.0	9.2
None	None	None	None	None	None	None	None	None	None

`cite` is uniformly ignored by all browsers in a visual sense.

rb

SPEC		
deprecated	empty	version
NO	NO	XHTML 1.1
BROWSER SUPPORT		
IE5.5+	FF2	Saf3	Op9.2
FULL	NONE	NONE	NONE

```
<rb>
</rb>
```

Example

An example usage of rb:

```
<ruby>
 <rb>家辺 勝文</rb>
 <rt>liaison</rt>
</ruby>
```

The `rb` element is a child element of the `ruby` (p. 216) element, and is used to contain the characters that require pronunciation help or are displayed as a learning aid.

For simple ruby markup, only one rb element may appear. However, there are more complex mechanisms for marking up ruby—including the use of the rbc (p. 208) element—which do allow for the presence of multiple instances of the rb element.

Use This For ...

This element is used to contain foreign characters that require annotation.

Compatibility

Internet Explorer			Firefox			Safari			Opera
5.5	6.0	7.0	1.0	1.5	2.0	1.3	2.0	3.0	9.2
Full	Full	Full	None	None	None	None	None	None	None

Only Internet Explorer offers any support for text marked up using ruby at this time. Other browsers ignore the markup and display the ruby text in the order in which it appears in the source.

Other Relevant Stuff

 ruby (p. 216)

provides a mechanism for annotating foreign characters

 rbc (p. 208)

defines the ruby base container for complex ruby markup

Text Formatting Elements

rbc

```
<rbc>
</rbc>
```

SPEC		
deprecated	empty	version
NO	NO	XHTML 1.1
BROWSER SUPPORT			
IE5.5+	FF2	Saf3	Op9.2
BUGGY	NONE	NONE	NONE

Example

Consider this example usage of rbc:

```
<ruby xml:lang="ja">
  <rbc>
    <rb>斎</rb>
    <rb>藤</rb>
    <rb>信</rb>
    <rb>男</rb>
  </rbc>
  <rtc class="reading">
    <rt>さい</rt>
    <rt>とう</rt>
    <rt>のぶ</rt>
    <rt>お</rt>
  </rtc>
  <rtc class="annotation">
    <rt rbspan="4" xml:lang="en">W3C
    Associate Chairman</rt>
  </rtc>
</ruby>
```

The rbc (ruby base container) element groups a collection of rb (p. 206) elements that will have related annotations in a subsequent rtc (p. 214) container. In the example shown above, which was taken from the W3C documentation, the rbc contains four Japanese characters (the more complex kanji symbols), each of which has its own rb element. Meanwhile, the ruby annotations inside the related rt (p. 211) elements are written in hiragana syllables (known as furigana when used for this purpose). Finally, there's an English annotation that spans all four of the previous rb and rt (p. 211) elements.

The intended rendering of this code is shown in Figure 5.21. However, only the first image in the example is behaving—and that's because it's a suggested rendering in the W3C documentation. The code's true rendering is shown in the following two images, which are taken from Internet Explorer and Firefox, respectively.

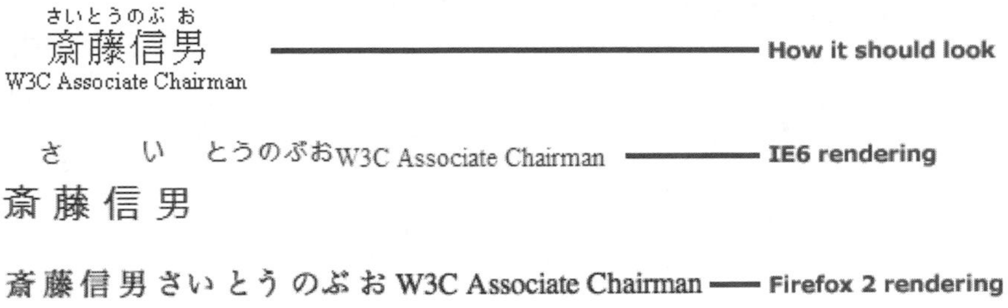

さいとうのぶ お
斎藤信男 ——————————————————— **How it should look**
W3C Associate Chairman

さ　　い　とうのぶおW3C Associate Chairman ——— **IE6 rendering**
斎 藤 信 男

斎藤信男 さい とう のぶ お W3C Associate Chairman —— **Firefox 2 rendering**

Figure 5.21: Poor levels of support for `rbc` and `rtc` elements

Use This For ...

This element is used to contain multiple `rb` (ruby base text) elements in complex ruby annotations.

Compatibility

Internet Explorer			Firefox			Safari			Opera
5.5	6.0	7.0	1.0	1.5	2.0	1.3	2.0	3.0	9.2
Buggy	Buggy	Buggy	None	None	None	None	None	None	None

Only Internet Explorer offers any support for text marked up using `ruby` at this time. Other browsers ignore the markup and display the ruby text in the order in which it appears in the source.

Other Relevant Stuff

`ruby` (p. 216)

provides a mechanism for annotating foreign characters

`rtc` (p. 214)

defines a ruby text container for complex ruby markup

`rb` (p. 206)

specifies ruby base text

rp

```
<rp>
</rp>
```

SPEC		
deprecated	empty	version
NO	NO	XHTML 1.1
BROWSER SUPPORT		
IE5.5+	FF2	Saf3	Op9.2
FULL	NONE	NONE	NONE

Example

Consider this example usage of rp:

```
<ruby>
 <rb>家辺 勝文</rb>
 <rt><rp>(</rp>liaison<rp>)</rp></rt>
</ruby>
```

Despite having been defined as far back as 2001, ruby doesn't enjoy great support in browsers. For a change, Internet Explorer is ahead of the game on this one! Created in light of the fact that not all browsers will understand ruby, the rp element may be used to present content to users who are viewing the ruby text on a browser that doesn't understand or support ruby, but removes that content for browsers that *do* support ruby. The content inside the rp element should be an opening or closing parenthesis, although there's no definitive rule about which character should be used. It's most likely that you'll use "(",")","[" or "]".

The effect of using rp can be seen in Figure 5.22.

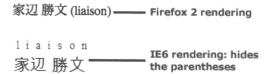

Figure 5.22: The ruby rp element hiding parentheses in supporting browsers

Use This For ...

This element is used to contain the annotation that relates to the foreign characters (contained in the rb element) which require annotation.

Compatibility

Internet Explorer			Firefox			Safari			Opera
5.5	6.0	7.0	1.0	1.5	2.0	1.3	2.0	3.0	9.2
Full	Full	Full	None	None	None	None	None	None	None

Only Internet Explorer offers any support for text marked up using ruby at this time. Other browsers ignore the markup and display the ruby text in the order in which it appears in the source.

Other Relevant Stuff

 ruby (p. 216)

provides a mechanism for annotating foreign characters

 rtc (p. 214)

defines a ruby text container for complex ruby markup

 # rt

SPEC		
deprecated	empty	version
NO	NO	XHTML 1.1
BROWSER SUPPORT			
IE5.5+	FF2	Saf3	Op9.2
FULL	NONE	NONE	NONE

```
<rt rbspan="number">
</rt>
```

Example

Here's rt in action:

```
<ruby>
 <rb>家辺 勝文</rb>
 <rt>liaison</rt>
</ruby>
```

The rt element is a child element of the ruby (p. 216) element and contains the annotation that will be displayed to the user on screen, ideally beside or above the base text (rb) which requires the annotation.

Text Formatting Elements

For simple ruby markup, only one rt element may appear. However, there are more complex mechanisms for marking up ruby, using the rtc (p. 214) element, which do allow for multiple instances of the rt element.

Use This For ...

This element is used to contain the annotation that relates to the foreign characters (contained in the rb element) that require annotation.

Compatibility

Internet Explorer			Firefox			Safari			Opera
5.5	6.0	7.0	1.0	1.5	2.0	1.3	2.0	3.0	9.2
Full	Full	Full	None	None	None	None	None	None	None

Only Internet Explorer offers any support for text marked up using ruby at this time. Other browsers ignore the markup and display the ruby text in the order in which it appears in the source.

Other Relevant Stuff

 ruby (p. 216)

provides a mechanism for annotating foreign characters

 rtc (p. 214)

defines a ruby text container for complex ruby markup

rbspan _for_ <rt>

rbspan="_number_"

SPEC		
deprecated	required	version
NO	NO	XHTML 1.1
BROWSER SUPPORT		
IE7	FF2	Saf3	Op9.2
NONE	NONE	NONE	NONE

Example

In this code, the English annotation is set to span all four of the Japanese characters:

```
<ruby xml:lang="ja">
  <rbc>
    <rb>斎</rb>
    <rb>藤</rb>
    <rb>信</rb>
    <rb>男</rb>
  </rbc>
  <rtc class="reading">
    <rt>さい</rt>
    <rt>とう</rt>
    <rt>のぶ</rt>
    <rt>お</rt>
  </rtc>
  <rtc class="annotation">
    <rt rbspan="4" xml:lang="en">W3C
    Associate Chairman</rt>
  </rtc>
</ruby>
```

The rbspan attribute allows you to specify, using their respective rb (p. 206) elements, the number of characters in a previous ruby base container (rbc (p. 208)) that the annotation in this rt (p. 211) element relates to. To put that into context, consider the example shown above. The four Japanese characters collectively relate to the title of W3C Associate Chairman; hence, we make that annotation span four rb elements using rbspan="4".

Value

This attribute takes as its value a number that must tally with the number of rb elements contained inside the rbc element to which it relates.

Compatibility

Internet Explorer			Firefox			Safari			Opera
5.5	6.0	7.0	1.0	1.5	2.0	1.3	2.0	3.0	9.2
None	None	None	None	None	None	None	None	None	None

Only Internet Explorer offers any support for text marked up using ruby at this time. Other browsers ignore the markup and display the ruby text in the order in which it appears in the source.

rtc

```
<rtc>
</rtc>
```

SPEC		
deprecated	empty	version
NO	NO	XHTML 1.1
BROWSER SUPPORT		
IE5.5+	FF2	Saf3	Op9.2
BUGGY	NONE	NONE	NONE

Example

Consider this example usage of rtc:

```
<ruby xml:lang="ja">
  <rbc>
    <rb>斎</rb>
    <rb>藤</rb>
    <rb>信</rb>
    <rb>男</rb>
  </rbc>
  <rtc class="reading">
    <rt>さい</rt>
    <rt>とう</rt>
    <rt>のぶ</rt>
    <rt>お</rt>
  </rtc>
  <rtc class="annotation">
    <rt rbspan="4" xml:lang="en">W3C
    Associate Chairman</rt>
  </rtc>
</ruby>
```

The rtc (ruby text container) element groups a collection of rt (p. 211) elements that hold the annotations related to the contents of the rbc (p. 208) container. The example above contains four Japanese characters (the more complex Kanji symbols), each with its own rb element, while the ruby annotations inside the related rt

(p. 211) elements are written in hiragana syllables (known as furigana when used for this purpose). In the example shown above, which was taken from the W3C documentation, there are two `rtc` elements that provide Japanese and English annotations.

The intended rendering of this code is shown in Figure 5.21. However, only the first image in the example is behaving—and that's because it's a suggested rendering in the W3C documentation. The code's true rendering is shown in the following two images, which are taken from Internet Explorer and Firefox, respectively.

さいとうのぶ お
斎藤信男 ——————————————— **How it should look**
W3C Associate Chairman

さ   い   とうのぶおW3C Associate Chairman ——— **IE6 rendering**
斎 藤 信 男

斎 藤 信 男 さい とう のぶ お W3C Associate Chairman —— **Firefox 2 rendering**

Figure 5.23: Poor levels of support for `rbc` and `rtc` elements

Use This For ...

This element is used to contain multiple `rt` elements in complex ruby annotations.

Compatibility

Internet Explorer			Firefox			Safari			Opera
5.5	6.0	7.0	1.0	1.5	2.0	1.3	2.0	3.0	9.2
Buggy	Buggy	Buggy	None	None	None	None	None	None	None

Only Internet Explorer offers any support for text marked up using `ruby` at this time. Other browsers ignore the markup and display the ruby text in the order in which it appears in the source.

Other Relevant Stuff

 `ruby` (p. 216)

provides a mechanism for annotating foreign characters

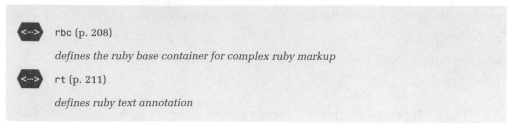

rbc (p. 208)

defines the ruby base container for complex ruby markup

rt (p. 211)

defines ruby text annotation

ruby

```
<ruby>
</ruby>
```

SPEC		
deprecated	empty	version
NO	NO	XHTML 1.1
BROWSER SUPPORT		
IE5.5+	FF2	Saf3	Op9.2
PARTIAL	NONE	NONE	NONE

Example

Here's an example of ruby in action:

```
<p>
 <ruby>
  <rb>家辺 勝文</rb>
  <rt>liaison</rt>
 </ruby>
</p>
```

The ruby element provides a mechanism for annotating characters of East Asian languages (Japanese, Chinese, Korean, and so on). Typically, these annotations appear in a smaller typeface above or beside the regular text, as Figure 5.24 shows.

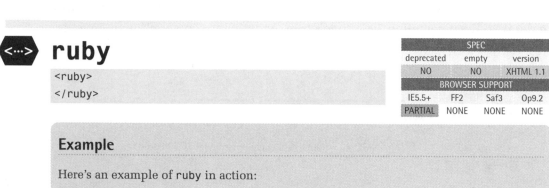

Figure 5.24: Ruby text as shown in Internet Explorer (supported) and Firefox (not supported)

The ruby element contains rb (p. 206) and rt (p. 211) elements, which relate to ruby base text, and the annotation for that base text, respectively. The ruby element may also contain the rp (p. 210) element (ruby parentheses) which is used to provide some visual help for non ruby-supporting browsers.

Use This For ...

This element is used to provide help with users' pronunciation of obscure characters, or as a language learning aid.

Compatibility

Internet Explorer			Firefox			Safari			Opera
5.5	6.0	7.0	1.0	1.5	2.0	1.3	2.0	3.0	9.2
Partial	Partial	Partial	None	None	None	None	None	None	None

Only Internet Explorer offers any support for text marked up using ruby at this time. Other browsers ignore the markup and display the ruby text in the order in which it appears in the source.

Other Relevant Stuff

 rb (p. 206)

specifies ruby base text

 rt (p. 211)

defines ruby text annotation

---

 s

```
<s>
</s>
```

SPEC		
deprecated	empty	version
YES	NO	HTML 3
BROWSER SUPPORT		
IE5.5+	FF1+	Saf1.3+	Op9.2+
FULL	FULL	FULL	FULL

The s is identical in purpose to the strike (p. 222) element.

For more information, visit http://reference.sitepoint.com/html/s/.

Other Relevant Stuff

 del (p. 182)

identifies deleted content

 strike (p. 222)

renders text with a horizontal strike (line) through the middle

samp

```
<samp>
</samp>
```

SPEC		
deprecated	empty	version
NO	NO	HTML 2
BROWSER SUPPORT			
IE5.5+	FF1+	Saf1.3+	Op9.2+
FULL	FULL	FULL	FULL

Example

In this example, a support site provides an explanation of a 404 error:

```
<p>If the browser spits out an error message such as
   <samp>HTTP 404 - File not found</samp>,
   you may simply have typed the address incorrectly.</p>
```

The samp element's purpose is to identify a sample of characters that form the output or result of some process. It's not often seen in practice, but would most probably be encountered in an online technical manual or support site of some kind.

The example code would render as shown in Figure 5.25.

If the browser spits out an error message such as HTTP 404 - File not found, you may simply have typed the address incorrectly.

Figure 5.25: Browser output of samp element

Use This For ...

This element is used to mark up a sequence of characters or a phrase that forms the output of some kind of machine or computer process.

Compatibility

Internet Explorer			Firefox			Safari			Opera
5.5	6.0	7.0	1.0	1.5	2.0	1.3	2.0	3.0	9.2
Full	Full	Full	Full	Full	Full	Full	Full	Full	Full

The samp has good browser support: most of the major browsers render it in a fixed-width font.

small

```
<small>
</small>
```

SPEC

	SPEC	
deprecated	empty	version
NO	NO	HTML 2
BROWSER SUPPORT		
IE5.5+	FF1+	Saf1.3+	Op9.2+
FULL	FULL	FULL	FULL

Example

Here's an example of the small element in use (nested):

```
<p>Mark tried to get out of buying a round of drinks by getting
    progressively quieter as he talked: "Right, I'm off to stretch my
    legs and then get a bag of peanuts ... <small>back in a minute ...
    <small>everyone OK for a drink?</small></small></p>
```

The small element is a text formatting control that reduces the size of the enclosed text by one size decrement (based on the old HTML font sizes 1 through 7). Each nested small element will further decrement the size.

This element is not deprecated, but is used less frequently now, as there are better methods for controlling text size (such as CSS), and because the small element provides no semantic value for any enclosed text—it simply states that the text needs to be smaller.

The example code above would render as shown in Figure 5.26.

Mark tried to get out of buying a round of drinks by getting progressively quieter as he talked: "Right, I'm off to stretch my legs and then get a bag of peanuts ... back in a minute ... everyone OK for a drink?

Figure 5.26: Displaying text to which small is applied

Some people argue that small can be used to indicate content that's less important than that nearby. While there is nothing in the current HTML specification to support it, the HTML5 draft proposal states that, "The small element represents small print (part of a document often describing legal restrictions, such as copyrights or other disadvantages), or other side comments." As such, its meaning and usage appears to be changing.

Use This For ...

This element is used to affect text content of any kind.

Compatibility

Internet Explorer			Firefox			Safari			Opera
5.5	6.0	7.0	1.0	1.5	2.0	1.3	2.0	3.0	9.2
Full	Full	Full	Full	Full	Full	Full	Full	Full	Full

As one of the earliest formatting elements, `small` has full browser support.

Other Relevant Stuff

 big (p. 177)

increases the font size of text

 # span

SPEC		
deprecated	empty	version
NO	NO	HTML 4
BROWSER SUPPORT		
IE5.5+	FF1+	Saf1.3+	Op9.2+
FULL	FULL	FULL	FULL

```
<span>
</span>
```

Example

Here's an example of the `span` element being used for CSS styling purposes:

```
.brandname {font-style:italic;color:#006;text-transform:uppercase;}
    ⋮
<p>There were various brands represented at the
    conference, including <span class="brandname">Adobe</span>,
    <span class="brandname">Microsoft</span>, <span
    class="brandname">Apple</span>, and <span
    class="brandname">Intel</span>.</p>
```

For an element that offers no semantic information about the content inside and also provides no styling change, or any other visual change to speak of, the lowly `span` element is one of the most useful elements in your HTML toolbox.

When you wrap text with an opening <span> and closing </span>, you're simply providing a hook—one that allows you to add styles (by adding a class attribute and using CSS to define the look of that class), or interact with the element via JavaScript and the Document Object Model (DOM).

In the example shown here, the author has decided that all brand names should be classed as "brandname" and styled differently via CSS, in italic, uppercase letters, as Figure 5.27 shows.

There were various brands represented at the conference, including *ADOBE*, *MICROSOFT*, *APPLE*, and *INTEL*.

Figure 5.27: Company names styled via span elements

A span is an inline element, and must only contain text content or nested inline or phrase elements. It shouldn't be used to surround block-level elements—a usage that's often seen in Content Management Systems which attempt to apply styling to almost any element by throwing a span around it.

The span is closely related to the div (p. 44) element, which is a block-level generic container, as opposed to span, which is an inline generic container.

A note of caution: it's not unheard of for people to go crazy with spans, using them all over the place. span-itis is a bad practice—it's just as bad as a dose of div-itis. Be sure to check that you're using the span element appropriately. For example, if you find yourself applying spans like this, you're in trouble:

```
He said it was <span class="important">really</span> important
    to know the difference.
```

It's clear that in the example above, the em (p. 189) element would have been more appropriate, as it implies emphasis in all browsers. On the other hand, without CSS styling, <span class="important"> would be all but meaningless.

Use This For ...

This element can be used to mark up text content of any kind.

Compatibility

Internet Explorer			Firefox			Safari			Opera
5.5	6.0	7.0	1.0	1.5	2.0	1.3	2.0	3.0	9.2
Full	Full	Full	Full	Full	Full	Full	Full	Full	Full

The span has full support in the browsers tested.

Other Relevant Stuff

 div (p. 44)

divides a page into separate sections

strike

```
<strike>
</strike>
```

SPEC		
deprecated	empty	version
NO	NO	HTML 4
BROWSER SUPPORT		
IE5.5+	FF1+	Saf1.3+	Op9.2+
FULL	FULL	FULL	FULL

The strike element will create a horizontal strike (or line) straight through any text and whitespace it contains. It provides no semantic meaning about the text affected, and is similar to b (p. 173) and i (p. 191) in that respect.

For more information, visit http://reference.sitepoint.com/html/strike/.

Other Relevant Stuff

 del (p. 182)

identifies deleted content

 s (p. 217)

renders text with a horizontal strike (line) through the middle

strong

```
<strong>
</strong>
```

SPEC		
deprecated	empty	version
NO	NO	HTML 2
BROWSER SUPPORT		
IE5.5+	FF1+	Saf1.3+	Op9.2+
FULL	FULL	FULL	FULL

Example

An example of strong at work:

```
<p>Look for the sign that says
   <strong>turn left<strong>, then turn left!</p>
```

The strong element is used to emphasize a phrase of text content. It typically renders the text contained in a bold, non-italicized font like that shown in Figure 5.28.

Look for the sign that says turn left, then turn left!

Figure 5.28: The phrase "turn left" highlighted with the strong element

Use This For ...

This element is used to highlight significant sections of content, possibly in body copy. It may also be used to emphasize key page elements; for example, the current navigation item in a list.

Compatibility

Internet Explorer			Firefox			Safari			Opera
5.5	6.0	7.0	1.0	1.5	2.0	1.3	2.0	3.0	9.2
Full	Full	Full	Full	Full	Full	Full	Full	Full	Full

As one of the earliest formatting elements, strong has full browser support.

Other Relevant Stuff

 em (p. 189)

signifies emphasized content

sub

```
<sub>
</sub>
```

SPEC		
deprecated	empty	version
NO	NO	HTML 2
BROWSER SUPPORT		
IE5.5+ FF1+ Saf1.3+ Op9.2+		
FULL FULL FULL FULL		

Example

Here's an example of the sub element used for chemical formulas:

```
<p>That's not just water. That's not just H<sub>2</sub>0. That's
    H<sub>2</sub>-woah!</p>
```

The sub element is used to define subscript—text which appears half a character's height below the baseline of the line it's on, and is most often used in mathematical or chemical formulae.

The example HTML, where the number 2 is defined as subscript, would render on screen as shown in Figure 5.29.

That's not just water. That's not just H_2O. That's H_2-woah!

Figure 5.29: An example of sub

Use This For ...

This element can be applied to any text content, but is likely to be limited to scientific or niche content.

Compatibility

Internet Explorer			Firefox			Safari			Opera
5.5	6.0	7.0	1.0	1.5	2.0	1.3	2.0	3.0	9.2
Full	Full	Full	Full	Full	Full	Full	Full	Full	Full

The sub element enjoys good browser support.

Other Relevant Stuff

 sup (p. 225)

specifies superscript text

sup

```
<sup>
</sup>
```

SPEC		
deprecated	empty	version
NO	NO	HTML 2
BROWSER SUPPORT		
IE5.5+ FF1+ Saf1.3+ Op9.2+		
FULL FUIL FULL FULL		

Example

Here's an example in which the sup element is used for the purpose of indicating a footnote reference:

```
<p>This document is a summary of findings. More details on the
    previous cases can be found in the referenced 'Prior Art'
    <sup>1</sup> and 'Intellectual Property History'<sup>2</sup>
    documents.</p>
```

The sup element is used to define superscript—text that appears half a character's height above the baseline of the line it's on. It's most often used in mathematical formulas, or for the purposes of indicating footnote references.

The example would render on screen as shown in Figure 5.30.

This document is a summary of findings. More details on the previous cases can be found in the referenced 'Prior Art'[1] and 'Intellectual Property History'[2] documents.

Figure 5.30: An example of sup at work

Use This For ...

This element can be applied to any text content, but its use is likely to be limited to footnote and mathematical applications.

Text Formatting Elements

Compatibility

Internet Explorer			Firefox			Safari			Opera
5.5	6.0	7.0	1.0	1.5	2.0	1.3	2.0	3.0	9.2
Full	Full	Full	Full	Full	Full	Full	Full	Full	Full

The sup element enjoys good browser support.

Other Relevant Stuff

 sub (p. 224)

specifies subscript text

 # tt

	SPEC	
deprecated	empty	version
NO	NO	HTML 2
BROWSER SUPPORT		
IE5.5+	FF1+	Saf1.3+	Op9.2+
FULL	FULL	FULL	FULL

```
<tt>
</tt>
```

Example

You might use tt to describe the output from an archaic sports scores system:

```
<p>The scores rolled in underneath the moustached face of Dickie
    Davies, hot off the teletype machines that someone was operating
    deep in the dungeons of ITV: &quot;<tt>Heart of Midlothian: 4,
    Queen of the South: 2, Plymouth Argyle 3 …</tt>&quot;</p>
```

Much like the b (p. 173) and i (p. 191) elements, tt provides no semantic information about the text it encloses—it is purely used for text formatting purposes. tt is short for teletype, and instructs the browser to render the text similarly to that produced by old-style teletype machines, which is understood to be a fixed-width (monospace) font. Most browsers will render tt content in Courier typeface.

Use This For ...

It's best not to use this element at all! While you may have text content that needs fixed width formatting, you'd be well advised to define a class in your CSS file, and style it using a monospace font.

Compatibility

Internet Explorer			Firefox			Safari			Opera
5.5	6.0	7.0	1.0	1.5	2.0	1.3	2.0	3.0	9.2
Full	Full	Full	Full	Full	Full	Full	Full	Full	Full

The tt element has good browser support: all the major browsers render it in a fixed-width font, which is usually Courier.

Other Relevant Stuff

 pre (p. 202)

defines preformatted text in which whitespace and line breaks are preserved

 # u

```
<u>
</u>
```

SPEC		
deprecated	empty	version
YES	NO	HTML 2
BROWSER SUPPORT		
IE5.5+	FF1+	Saf1.3+	Op9.2+
FULL	FULL	FULL	FULL

The u element (short for underline) simply styles the text it contains with a solid underline, but offers no semantic meaning about the text contained. This element is, therefore, purely presentational in nature.

For more information, visit http://reference.sitepoint.com/html/u/.

Other Relevant Stuff

 strong (p. 223)

signifies strongly emphasized content

 em (p. 189)

signifies emphasized content

 a (p. 146)

defines an anchor (or hyperlink)

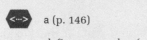 # var

```
<var>
</var>
```

SPEC		
deprecated	empty	version
NO	NO	HTML 2
BROWSER SUPPORT			
IE5.5+	FF1+	Saf1.3+	Op9.2+
FULL	FULL	FULL	FULL

Example

In the following example, a customer is asked to enter two pieces of information, which are marked up as variables:

```
<p>To get access to the system you first need to enter your
    username, e.g. <var>monkeyboy123</var>, followed by your unique
    6-digit customer ID beginning with C, e.g. <var>C13345</var>.</p>
```

The var element is used to indicate that the text is a variable and shouldn't be taken literally. Instead, it's an example that should be replaced with your own value.

The example code would render as shown in Figure 5.31.

To get access to the system you first need to enter your username, e.g. *monkeyboy123*, followed by your unique 6-digit customer ID beginning with C, e.g. *C13345*.

Figure 5.31: An example usage of var

Use This For ...

This element is used to indicate that the phrase is a variable of some kind—most likely in the context of showing an example value, as illustrated in the example HTML above.

Compatibility

Internet Explorer			Firefox			Safari			Opera
5.5	6.0	7.0	1.0	1.5	2.0	1.3	2.0	3.0	9.2
Full	Full	Full	Full	Full	Full	Full	Full	Full	Full

The var has good browser support; most of the major browsers render the variable in italics (similar to other reference-type phrase elements, such as cite (p. 179) and dfn (p. 187)).

wbr

`<wbr>`

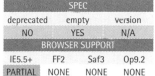

SPEC		
deprecated	empty	version
NO	YES	N/A
BROWSER SUPPORT		
IE5.5+	FF2	Saf3	Op9.2
PARTIAL	NONE	NONE	NONE

The wbr element is used in sections marked up with the nobr (p. 199) element. It is used to suggest to the browser or other user agent the point within a word at which it would be most appropriate to break that word, inserting a hyphen.

For more information, visit http://reference.sitepoint.com/html/wbr/.

Other Relevant Stuff

 nobr (p. 199)

identifies content that is not to be broken or wrapped

xmp

`<xmp>`
`</xmp>`

SPEC		
deprecated	empty	version
YES	NO	HTML 2
BROWSER SUPPORT		
IE5.5+	FF1+	Saf1.3+	Op9.2+
PARTIAL	PARTIAL	PARTIAL	PARTIAL

The xmp element was originally intended for marking up example text as it might appear on an 80-column display unit. xmp is similar to pre (p. 202) in that it honors carriage returns, spaces, and tabs, and treats markup characters as literal text. It is also a block-level element, and will therefore create a line break before the opening `<xmp>` and after the closing `</xmp>`.

Text Formatting Elements

For more information, visit http://reference.sitepoint.com/html/xmp/.

Other Relevant Stuff

 pre (p. 202)

defines preformatted text in which whitespace and line breaks are preserved

Chapter 6

Form Elements

This section describes the controls that may be used within the context of a `form`, and which allow the user to enter data that's submitted for processing by the server.

 ## button

```
<button name="string" type=" { button | reset |
submit } " value="value">
</button>
```

SPEC		
deprecated	empty	version
NO	NO	HTML 4
BROWSER SUPPORT			
IE5.5+	FF1+	Saf1.3+	Op9.2+
BUGGY	FULL	FULL	FULL

Example

Here, the phrase including the `em` element is a clickable `button`:

```
<form>
  <button>I am <em>really</em> sure I want to proceed</button>
</form>
```

The `button` form control is an attempt at improving the humble `"submit"` button (`input type="submit"`), which can only contain one line of text (the `value` attribute (p. 275)), and places certain limitations on the possibilities for CSS styling. It's possible to wrap the `button` element around a whole collection of HTML elements, encapsulating the entire area as a single, clickable element. Of course, it's not necessarily wise to cram too much into the button, but some helpful effects *are* possible. For example, this control could be used to add emphasis to part of the button text, as Figure 6.1 shows.

I am *really* sure I want to proceed

Figure 6.1: Formatting part of the button text differently from the rest

By default, the `button` will act as a `"submit"` button, but we can set it, via the `type` (p. 239) attribute, to be a `"reset"` or a simple `"button"` (with no default action—we'd need to use JavaScript to add behavior in this case).

Use This For ...

This control is used in cases where a simple `"submit"` button isn't capable of containing the information required, or where CSS styling requirements can't be met by a simple `"submit"` button.

Compatibility

Internet Explorer			Firefox			Safari			Opera
5.5	6.0	7.0	1.0	1.5	2.0	1.3	2.0	3.0	9.2
Buggy	Buggy	Buggy	Full	Full	Full	Full	Full	Full	Full

This element type isn't particularly well supported and has limited practical value.

Rendering of the button and its contents varies, but Internet Explorer appears to provide the worst rendering.

Other Relevant Stuff

 input (p. 253)

defines the input control for a form

accesskey *for <button>*

```
accesskey="key"
```

SPEC		
deprecated	required	version
NO	NO	HTML 4
BROWSER SUPPORT		
IE5.5+ FF1+	Saf1.3+	Op9.2+
FULL FULL	FULL	FULL

Example

This code assigns the accesskey for this button to the "s" key:

```
<form>
  <button accesskey="s" title="Accesskey = s">I am
      <em>really</em> sure I want to proceed</button>
</form>
```

The accesskey attribute allows the user to activate a control on a page using a keyboard shortcut. This may save time for users who would otherwise need to tab through a series of form controls or move the mouse to get to the desired link. The key combination that activates the link to which the accesskey is applied varies depending on the platform and browser combination. For IE/Windows, users press Alt + accesskey, while Firefox/Windows users press Alt + Shift + accesskey; users of most Mac browsers press Ctrl + accesskey; in Opera, pressing Shift + Esc displays a list of links for which accesskey attributes are defined, allowing users to choose the key they want to use.

Generally speaking, browsers don't indicate that an accesskey attribute is defined for a form control, and this lack of discoverability is a problem. The most common method for indicating the accesskey value is to place it in a title (p. 506) attribute of the element to which it's applied. However, for this approach to work, the user must mouse over the element in question. You may want to state the accesskey value in some other way—for example:

```
<form>
<button accesskey="s" title="Accesskey = s">I am
<em>really</em> sure I want to proceed [accesskey = s]</button>
</form>
```

Form Elements

Admittedly, this may not be practical or cosmetically pleasing, but without this hint, the user may never realize that an `accesskey` is available.

Value

This attribute takes as its value a single character, which can be numerical, alphabetical, or even a symbol.

Compatibility

Internet Explorer			Firefox			Safari			Opera
5.5	6.0	7.0	1.0	1.5	2.0	1.3	2.0	3.0	9.2
Full	Full	Full	Full	Full	Full	Full	Full	Full	Full

There is some variety in the way that the `accesskey` is activated. The biggest problem with this attribute is that the keystrokes you've defined may clash with other technologies. For example, a user may have assistive technology (such as a screen reader or screen magnifier) that shares keystrokes with those that you've defined in the `accesskey` attribute. In addition, different language browsers use different "accelerator keys" for their own menu options, and these may also clash with the access keys you've defined. In such cases, the `accesskey` may not work as you intended for all users, and as such, many web standards advocates strongly discourage its use. However, `accesskey` can have a role in documents that are used in controlled environments, such as intranets or for point-of-sale environments, in which you know exactly which browsers and languages the users can access. In such cases, using a standard set of `accesskey` attributes may be of great benefit.

disabled *for <button>*

```
disabled="disabled"
```

	SPEC	
deprecated	required	version
NO	NO	HTML 4
BROWSER SUPPORT		
IE5.5+	FF1+	Saf1.3+	Op9.2+
FULL	FULL	FULL	FULL

Example

The `disabled` attribute used in this code will stop the `button` from being usable:

```
<form>
  <button accesskey="s" disabled="disabled">I am
    <em>really</em> sure I want to proceed [accesskey = s]</button>
</form>
```

The `disabled` attribute stops the user from interacting with the `form` control. In this case, it stops the user clicking on the `button`, or tabbing to it using the keyboard—it prevents the user from activating the control.

The most likely use for this attribute is to disable a `button` until such a time as some other condition has been met (for instance, a checkbox is ticked to confirm the acceptance of terms and conditions). At that point, JavaScript would be required to removed the `"disabled"` value and make the form control usable.

Value

The only value this attribute can take is `"disabled"`.

Compatibility

Internet Explorer			Firefox			Safari			Opera
5.5	6.0	7.0	1.0	1.5	2.0	1.3	2.0	3.0	9.2
Full	Full	Full	Full	Full	Full	Full	Full	Full	Full

It causes no compatibility issues, and has excellent support across all tested browsers.

Form Elements

name *for <button>*

`name="string"`

SPEC		
deprecated	required	version
NO	NO	HTML 4
BROWSER SUPPORT			
IE5.5+	FF1+	Saf1.3+	Op9.2+
FULL	FULL	FULL	FULL

Example

The `name` attribute is used here to specify a name by which to reference form data:

```
<form>
  <button name="btnProceed">I am
      <em>really</em> sure I want to proceed</button>
</form>
```

The `name` attribute is used to reference `form` data after it's submitted, and to reference the data using JavaScript on the client side. Unlike the `id` attribute, which must be given a unique value each time it's applied to a new form control, a `name` attribute with a given value may be applied to numerous form controls (although in practice this approach is *only* used with radio `input` buttons). Note that only `form` elements which have a `name` attribute will have their values passed through to the page or script specified in the `form`'s `action` attribute.

You may wish to apply the same name to multiple buttons. In the example below, two `button`s have the same `name` value (`"dowhat"`), but each submits a different `"value"` (`"save"` or `"publish"`):

```
<button name="dowhat" value="save"
    id="action-save">Save Draft</button>
<button name="dowhat" value="publish"
    id="action-publish">Publish</button>
```

Using the same `name` value ensures that only one of the two possible `values` is submitted, and each button can be uniquely identified (perhaps for the purposes of rendering the different actions with different CSS styles).

Value

The name attribute takes as its value any name that the developer chooses, as long as it doesn't contain spaces or special characters.

Compatibility

Internet Explorer			Firefox			Safari			Opera
5.5	6.0	7.0	1.0	1.5	2.0	1.3	2.0	3.0	9.2
Full	Full	Full	Full	Full	Full	Full	Full	Full	Full

It causes no compatibility issues, and has excellent support across all tested browsers.

tabindex *for <button>*

```
tabindex="number"
```

SPEC		
deprecated	required	version
NO	NO	HTML 3.02
BROWSER SUPPORT		
IE5.5+	FF1+	Saf1.3+	Op9.2+
FULL	FULL	FULL	FULL

Example

This code sets the tabindex for the button control:

```
<form>
  <button tabindex="4">I am
      <em>really</em> sure I want to proceed</button>
</form>
```

The tabindex is used to define a sequence that users follow when they use the Tab key to navigate through a page. By default, the natural tabbing order will match the source order in the markup. In certain circumstances it may be necessary to override the default tabbing order, but it's strongly recommended that you craft a page in a logical flow and let the browser work through it in the default order—an approach that negates the need for the tabindex attribute.

A tabindex can start at 0 and increment in any value. As such, the sequence 1, 2, 3, 4, 5 would be fine, as would 10, 20, 30, 40, 50. If you need to introduce a tabindex, it's advisable to use a sequence that contains intervals (like the second example provided), as this will give you the opportunity to inject other controls later if need be (for example, 10, 15, 20) without having to reindex all the `tabindex` values on the page. Should a given `tabindex` value be applied to more than one element in error, the tabbing order of those affected elements will be as per the source markup order.

If a `tabindex` is set anywhere on a page—even if it's the hundredth link or the fiftieth form control—the tab order will start at the element with the lowest `tabindex` value, and work through the increments. Only *then* will the tab order take in the remaining elements for which no `tabindex` has been set. As such, great care must be taken to ensure that adding a `tabindex` doesn't harm the usability of the page as a whole.

If the `disabled` attribute is set on an element which has a `tabindex`, that `tabindex` will be ignored.

Value

This attribute takes a numerical value only.

Compatibility

Internet Explorer			Firefox			Safari			Opera
5.5	6.0	7.0	1.0	1.5	2.0	1.3	2.0	3.0	9.2
Full	Full	Full	Full	Full	Full	Full	Full	Full	Full

It causes no compatibility issues, and has excellent support across all tested browsers.

"...." type *for <button>*

```
type=" { button | reset | submit } "
```

	SPEC	
deprecated	required	version
NO	NO	HTML 4
BROWSER SUPPORT		
IE5.5+ FF1+	Saf1.3+	Op9.2+
BUGGY FULL	FULL	FULL

Example

The type is set to "reset" for this button:

```
<form>
  <button type="reset">
    <strong>Clear all data</strong> in this form
  </button>
</form>
```

Just as different types of button may be specified for the input (p. 253) element ("button", "reset", and "submit"), we can specify different button types for the button element—even though it may be a little confusing to see input type="button" and button type="button"! If no type is specified, the default behavior is identical to "submit".

Value

Possible values for type are "button", "reset", and "submit".

Compatibility

Internet Explorer			Firefox			Safari			Opera
5.5	6.0	7.0	1.0	1.5	2.0	1.3	2.0	3.0	9.2
Buggy	Buggy	Buggy	Full	Full	Full	Full	Full	Full	Full

The support for this element-specific attribute is good (where the browser supports the element itself).

However, Internet Explorer incorrectly defaults to type="button" rather than "submit" (which is why its support is described as buggy).

Form Elements

 **value** *for <button>*

```
value="value"
```

	SPEC	
deprecated	required	version
NO	NO	HTML 2
BROWSER SUPPORT			
IE5.5+	FF1+	Saf1.3+	Op9.2+
BUGGY	FULL	FULL	FULL

Example

This markup defines different `value` attributes for two submit `buttons`:

```
<form>
  ⋮
  <button accesskey="b" name="cmdsubmitter1"
      type="submit" value="blue">
      Take the <strong style="color:blue;">blue</strong> pill
  </button>
  <button accesskey="r" name="cmdsubmitter2"
      type="submit" value="red">
      Take the <strong style="color:red;">red</strong> pill
  </button>
</form>
```

The `button` element has the potential to encapsulate a number of different HTML elements and a range of content. HTML authors are unable to access the data submitted via this element. The `value` attribute can be used to alleviate this issue, although the most common scenario sees `value` used to identify which of a series of `button` elements a user clicked on, and to behave accordingly, as suggested in the example above.

Value

This attribute can take any name or value that the developer chooses.

Compatibility

Internet Explorer			Firefox			Safari			Opera
5.5	6.0	7.0	1.0	1.5	2.0	1.3	2.0	3.0	9.2
Buggy	Buggy	Buggy	Full	Full	Full	Full	Full	Full	Full

The support for this element-specific attribute is good (where the browser supports the element itself).

Internet Explorer misbehaves slightly with the `value` attribute—it incorrectly submits the text content that's contained within the opening `<button>` and closing `</button>` tags, rather than that contained in the `value` attribute. In addition, Internet Explorer doesn't seem to care which of the `button` elements in a group was pressed—no matter which one the user presses, you'll only get the data associated with the final `button` in the group!

fieldset

```
<fieldset>
</fieldset>
```

SPEC		
deprecated	empty	version
NO	NO	HTML 4
BROWSER SUPPORT			
IE5.5+	FF1+	Saf1.3+	Op9.2+
FULL	FULL	FULL	FULL

Example

This `fieldset` element is used to group three related XFN attributes (see the Microformats section regarding XFN[1]):

```
<form>
  <fieldset>
      <legend>Friendship</legend>
      <input type="radio" name="radFriendship" value="Not_Applicable"
          id="radFriendNot_Applicable"/>
      <label for="radFriendNot_Applicable">Not_Applicable</label>
      <input type="radio" name="radFriendship" value="acquaintance"
          id="radFriendaquaintence"/>
      <label for="radFriendaquaintence">acquaintance</label>
      <input type="radio" name="radFriendship" value="friend"
          id="radFriendfriend"/>
    <label for="radFriendfriend">friend</label>
  </fieldset>
    ⋮
</form>
```

The `fieldset` is a useful tool for organizing and grouping related items within a `form`, and has been used for a long time in desktop applications. When it's combined with the `legend` (p. 282) (which is contained inside the `fieldset`, and is a required element if you use the `fieldset`), it has the effect of creating a box around the

---

[1] http://reference.sitepoint.com/html/xfn/

grouped items and showing a description to the right of each item, as shown in Figure 6.2.

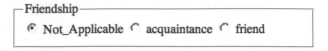

Figure 6.2: A fieldset with the legend of "Friendship" grouping related items in a form

It's also possible to nest fieldsets as a means to subgroup items, as shown in Figure 6.3.

Figure 6.3: Nested fieldsets, as shown on Accessify.com's Markup Maker tool

Use This For ...

The `fieldset` attribute is used to logically group data items that share some characteristics. For example, you may wrap a `fieldset` around personal details, and another around work details, when capturing information about a visitor in an application form.

Compatibility

Internet Explorer			Firefox			Safari			Opera
5.5	6.0	7.0	1.0	1.5	2.0	1.3	2.0	3.0	9.2
Full	Full	Full	Full	Full	Full	Full	Full	Full	Full

It causes no compatibility issues, and has excellent support across all tested browsers.

Other Relevant Stuff

 legend (p. 282)

defines caption text for form controls that are grouped by the fieldset *element*

form

```
<form action="uri" enctype=""
{ application/x-www-form-urlencoded |
multipart/form-data | text/plain } " method=" { get
| post } ">
</form>
```

SPEC		
deprecated	empty	version
NO	NO	HTML 2
BROWSER SUPPORT		
IE5.5+	FF1+	Saf1.3+	Op9.2+
FULL	FULL	FULL	FULL

Example

Here's a simple booking form:

```
<form action="form-to-email.php" method="post" action="post">
  <div>
    <label for="txtname">Name:</label>
    <input type="text" name="txtname" id="txtname"/>
  </div>
  <div>
    <label for="txtcontacttel">Contact Tel:</label>
    <input type="text" name="txtcontacttel" id="txtcontacttel"/>
  </div>
  <div>
    <input type="submit" name="cmdSubmit" id="cmdSubmit"
        value="Send booking details"/>
  </div>
</form>
```

The form element is the container that defines the start and end points for a form
that a site visitor can fill in. Any fields that are located between the opening <form>

Form Elements

and closing </form> tags will be associated with this form. It's possible to have multiple form elements on a page.

form is a block-level element, which means that it will take up the full width of the page (or the containing element) and create a break before and after itself. However, without additional CSS styling, there's no discernible boundary between it and the surrounding markup (for example, the form has no border or background color).

Information can be captured in the form using many different form-specific elements. These controls include the input (p. 253) element, as well as textarea (p. 306), select (p. 296), and button (p. 231). There are also labeling and grouping controls, which include the fieldset (p. 241), legend (p. 282), and label (p. 277) elements.

Use This For ...

This element is used to capture user information (shipping address details, credit card information, customer names and titles, and so on). form may also be used for the purposes of navigation. Although it's not the original intent of forms, this application isn't unusual. For example, you might use select lists as navigation menus, and have the user press a **Go** button to activate the menu item.

Compatibility

Internet Explorer			Firefox			Safari			Opera
5.5	6.0	7.0	1.0	1.5	2.0	1.3	2.0	3.0	9.2
Full	Full	Full	Full	Full	Full	Full	Full	Full	Full

It causes no compatibility issues, and has excellent support across all tested browsers.

In addition to the attributes listed here is one other that deserves a mention: autocomplete is an Internet Explorer-only attribute which can be used to enable or prevent form information from being stored and recalled later using that browser's autocomplete facility. The value for autocomplete can be "on" or "off".

Other Relevant Stuff

   input (p. 253)

defines the input control for a form

textarea (p. 306)

creates a multiline text input field

 select (p. 296)

defines a selection list (for single or multiple selections)

 button (p. 231)

groups a selection of elements together into a clickable form element

 fieldset (p. 241)

groups related form controls

 legend (p. 282)

defines caption text for form controls that are grouped by the fieldset element

 label (p. 277)

specifies descriptive text for the associated form control

accept-charset *for <form>*

`accept-charset="character set"`

SPEC		
deprecated	required	version
NO	NO	HTML 2
BROWSER SUPPORT		
IE5.5+	FF1+	Saf1.3+	Op9.2+
BUGGY	FULL	FULL	FULL

Example

In this form, we tell the server to accept Windows-only character sets (which isn't a brilliant idea, to be honest):

```
<form action="form-to-email.php" method="post"
    accept-charset="windows-1252">
  <div>
    <label for="txtname">Name:</label>
    <input type="text" name="txtname" id="txtname"/></span>
  </div>
    ⋮
</form>
```

The accept-charset attribute specifies the character encodings that the server can handle or process for input data.

Form Elements

Value

This attribute can accept a space- and/or comma-delimited list of charset values. The default value for this attribute is the reserved string "UNKNOWN." Browsers may interpret this value as the character encoding specified in the head of the document.

Compatibility

Internet Explorer			Firefox			Safari			Opera
5.5	6.0	7.0	1.0	1.5	2.0	1.3	2.0	3.0	9.2
Buggy	Buggy	Buggy	Full	Full	Full	Full	Full	Full	Full

Internet Explorer's support for `accept-charset` is buggy. If the attribute's specified as `"ISO-8859-1"`, IE will happily send data encoded as `"Windows-1252"`.

 **action** *for <form>*

`action="uri"`

SPEC		
deprecated	required	version
NO	YES	HTML 2
BROWSER SUPPORT		
IE5.5+	FF1+	Saf1.3+	Op9.2+
FULL	FULL	FULL	FULL

Example

Here, the `action` attribute tells the browser to send the `form` data to a form-handling PHP page (which will presumably convert the form data to something more email-friendly):

```
<form action="form-to-email.php" method="post"
    accept-charset="windows-1252">
  <div>
    <label for="txtname">Name:</label>
    <input type="text" name="txtname" id="txtname"/>
  </div>
  ⋮
</form>
```

A `form` is useless unless some kind of processing takes place after the `form` is submitted. The `action` attribute is used to inform the browser what page (or script) to call once the `"submit"` button is pressed.

Value

This element takes as its value a URL to a document that may be on the same server (for example, a shared CGI folder that has various form-processing scripts), or even a page or script on an entirely separate server (perhaps a free form-handling service).

Compatibility

Internet Explorer			Firefox			Safari			Opera
5.5	6.0	7.0	1.0	1.5	2.0	1.3	2.0	3.0	9.2
Full	Full	Full	Full	Full	Full	Full	Full	Full	Full

It causes no compatibility issues, and has excellent support across all tested browsers.

In addition to allowing a URL value, some browsers will understand a `mailto:` URL, which will open the email client on the user's computer and generate a new message, but this isn't a particularly slick way of managing `form` data. It's a much better approach to use server-side processing to ensure consistent behavior across browsers.

enctype *for <form>*

```
enctype=" { application/x-www-form-urlencoded |
multipart/form-data | text/plain } "
```

SPEC		
deprecated	required	version
NO	NO	HTML 2

BROWSER SUPPORT			
IE5.5+	FF1+	Saf1.3+	Op9.2+
FULL	FULL	FULL	FULL

Example

In this example, the `enctype` attribute tells the browser to send form data unencoded:

```
<form action="address.php" method="get" enctype="text/plain">
  <div>
    <label for="txtname">Full Name:</label>
    <input type="text" name="txtname" id="txtname"/>
  </div>
  <div>
    <label for="txtcontacttel">Contact Tel:</label>
    <input type="text" name="txtcontacttel" id="txtcontacttel"/>
  </div>
  <div>
    <input type="submit" name="cmdSubmit" id="cmdSubmit"
        value="Send personal details"/>
  </div>
</form>
```

The `enctype` attribute's purpose is to indicate how `form` data should be encoded prior to it being sent to the location defined in the `action` (p. 246) attribute. By default, form data is encoded so that spaces are converted to "+" symbols, and special characters—for example, apostrophes, percentage and other symbols, and so on—are converted to their ASCII HEX equivalents.

Value

The default value (which is assumed, and doesn't need to be set explicitly) is `"application/x-www-form-urlencoded"`. It ensures that all characters are encoded before they're sent to the server. The other possible values are `"multipart/form-data"`, which is required when you're using forms that have a file upload control (it ensures that no character conversion takes place, and transfers `form` data as a compound MIME document), and `"text/plain"`, which converts spaces to "+" symbols, but doesn't HEX-encode special characters such as apostrophes.

Compatibility

Internet Explorer			Firefox			Safari			Opera
5.5	6.0	7.0	1.0	1.5	2.0	1.3	2.0	3.0	9.2
Full	Full	Full	Full	Full	Full	Full	Full	Full	Full

It causes no compatibility issues, and has excellent support across all tested browsers.

 **method** *for <form>*

	SPEC		
deprecated	required	version	
NO	NO	HTML 2	
BROWSER SUPPORT			
IE5.5+	FF1+	Saf1.3+	Op9.2+
FULL	FULL	FULL	FULL

```
method=" { get | post } "
```

Example

Here, we use the `method` attribute to tell the browser to append data to the URL via the "`get`" method:

```
<form action="address.php" method="get">
  <div>
    <label for="txtname">Full Name:</label>
    <input type="text" name="txtname" id="txtname"/></span>
  </div>
  <div>
    <label for="txtcontacttel">Contact Tel:</label>
    <input type="text" name="txtcontacttel" id="txtcontacttel"/>
  </div>
  <div>
    <input type="submit" name="cmdSubmit" id="cmdSubmit"
        value="Send personal details"/>
  </div>
</form>
```

The `form`'s `method` attribute instructs the browser to send data on to the page or script (identified in the `action` attribute) either as information appended in the URL, using "`get`" (which is useful for form submissions for which you subsequently want to bookmark the results), or packaged as an HTTP post transaction, using "`post`".

The "`get`" method has a couple of shortfalls that you should be aware of. Firstly, there's a limit to how much data you can place in a URL (it varies between browsers, and also between servers), and as a result, you can't rely on the information to be

Form Elements

correctly transferred or processed. Secondly, passing sensitive information in this way is a security issue, yet passwords are all too often passed in this way (a crazy practice—anyone could look over the user's shoulder and read the password).

The `"post"` method may require a little more processing on the server, and `form` submissions made in this way can't be bookmarked. However, the `"post"` method is a more robust solution, and doesn't suffer the size limitations that `"get"` does.

Value

This attribute accepts `"get"` and `"post"` values only.

Compatibility

Internet Explorer			Firefox			Safari			Opera
5.5	6.0	7.0	1.0	1.5	2.0	1.3	2.0	3.0	9.2
Full	Full	Full	Full	Full	Full	Full	Full	Full	Full

It causes no compatibility issues, and has excellent support across all tested browsers.

 name *for <form>*

	SPEC	
deprecated	required	version
NO	NO	HTML 2
BROWSER SUPPORT		
IE5.5+	FF1+	Saf1.3+	Op9.2+
FULL	FULL	FULL	FULL

`name="string"`

Example

The `name` attribute provides a means by which we can reference form data:

```
<form action="search.php" method="post"
    target="searchresults" name="frmSearch">
  <label for="txtsearch">Search for</label>
  <input type="text" name="txtsearch" id="txtsearch"/>
  <input type="submit" name="cmdSubmit"
      id="cmdSubmit" value="Search"/>
</form>
```

The `form`'s `name` attribute is just one way to provide a reference for form data. There are several options for achieving the same goal in JavaScript—using collections, or using the `id` or `name` attributes—but using the `name` attribute provides the greatest level of compatibility, as all browsers support it (which is not the case with the `id` attribute). It's not uncommon to see a form for which both `name` and `id` attributes are specified with identical values.

Value

This attribute can take any name that the developer chooses, though the name can't contain spaces or special characters.

Compatibility

Internet Explorer			Firefox			Safari			Opera
5.5	6.0	7.0	1.0	1.5	2.0	1.3	2.0	3.0	9.2
Full	Full	Full	Full	Full	Full	Full	Full	Full	Full

It causes no compatibility issues, and has excellent support across all tested browsers.

 # target *for <form>*

```
target=" { _blank | frame name | _parent | _self |
_top } "
```

	SPEC	
deprecated	required	version
YES	NO	HTML 2
BROWSER SUPPORT		
IE5.5+	FF1+	Saf1.3+	Op9.2+
FULL	FULL	FULL	FULL

Example

This `target` attribute instructs the browser to process the `form` in a `frame` (p. 493) with a custom `name` of `"searchresults"`:

```
<form action="search.php" method="post" target="searchresults">
  <label for="txtsearch">Search for</label>
  <input type="text" name="txtsearch" id="txtsearch"/>
  <input type="submit" name="cmdSubmit" id="cmdSubmit" value="Search"/>
</form>
```

The `target` attribute is deprecated, and, like the use of `frameset` (p. 494) for layout purposes, it's no longer widely used. However, if you do find yourself having to maintain a frameset-based web site, you may wish to present the results of a `form` submission in a separate `frame` (p. 493). For example, you might work with a two-framed page that displays the search `form` in the first `frame` and the search results in the second `frame`, refreshing only the results frame each time the form is submitted.

Value

Possible values for this attribute include:

- `"_blank"`, which sends the results to a completely new window
- `"frame-name"`, which sends the results to a frame with a custom name
- `"_parent"`, which sends the results to the current `frame`'s parent `frameset`
- `"_self"`, which displays the form's submission results in the same frame[2]
- `"_top"`, which sends results to the top-level `frameset` (in effect, the whole browser window), no matter how many nested levels down the hierarchy the current `frame` is

Compatibility

Internet Explorer			Firefox			Safari			Opera
5.5	6.0	7.0	1.0	1.5	2.0	1.3	2.0	3.0	9.2
Full	Full	Full	Full	Full	Full	Full	Full	Full	Full

It causes no compatibility issues, and has excellent support across all tested browsers.

---

[2] Note that this value isn't normally required. The `target` is assumed to be the same window, unless the `base` (p. 77) element specifies the `target` to be a different window or frame, in which case you'd need to override the `base` value using `"_self"`, like so: `<base target="searchresults"/>`.

input

```
<input name="string" type=" { button | checkbox |
file | hidden | image | password | radio | reset |
submit | text } " value="value" />
```

SPEC		
deprecated	empty	version
NO	YES	HTML 2
BROWSER SUPPORT		
IE5.5+ FF1+	Saf1.3+	Op9.2+
FULL FULL	FULL	FULL

Example

Here's a simple text input (see type (p. 269) for other input examples):

```
<form>
  <label for="firstname">First name</label>
  <input type="text" name="firstname" id="firstname"/>
</form>
```

Describing the input element simply is not straightforward, as there is much variation in the way an input appears—and the attributes it uses or requires—depending on the type attribute specified. But whatever the type, the feature that's common to all input elements is that they allow users to enter data.

The specific features of each kind of input are covered in the type attribute section (p. 269) of this reference. Other type-specific attributes are indicated as such in their own sections.

Use This For ...

The input element is used to capture user information. The kind of control that's used will vary on a case-by-case basis, as explained in type (p. 269).

Compatibility

Internet Explorer			Firefox			Safari			Opera
5.5	6.0	7.0	1.0	1.5	2.0	1.3	2.0	3.0	9.2
Full	Full	Full	Full	Full	Full	Full	Full	Full	Full

It causes no compatibility issues, and has excellent support across all tested browsers.

Form Elements

Other Relevant Stuff

 input (p. 253)

defines the input control for a form

 accept *for <input>*

`accept="MIME type"`

SPEC		
deprecated	required	version
NO	NO	HTML 2
BROWSER SUPPORT			

IE5.5+	FF1+	Saf1.3+	Op9.2+
BUGGY	BUGGY	BUGGY	BUGGY

Example

Here, the `accept` attribute is used in a file upload `input` (p. 270):

```
<input type="file" name="picture" id="picture"
    accept="image/jpeg"/>
```

The `accept` attribute is used to filter the types of files that can be submitted through a file upload input. Browser support for this attribute is inconsistent, however, and the job of validating file uploads is best left to the server.

Value

The attribute takes a MIME type in the format type/subtype—for example, `"text/html"`, `"image/x-rgb"`, or `"application/java"`. Multiple values can be applied, but they must be comma-separated.

Compatibility

Internet Explorer			Firefox			Safari			Opera
5.5	6.0	7.0	1.0	1.5	2.0	1.3	2.0	3.0	9.2
Buggy	Buggy	Buggy	Buggy	Buggy	Buggy	Buggy	Buggy	Buggy	Buggy

This element is poorly supported and should not be relied upon.

accesskey *for <input>*

`accesskey="key"`

SPEC		
deprecated	required	version
NO	NO	HTML 4
BROWSER SUPPORT			
IE5.5+	FF1+	Saf1.3+	Op9.2+
FULL	FULL	FULL	FULL

Example

The `accesskey` for this `input` is assigned to `"f"`:

```
<label for="firstname">First name</label>
<input type="text" name="firstname" id="firstname" accesskey="f" />
```

The `accesskey` attribute allows the user to activate a control on a page using a keyboard shortcut. This may save time for users who would otherwise need to tab through a series of form controls or move the mouse to get to the desired link. The key combination that activates the link to which the `accesskey` is applied varies depending on the platform and browser combination. For IE/Windows, users press Alt + `accesskey`, while Firefox/Windows users press Alt + Shift + `accesskey`; users of most Mac browsers press Ctrl + `accesskey`; in Opera, pressing Shift + Esc displays a list of links for which `accesskey` attributes are defined, allowing users to choose the key they want to use.

Generally speaking, browsers don't indicate that an `accesskey` attribute is defined for a form control, and this lack of discoverability is a problem. The most common method for indicating the `accesskey` value is to place it in a `title` (p. 506) attribute of the element to which it's applied. However, for this approach to work, the user must mouse over the element in question. You may want to state the `accesskey` value in some other way—for example:

```
<label for="firstname">First name [access key = f]</label>
<input type="text" name="firstname" id="firstname" accesskey="f" />
```

Admittedly, this may not be practical or cosmetically pleasing, but without this hint, the user may never realize that an `accesskey` is available.

Value

This attribute takes as its value a single character, which can be numerical, alphabetical, or even a symbol.

Compatibility

Internet Explorer			Firefox			Safari			Opera
5.5	6.0	7.0	1.0	1.5	2.0	1.3	2.0	3.0	9.2
Full	Full	Full	Full	Full	Full	Full	Full	Full	Full

There is some variety in the way that the accesskey is activated. The biggest problem with this attribute is that the keystrokes you've defined may clash with other technologies. For example, a user may have assistive technology (such as a screen reader or screen magnifier) that shares keystrokes with those that you've defined in the accesskey attribute. In addition, different language browsers use different "accelerator keys" for their own menu options, and these may also clash with the access keys you've defined. In such cases, the accesskey may not work as you intended for all users, and as such, many web standards advocates strongly discourage its use. However, accesskey can have a role in documents that are used in controlled environments, such as intranets or for point-of-sale environments, in which you know exactly which browsers and languages the users can access. In such cases, using a standard set of accesskey attributes may be of great benefit.

align *for `<input>`*

```
align=" { bottom | left | middle | right | top } "
```

SPEC		
deprecated	required	version
YES	NO	HTML 2
BROWSER SUPPORT			
IE5.5+	FF1+	Saf1.3+	Op9.2+
PARTIAL	PARTIAL	PARTIAL	PARTIAL

Example

The `align` attribute for this input is set to `"right"`:

```
<form>
  ⋮
  <input type="image" src="submit.jpg" alt="Submit your details"
    align="right"/>
  <p>This a load of explanatory text that we need at the end of the
    form. This a load of explanatory text that we need at the end of
    the form. This a load of explanatory text that we need at the end
    of the form. </p>
</form>
```

Instead of using a button to submit `form` details, you may wish to use an image (see image `input` (p. 271) for more details). Just as you can align the `img` (p. 333) element in HTML, you do the same for one used as an `input`. However, the use of this attribute isn't recommended; instead, use CSS to align the image. Without CSS, you have limited control over design, as Figure 6.4 shows, where the text wraps around the image unattractively.

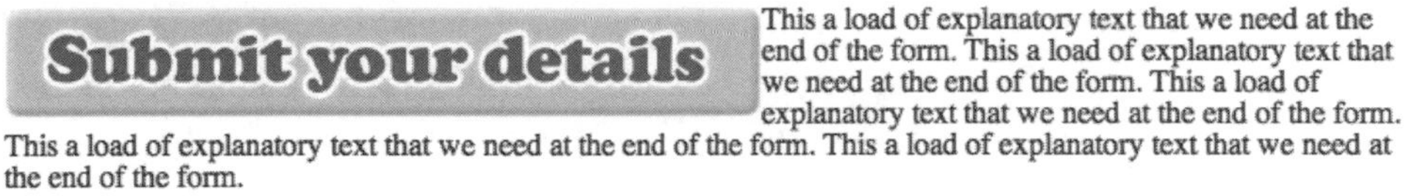

Submit your details This a load of explanatory text that we need at the end of the form. This a load of explanatory text that we need at the end of the form. This a load of explanatory text that we need at the end of the form.
This a load of explanatory text that we need at the end of the form. This a load of explanatory text that we need at the end of the form.

Figure 6.4: An `input` of `type` `"image"`, aligned left

Value

Possible values for this attribute include `"bottom"`, `"left"`, `"middle"`, `"right"`, and `"top"`. The browser default is `"left"`.

Form Elements

Compatibility

Internet Explorer			Firefox			Safari			Opera
5.5	6.0	7.0	1.0	1.5	2.0	1.3	2.0	3.0	9.2
Partial	Partial	Partial	Partial	Partial	Partial	Partial	Partial	Partial	Partial

This attribute is now deprecated, and is highly presentational in its nature. The desired visual effects can all be achieved with CSS and, as such, this attribute shouldn't be used—it's presented here for informational purposes only.

 alt *for <input>*

```
alt="string"
```

SPEC		
deprecated	required	version
NO	NO	HTML 2
BROWSER SUPPORT		
IE5.5+ FF1+ Saf3 Op9.2+		
FULL FULL NONE FULL		

Example

This code shows the `alt` attribute for a form's image submit `input`:

```
<form>
    ⋮
  <input type="image" src="submit.jpg"
      alt="Submit your details"/>
</form>
```

In the event that the user cannot view the image you've used—perhaps because he or she is using a very slow connection, you've included an incorrect `src` (p. 266) attribute, or because the user is visually impaired and is accessing the content using a screen reader—the `alt` attribute provides alternative information, as Figure 6.5 shows (that screenshot taken from IE6 on Windows XP).

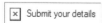

Figure 6.5: The alternative text showing for a missing image submit button

The `alt` attribute should be considered to be required when the `type` attribute is set to `"image"`, although that requirement cannot be expressed in an SGML DTD (hence, this isn't shown as a required attribute—it depends on context).

Value

The attribute value comprises text that's equivalent to the content of the image. As such, the text should state clearly the effect of pressing the button (or image).

Compatibility

Internet Explorer			Firefox			Safari			Opera
5.5	6.0	7.0	1.0	1.5	2.0	1.3	2.0	3.0	9.2
Full	Full	Full	Full	Full	Full	None	None	None	Full

Generally, good support is provided for `alt`, but Safari doesn't display suitable alternative content when the image fails to load (it simply displays a rather unhelpful question mark).

checked *for <input>*

```
checked="checked"
```

SPEC		
deprecated	required	version
NO	NO	HTML 2
BROWSER SUPPORT			
IE5.5+	FF1+	Saf1.3+	Op9.2+
FULL	FULL	FULL	FULL

Example

This `checked` attribute is applied to a newsletter signup checkbox:

```
<form>
  <input type="checkbox" name="chknewsletter" id="chknewsletter"
     checked="checked"/>
  <label for="chknewsletter">Send me the monthly newsletter</label>
</form>
```

In some circumstances, you may need to present one or more checkboxes in such a way that the state of the control at the point of page load is checked, and the user has to opt out rather than opting in. Or perhaps you're presenting the user with a `form`—including a series of checkboxes—that he or she has previously filled in, and you want to preserve the state of the selections that were made. The `checked` attribute allows you to set the checked state to "on" by default.

The checked attribute is also used for radio input controls. Unlike the checkbox, only one in a range of related radio inputs can be selected (see the section on radio inputs in type (p. 269) for more on this), and the checked attribute is used to identify which one is selected. If you accidentally mark as "checked" a number of radio inputs that share a given name attribute, the last one that's marked as such will be selected.

Note that the checkbox's appearance differs between browsers and operating systems—in some, the checked checkbox appears as a ticked or checked box, while in others, it's a crossed box. A radio input that's "checked" will almost certainly *not* look like a tick or a check, but let's not get hung up on appearances. The key is to know that the right control is selected!

Value

"checked" is the only possible value. If the input should be unchecked, simply omit the attribute entirely.

Compatibility

Internet Explorer			Firefox			Safari			Opera
5.5	6.0	7.0	1.0	1.5	2.0	1.3	2.0	3.0	9.2
Full	Full	Full	Full	Full	Full	Full	Full	Full	Full

It causes no compatibility issues, and has excellent support across all tested browsers.

disabled *for <input>*

`disabled="`*`disabled`*`"`

SPEC		
deprecated	required	version
NO	NO	HTML 4
BROWSER SUPPORT			
IE5.5+	FF1+	Saf1.3+	Op9.2+
FULL	FULL	FULL	FULL

Example

The `disabled` attribute stops this checkbox `input` from being used:

```
<form>
  <input type="checkbox" name="chknewsletter" id="chknewsletter"
      checked="checked" disabled="disabled"/>
  <label for="chknewsletter">Send me the monthly newsletter</label>
</form>
```

The `disabled` attribute prevents the user from interacting with the form control to which it's applied. In this case, it stops the user from clicking on the `checkbox`, or tabbing to it with the keyboard, so the user can't activate the control.

The most likely use for this attribute is to disable a `checkbox` until such a time as some other condition has been met, at which point JavaScript would be required to removed the `"disabled"` value, making the form control usable again.

Value

`"disabled"` is only possible value for this attribute. If the `input` should be enabled, simply omit the attribute entirely.

Compatibility

Internet Explorer			Firefox			Safari			Opera
5.5	6.0	7.0	1.0	1.5	2.0	1.3	2.0	3.0	9.2
Full	Full	Full	Full	Full	Full	Full	Full	Full	Full

It causes no compatibility issues, and has excellent support across all tested browsers.

maxlength *for <input>*

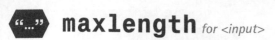

```
maxlength="number"
```

SPEC		
deprecated	required	version
NO	NO	HTML 2
BROWSER SUPPORT		
IE5.5+	FF1+	Saf1.3+	Op9.2+
FULL	FULL	FULL	FULL

Example

This `maxlength` attribute restricts entries in this password field to a maximum of four characters:

```
<form>
  <label for="pin">Your 4-digit PIN:</label>
  <input type="password" name="pin" id="pin"
     maxlength="4" size="6"/>
   ⋮
</form>
```

While it's possible to use JavaScript to validate `form` data entry, this approach can't be relied upon (JavaScript may be disabled, and form data may not be trustworthy if the client has been affected by a nefarious script). Server—side validation is a much safer option, and could be used, among other things, to check that the amount of data submitted isn't too long. The `maxlength` attribute provides a means for reducing the likelihood that too much data will be sent to the server for processing, and also provides some degree of usability enhancement—users can clearly see when they've reached the maximum character length for an input, as although they're typing, nothing more is being entered into the field.

Value

The value for this attribute is a number which represents the total characters that can be submitted.

Compatibility

Internet Explorer			Firefox			Safari			Opera
5.5	6.0	7.0	1.0	1.5	2.0	1.3	2.0	3.0	9.2
Full	Full	Full	Full	Full	Full	Full	Full	Full	Full

It causes no compatibility issues, and has excellent support across all tested browsers.

name for <input>

`name="string"`

SPEC		
deprecated	required	version
NO	NO	HTML 2
BROWSER SUPPORT			
IE5.5+	FF1+	Saf1.3+	Op9.2+
FULL	FULL	FULL	FULL

Example

This name attribute, which is set to `"pin"`, provides a means for referencing the input data:

```
<form>
  <label for="pin">Your 4-digit PIN:</label>
  <input type="password" name="pin" id="pin" maxlength="4" size="6"/>
    ⋮
</form>
```

The name attribute is used to reference form data after it's submitted, and to reference the data using JavaScript on the client side. Unlike the id attribute, which must be given a unique value each time it's applied to a new form control, a name attribute with a given value may be applied to numerous form controls (although in practice this approach is *only* used with radio input buttons). Note that only form elements which have a name attribute will have their values passed through to the page or script specified in the form's action attribute.

Value

This attribute takes any name that the developer chooses, as long as it doesn't contain any spaces or special characters.

Compatibility

Internet Explorer			Firefox			Safari			Opera
5.5	6.0	7.0	1.0	1.5	2.0	1.3	2.0	3.0	9.2
Full	Full	Full	Full	Full	Full	Full	Full	Full	Full

It causes no compatibility issues, and has excellent support across all tested browsers.

Form Elements

readonly *for <input>*

`readonly="readonly"`

SPEC		
deprecated	required	version
NO	NO	HTML 3.02
BROWSER SUPPORT			
IE5.5+	FF1+	Saf1.3+	Op9.2+
FULL	FULL	FULL	FULL

Example

This `readonly` attribute prevents the `input` `value` of `"Southampton"` from being changed:

```
<form>
  <label for="town">Postal Town:</label>
  <input type="text" name="town" id="town" readonly="readonly"
      value="Southampton"/>
</form>
```

The `"readonly"` attribute stops the user from changing the value of an `input` (in the case of a text input or password), but *doesn't* prevent the user from interacting with the form control content. It's still possible for the user to click inside the `input`, tab to it, highlight the text inside it, and even copy and paste that content—it's just that the value can't be changed or cleared.

This attribute is most commonly used to stop the user from interfering with the value of an `input` until some other condition has been met (for example, until a checkbox is ticked to confirm the user's acceptance of terms and conditions). At that point, JavaScript would be required to removed the `"readonly"` value, making the form control completely usable.

Value

`"readonly"` is the only possible value for this attribute.

Compatibility

Internet Explorer			Firefox			Safari			Opera
5.5	6.0	7.0	1.0	1.5	2.0	1.3	2.0	3.0	9.2
Full	Full	Full	Full	Full	Full	Full	Full	Full	Full

It causes no compatibility issues, and has excellent support across all tested browsers.

"..." **size** *for <input>*

`size="number"`

SPEC		
deprecated	required	version
NO	NO	HTML 2
BROWSER SUPPORT		
IE5.5+	FF1+	Saf1.3+	Op9.2+
FULL	FULL	FULL	FULL

Example

Here, the `size` attribute is set to `"6"` for a field that only requires four characters:

```
<form>
  <label for="pin">Your 4-digit PIN:</label>
  <input type="password" name="pin" id="pin" maxlength="4" size="6"/>
  ⋮
</form>
```

The `size` attribute is used to set the width of a text or password input field. The length of these fields is determined by the number of characters that should be visible, as Figure 6.6 shows.

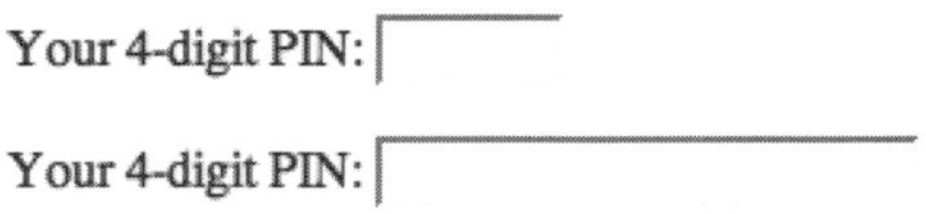

Figure 6.6: Two inputs, the first with a size of 6, the second with no size specified

Given the presentational nature of this attribute, it's best avoided. Instead, use CSS to define field widths using more precise measurements.

Value

This attribute takes a number that reflects the field's width in characters—for example, `"5"`, `"10"`, and so on.

Compatibility

Internet Explorer			Firefox			Safari			Opera
5.5	6.0	7.0	1.0	1.5	2.0	1.3	2.0	3.0	9.2
Full	Full	Full	Full	Full	Full	Full	Full	Full	Full

It causes no compatibility issues, and has excellent support across all tested browsers.

src *for <input>*

`src="uri"`

SPEC		
deprecated	required	version
NO	NO	HTML 2
BROWSER SUPPORT		
IE5.5+	FF1+	Saf1.3+	Op9.2+
FULL	FULL	FULL	FULL

Example

The `src` attribute for this image input shows that the image resides in the same directory as the web page that references it:

```
<form>
  ⋮
  <input type="image" src="submit.jpg" alt="Submit your details"/>
</form>
```

The `src` attribute tells the browser where to look for the image that should be presented to the user. This image may be located in the same directory as the page that's referencing the file, in another directory on the same server, or on another server entirely.

The example specifies an image that's located in the same directory as the web page that's calling it, but if the submit image was located in a directory that was one level higher than the referencing document, the syntax would be as follows:

```
<input type="image" src="../submit.jpg"
    alt="Submit your details"/>
```

Here, `../` equates to "move up one directory in the hierarchy."

You can also reference an image relative to the web site's root (the folder or file after the domain name):

```
<input type="image" src="/submit.jpg"
    alt="Submit your details"/>
```

This attribute markup basically says, "display the image **submit.jpg** that can be found in **www.mydomain.com**/." This is a very handy way of referencing files, as you can move the document containing the submit image to another location on the file system without having to change the link.

If you were referencing an image that's held on another server, you'd express the src using a complete URI, as follows:

```
<input type="image" src="http://www.some-domain.com/submit.jpg"
    alt="Submit your details"/>
```

Value

This attribute takes as its value the location of the button image relative to the referencing document, relative to the server root, or as a complete URI containing **http://** or **https://**, the server name, and the path to the document on that server.

Compatibility

Internet Explorer			Firefox			Safari			Opera
5.5	6.0	7.0	1.0	1.5	2.0	1.3	2.0	3.0	9.2
Full	Full	Full	Full	Full	Full	Full	Full	Full	Full

It causes no compatibility issues, and has excellent support across all tested browsers.

tabindex *for <input>*

```
tabindex="number"
```

SPEC		
deprecated	required	version
NO	NO	HTML 3.02
BROWSER SUPPORT		
IE5.5+	FF1+	Saf1.3+	Op9.2+
FULL	FULL	FULL	FULL

Example

The tabindex is set for the form control below:

```
<form>
  ⋮
  <label for="pin">Your 4-digit PIN:</label>
  <input type="password" name="pin" id="pin" tabindex="2"/>
  ⋮
</form>
```

The `tabindex` is used to define a sequence that users follow when they use the Tab key to navigate through a page. By default, the natural tabbing order will match the source order in the markup. In certain circumstances it may be necessary to override the default tabbing order, but it's strongly recommended that you craft a page in a logical flow and let the browser work through it in the default order—an approach that negates the need for the `tabindex` attribute.

A `tabindex` can start at 0 and increment in any value. As such, the sequence 1, 2, 3, 4, 5 would be fine, as would 10, 20, 30, 40, 50. If you need to introduce a `tabindex`, it's advisable to use a sequence that contains intervals (like the second example provided), as this will give you the opportunity to inject other controls later if need be (for example, 10, 15, 20) without having to reindex all the `tabindex` values on the page. Should a given `tabindex` value be applied to more than one element in error, the tabbing order of those affected elements will be as per the source markup order.

If a `tabindex` is set anywhere on a page—even if it's the hundredth link or the fiftieth form control—the tab order will start at the element with the lowest `tabindex` value, and work through the increments. Only *then* will the tab order take in the remaining elements for which no `tabindex` has been set. As such, great care must be taken to ensure that adding a `tabindex` doesn't harm the usability of the page as a whole.

If the `disabled` attribute is set on an element which has a `tabindex`, that `tabindex` will be ignored.

Value

This attribute can take only a number as its value.

Compatibility

Internet Explorer			Firefox			Safari			Opera
5.5	6.0	7.0	1.0	1.5	2.0	1.3	2.0	3.0	9.2
Full	Full	Full	Full	Full	Full	Full	Full	Full	Full

It causes no compatibility issues, and has excellent support across all tested browsers.

type *for <input>*

```
type=" { button | checkbox | file | hidden | image
| password | radio | reset | submit | text } "
```

SPEC		
deprecated	required	version
NO	NO	HTML 2
BROWSER SUPPORT		
IE5.5+	FF1+	Saf1.3+	Op9.2+
FULL	FULL	FULL	FULL

Example

The type is set to "text" for this input:

```
<input type="text" name="txtsearch" id="txtsearch" size="20"/>
```

Of all the attributes that can be applied to an input, the type attribute is the one that has the biggest impact. With a change of this value, the appearance and behavior of the input can change dramatically, from a simple text input or a masked password field, to controls such as radio buttons, checkboxes, and even images. The possible values and their applications are detailed in the list below:

"button"   This is a simple clickable button that doesn't actually *do* anything per se (unlike a **Submit** button, which sends the form data to the location defined in action (p. 246)). The input button type is usually used along with JavaScript to trigger some kind of behavior (for example, using a button to open a help page in a new window). Here's a button definition:

```
<input type="button" value="Click me. I basically do
    nothing"/>
```

"checkbox"   This type of input is used when you need users to answer a question with a yes or no response. There's no way that users can enter any data of their own—their action is simply a case of checking or unchecking the box. When the form is submitted, the server will be interested in the value attribute attached to the control, and the state of the checkbox (checked or unchecked (p. 259)). When you're specifying a checkbox

Form Elements

input, the control should come first, and be followed by the associated text, as shown in Figure 6.7:

```
<input type="checkbox" name="chknewsletter"
    id="chknewsletter" value="newsletter-opt-in"/>
  <label for="chknewsletter">Send me the monthly
      newsletter</label>
```

☑ **Send me the monthly newsletter**

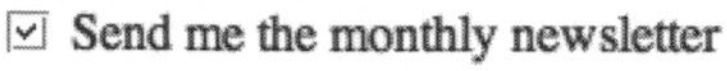

Figure 6.7: A checked (or ticked) checkbox

"file"   This input type is used for file uploads. When the attribute is set to "file", two controls appear in the browser: a field that looks similar to a text input, and a button control that's labeled **Browse...**. The text that appears on this button can't be changed, and a file upload control is generally difficult to style with CSS. The file upload control has an optional attribute, accept (p. 254), which is used to define the kinds of files that may be uploaded.

Figure 6.8 shows the rendering of the below markup, which creates a file upload control:

```
<input type="file" name="picture" id="picture"
    accept="image/jpeg, image/gif"/>
```

| Browse... |

Figure 6.8: A file upload control

"hidden"   A hidden form input is one that, though it doesn't appear on the page, can be used for storing a value (p. 275). The value in a hidden field may be set at page-load time (it may be written using server-side scripting, as in the example below), or it may be entered or changed dynamically, via JavaScript.

Here's an example in which the "hidden" input element obtains its value from a PHP variable called $strCustomerId:

```
<input type="hidden" name="hdnCustId"
    value="<?php echo $strCustomerId; ?>"/>
```

"image" The image input type is used in place of a standard submit button, which may be a bit boring and conservative for your form design (or perhaps your marketing department is demanding something a little more "on brand"). When using an input of type "image", you'll also need to specify a src (p. 266) (where the image can be found) and an alt (p. 258) attribute (alternative text for the image, in case it's missing or cannot be viewed for some other reason):

```
<input type="image" src="submit.jpg"
    alt="Submit your details"/>
```

"password" The password field is almost identical to the standard text input (p. 273):

```
<input type="password" name="pin" id="pin"
    maxlength="4" size="6"/>
```

The password input has exactly the same set of attributes as the text input, but differs visually in that characters entered in this type of field are masked in the browser, so that entered characters appear as asterisks or blobs, as shown in Figure 6.9.

Your 4-digit PIN: ****

Figure 6.9: A masked password field

"radio" The "radio" button control is arguably the most complex type of input control. To explain how this control works, it's worth thinking about the origin of its name. In old-fashioned radio sets, tuning between stations wasn't achieved by using the "scan" facility, or even rotating a dial. Rather, a series of buttons that were linked to a handful of radio stations could be chosen, one at a time—pressing one button in the range would cause any other button to pop out. The same effect is in play here. Only one control can be selected from a range, and if you select another, the previously selected input is deselected. For this control to work, though, each radio button in the range that you want

Form Elements

users to choose from must have the same name (p. 263) attribute, as shown below. With a radio input, the control should come first, followed by the associated text:

```
<div><input type="radio" name="station" id="rad1"
    value="Radio 1"/> <label for="rad1">Radio
1</label></div>
<div><input type="radio" name="station" id="rad2"
    value="Radio 2"/> <label for="rad2">Radio
2</label></div>
<div><input type="radio" name="station" id="rad3"
    value="XFM"/> <label for="rad3">XFM</label></div>
<div><input type="radio" name="station" id="rad4"
    value="4Music"/> <label for="rad4">4Music</label></div>
```

The browser representation is shown in Figure 6.10.

    ◯ Radio 1
    ◯ Radio 2
    ◯ XFM
    ◉ 4Music

Figure 6.10: Radio buttons

Because each control has the same name (in this case, "station"), only one can be picked from the list. The value for each control differs, though, so if users chose "XFM" as their favorite radio station in the example above, that would be the value associated with the field name of "station". Also note that, unlike all the other form markup examples, the name and id values differ for *this* type of control. The id is used for the purposes of linking the control to its label text, and *must* be unique.

"reset"   The "reset" input is visually similar to the "button" and "submit" types—it's like a button control that can be clicked on or pressed, and accepts no data from the user. However, a reset control is a very destructive control to introduce to a web page, as pressing it will clear all the data already entered into the form in which the reset button resides, usually causing a fair amount of user rage! While the use of this control constitutes perfectly valid HTML, it's used less and less these days, as it's too easy for users to accidentally action the reset button with either a mouse click or while tabbing through the page with the keyboard. If you do feel that a `"reset"` button is warranted, consider adding some JavaScript to the page—something that can double-check the pressing of the button with a message that asks, "Are you sure you want to clear everything and start again?" However, it's probably best to avoid this input, letting users easily refresh or reload a page to start again, if they want to. The markup below shows a reset button:

```
<input type="reset" name="cmdReset" id="cmdReset"
    value="Clear form data"/>
```

`"submit"`   This is the magic button—the one that users press to send all the form data they've entered. Once it's clicked, there's no going back! The `"submit"` input displays the text that you specify in the `value` (p. 275) attribute, but if no `value` is specified, the button face will simply display the word Submit. The markup below creates a submit button that displays the words **Send this Application**:

```
<input type="submit" name="cmdSubmit" id="cmdSubmit"
    value="Send this application"/>
```

`"text"`   This is the most common kind of `input` that you'll encounter on the Web, and that you'll need most often as you're building your own forms. The `"text"` input creates a single-line box that the user can enter text into, and has a number of attributes, such as `size` (p. 265), `maxlength` (p. 262), `disabled` (p. 261), `readonly` (p. 264), `name` (p. 263), and `tabindex` (p. 267).

Value

The possible values for `type` include `"button"`, `"checkbox"`, `"file"`, `"hidden"`, `"image"`, `"password"`, `"radio"`, `"reset"`, `"submit"`, and `"text"`.

Form Elements

Compatibility

Internet Explorer			Firefox			Safari			Opera
5.5	6.0	7.0	1.0	1.5	2.0	1.3	2.0	3.0	9.2
Full	Full	Full	Full	Full	Full	Full	Full	Full	Full

It causes no compatibility issues, and has excellent support across all tested browsers.

usemap *for <input>*

```
usemap="#map name"
```

SPEC		
deprecated	required	version
NO	NO	HTML 2
BROWSER SUPPORT		
IE5.5+	FF1+	Saf1.3+	Op9.2+
PARTIAL	PARTIAL	PARTIAL	PARTIAL

Example

The usemap attribute below references a map named "sections":

```
<map name="sections">
  <area shape="circle" coords="70,84,51" href="/default.html"/>
  <area shape="rect" coords="25,180,125,280" href="/about.html"/>
  ⋮
</map>
  ⋮
<form>
  ⋮
  <input type="image" src="submit.jpg" alt="Submit your details"
      usemap="#sections"/>
</form>
```

The usemap attribute, which is only applied to an input of type "image", allows the author to specify a different outcome depending on the area of the image that the user clicks on.

Value

A reference to the map's name attribute takes the form of an # character followed by the "name" of the map:

```
usemap="#sections"
```

Compatibility

Internet Explorer			Firefox			Safari			Opera
5.5	6.0	7.0	1.0	1.5	2.0	1.3	2.0	3.0	9.2
Partial	Partial	Partial	Partial	Partial	Partial	Partial	Partial	Partial	Partial

This element type isn't particularly well supported and has limited practical value.

In all the browsers that were tested, clicking on the input image caused the form to submit, but with additional *x* and *y* coordinates appended to the form data, which suggests that the browsers were at least recognizing the notion that the image was being used as a map. Firefox and Opera were the only browsers that additionally honored the coordinates in the associated `area` element.

The HTML specifications regarding this attribute were vague as to its use, and its usage has been extremely limited. As such, it has been dropped from the HTML 5 draft.

 # **value** *for <input>*

SPEC		
deprecated	required	version
NO	NO	HTML 2
BROWSER SUPPORT		
IE5.5+	FF1+	Saf1.3+	Op9.2+
FULL	FULL	FULL	FULL

```
value="value"
```

Example

This code sets a predefined `value` of `"Enter search phrase"` for a text input:

```
<input type="text" name="search" value="Enter search phrase"/>
```

The `value` attribute is used and displayed differently depending on the type of form control (p. 269) to which it's applied, as detailed below:

- `type = "button"`, `"submit"`, `"reset"`

   The text stated in the `value` attribute is used as the button's text, and can't be changed by the user (although it could be changed dynamically via JavaScript).

- `type = "text"`, `"password"`

The `value` will appear inside the `form` control and may be overtyped, copied, or cut by the user. Note that if it's displayed in the password field, it will be obfuscated, but the correct number of characters will appear nonetheless.

▣ type = "radio", "checkbox", "image", "hidden"

The `value` won't be displayed to the user, nor can it be changed, but it will be associated with the control, and it's the `value` that's passed on when the `form` is submitted.

Note that the properties chart doesn't show the `value` attribute as being required for all input types, but in the case of radio and checkbox input types, `value` *is* required.

Value

This attribute can take any name or value of the developer's choosing.

Compatibility

Internet Explorer			Firefox			Safari			Opera
5.5	6.0	7.0	1.0	1.5	2.0	1.3	2.0	3.0	9.2
Full	Full	Full	Full	Full	Full	Full	Full	Full	Full

It causes no compatibility issues, and has excellent support across all tested browsers.

 # isindex

```
<isindex action="uri" href="uri" prompt="string" />
```

SPEC		
deprecated	empty	version
YES	YES	HTML 2
BROWSER SUPPORT		
IE5.5+	FF1+	Saf1.3+	Op9.2
PARTIAL	PARTIAL	PARTIAL	NONE

The `isindex` element is a deprecated and poorly supported method for providing a searchable index related to the current document. There's not much to say about this element, given the current lack of support for it.

For more information, visit http://reference.sitepoint.com/html/isindex/

Other Relevant Stuff

 input (p. 253)

defines the input control for a form

 # `label`

```
<label for="field ID">
</label>
```

SPEC		
deprecated	empty	version
NO	NO	HTML 4
BROWSER SUPPORT			

IE5.5+	FF1+	Saf3+	Op9.2+
FULL	FULL	FULL	FULL

Example

Here, the `label` element links the text "Not Applicable" with the form control that has the `id` of `"b"`:

```
<input type="radio" name="radFriendship" value="Not_Applicable" id="b"/>
<label for="b">Not_Applicable</label>
```

The `label` element is invisible to users (unless it's styled with CSS, or behavior is attached to it via JavaScript and the DOM). By default, applying a `label` to a form control's descriptive text makes no difference to its visual appearance. However, there are other benefits to be gained by explicitly linking the text to the form control using the `label`:

- It provides a usability improvement for mouse users. In the majority of current web browsers, the text that's associated with a given form control (by being contained within the `<label>` and `</label>` tags) also becomes a clickable area. Thus, if the form control is something small, like a checkbox or radio button, you can massively increase the "hit area" for the mouse user by applying a `label` to it.

- It improves accessibility. By adding a `label` to all controls, you make the controls' purpose clear to users of assistive technology (for example, visually impaired users reading the page through a screen reader). If the form controls aren't linked to their associated text descriptions in this way, the assistive technology may

Form Elements

need to hazard a guess as to which control goes with which description, depending on the layout of the web page and/or the source order of the markup to make its interpretation.

Note that there are two ways in which you can use the `label` element, both of which are detailed in the section on the `for` (p. 280) attribute.

Use This For ...

`label` is used to link the descriptive text for a given form control directly to that control.

Compatibility

Internet Explorer			Firefox			Safari			Opera
5.5	6.0	7.0	1.0	1.5	2.0	1.3	2.0	3.0	9.2
Full	Full	Full	Full	Full	Full	None	None	Full	Full

Every browser listed supports this element type.

Safari 2 and earlier versions didn't support the feature that allows users to click on a label to focus on the associated form control, but thankfully, this functionality was added in version 3.

accesskey _for <label>_

```
accesskey="key"
```

SPEC		
deprecated	required	version
NO	NO	HTML 4
BROWSER SUPPORT		
IE5.5+	FF1+	Saf3+	Op9.2
FULL	FULL	FULL	NONE

Example

The `accesskey` for the radio button control in this example is assigned to `"b"`:

```
<input type="radio" name="radFriendship" value="Not_Applicable"
    id="b"/>
<label for="b" accesskey="b">Not_Applicable</label>
```

The `accesskey` attribute allows the user to activate a control on a page using a keyboard shortcut. This may save time for users who would otherwise need to tab through a series of form controls or move the mouse to get to the desired link. The key combination that activates the link to which the `accesskey` is applied varies depending on the platform and browser combination. For IE/Windows, users press Alt + `accesskey`, while Firefox/Windows users press Alt + Shift + `accesskey`; users of most Mac browsers press Ctrl + `accesskey`; in Opera, pressing Shift + Esc displays a list of links for which `accesskey` attributes are defined, allowing users to choose the key they want to use.

Generally speaking, browsers don't indicate that an `accesskey` attribute is defined for a form control, and this lack of discoverability is a problem. The most common method for indicating the `accesskey` value is to place it in a `title` (p. 506) attribute of the element to which it's applied. However, for this approach to work, the user must mouse over the element in question. You may want to state the `accesskey` value in some other way—for example:

```
<input type="radio" name="radFriendship" value="Not_Applicable"
    id="b"/>
<label for="b" accesskey="b">Not_Applicable
    [access key = b]</label>
```

Admittedly, this may not be practical or cosmetically pleasing, but without this hint, the user may never realize that an `accesskey` is available.

Value

This attribute takes as its value a single character, which can be numerical, alphabetical, or even a symbol.

Compatibility

Internet Explorer			Firefox			Safari			Opera
5.5	6.0	7.0	1.0	1.5	2.0	1.3	2.0	3.0	9.2
Full	Full	Full	Full	Full	Full	None	None	Full	None

There is some variety in the way that the `accesskey` is activated. The biggest problem with this attribute is that the keystrokes you've defined may clash with other technologies. For example, a user may have assistive technology (such as a screen reader or screen magnifier) that shares keystrokes with those that you've defined in the `accesskey` attribute. In addition, different language browsers use different "accelerator keys" for their own menu options, and these may also clash with the access keys you've defined. In such cases, the `accesskey` may not work as you intended for all users, and as such, many web standards advocates strongly discourage its use. However, `accesskey` can have a role in documents that are used in controlled environments, such as intranets or for point-of-sale environments, in which you know exactly which browsers and languages the users can access. In such cases, using a standard set of `accesskey` attributes may be of great benefit.

for *for <label>*

```
for="field ID"
```

SPEC		
deprecated	required	version
NO	YES	HTML 4
BROWSER SUPPORT			
IE5.5+	FF1+	Saf3+	Op9.2+
FULL	FULL	FULL	FULL

Example

This `for` attribute points to a `form` control with the `id` of `"b"`:

```
<input type="radio" name="radFriendship" value="Not_Applicable"
    id="b"/>
<label for="b" accesskey="b">Not_Applicable</label>
```

The `for` attribute is the glue that binds the text contained inside the `label` element to the form control to which it relates. There's another way that descriptive text can be linked to a form control: instead of using a `for` attribute, the opening `<label>` and closing `</label>` tags can be wrapped around the form control. In that instance, the example code would look like this:

```
<label accesskey="b"><input type="radio" name="radFriendship"
    value="Not_Applicable" id="b"/> Not_Applicable</label>
```

Finally, you could take the belt-and-braces approach and do *both*: wrap the `label` around the form control *and* link it using the `for` attribute:

```
<label for="b" accesskey="b"><input type="radio"
    name="radFriendship" value="Not_Applicable" id="b"/>
    Not_Applicable</label>
```

Note that the former method—using the `for` attribute—is by far the safer option (at least one screen reader, Window Eyes, is not able to make the correct association when the `label` is wrapped around the related text).

Value

This attribute takes as its value a reference to an existing (and valid) `id` of a form control.

Compatibility

Internet Explorer			Firefox			Safari			Opera
5.5	6.0	7.0	1.0	1.5	2.0	1.3	2.0	3.0	9.2
Full	Full	Full	Full	Full	Full	None	None	Full	Full

The `for` attribute is more widely supported than the approach that involves simply wrapping the `label` around the control, and is the preferred method. It's also more flexible, as the text and control may be separated by other HTML structural elements that would make it impossible to wrap the inline `label` around the control and the associated text.

Form Elements

legend

```
<legend>
</legend>
```

SPEC		
deprecated	empty	version
NO	NO	HTML 4
BROWSER SUPPORT			
IE5.5+	FF1+	Saf1.3+	Op9.2+
FULL	FULL	FULL	FULL

Example

This `legend` element identifies three related XFN attributes (the online reference[4] has more on XFN):

```
<form>
  <fieldset>
    <legend>Friendship</legend>
    <input type="radio" name="radFriendship" value="Not_Applicable"
        id="radFriendNot_Applicable"/>
    <label for="radFriendNot_Applicable">Not_Applicable</label>
    <input type="radio" name="radFriendship" value="acquaintance"
        id="radFriendaquaintence"/>
    <label for="radFriendaquaintence">acquaintance</label>
    <input type="radio" name="radFriendship" value="friend"
        id="radFriendfriend"/>
    <label for="radFriendfriend">friend</label>
  </fieldset>
  ⋮
</form>
```

The `legend` is used to provide the caption text for grouped form controls and text contained in a `fieldset` (p. 241). By default, the text appears on the left, *over* the boxed outline that the fieldset creates, as Figure 6.2 shows (the word "Friendship" is the content). No other content may appear between the opening `<fieldset>` tag and the opening `<legend>` tag—only whitespace is allowed.

Figure 6.11: A fieldset with the legend "Friendship" grouping related items in the form

---

[4] http://reference.sitepoint.com/html/xfn/

Use This For ...

Use this element to give a name to the grouped `form` (p. 243) elements. There are no hard rules about what goes inside the `<legend>` and `</legend>` tags, but take care: some browsers have a hard time applying styles to the `legend`, so it's good practice to keep the text content as succinct as possible, in order to avoid styling problems. Another reason to keep the text short is that this is best for screen reader users who may have to listen to the announcement of the `legend` text before every form input inside the `fieldset` related to the `legend`.

Compatibility

Internet Explorer			Firefox			Safari			Opera
5.5	6.0	7.0	1.0	1.5	2.0	1.3	2.0	3.0	9.2
Full	Full	Full	Full	Full	Full	Full	Full	Full	Full

It causes no compatibility issues, and has excellent support across all tested browsers.

Other Relevant Stuff

 `fieldset` (p. 241)

groups related form controls

accesskey _for <legend>_

`accesskey="key"`

SPEC		
deprecated	required	version
NO	NO	HTML 4
BROWSER SUPPORT		
IE6+	FF2	Saf3	Op9.2
PARTIAL	NONE	NONE	NONE

Example

The `accesskey` for this group of controls is assigned to `"1"`:

```
<form>
  <fieldset>
    <legend accesskey="1">Friendship</legend>
    <input type="radio" name="radFriendship" value="Not_Applicable"
        id="radFriendNot_Applicable"/>
    <label for="radFriendNot_Applicable">Not_Applicable</label>
    <input type="radio" name="radFriendship" value="acquaintance"
        id="radFriendaquaintence"/>
    <label for="radFriendaquaintence">acquaintance</label>
    <input type="radio" name="radFriendship" value="friend"
        id="radFriendfriend"/>
    <label for="radFriendfriend">friend</label>
  </fieldset>
</form>
```

The `accesskey` attribute allows the user to activate a control on a page using a keyboard shortcut. This may save time for users who would otherwise need to tab through a series of form controls or move the mouse to get to the desired link. The key combination that activates the link to which the `accesskey` is applied varies depending on the platform and browser combination. For IE/Windows, users press Alt + `accesskey`, while Firefox/Windows users press Alt + Shift + `accesskey`; users of most Mac browsers press Ctrl + `accesskey`; in Opera, pressing Shift + Esc displays a list of links for which `accesskey` attributes are defined, allowing users to choose the key they want to use.

Generally speaking, browsers don't indicate that an `accesskey` attribute is defined for a form control, and this lack of discoverability is a problem. The most common method for indicating the `accesskey` value is to place it in a `title` (p. 506) attribute of the element to which it's applied. However, for this approach to work, the user must mouse over the element in question. You may want to state the `accesskey` value in some other way—for example:

```
<legend accesskey="1">Friendship [access key = 1]</legend>
```

Admittedly, this may not be practical or cosmetically pleasing, but without this hint, the user may never realize that an `accesskey` is available.

Value

This attribute takes as its value a single character, which can be numerical, alphabetical, or even a symbol.

Compatibility

Internet Explorer			Firefox			Safari			Opera
5.5	6.0	7.0	1.0	1.5	2.0	1.3	2.0	3.0	9.2
None	Partial	Partial	None	None	None	None	None	None	None

There is some variety in the way that the `accesskey` is activated. The biggest problem with this attribute is that the keystrokes you've defined may clash with other technologies. For example, a user may have assistive technology (such as a screen reader or screen magnifier) that shares keystrokes with those that you've defined in the `accesskey` attribute. In addition, different language browsers use different "accelerator keys" for their own menu options, and these may also clash with the access keys you've defined. In such cases, the `accesskey` may not work as you intended for all users, and as such, many web standards advocates strongly discourage its use. However, `accesskey` can have a role in documents that are used in controlled environments, such as intranets or for point-of-sale environments, in which you know exactly which browsers and languages the users can access. In such cases, using a standard set of `accesskey` attributes may be of great benefit.

Form Elements

 **align** *for <legend>*

`align=" { bottom | left | right | top } "`

SPEC		
deprecated	required	version
YES	NO	HTML 4
BROWSER SUPPORT		
IE5.5+	FF1+	Saf1.3+	Op9.2
PARTIAL	PARTIAL	PARTIAL	NONE

Example

The `align` attribute for this group of controls is set to `"right"`:

```
<form>
  <fieldset>
    <legend accesskey="1" align="right">Friendship</legend>
    <input type="radio" name="radFriendship" value="Not_Applicable"
        id="radFriendNot_Applicable"/>
    <label for="radFriendNot_Applicable">Not_Applicable</label>
    <input type="radio" name="radFriendship" value="acquaintance"
        id="radFriendaquaintence"/>
    <label for="radFriendaquaintence">acquaintance</label>
    <input type="radio" name="radFriendship" value="friend"
        id="radFriendfriend"/>
    <label for="radFriendfriend">friend</label>
  </fieldset>
</form>
```

The `align` attribute is intended to enable finer positioning of the text in relation to the `fieldset`'s boxed outline. In practice, though, you won't find much use for this attribute, as it's deprecated and poorly supported. Aside from the default position (top, left), few of the tested browsers paid any attention to any of the other values, aside from the `"right"` alignment, as Figure 6.12 shows.

Figure 6.12: A right-aligned `legend` element

Value

This attribute accepts as its values `"bottom"`, `"left"`, `"right"`, and `"top"`. The browser default is `"left"`.

Compatibility

Internet Explorer			Firefox			Safari			Opera
5.5	6.0	7.0	1.0	1.5	2.0	1.3	2.0	3.0	9.2
Partial	Partial	Partial	Partial	Partial	Partial	Partial	Partial	None	None

This attribute is poorly supported and highly presentational. CSS should be used to control appearance instead.

optgroup

```
<optgroup label="string">
</optgroup>
```

SPEC		
deprecated	empty	version
NO	NO	HTML 4
BROWSER SUPPORT		
IE5.5+	FF1+	Saf1.3+	Op9.2+
FULL	FULL	FULL	FULL

Example

In this select list, food types are grouped together with optgroup elements:

```
<form>
  <select name="favoritefood">
    <optgroup label="Dairy products">
      <option>Cheese</option>
      <option>Egg</option>
    </optgroup>
    <optgroup label="Vegetables">
      <option>Cabbage</option>
      <option>Lettuce</option>
      <option>Beans</option>
      <option>Onions</option>
      <option>Courgettes</option>
    </optgroup>
    ⋮
  </select>
</form>
```

In longer select (p. 296) lists, it may be beneficial to subgroup related items in much the same way as you might organize list content by nesting those lists. You effectively create a series of categories, and items that fit into each category. The optgroup element allows you to do this in select lists, helping to visually clarify the organization of list items, although browsers use a range of different visual styles to indicate related groups of options, as Figure 6.13 shows.

Figure 6.13: Optgroups rendered in IE (Windows), Firefox, Opera, and IE5.2 Mac

Note that optgroup is only used to identify related items visually. It contains no useful data, nor can users click on an option group as they could an individual option.

Use This For ...

This element is used to group related items as a means to enhance the clarity of information presented to the user.

Compatibility

Internet Explorer			Firefox			Safari			Opera
5.5	6.0	7.0	1.0	1.5	2.0	1.3	2.0	3.0	9.2
Full	Full	Full	Full	Full	Full	Full	Full	Full	Full

It causes no compatibility issues, and has excellent support across all tested browsers.

Other Relevant Stuff

 option (p. 290)

defines an item in a select *list*

label *for <optgroup>*

`label="string"`

	SPEC	
deprecated	required	version
NO	YES	HTML 4
BROWSER SUPPORT		
IE5.5+	FF1+	Saf1.3+ Op9.2+
FULL	FULL	FULL FULL

Example

This required `label` attribute identifies a group of options as `"Dairy products"`:

```
<form>
  <select name="favoritefood">
    <optgroup label="Dairy products">
      <option>Cheese</option>
      <option>Egg</option>
    </optgroup>
  </select>
</form>
```

The `label` attribute is used to identify the contents—the `option` elements—of the `optgroup`. The rendering of the `optgroup`'s `label` differs between browsers, as Figure 6.13 shows.

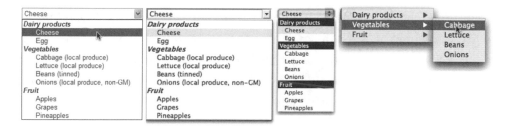

Figure 6.14: Example browser output of the `optgroup` label

Value

This attribute takes a (preferably short) description or classification of the contained `option` elements.

Compatibility

Internet Explorer			Firefox			Safari			Opera
5.5	6.0	7.0	1.0	1.5	2.0	1.3	2.0	3.0	9.2
Full	Full	Full	Full	Full	Full	Full	Full	Full	Full

Every browser listed supports this attribute.

option

```
<option selected="selected" value="value">
</option>
```

SPEC		
deprecated	empty	version
NO	NO	HTML 2
BROWSER SUPPORT			
IE5.5+	FF1+	Saf1.3+	Op9.2+
FULL	FULL	FULL	FULL

Example

This code produces a simple `select` list in which the `option` elements are highlighted:

```
<form>
  <label for="favoritefood">Favorite food</label>
  <select name="favoritefood" id="favoritefood">
    <option>Cheese</option>
    <option>Egg</option>
    <option>Cabbage</option>
    ⋮
  </select>
</form>
```

Each `option` in a `select` element represents an option that the user can choose. The text contained between the opening `<option>` and closing `</option>` tags is displayed to the user, while the `value` (p. 275) attribute contains the actual data that will be sent when the `form` is submitted. The `selected` (p. 294) attribute is useful for preselecting a list option at page load.

Use This For ...

The `option` element is used to create a single option in a `select` list. It would primarily be used for data capture purposes, but may also be used to create navigation. `select` lists are sometimes used for this purpose, with the destination presented as text content within the opening `<option>` and closing `</option>` tags, and the address, or URL, specified by the `value` attribute.

Compatibility

Internet Explorer			Firefox			Safari			Opera
5.5	6.0	7.0	1.0	1.5	2.0	1.3	2.0	3.0	9.2
Full	Full	Full	Full	Full	Full	Full	Full	Full	Full

It causes no compatibility issues, and has excellent support across all tested browsers.

Other Relevant Stuff

 optgroup (p. 287)

groups related option elements contained in a select list

disabled *for <option>*

```
disabled="disabled"
```

	SPEC	
deprecated	required	version
NO	NO	HTML 3.02
BROWSER SUPPORT		
IE7	FF1+	Saf3+	Op9.2+
NONE	FULL	FULL	FULL

Example

The disabled attribute stops the "Cabbage" and "Lettuce" option elements from being used:

```
<form>
  <label for="favoritefood">Favorite food</label>
  <select name="favoritefood" id="favoritefood">
    <option>Cheese</option>
    <option>Egg</option>
    <option disabled="disabled">Cabbage</option>
    <option disabled="disabled">Lettuce</option>
    ⋮
  </select>
</form>
```

The disabled attribute stops the user from interacting with specific options in the select list. When using the up and down arrow keys, users will simply skip over any disabled options; nor can they click on disabled options with the mouse.

The most likely application for this attribute is to disable certain choices in the list until some other condition has been met (until a checkbox is checked, for example, which widens the potential choices the user may make). At this point, JavaScript would be required to removed the `"disabled"` values, making those options selectable. Figure 6.15 shows the effect of disabling specific `option` elements.

Figure 6.15: A select list in which two options disabled

Value

The only value that `disabled` can take `"disabled"`.

Compatibility

Internet Explorer			Firefox			Safari			Opera
5.5	6.0	7.0	1.0	1.5	2.0	1.3	2.0	3.0	9.2
None	None	None	Full	Full	Full	None	None	Full	Full

This attribute is poorly supported and should not be relied upon.

 **label** *for <option>*

`label="string"`

SPEC		
deprecated	required	version
NO	NO	HTML 2
BROWSER SUPPORT		
IE7+	FF2	Saf1.3+	Op9.2
FULL	NONE	FULL	NONE

Example

This `label` attribute presents a simpler version of the `option` content:

```
<form>
  <label for="favoritefood">Favorite food</label>
  <select name="favoritefood" id="favoritefood">
    ⋮
    <optgroup label="Vegetables">
      <option label="Cabbage">Cabbage (local produce)</option>
      <option label="Lettuce">Lettuce (local produce)</option>
      <option label="Beans">Beans (tinned)</option>
      <option label="Onions">Onions (local produce, non-GM)</option>
    </optgroup>
    ⋮
  </select>
</form>
```

The `label` attribute provides a means for presenting a shortened version of an `option` when it appears within an `optgroup` (which, depending on the browser, may display in a hierarchical layout or some other modified layout). The `optgroups` rendering is shown in Figure 6.16.

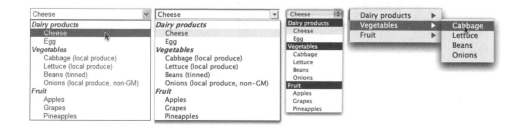

Figure 6.16: optgroup and option label rendering in IE, Firefox, Opera, and IE5 (Mac)

Value

This attribute takes an abbreviated version of the `option` content.

Form Elements

Compatibility

Internet Explorer			Firefox			Safari			Opera
5.5	6.0	7.0	1.0	1.5	2.0	1.3	2.0	3.0	9.2
None	None	Full	None	None	None	Full	Full	Full	None

This attribute is poorly supported and has limited practical value.

selected *for <option>*

```
selected="selected"
```

SPEC		
deprecated	required	version
NO	NO	HTML 2
BROWSER SUPPORT		
IE5.5+ FF1+ Saf1.3+ Op9.2+		
FULL FULL FULL FULL		

Example

This selected attribute is used to choose the second option:

```
<form>
  <label for="favoritefood">Favorite food</label>
  <select name="favoritefood" id="favoritefood" disabled="disabled">
    <option>Cheese</option>
    <option selected="selected">Egg</option>
    <option>Cabbage</option>
    ⋮
  </select>
</form>
```

The selected attribute is used to preselect an option in a select list, usually at page-load time (although you could use JavaScript to change the selected option dynamically, after page load).

You might use this attribute when an error is found in a user-submitted form (p. 243), and you want the user to reenter data into a field in the redisplayed page. It would be irritating for the user to have to reselect selections that had previously been made from lists; the selected attribute takes care of that particular conundrum.

Value

The only possible value for this attribute is "selected".

Compatibility

Internet Explorer			Firefox			Safari			Opera
5.5	6.0	7.0	1.0	1.5	2.0	1.3	2.0	3.0	9.2
Full	Full	Full	Full	Full	Full	Full	Full	Full	Full

It causes no compatibility issues, and has excellent support across all tested browsers.

value *for <option>*

`value="value"`

SPEC		
deprecated	required	version
NO	NO	HTML 2
BROWSER SUPPORT		
IE5.5+ FF1+	Saf1.3+	Op9.2+
FULL FULL	FULL	FULL

Example

In this example, `value` attributes are specified for a series of `options`:

```
<form>
  <label for="favoritefood">Favorite food</label>
  <select name="favoritefood" id="favoritefood" disabled="disabled">
    <option value="1">Cheese</option>
    <option value="2">Egg</option>
    <option value="3">Cabbage</option>
    ⋮
  </select>
</form>
```

The content contained between the opening `<option>` and closing `</option>` tags is the user-friendly version that's displayed on screen, but it's what's inside the `value` that's important to the processing application on the server. In the example above, different foods are displayed on screen, but they have `value`s of `"1"`, `"2"`, and `"3"`, which should match up with values in a database. If the `value` attribute isn't present, the content (`"Cheese"`, `"Egg"`, and `"Cabbage"` in this example) will be passed as a `"value"` instead.

Value

This attribute takes any name or value that the developer chooses.

Compatibility

Internet Explorer			Firefox			Safari			Opera
5.5	6.0	7.0	1.0	1.5	2.0	1.3	2.0	3.0	9.2
Full	Full	Full	Full	Full	Full	Full	Full	Full	Full

It causes no compatibility issues, and has excellent support across all tested browsers.

select

```
<select multiple="multiple" name="string"
size="number">
</select>
```

SPEC		
deprecated	empty	version
NO	NO	HTML 2
BROWSER SUPPORT		
IE5.5+	FF1+	Saf1.3+	Op9.2+
FULL	FULL	FULL	FULL

Example

This example shows a very simple select element:

```
<form>
  <label for="favoritefood">Favorite food</label>
  <select name="favoritefood" id="favoritefood">
    <option>Cheese</option>
    <option>Egg</option>
    <option>Cabbage</option>
    ⋮
  </select>
</form>
```

The select form control is a container for a series of option (p. 290) elements that display in the browser as a pull-down menu (that is, a drop-down list). Unless you use the multiple (p. 301) attribute, the control will allow the user to pick just one item from the list of options that's generated by the contents of the nested option elements. The select renders slightly differently depending on the browser and operating system in use, and is well known as a troublesome HTML element to style with CSS (because the display is inherited from the operating system, rather than provided by the browser). If there isn't enough room on the page for the list to display below the control, it will open up *above* it. Figure 6.17 shows an expanded (opened) select list in Firefox.

Figure 6.17: An expanded select list

Use This For ...

This element is used to allow visitors to make selections from a long list of items. The alternative approach would involve the use of radio input selections, but this would require all the options to be displayed on the page at once; select controls generally display in a smaller amount of page real estate.

Compatibility

Internet Explorer			Firefox			Safari			Opera
5.5	6.0	7.0	1.0	1.5	2.0	1.3	2.0	3.0	9.2
Full	Full	Full	Full	Full	Full	Full	Full	Full	Full

It causes no compatibility issues, and has excellent support across all tested browsers.

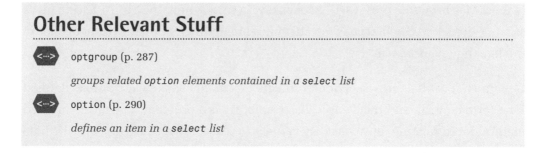

Other Relevant Stuff

optgroup (p. 287)

groups related option elements contained in a select list

option (p. 290)

defines an item in a select list

Form Elements

accesskey *for <select>*

`accesskey="key"`

SPEC		
deprecated	required	version
NO	NO	HTML 4
BROWSER SUPPORT		
IE5.5+	FF1+	Saf1.3+	Op9.2+
FULL	FULL	FULL	FULL

Example

The `accesskey` for this `select` is assigned to `"f"`:

```
<form>
  <label for="favoritefood">Favorite food</label>
  <select name="favoritefood" id="favoritefood" accesskey="f">
    <option>Cheese</option>
    <option>Egg</option>
    <option>Cabbage</option>
    ⋮
  </select>
</form>
```

The `accesskey` attribute allows the user to activate a control on a page using a keyboard shortcut. This may save time for users who would otherwise need to tab through a series of form controls or move the mouse to get to the desired link. The key combination that activates the link to which the `accesskey` is applied varies depending on the platform and browser combination. For IE/Windows, users press Alt + `accesskey`, while Firefox/Windows users press Alt + Shift + `accesskey`; users of most Mac browsers press Ctrl + `accesskey`; in Opera, pressing Shift + Esc displays a list of links for which `accesskey` attributes are defined, allowing users to choose the key they want to use.

Generally speaking, browsers don't indicate that an `accesskey` attribute is defined for a form control, and this lack of discoverability is a problem. The most common method for indicating the `accesskey` value is to place it in a `title` (p. 506) attribute of the element to which it's applied. However, for this approach to work, the user must mouse over the element in question. You may want to state the `accesskey` value in some other way—for example:

```
<label for="favoritefood">Favorite food [access key = f]</label>
<select name="favoritefood" id="favoritefood" accesskey="f">
```

Admittedly, this may not be practical or cosmetically pleasing, but without this hint, the user may never realize that an accesskey is available.

Value

This attribute takes as its value a single character, which can be numerical, alphabetical, or even a symbol.

Compatibility

Internet Explorer			Firefox			Safari			Opera
5.5	6.0	7.0	1.0	1.5	2.0	1.3	2.0	3.0	9.2
Full	Full	Full	Full	Full	Full	Full	Full	Full	Full

There is some variety in the way that the accesskey is activated. The biggest problem with this attribute is that the keystrokes you've defined may clash with other technologies. For example, a user may have assistive technology (such as a screen reader or screen magnifier) that shares keystrokes with those that you've defined in the accesskey attribute. In addition, different language browsers use different "accelerator keys" for their own menu options, and these may also clash with the access keys you've defined. In such cases, the accesskey may not work as you intended for all users, and as such, many web standards advocates strongly discourage its use. However, accesskey can have a role in documents that are used in controlled environments, such as intranets or for point-of-sale environments, in which you know exactly which browsers and languages the users can access. In such cases, using a standard set of accesskey attributes may be of great benefit.

Form Elements

 **disabled** *for <select>*

`disabled="disabled"`

SPEC		
deprecated	required	version
NO	NO	HTML 3.02
BROWSER SUPPORT		
IE5.5+	FF1+	Saf1.3+	Op9.2+
FULL	FULL	FULL	FULL

Example

This `disabled` attribute prevents the `select` from being used:

```
<form>
  <label for="favoritefood">Favorite food</label>
  <select name="favoritefood" id="favoritefood"
      disabled="disabled">
   <option>Cheese</option>
   <option>Egg</option>
   <option>Cabbage</option>
   ⋮
  </select>
</form>
```

The `disabled` attribute stops the user from interacting with the form control. In this case, it prevents the user from clicking on the `select`, or tabbing to it with the keyboard, so the user is prevented from changing the value.

The most likely application for this attribute is to disable a `select` until such a time as some other condition has been met (for example, a user clicks on a checkbox to confirm terms and conditions). At that point, JavaScript would be required to removed the `"disabled"` value, making the form control usable.

Value

The only value this attribute can take is `"disabled"`.

Compatibility

Internet Explorer			Firefox			Safari			Opera
5.5	6.0	7.0	1.0	1.5	2.0	1.3	2.0	3.0	9.2
Full	Full	Full	Full	Full	Full	Full	Full	Full	Full

It causes no compatibility issues, and has excellent support across all tested browsers.

multiple *for <select>*

`multiple="*multiple*"`

SPEC		
deprecated	required	version
NO	NO	HTML 3.02
BROWSER SUPPORT		
IE5.5+	FF1+	Saf1.3+	Op9.2+
FULL	FULL	FULL	FULL

Example

This example shows a `multiple` attribute applied to a `select` list:

```
<form>
  <label for="favoritefood">Favorite food</label>
  <select name="favoritefood" id="favoritefood"
      multiple="multiple" size="10">
    <option>Cheese</option>
    <option>Egg</option>
    <option>Cabbage</option>
    ⋮
  </select>
</form>
```

When the `multiple` attribute is combined with the `size` (p. 303) attribute, the user is able to select multiple, noncontiguous items from the list of options. To do this, the user must use a modifier key; for most Windows browsers, users would press Control while they clicked, while users of Mac browsers would press Command while they clicked. The user's selection may appear as shown in Figure 6.18—this screenshot was taken using Firefox on Mac, but the highlight colour may vary depending on user preferences.

Figure 6.18: Selecting multiple items

Note that in the example shown, there is no formatting in the form of CSS, or `br` (p. 40) or `div` (p. 44) elements, so the label text appears to be aligned with the base of the `select` element. Naturally, you'd want to rectify this, but I've presented it this way so that you're aware of the default layout.

Multiple `select` lists aren't very common, and it may be better to provide such choices in the form of checkboxes. If you use a multiple `select` list, you'll almost always need to provide instructions to tell the user how to select multiple items—and those instructions will need to be relevant to the browsers and operating systems in use, which ultimately means there's more room for user error.

Value

The only possible value for this attribute is `"multiple"`.

Compatibility

Internet Explorer			Firefox			Safari			Opera
5.5	6.0	7.0	1.0	1.5	2.0	1.3	2.0	3.0	9.2
Full	Full	Full	Full	Full	Full	Full	Full	Full	Full

It causes no compatibility issues, and has excellent support across all tested browsers.

name *for <select>*

```
name="string"
```

SPEC		
deprecated	required	version
NO	NO	HTML 2
BROWSER SUPPORT			
IE5.5+	FF1+	Saf1.3+	Op9.2+
FULL	FULL	FULL	FULL

Example

The `name` attribute of `"favoritefood"` provides a means for referencing the `select`'s data:

```
<form>
  <label for="favoritefood">Favorite food</label>
  <select name="favoritefood" id="favoritefood">
    <option>Cheese</option>
    <option>Egg</option>
    <option>Cabbage</option>
    ⋮
  </select>
</form>
```

The name attribute is used to reference form data after it's submitted, and to reference the data using JavaScript on the client side. Unlike the id attribute, which must be given a unique value each time it's applied to a new form control, a name attribute with a given value may be applied to numerous form controls (although in practice this approach is *only* used with radio input buttons). Note that only form elements which have a name attribute will have their values passed through to the page or script specified in the form's action attribute.

Value

This attribute takes as its value any name that the developer chooses, as long as that name doesn't contain spaces or special characters.

Compatibility

Internet Explorer			Firefox			Safari			Opera
5.5	6.0	7.0	1.0	1.5	2.0	1.3	2.0	3.0	9.2
Full	Full	Full	Full	Full	Full	Full	Full	Full	Full

It causes no compatibility issues, and has excellent support across all tested browsers.

 size *for <select>*

```
size="number"
```

SPEC		
deprecated	required	version
NO	NO	HTML 2
BROWSER SUPPORT		
IE5.5+	FF1+	Saf1.3+	Op9.2+
FULL	FULL	FULL	FULL

Example

This size attribute displays five options in the list:

```
<form>
  <label for="favoritefood">Favorite food</label>
  <select name="favoritefood" id="favoritefood"
      multiple="multiple" size="5">
    <option>Cheese</option>
    <option>Egg</option>
    <option>Cabbage</option>
    ⋮
  </select>
</form>
```

Form Elements

The `size` attribute is normally used in conjunction with the `multiple` (p. 301) attribute to define the number of options that will be displayed in the list at any time. The `size` attribute can also be used without a multiple selection list, but this usage isn't common.

If the `size` is set to `"1"`, or omitted entirely, the select will render as a pull-down list. If the value is greater than `"1"`, the `select` renders as list of options. If the value of the `size` attribute is lower than the number of `option` elements contained in the `select` list, the browser will display a scroll bar control to indicate that there are more options to view or action below, as Figure 6.19 shows.

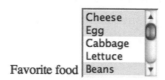

Figure 6.19: A select list on which `multiple` is set, which has a `size` of `"5"`

Value

This attribute takes as its value a number, such as `"5"`, `"10"`, and so on.

Compatibility

Internet Explorer			Firefox			Safari			Opera
5.5	6.0	7.0	1.0	1.5	2.0	1.3	2.0	3.0	9.2
Full	Full	Full	Full	Full	Full	Full	Full	Full	Full

It causes no compatibility issues, and has excellent support across all tested browsers.

tabindex *for <select>*

```
tabindex="number"
```

SPEC		
deprecated	required	version
NO	NO	HTML 3.02
BROWSER SUPPORT			
IE5.5+	FF1+	Saf1.3+	Op9.2+
FULL	FULL	FULL	FULL

Example

The `tabindex` is set for both form controls in this example:

```
<form>
  <label for="perfectday">Describe your perfect day:</label>
  <textarea id="perfectday" tabindex="1" name="perfectday"
      accesskey="d" cols="40" rows="10">Sitting by the beach,
      sipping a cocktail</textarea>
  <input type="submit" value="Tell us" tabindex="2"/>
</form>
```

The `tabindex` is used to define a sequence that users follow when they use the Tab key to navigate through a page. By default, the natural tabbing order will match the source order in the markup. In certain circumstances it may be necessary to override the default tabbing order, but it's strongly recommended that you craft a page in a logical flow and let the browser work through it in the default order—an approach that negates the need for the `tabindex` attribute.

A `tabindex` can start at 0 and increment in any value. As such, the sequence 1, 2, 3, 4, 5 would be fine, as would 10, 20, 30, 40, 50. If you need to introduce a `tabindex`, it's advisable to use a sequence that contains intervals (like the second example provided), as this will give you the opportunity to inject other controls later if need be (for example, 10, 15, 20) without having to reindex all the `tabindex` values on the page. Should a given `tabindex` value be applied to more than one element in error, the tabbing order of those affected elements will be as per the source markup order.

If a `tabindex` is set anywhere on a page—even if it's the hundredth link or the fiftieth form control—the tab order will start at the element with the lowest `tabindex` value, and work through the increments. Only *then* will the tab order take in the remaining elements for which no `tabindex` has been set. As such, great care must be taken to ensure that adding a `tabindex` doesn't harm the usability of the page as a whole.

If the `disabled` attribute is set on an element which has a `tabindex`, that `tabindex` will be ignored.

Value

The `tabindex` attribute takes numerical values only .

Compatibility

Internet Explorer			Firefox			Safari			Opera
5.5	6.0	7.0	1.0	1.5	2.0	1.3	2.0	3.0	9.2
Full	Full	Full	Full	Full	Full	Full	Full	Full	Full

It causes no compatibility issues, and has excellent support across all tested browsers.

textarea

```
<textarea cols="number" name="string" rows="number">
</textarea>
```

SPEC		
deprecated	empty	version
NO	NO	HTML 4
BROWSER SUPPORT		
IE5.5+	FF1+	Saf1.3+	Op9.2+
FULL	FULL	FULL	FULL

Example

This example shows a very simple `textarea` to which no layout or formatting is applied:

```
<form>
  <label for="perfectday">Describe your perfect day:</label>
  <textarea id="perfectday"></textarea>
  <input type="submit" value="Tell us"/>
</form>
```

A `textarea` is similar to the text `input` (p. 273), but allows the person who's filling in the form to enter multiple lines of information, rather than a single line, and thus is better for free-form text entry. However, unlike the `input` element (in all its different types), the `textarea` has an opening `<textarea>` and closing `</textarea>` tag. It's not possible to insert any kind of markup inside the `textarea`—only text content is allowed. However, when users complete the form, they may potentially enter any characters, including accented characters, foreign characters, or markup. As such, it's important to state which kinds of content you'll allow the user to enter into the `textarea`, and it's even more important to effectively validate any content that's entered in to a `textarea` when it's submitted. The example above shows that, if no styles are applied via CSS, and `br` (p. 40) and `div` (p. 44) elements aren't used, the `textarea` lines up with the neighbouring elements along its base, as Figure 6.20 shows.

Figure 6.20: A simple, unformatted textarea

The size of the `textarea` can be changed in a couple of ways, should the default size be insufficient. The old-fashioned method involves the use of the `cols` (p. 310) and `rows` (p. 314) attributes which, unsurprisingly, define the number of horizontal input lines (rows) and the width of the `textarea` in terms of columns. This is a slightly clumsy and simplistic way of controlling the element's size, but these are required attributes and they can't simply be dropped. However, browser support for styling the `textarea` via CSS is excellent, so you can override these attributes and let CSS do the heavy lifting (for example, setting the width to 100% of the container—a much more useful method of sizing).

Use This For ...

This element can be used to capture any data that may vary in size. For instance, it might be used to add a comment on a blog, enter biography information, write a review, or apply for a job. The possibilities for its use are almost endless!

Compatibility

Internet Explorer			Firefox			Safari			Opera
5.5	6.0	7.0	1.0	1.5	2.0	1.3	2.0	3.0	9.2
Full	Full	Full	Full	Full	Full	Full	Full	Full	Full

It causes no compatibility issues, and has excellent support across all tested browsers.

Form Elements

Other Relevant Stuff

 input (p. 253)

defines the input control for a form

 # accesskey *for <textarea>*

`accesskey="key"`

SPEC		
deprecated	required	version
NO	NO	HTML 4
BROWSER SUPPORT			
IE7	FF2	Saf3	Op9.2
NONE	NONE	NONE	NONE

Example

The `accesskey` for this group of controls is assigned to `"d"`:

```
<form>
  <label for="perfectday">Describe your perfect day:</label>
  <textarea id="perfectday" accesskey="d"></textarea>
  <input type="submit" value="Tell us"/>
</form>
```

The `accesskey` attribute allows the user to activate a control on a page using a keyboard shortcut. This may save time for users who would otherwise need to tab through a series of form controls or move the mouse to get to the desired link. The key combination that activates the link to which the `accesskey` is applied varies depending on the platform and browser combination. For IE/Windows, users press Alt + `accesskey`, while Firefox/Windows users press Alt + Shift + `accesskey`; users of most Mac browsers press Ctrl + `accesskey`; in Opera, pressing Shift + Esc displays a list of links for which `accesskey` attributes are defined, allowing users to choose the key they want to use.

Generally speaking, browsers don't indicate that an `accesskey` attribute is defined for a form control, and this lack of discoverability is a problem. The most common method for indicating the `accesskey` value is to place it in a `title` (p. 506) attribute of the element to which it's applied. However, for this approach to work, the user must mouse over the element in question. You may want to state the `accesskey` value in some other way—for example:

```
<form>
  <label for="perfectday">Describe your perfect day
    [access key = d]:</label>
  <textarea id="perfectday" accesskey="d"></textarea>
  <input type="submit" value="Tell us"/>
</form>
```

Admittedly, this may not be practical or cosmetically pleasing, but without this hint, the user may never realize that an `accesskey` is available.

Value

This attribute takes as its value a single character, which can be numerical, alphabetical, or even a symbol.

Compatibility

Internet Explorer			Firefox			Safari			Opera
5.5	6.0	7.0	1.0	1.5	2.0	1.3	2.0	3.0	9.2
None	None	None	None	None	None	None	None	None	None

There is some variety in the way that the `accesskey` is activated. The biggest problem with this attribute is that the keystrokes you've defined may clash with other technologies. For example, a user may have assistive technology (such as a screen reader or screen magnifier) that shares keystrokes with those that you've defined in the `accesskey` attribute. In addition, different language browsers use different "accelerator keys" for their own menu options, and these may also clash with the access keys you've defined. In such cases, the `accesskey` may not work as you intended for all users, and as such, many web standards advocates strongly discourage its use. However, `accesskey` can have a role in documents that are used in controlled environments, such as intranets or for point-of-sale environments, in which you know exactly which browsers and languages the users can access. In such cases, using a standard set of `accesskey` attributes may be of great benefit.

Form Elements

cols *for <textarea>*

`cols="number"`

	SPEC	
deprecated	required	version
NO	YES	HTML 2
BROWSER SUPPORT		
IE5.5+	FF1+	Saf1.3+	Op9.2+
FULL	FULL	FULL	FULL

Example

The `cols` attribute for this `textarea` is set to "40" characters:

```
<form>
  <label for="perfectday">Describe your perfect day:</label>
  <textarea id="perfectday" accesskey="d" cols="40"></textarea>
  <input type="submit" value="Tell us"/>
</form>
```

The `cols` attribute defines the width of the `textarea`, the value of which reflects the number of characters that can be entered (although how well this actually matches up to the actual number of characters displayed width-wise is debatable, as the font style for characters may change with the style specified for this element in the CSS). If `cols` isn't specified at all (even though it's a required attribute), the `textarea` will render with a width of 20 characters. Applying a value of "40" to the `cols` attribute doubles the available width, as Figure 6.21 shows.

Figure 6.21: Two `textarea`s, the first without a `cols` attribute, the second with `cols` set to "40"

Note that `cols` is a required attribute, as is `rows` (p. 314), so you shouldn't *replace* it with CSS styling. Instead, the CSS should *override* the size defined in this attribute. Without this attribute, your page can't possibly validate (and besides, it's helpful for users who are browsing with CSS switched off).

Value

This attribute takes as its value a number only—it can't take percentages or other values.

Compatibility

Internet Explorer			Firefox			Safari			Opera
5.5	6.0	7.0	1.0	1.5	2.0	1.3	2.0	3.0	9.2
Full	Full	Full	Full	Full	Full	Full	Full	Full	Full

It causes no compatibility issues, and has excellent support across all tested browsers.

disabled *for <textarea>*

```
disabled="disabled"
```

SPEC		
deprecated	required	version
NO	NO	HTML 3.02
BROWSER SUPPORT		
IE5.5+	FF1+	Saf1.3+	Op9.2+
FULL	FULL	FULL	FULL

Example

The `disabled` attribute prevents the `textarea` from being used:

```
<form>
  <label for="perfectday">Describe your perfect day:</label>
  <textarea id="perfectday" disabled="disabled" name="perfectday"
      accesskey="d" cols="40" rows="10"></textarea>
  <input type="submit" value="Tell us"/>
</form>
```

The `disabled` attribute stops the user from interacting with the `form` control. In this case, it prevents the user from clicking on the `textarea`, tabbing to it with the keyboard, or gaining access to any default text that appears inside the `textarea`.

The most likely application for this attribute is to disable a `textarea` until such a time as some other condition has been met (for example, a checkbox is ticked to confirm the user's acceptance of terms and conditions). At this point, JavaScript would be required to removed the `"disabled"` value, making the form control usable.

Value

"`disabled`" is the only value this attribute can accept.

Compatibility

Internet Explorer			Firefox			Safari			Opera
5.5	6.0	7.0	1.0	1.5	2.0	1.3	2.0	3.0	9.2
Full	Full	Full	Full	Full	Full	Full	Full	Partial	Full

It causes no compatibility issues, and has excellent support across all tested browsers.

name *for <textarea>*

```
name="string"
```

SPEC		
deprecated	required	version
NO	NO	HTML 2
BROWSER SUPPORT		
IE5.5+	FF1+	Saf1.3+	Op9.2+
FULL	FULL	FULL	FULL

Example

The name attribute provides a means for referencing form data—in this case, "`perfectday`":

```
<form>
  <label for="perfectday">Describe your perfect day:</label>
  <textarea id="perfectday" name="perfectday" accesskey="d"
      cols="40" rows="10"></textarea>
  <input type="submit" value="Tell us"/>
</form>
```

The name attribute is used to reference form data after it's submitted, and to reference the data using JavaScript on the client side. Unlike the id attribute, which must be given a unique value each time it's applied to a new form control, a name attribute with a given value may be applied to numerous form controls (although in practice this approach is *only* used with radio input buttons). Note that only form elements which have a name attribute will have their values passed through to the page or script specified in the form's action attribute.

Value

This attribute can take as its value any name of the developer's choosing, so long as that name doesn't contain spaces or special characters.

Compatibility

Internet Explorer			Firefox			Safari			Opera
5.5	6.0	7.0	1.0	1.5	2.0	1.3	2.0	3.0	9.2
Full	Full	Full	Full	Full	Full	Full	Full	Full	Full

It causes no compatibility issues, and has excellent support across all tested browsers.

readonly *for <textarea>*

```
readonly="readonly"
```

SPEC		
deprecated	required	version
NO	NO	HTML 3.02
BROWSER SUPPORT		
IE5.5+	FF1+	Saf1.3+	Op9.2+
FULL	FULL	FULL	FULL

Example

The readonly attribute below prevents the textarea content from being changed:

```
<form>
  <label for="perfectday">Describe your perfect day:</label>
  <textarea id="perfectday" readonly="readonly" name="perfectday"
      accesskey="d" cols="40" rows="10">
    Sitting by the beach, sipping a cocktail</textarea>
  <input type="submit" value="Tell us"/>
</form>
```

The "readonly" attribute stops the user from changing the content, but *doesn't* stop the user from interacting with the form control content. It's still possible to click inside the textarea, tab to it, highlight the text inside it, and even to copy and paste that content—it just can't be changed.

The most likely application for this attribute is to stop the user from interfering with the content inside a textarea until such a time as some other condition has been met (for example, a checkbox is checked to confirm the user's acceptance of

Form Elements

terms and conditions). At this point, JavaScript would be required to remove the `"readonly"` value, making the form control completely usable.

Value

`"readonly"` is the only possible value for this attribute.

Compatibility

Internet Explorer			Firefox			Safari			Opera
5.5	6.0	7.0	1.0	1.5	2.0	1.3	2.0	3.0	9.2
Full	Full	Full	Full	Full	Full	Full	Full	Full	Full

It causes no compatibility issues, and has excellent support across all tested browsers.

rows *for <textarea>*

`rows="number"`

	SPEC		
deprecated	required		version
NO	YES		HTML 2
BROWSER SUPPORT			
IE5.5+	FF1+	Saf1.3+	Op9.2+
FULL	FULL	FULL	FULL

Example

The rows attribute for this `textarea` is set to `"10"`:

```
<form>
  <label for="perfectday">Describe your perfect day:</label>
  <textarea id="perfectday" accesskey="d" cols="40" rows="10">
  </textarea>
  <input type="submit" value="Tell us"/>
</form>
```

The rows attribute defines the number of lines of text that are visible in the `textarea`. However, how well this actually matches up to the number of characters displayed height-wise is debatable, as the font style for characters may vary between browsers—especially if the style is changed by CSS. If no rows attribute is specified (even though it's a *required* attribute), the `textarea` will render with approximately three visible lines of text. If you provide a rows value of `"10"`, the `textarea` appears just over three times taller than the default height, as Figure 6.22 shows.

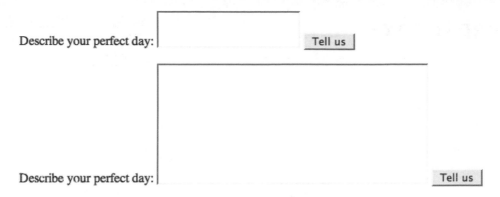

Figure 6.22: Two textareas, the first without a rows attribute, the second with rows set to "10"

Note that rows is a required attribute, as is cols (p. 310), so you shouldn't *replace* it with CSS styling. Instead, the CSS should *override* the size defined in this attribute. Without this attribute, your page can't possibly validate (and besides, it's helpful for users who are browsing with CSS switched off).

Value

This attribute accepts a number only—it won't accept percentages or other values.

Compatibility

Internet Explorer			Firefox			Safari			Opera
5.5	6.0	7.0	1.0	1.5	2.0	1.3	2.0	3.0	9.2
Full	Full	Full	Full	Full	Full	Full	Full	Full	Full

It causes no compatibility issues, and has excellent support across all tested browsers.

tabindex *for <textarea>*

```
tabindex="number"
```

SPEC		
deprecated	required	version
NO	NO	HTML 3.02
BROWSER SUPPORT			
IE5.5+	FF1+	Saf1.3+	Op9.2+
FULL	FULL	FULL	FULL

Example

The `tabindex` is set for both form controls below:

```
<form>
  <label for="perfectday">Describe your perfect day:</label>
  <textarea id="perfectday" tabindex="1" name="perfectday"
    accesskey="d" cols="40" rows="10">
    Sitting by the beach, sipping a cocktail</textarea>
  <input type="submit" value="Tell us" tabindex="2"/>
</form>
```

The `tabindex` is used to define a sequence that users follow when they use the Tab key to navigate through a page. By default, the natural tabbing order will match the source order in the markup. In certain circumstances it may be necessary to override the default tabbing order, but it's strongly recommended that you craft a page in a logical flow and let the browser work through it in the default order—an approach that negates the need for the `tabindex` attribute.

A `tabindex` can start at 0 and increment in any value. As such, the sequence 1, 2, 3, 4, 5 would be fine, as would 10, 20, 30, 40, 50. If you need to introduce a `tabindex`, it's advisable to use a sequence that contains intervals (like the second example provided), as this will give you the opportunity to inject other controls later if need be (for example, 10, 15, 20) without having to reindex all the `tabindex` values on the page. Should a given `tabindex` value be applied to more than one element in error, the tabbing order of those affected elements will be as per the source markup order.

If a `tabindex` is set anywhere on a page—even if it's the hundredth link or the fiftieth form control—the tab order will start at the element with the lowest `tabindex` value, and work through the increments. Only *then* will the tab order take in the remaining elements for which no `tabindex` has been set. As such, great care must be taken to ensure that adding a `tabindex` doesn't harm the usability of the page as a whole.

If the `disabled` attribute is set on an element which has a `tabindex`, that `tabindex` will be ignored.

Value

This attribute accepts a number value only.

Compatibility

Internet Explorer			Firefox			Safari			Opera
5.5	6.0	7.0	1.0	1.5	2.0	1.3	2.0	3.0	9.2
Full	Full	Full	Full	Full	Full	Full	Full	Full	Full

It causes no compatibility issues, and has excellent support across all tested browsers.

Chapter 7

Image and Media Elements

Once upon a time, in the dim, distant past, the Web was little more than a bunch of boring academic documents that were exciting to the handful of scientists and physicists who were technically capable of putting such documents together and able to configure a cranky old dial-up modem. Then along came the `img` (p. 333) element, and the Web started its transformation into the form we know and love today.

Yes, that's a *slight* oversimplification of how we got from A to B, but in all seriousness, until the elements detailed in *this* section were included in the W3C specs, and then in web browsers (or sometimes the other way around), the Web didn't have much to offer in the way of eye candy.

The elements in this section provide many opportunities to liven up a web page, whether that be to add a few images (using the `img` element), perhaps add a Flash movie or some other multimedia item using the `object` (p. 357) or `embed` (p. 332) elements, or create interactive maps that users can navigate through using the `map` (p. 354) and `area` (p. 320) elements.

applet

```
<applet archive="uri" code="uri" codebase="uri"
height=" { number | percentage } "width=" { number
| percentage } ">
</applet>
```

SPEC		
deprecated	empty	version
YES	NO	HTML 3.2
BROWSER SUPPORT			
IE5.5+	FF1+	Saf1.3+	Op9.2+
PARTIAL	PARTIAL	PARTIAL	PARTIAL

The `applet` element's purpose is to embed small Java applications (or applets—little apps) into the flow of a page. If any `param` (p. 378) elements are specified in the `applet` tag, they must be placed before all other content. This element has been replaced by the much more flexible, and non-Java-specific `object` (p. 357) element.

For more information, see http://reference.sitepoint.com/html/applet/.

Other Relevant Stuff

 object (p. 357)

specifies a generic, multipurpose container for a media object

area

```
<area alt="string" coords="coordinates" href="uri"
shape=" { circle | default | poly | rect } "/>
```

SPEC		
deprecated	empty	version
NO	YES	HTML 3.2
BROWSER SUPPORT			
IE5.5+	FF1+	Saf1.3+	Op9.2+
FULL	FULL	FULL	FULL

Example

This code identifies one `area` element within an image `map`:

```
<map name="bigthings" id="bigthings">
  <area shape="rect" coords="35,4,205,108"
      href="http://en.wikipedia.org/wiki/Australia's_Big_Things"
      alt="Australia's Big Things (on Wikipedia)"/>
   ⋮
</map>
<p><img src="giant-prawn.jpg" alt="The Giant Prawn at Ballina"
    border="0" usemap="#bigthings"/></p>
```

We use the `area` element to define each hotspot that's clickable or actionable and will act as a link within a client-side image `map`. The behavior of a hotspot is similar to a normal link (the `a` (p. 146) element) in that it can be activated with a mouse click or the keyboard, and it's used to link to another web page or resource; it's also similar to the image element because, as it defines a specific area of a larger image, it requires us to set an `alt` (p. 323) attribute for those using non-visual browsers.

The hit, or actionable, area of the image is defined using a combination of the `shape` (p. 328) and `coords` (p. 325) attributes, which create the hit area boundaries as a sequence of *x,y* coordinate pairings.

Use This For ...

This element is used to create clickable or actionable areas on an image. For example, you might use it to create a graphically rich navigation mechanism such as a map on which the different countries or regions are the clickable areas.

Note that not every `area` needs to be actionable. It's perfectly acceptable to use `area` *without* an `href` attribute for the purposes of outlining a given area, and for providing additional help in the form of a tooltip created using the `title` (p. 506) attribute. However, this technique is inaccessible to people who use anything other than a mouse to navigate the web page, since there will be no mouse hover event for those users—the usual trigger for the tooltip display.

Compatibility

Internet Explorer			Firefox			Safari			Opera
5.5	6.0	7.0	1.0	1.5	2.0	1.3	2.0	3.0	9.2
Full	Full	Full	Full	Full	Full	Full	Full	Full	Full

It causes no compatibility issues, and has excellent support across all tested browsers.

Other Relevant Stuff

 map (p. 354)

   defines a client-side image map

accesskey *for* *<area>*

`accesskey="key"`

SPEC		
deprecated	required	version
NO	NO	HTML 4
BROWSER SUPPORT			
IE5.5+	FF1+	Saf1.3+	Op9.2+
FULL	FULL	FULL	FULL

Example

Here, the first `area` has an `accesskey` of "b" defined:

```
<map name="bigthings" id="bigthings">
  <area shape="rect" coords="35,4,205,108"
      href="http://en.wikipedia.org/wiki/Australia's_Big_Things"
      alt="Australia's Big Things (on Wikipedia)" accesskey="b"/>
    ⋮
</map>
<p><img src="giant-prawn.jpg" alt="The Giant Prawn at Ballina"
    border="0" usemap="#bigthings"/></p>
```

The `accesskey` attribute allows the user to activate a control on a page using a keyboard shortcut. This may save time for users who would otherwise need to tab through a series of form controls or move the mouse to get to the desired link. The key combination that activates the link to which the `accesskey` is applied varies depending on the platform and browser combination. For IE/Windows, users press Alt + `accesskey`, while Firefox/Windows users press Alt + Shift + `accesskey`; users of most Mac browsers press Ctrl + `accesskey`; in Opera, pressing Shift + Esc displays a list of links for which `accesskey` attributes are defined, allowing users to choose the key they want to use.

Generally speaking, browsers don't indicate that an `accesskey` attribute is defined for a form control, and this lack of discoverability is a problem. The most common method for indicating the `accesskey` value is to place it in a `title` (p. 506) attribute of the element to which it's applied. However, for this approach to work, the user must mouse over the element in question. You may want to state the `accesskey` value in some other way—for example:

```
<p>Press <kbd>b</kbd> to go to Australia's Big Things (on
Wikipedia).</p>
```

Value

This attribute takes as its value a single character, which can be numerical, alphabetical, or even a symbol.

Compatibility

Internet Explorer			Firefox			Safari			Opera
5.5	6.0	7.0	1.0	1.5	2.0	1.3	2.0	3.0	9.2
Full	Full	Full	Full	Full	Full	Full	Full	Full	Full

There's some variety in the way that the accesskey is activated, but generally speaking, it can work well. The downside of using this attribute is that keystrokes defined may clash with those of other technologies. For example, an assistive device such as a screen reader or magnifier may have designated for certain purposes the keystrokes that you've defined in the accesskey attribute. In addition, different language browsers use different "accelerator keys" for their own menu options, which may also clash with those you've defined. As a result of these clashes, the accesskey may not work as expected for all users. However, it may be very useful for controlled environments such as intranets, where you know exactly what browsers and languages are in use.

alt *for <area>*

```
alt="string"
```

SPEC		
deprecated	required	version
NO	YES	HTML 3.2
BROWSER SUPPORT		
IE7	FF2	Saf3	Op9.2
NONE	NONE	NONE	NONE

Example

This alt attribute explains the link destination—a Wikipedia entry:

```
<map name="bigthings" id="bigthings">
  <area shape="rect" coords="35,4,205,108"
     href="http://en.wikipedia.org/wiki/Australia's_Big_Things"
     alt="Australia's Big Things (on Wikipedia)"/>
  ⋮
</map>
<p><img src="giant-prawn.jpg" alt="The Giant Prawn at Ballina"
border="0" usemap="#bigthings"/></p>
```

In the event that the user can't view the image—perhaps because he or she is accessing your page over a very slow connection, because an incorrect `src` (p. 348) attribute has been defined, or because the user is visually impaired and is accessing the content using a screen reader—the `alt` attribute provides alternative content that can be displayed instead of the image.

Thus, an `alt` attribute applied to the `area` element will render over that `area` if the image isn't displayed.

Value

This attribute takes as its value text that's equivalent to the purpose or destination of the link (as defined by the `href` (p. 326) attribute). For a full rundown of how best to handle content inside the `alt` attribute, refer to the `alt` (p. 337) element type.

Compatibility

Internet Explorer			Firefox			Safari			Opera
5.5	6.0	7.0	1.0	1.5	2.0	1.3	2.0	3.0	9.2
None	None	None	None	None	None	None	None	None	None

Unlike the `img`'s `alt` attribute (p. 337), support for the `alt` attribute's application to the `area` element is poor. In cases where the image was unavailable, only the `img`'s `alt` attribute was displayed by the tested browsers. The alternative text for the clickable areas defined by the `area` elements' `alt` attributes wasn't rendered by any browser except Opera 9.5.

coords *for <area>*

SPEC		
deprecated	required	version
NO	NO	HTML 3.2
BROWSER SUPPORT		
IE5.5+	FF1+	Saf1.3+	Op9.2+
FULL	FULL	FULL	FULL

```
coords="coordinates"
```

Example

This coords attribute defines the top-left and bottom-right coordinates for a rectangular shape:

```
<map name="bigthings" id="bigthings">
  <area shape="rect" coords="35,4,205,108"
      href="http://en.wikipedia.org/wiki/Australia's_Big_Things"
      alt="Australia's Big Things (on Wikipedia)"/>
  ⋮
</map>
<p><img src="giant-prawn.jpg" alt="The Giant Prawn at Ballina"
border="0" usemap="#bigthings"/></p>
```

The coords attribute tells the browser the shape of the hotspot. Its use depends on the type of shape (p. 328) that's being applied, as detailed below.

Value

The values that are used in the coords attribute are as follows:

- For rectangular shapes ("rect"), the coords attribute will take four values: $x1$, $y1$, $x2$, and $y2$. These values define the top-left corner of the rectangle (how many pixels along and down from the image's top-left corner the boundary will appear), and the bottom-right corner (how many pixels along and up from the image's bottom-right corner the boundary will appear).

- For circular shapes ("circ"), three values are required: x, y, and r. The x and y coordinates tell the browser where the circle's center point is, while the r value specifies the radius of the circle.

- Polygonal shapes ("poly"), which are almost always created using a WYSIWYG HTML editor such as Dreamweaver, are defined by a series of x, y coordinates, each of which relates to a point on the polygon's outline.

Compatibility

Internet Explorer			Firefox			Safari			Opera
5.5	6.0	7.0	1.0	1.5	2.0	1.3	2.0	3.0	9.2
Full	Full	Full	Full	Full	Full	Full	Full	Full	Full

It causes no compatibility issues, and has excellent support across all tested browsers.

href *for <area>*

```
href="uri"
```

SPEC		
deprecated	required	version
NO	NO	HTML 3.2
BROWSER SUPPORT			
IE5.5+	FF1+	Saf1.3+	Op9.2+
FULL	FULL	FULL	FULL

Example

The href below defines a link to a page on Wikipedia:

```
<map name="bigthings" id="bigthings">
  <area shape="rect" coords="35,4,205,108"
      href="http://en.wikipedia.org/wiki/Australia's_Big_Things"
      alt="Australia's Big Things (on Wikipedia)"/>
  ⋮
</map>
<p><img src="giant-prawn.jpg" alt="The Giant Prawn at Ballina"
border="0" usemap="#bigthings"/></p>
```

The href defines the destination of the link for this area. It may be a web page in the same directory, a page somewhere else on the same server, a location within the current page, or a document stored on another server.

For a full description of the href attribute, refer to the entry for the a element's href (p. 153)—its usage and syntax is exactly the same when applied to an area.

Value

This attribute takes as its value the location of the destination document relative to the referencing document, relative to the server root, or as a complete URI containing the http:// protocol, the server name, and the path to the document on that server. It may also contain reference to the ftp: or mailto: protocols.

Compatibility

Internet Explorer			Firefox			Safari			Opera
5.5	6.0	7.0	1.0	1.5	2.0	1.3	2.0	3.0	9.2
Full	Full	Full	Full	Full	Full	Full	Full	Full	Full

It causes no compatibility issues, and has excellent support across all tested browsers.

 **nohref** *for <area>*

SPEC		
deprecated	required	version
NO	NO	HTML 2
BROWSER SUPPORT		
IE7	FF2	Saf3	Op9.2
NONE	NONE	NONE	NONE

`nohref="nohref"`

Example

The `nohref` attribute is used here in place of an `href`:

```
<map name="bigthings" id="bigthings">
  <area shape="rect" coords="35,4,205,108"
      nohref="nohref"
      alt="The giant prawn, another of Australia's Big Things"/>
  ⋮
</map>
<p><img src="giant-prawn.jpg" alt="The Giant Prawn at Ballina"
border="0" usemap="#bigthings"/></p>
```

The `nohref` attribute is intended to inform the browser that an `href` attribute isn't present, when in fact you could more easily do that by, well, not including an `href`!

The example shows the specification of the `nohref` in XHTML-compliant syntax, with an attribute and value pairing, but it can be used as an attribute on its own in HTML, as shown below:

```
<map name="bigthings" id="bigthings">
  <area shape="rect" coords="35,4,205,108" nohref
      alt="The giant prawn, another of Australia's Big Things"/>
  ⋮
```

Image and Media Elements

```
</map>
<p><img src="giant-prawn.jpg" alt="The Giant Prawn at Ballina"
border="0" usemap="#bigthings"/></p>
```

Value

`"nohref"` is the only value this attribute can take.

Compatibility

Internet Explorer			Firefox			Safari			Opera
5.5	6.0	7.0	1.0	1.5	2.0	1.3	2.0	3.0	9.2
None	None	None	None	None	None	None	None	None	None

The HTML specifications provide no indication as to what browsers should do with this attribute, so it's difficult to say which browsers are and aren't compatible. All the tested browsers have been described as providing no support for this attribute, although given that they have no guide on what they should be doing to support it, this seems unfair.

In essence, this attribute is entirely useless, and you have little to gain from using it.

 **shape** *for <area>*

SPEC		
deprecated	required	version
NO	NO	HTML 3.2
BROWSER SUPPORT			
IE5.5+	FF1+	Saf1.3+	Op9.2+
FULL	FULL	FULL	FULL

```
shape=" { circle | default | poly | rect } "
```

Example

This **shape** attribute is set to `"rect"`, for rectangle:

```
<map name="bigthings" id="bigthings">
  <area shape="rect" coords="35,4,205,108"
      href="http://en.wikipedia.org/wiki/Australia's_Big_Things"
      alt="Australia's Big Things (on Wikipedia)"/>
  ⋮
</map>
<p><img src="giant-prawn.jpg" alt="The Giant Prawn at Ballina"
border="0" usemap="#bigthings"/></p>
```

The shape attribute allows the author to define some simple area hotspots, using "rect" or "default" for rectangles, and "circle" or "poly" for more complex polygon shapes. The coords attribute will differ depending on the type of shape that's specified; "circle" is the simplest, as it requires just three values, while "poly" is the most complex, as any number of coordinates may be specified for it.

Value

"circle", "default", "poly", and "rect" are the W3C-approved attribute values, but some browsers will also recognize variants of these, namely the abbreviated "circ", and the expanded "polygon" and "rectangle". It's best to stick to the approved attribute values, though.

Compatibility

Internet Explorer			Firefox			Safari			Opera
5.5	6.0	7.0	1.0	1.5	2.0	1.3	2.0	3.0	9.2
Full	Full	Full	Full	Full	Full	Full	Full	Full	Full

It causes no compatibility issues, and has excellent support across all tested browsers.

tabindex *for <area>*

tabindex="*number*"

SPEC		
deprecated	required	version
NO	NO	HTML 3.2
BROWSER SUPPORT		
IE5.5+ FF1+ Saf1.3+ Op9.2+		
FULL FULL FULL FULL		

Example

The tabindex is set to "3" for the link in the area below:

```
<map name="bigthings" id="bigthings">
  <area shape="rect" coords="35,4,205,108" tabindex="3"
      href="http://en.wikipedia.org/wiki/Australia's_Big_Things"
      alt="Australia's Big Things (on Wikipedia)"/>
  ⋮
</map>
<p><img src="giant-prawn.jpg" alt="The Giant Prawn at Ballina"
border="0" usemap="#bigthings"/></p>
```

The `tabindex` is used to define a sequence that users follow when they use the Tab key to navigate through a page. By default, the natural tabbing order will match the source order in the markup. In certain circumstances it may be necessary to override the default tabbing order, but it's strongly recommended that you craft a page in a logical flow and let the browser work through it in the default order—an approach that negates the need for the `tabindex` attribute.

A `tabindex` can start at 0 and increment in any value. As such, the sequence 1, 2, 3, 4, 5 would be fine, as would 10, 20, 30, 40, 50. If you need to introduce a `tabindex`, it's advisable to use a sequence that contains intervals (like the second example provided), as this will give you the opportunity to inject other controls later if need be (for example, 10, 15, 20) without having to reindex all the `tabindex` values on the page. Should a given `tabindex` value be applied to more than one element in error, the tabbing order of those affected elements will be as per the source markup order.

If a `tabindex` is set anywhere on a page—even if it's the hundredth link or the fiftieth form control—the tab order will start at the element with the lowest `tabindex` value, and work through the increments. Only *then* will the tab order take in the remaining elements for which no `tabindex` has been set. As such, great care must be taken to ensure that adding a `tabindex` doesn't harm the usability of the page as a whole.

If the `disabled` attribute is set on an element which has a `tabindex`, that `tabindex` will be ignored.

Value

This attribute takes a number value.

Compatibility

Internet Explorer			Firefox			Safari			Opera
5.5	6.0	7.0	1.0	1.5	2.0	1.3	2.0	3.0	9.2
Full	Full	Full	Full	Full	Full	Full	Full	Full	Full

It causes no compatibility issues, and has excellent support across all tested browsers.

target *for <area>*

SPEC		
deprecated	required	version
YES	NO	HTML 3.2
BROWSER SUPPORT			
IE5.5+	FF1+	Saf1.3+	Op9.2+
FULL	FULL	FULL	FULL

```
target=" { _blank | frame name | _parent | _self |
_top } "
```

Example

The target attribute for this area is set to "_top":

```
<map name="bigthings" id="bigthings">
  <area shape="rect" coords="35,4,205,108" target="_top"
      href="http://en.wikipedia.org/wiki/Australia's_Big_Things"
      alt="Australia's Big Things (on Wikipedia)"/>
  ⋮
</map>
<p><img src="giant-prawn.jpg" alt="The Giant Prawn at Ballina"
border="0" usemap="#bigthings"/></p>
```

The target attribute is deprecated and its use as a layout mechanism, like that of frameset (p. 494), is no longer common. However, if you do find yourself having to maintain a frameset-based web site, you may need to open links defined in area elements in frames or windows other than the one in which the image map resides.

Value

This attribute can take the following values:

"_blank" sends the results to a completely new window

"frame name" sends the results to a frame with a custom name

"_parent" sends the results to the parent frameset for the current frame

"_self" displays the form's submission results in the same frame (This attribute isn't normally required, as this is the default behavior unless the base (p. 77) element specifies otherwise. In that case, you'd need to override the specification using "_self", for example <base **target="searchresults"** />.)

"**_top**" sends the results to the absolute top-level `frameset` (in effect, the whole browser window), no matter how many nested levels down the current `frame` is located

Compatibility

Internet Explorer			Firefox			Safari			Opera
5.5	6.0	7.0	1.0	1.5	2.0	1.3	2.0	3.0	9.2
Full	Full	Full	Full	Full	Full	Full	Full	Full	Full

It causes no compatibility issues, and has excellent support across all tested browsers.

bgsound

```
<bgsound balance="number" loop="number" src="uri"
volume="number">
```

SPEC		
deprecated	empty	version
NO	YES	N/A
BROWSER SUPPORT			
IE5.5+	FF2	Saf3	Op9.2
FULL	NONE	NONE	NONE

The `bgsound` element is used to play an audio file when the page loads, and has a handful of attributes to control that file.

This is a nonstandard element (it was never defined in *any* standard), so there's little point in writing it to be XHTML-compliant, as it will never validate.

For more information, see http://reference.sitepoint.com/html/bgsound/.

embed

```
<embed alt="string" height=" { number |
percentage } " hidden=" { true | false } "
pluginspage="uri" src="uri" type="MIME type"
width="number">
</embed>
```

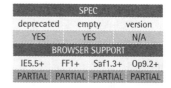

SPEC		
deprecated	empty	version
YES	YES	N/A
BROWSER SUPPORT			
IE5.5+	FF1+	Saf1.3+	Op9.2+
PARTIAL	PARTIAL	PARTIAL	PARTIAL

The `embed` element is a nonstandard but well-supported element that is used to embed multimedia content, including media types that might not normally be natively supported by the browser (it can also be used for embedding media that *are* supported, for example images in **.jpg**, **.gif**, or **.png** format).

For more information, visit http://reference.sitepoint.com/html/embed/.

Other Relevant Stuff

 object (p. 357)

specifies a generic, multipurpose container for a media object

 noembed (p. 357)

alternative content for browsers that do not support embed

 # img

```
<img alt="string" height=" { number | percentage } "
src="uri" width=" { number | percentage } " />
```

SPEC		
deprecated	empty	version
NO	YES	HTML 2
BROWSER SUPPORT			
IE5.5+	FF1+	Saf1.3+	Op9.2+
FULL	FULL	FULL	FULL

Example

Here's an img element for which only the required attributes are specified (src (p. 348) and alt (p. 337)):

```
<img src="giant-prawn.jpg" alt="The Giant Prawn at Ballina"/>
```

The img element provides a means for embedding an image in the document, which can be used for as many different purposes as your imagination allows. With just the couple of required attributes shown in the example, the img provides a reference to the image file to display, and a text alternative should the image not be available for whatever reason. A number of optional, and deprecated, attributes are covered below in detail.

As it's an empty element, the img element requires a trailing slash if it's to be XHTML-compliant, but it can be expressed in HTML as follows:

```
<img src="giant-prawn.jpg" alt="The Giant Prawn at Ballina">
```

As an image is an inline element, a break isn't created before or after it, so the following HTML would render with the text appearing on either side of the image:

```
<p>Driving along, we spotted a giant prawn <img
    src="giant-prawn.jpg" alt="The Giant Prawn at Ballina">,
    so we had to stop and take a closer look.</p>
```

The somewhat unsightly effect of this markup can be seen in Figure 7.1.

Driving along, we spotted a giant prawn , so we had to stop and take a closer look.

Figure 7.1: The image failing to create a break in the text

However, with CSS you can achieve great control over the `img` element, creating wrapping text with margins (or gutters, to use the print analogy), border styles, and more.

Some presentational attributes, which control alignment and dimensions, are covered below, but these effects are best controlled using CSS.

Use This For ...

This element is used to place illustrative images—pictures that convey some important information. It's not used for purely decorative images that don't offer any information, and which could easily be removed from the page without detriment to its content. Such noncritical, decorative images may be better implemented using the CSS `background-image` property.

This element can be used for photographs, charts and graphs, and maps. Even when it's used for images that may be difficult to accurately describe in words (for instance, a trend may be seen easily on a graph, but its meaning may be impossible to understand in the absence of the image, for whatever reason), it's important to ensure that an alternative description is available. See the sections on the `alt` (p. 337) and `longdesc` (p. 346) attributes for more information.

Compatibility

Internet Explorer			Firefox			Safari			Opera
5.5	6.0	7.0	1.0	1.5	2.0	1.3	2.0	3.0	9.2
Full	Full	Full	Full	Full	Full	Full	Full	Full	Full

It causes no compatibility issues, and has excellent support across all tested browsers.

Other Relevant Stuff

 input (p. 253)

defines the input control for a form

 ## align *for <img>*

	SPEC	
deprecated	required	version
YES	NO	HTML 2
BROWSER SUPPORT		
IE5.5+	FF1+	Saf1.3+	Op9.2+
FULL	FULL	FULL	FULL

`align=" { bottom | left | middle | right | top } "`

Example

The `align` attribute for this `img` is set to `"right"`:

```
<p><img src="giant-prawn.jpg" alt="The Giant Prawn at Ballina"
    align="right"/>Driving along, we spotted a giant prawn, so had to
    stop and take a closer look.</p>
```

The `align` attribute is used to specify how the image sits on the page in relation to surrounding text and other elements. It is a fairly rudimentary attribute—and a very presentational one—that allows you to move an image to the right or left, with text wrapping around it accordingly (although without surrounding whitespace, which generally produces quite an ugly result). You can also alter the adjacent text alignment so that the first line of the text aligns with the top, middle, or bottom of the image.

The example markup shown with a right-aligned image would appear as shown in Figure 7.2.

Figure 7.2: A right-aligned image

If the value were changed to `"top"`, the effect would be very different, as Figure 7.3 shows.

Figure 7.3: An image for which `align` is set to `"top"`

As the two examples show, the `align` attribute is no precision instrument when it comes to layout!

If an img is aligned "left" or "right", text will continue to wrap around it until it encounters either:

- a br (p. 40) element with a clear (p. 42) attribute
- any other element whose CSS clear property is set to "left", "right", or "both"

Value

"bottom", "left", "middle", "right", and "top" are the values that this attribute may take.

Nonstandard, proprietary attributes (which are still supported by Internet Explorer) that are acceptable include "absbottom", "absmiddle", "baseline", and "texttop".

Compatibility

Internet Explorer			Firefox			Safari			Opera
5.5	6.0	7.0	1.0	1.5	2.0	1.3	2.0	3.0	9.2
Full	Full	Full	Full	Full	Full	Full	Full	Full	Full

This attribute is now deprecated, and is highly presentational in its nature. The desired visual effects can all be achieved with CSS and, as such, this attribute shouldn't be used—it's presented here for informational purposes only.

 alt *for <img>*

alt="*string*"

SPEC		
deprecated	required	version
NO	YES	HTML 2
BROWSER SUPPORT		
IE5.5+	FF1+	Saf1.3+ Op9.2+
FULL	FULL	FULL FULL

Example

The alt attribute clearly explains what the image contains:

```
<img src="giant-prawn.jpg" alt="The Giant Prawn at Ballina" />
```

In the event that the user can't view the image—perhaps because he or she is accessing your page over a very slow connection, because an incorrect src (p. 348) attribute has been defined, or because the user is visually impaired and is accessing the content using a screen reader—the `alt` attribute provides alternative content that can be displayed instead of the image.

Value

This attribute takes as its value text that's equivalent to the content or purpose of the image:

- For an image that conveys important information, describe the image.
- For an image that's contained inside an a (p. 146) element, and is thus being used as a link, use an `alt` attribute that explains where the link goes, or what activating the link will do.
- For purely decorative images that offer no additional information to the page content, use an empty `alt` attribute:

```
alt=""
```

  Don't simply omit the `alt` attribute—it's required, and absence of an `alt` attribute can cause problems for screen readers, which, in an effort to provide information about the image, may read out the image's filename, for example.

- If an image is supplementary to the surrounding text, but isn't purely decorative, don't simply replicate the content from the surrounding text in the image's `alt` attribute. In this instance, you should use an empty `alt` attribute.
- If the image is a graphic, for example a chart or graph, and if the pattern or process illustrated in the image is explained alongside or nearby in text, apply an empty `alt` attribute to the image.

Compatibility

Internet Explorer			Firefox			Safari			Opera
5.5	6.0	7.0	1.0	1.5	2.0	1.3	2.0	3.0	9.2
Full	Full	Full	Full	Full	Full	Full	Full	Full	Full

It causes no compatibility issues, and has excellent support across all tested browsers.

Most browsers don't display the content of the alt attribute unless the image is actually missing—it is, after all, supposed to be an *alternative* to the image. Internet Explorer, however, will display the value for the alt in the form of a tooltip when the user mouses over the img element in question. This isn't the correct behavior, so be mindful of the fact that the other browsers are operating according to the specification, and it's Internet Explorer's interpretation that's slightly wrong. If you *do* want to create a tooltip effect on an image, use the title (p. 506) attribute.

Note that Internet Explorer and Opera don't deal with missing images very well, as Figure 7.4 shows (that screenshot was taken using IE6 on Windows XP).

 Driving along, we spotted a giant prawn, so had to stop and take a closer look.

Figure 7.4: Alternative text showing for a missing image in IE

Despite the fact that the image is absent, both of these browsers honor the height and width attributes of the missing image (if they're set) and display a placeholder frame. If the alt text takes up more space than the image's dimensions, neither shows the alternative text properly—it's a little like looking through a letterbox. Safari is even worse, displaying a question mark where the image should appear, and no alternative text. Arguably the best of the bunch is Firefox, which doesn't display a placeholder frame, and allows whatever space is required for the alternative text, making it a much more usable implementation.

"..." **border** *for <img>*

border="*number*"

SPEC		
deprecated	required	version
YES	NO	HTML 2
BROWSER SUPPORT			
IE5.5+	FF1+	Saf1.3+	Op9.2+
FULL	FULL	FULL	FULL

Example

This border attribute is set to "5":

```
<img src="giant-prawn.jpg" alt="The Giant Prawn at Ballina"
    border="5"/>
```

By default, an image will display without a border (unless it's contained inside an a (p. 146) element and CSS has *not* been used to remove the border). The `border` attribute rectifies this, and allows you to specify a border in pixels. Depending on the browser, the border will either be black, or will match the color of the document's text.

Figure 7.5: An image with a border thickness of five pixels

Value

This attribute takes as its value a number that represents the width of the border in pixels.

Compatibility

Internet Explorer			Firefox			Safari			Opera
5.5	6.0	7.0	1.0	1.5	2.0	1.3	2.0	3.0	9.2
Full	Full	Full	Full	Full	Full	Full	Full	Full	Full

Although support for this attribute is good, it's now deprecated, and is highly presentational in its nature. The desired visual effects can all be achieved with CSS and, as such, this attribute shouldn't be used—it's presented here for informational purposes only.

height *for <img>*

`height=" { number | percentage } "`

	SPEC	
deprecated	required	version
NO	NO	HTML 2
BROWSER SUPPORT		
IE5.5+	FF1+	Saf1.3+	Op9.2+
FULL	FULL	FULL	FULL

Image and Media Elements

Example

Here, the `height` attribute is set to `"30"`:

```
<img src="giant-prawn.jpg" alt="The Giant Prawn at Ballina"
    height="30"/>
```

An image doesn't require a `height` attribute, but it has its uses. The main use for specifying the `height` (and `width` (p. 353)) is to improve the user experience while a page is loading. If the dimensions are specified in the markup, as the page is loaded, the space required for the images is reserved by the browser; without this information, the browser doesn't know how big the image is, and can't allocate the appropriate space to it. On a slow-loading page, the effect can be quite disturbing, as content is constantly reflowed as each new image appears on the page.

The downside of specifying a `height` (and `width`) is that if you later decide to update an image that's used site-wide—for example, a company logo—you'd need to change the dimension attributes for each page of the site. Depending on how your web site is managed (manually, in a template-driven way, via a CMS, or through server-side includes), this may either be a minor niggle, or a real issue for you. It's a case of weighing up the pros and cons in each situation.

If the `height` attribute is set by itself, but no `width` attribute is set, the image will be rescaled proportionally, as shown by the three images (set to `"30"`, `"100"`, and `"200"` pixel widths, respectively) in Figure 7.6.

Figure 7.6: Rescaling an image by setting the `height` attribute alone

If, however, the correct `width` attribute is set, but the `height` differs, the image will appear stretched, as shown in Figure 7.7.

Figure 7.7: Stretched images resulting from the application of an incorrect `height` attribute

Note that it's not a good practice to rescale images in your markup. If you need an image with dimensions of 200×200 pixels, *don't* drop in an image of 1000×1000 pixels and use HTML attributes to rescale it. Not only does this approach force the user to download a large image that's rendered at a much smaller size on the web page, but the result is usually quite untidy. The correct method is to rescale the image in a graphics application first, and then place the correctly sized image on the page.

Value

This attribute takes a number representing the height of the image in pixels, or as a percentage of the containing element.

Compatibility

Internet Explorer			Firefox			Safari			Opera
5.5	6.0	7.0	1.0	1.5	2.0	1.3	2.0	3.0	9.2
Full	Full	Full	Full	Full	Full	Full	Full	Full	Full

It causes no compatibility issues, and has excellent support across all tested browsers.

hspace *for <img>*

`hspace="number"`

	SPEC	
deprecated	required	version
YES	NO	HTML 2
	BROWSER SUPPORT	
IE5.5+	FF1+	Saf1.3+	Op9.2+
FULL	FULL	FULL	FULL

Example

Here, the hspace attribute is set to "10" pixels around a left-aligned image:

```
<p><img src="giant-prawn.jpg" alt="The Giant Prawn at Ballina"
    align="left" hspace="10"/>Driving along, we spotted a giant prawn,
    so we had to stop and take a closer look.</p>
```

When an image is aligned (p. 335) left or right, text will flow around the image, but no space will appear between the text and the image edge. The hspace (and related vspace (p. 352)) attribute provides a little breathing space, but it applies space on both sides of the image, which is not entirely flexible, as Figure 7.8 shows.

Lorem ipsum dolor sit amet, consectetuer adipiscing elit. Nulla sapien neque, vulputate a, cursus consequat, ultricies eu, mi. Etiam est nibh, interdum ut, dapibus at, adipiscing eu, quam.

Driving along, we spotted a giant prawn, so we had to stop and take a closer look.

Quisque in eros ultrices risus gravida vestibulum. Maecenas adipiscing, lacus vel laoreet hendrerit, tortor diam viverra velit, id consectetuer orci purus id tortor.

Figure 7.8: An image to which an hspace of 10 is applied

Value

This attribute takes as its value a number that represents the width of spacing on either side of the image in pixels.

Compatibility

Internet Explorer			Firefox			Safari			Opera
5.5	6.0	7.0	1.0	1.5	2.0	1.3	2.0	3.0	9.2
Full	Full	Full	Full	Full	Full	Full	Full	Full	Full

Although support for this attribute is good, it's now deprecated, and is highly presentational in its nature. The desired visual effects can all be achieved with CSS and, as such, this attribute shouldn't be used—it's presented here for informational purposes only.

ismap *for <img>*

`ismap="ismap"`

SPEC		
deprecated	required	version
NO	NO	HTML 2
BROWSER SUPPORT		
IE5.5+	FF1+	Saf1.3+	Op9.2+
FULL	FULL	FULL	FULL

Example

The `ismap` attribute is set as follows:

```
<img src="giant-prawn.jpg" alt="The Giant Prawn at Ballina"
    ismap="ismap"/>
```

The `ismap` attribute is rarely seen, but when it is, it's used to indicate that the user's mouse actions over the image should be processed using a server-side image map. When the user clicks on an area of the image using the mouse (it can't be activated by keyboard controls), the coordinates are sent back to the server in the form of a query string in the URI.

It's far more common to see this behavior handled on the client side with the `usemap` (p. 350) attribute.

Value

`"ismap"` is the only value that this attribute can take.

Compatibility

Internet Explorer			Firefox			Safari			Opera
5.5	6.0	7.0	1.0	1.5	2.0	1.3	2.0	3.0	9.2
Full	Full	Full	Full	Full	Full	Full	Full	Full	Full

It causes no compatibility issues, and has excellent support across all tested browsers.

longdesc *for <img>*

`longdesc="uri"`

SPEC		
deprecated	required	version
NO	NO	HTML 2
BROWSER SUPPORT			
---	---	---	---
IE5.5+	FF1+	Saf1.3+	Op9.2+
PARTIAL	PARTIAL	PARTIAL	PARTIAL

Example

This `longdesc` attribute refers to a text file "prawn.txt":

```
<img src="giant-prawn.jpg" alt="The Giant Prawn at Ballina"
    longdesc="prawn.txt"/>
```

The `alt` (p. 337) attribute is intended to be a *short* alternative for the image, and shouldn't be used for lengthy descriptions of the image. The attribute that's used to provide a pointer to further information is `longdesc`. Unfortunately, it's so poorly supported that it's almost unusable (see below for more information).

Value

This attribute takes as its value the URL for a file that contains the extra descriptive text, most likely a simple **.txt** file.

Compatibility

Internet Explorer			Firefox			Safari			Opera
5.5	6.0	7.0	1.0	1.5	2.0	1.3	2.0	3.0	9.2
Partial	Partial	Partial	Partial	Partial	Partial	Partial	Partial	Partial	Partial

The `longdesc` attribute has almost no practical use, even with today's good, standards-aware browsers. Despite the best intentions, no browser on the support charts makes it clear to the user when extra information is available for the image in the form of a descriptive text file, and this level of indifference toward the attribute is likely to continue. Even the technology that would benefit the most from the presence of this attribute—assistive technology such as screen readers—is oblivious to the presence of a `longdesc`. Only Firefox appears to show a basic level of awareness of the attribute: if you right-click on the image and choose **Properties**, the `longdesc`'s file location is visible next to the **Description** title, as shown in Figure 7.9.

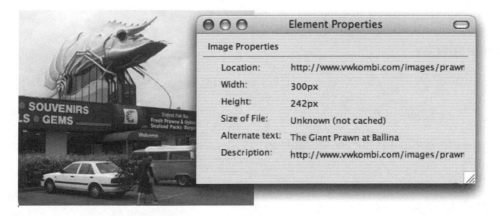

Figure 7.9: The `longdesc` shows in Firefox's contextual menu as the **Description**

A much safer option is to avoid this attribute altogether, and simply to create a link that anyone can access or see, perhaps linking from picture caption text.

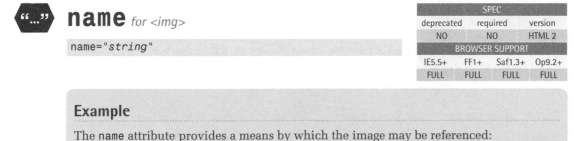

name *for <img>*

`name="string"`

SPEC		
deprecated	required	version
NO	NO	HTML 2
BROWSER SUPPORT			
IE5.5+	FF1+	Saf1.3+	Op9.2+
FULL	FULL	FULL	FULL

Example

The `name` attribute provides a means by which the image may be referenced:

```
<p><img src="giant-prawn.jpg" alt="The Giant Prawn at Ballina"
    name="giantprawn"/></p>
```

The `name` attribute is one method for referencing an `img` element using JavaScript (the alternative, more forward-thinking method is to reference it using the `id` (p. 501) attribute). It has historically been used for techniques such as image swaps for rollovers (which have since largely been replaced using CSS techniques).

Value

This attribute takes as its value any name that the developer chooses, as long as it doesn't contain spaces or special characters.

Compatibility

Internet Explorer			Firefox			Safari			Opera
5.5	6.0	7.0	1.0	1.5	2.0	1.3	2.0	3.0	9.2
Full	Full	Full	Full	Full	Full	Full	Full	Full	Full

It causes no compatibility issues, and has excellent support across all tested browsers.

 # src *for <img>*

```
src="uri"
```

	SPEC	
deprecated	required	version
NO	YES	HTML 2
BROWSER SUPPORT		
IE5.5+	FF1+	Saf1.3+	Op9.2+
FULL	FULL	FULL	FULL

Example

The src attribute for this image shows that the image is located in the same directory as the web page:

```
<img src="giant-prawn.jpg" alt="The Giant Prawn at Ballina"/>
```

The src attribute instructs the browser where on the server it should look for the image that's to be presented to the user. This may be an image in the same directory, an image somewhere else on the same server, or an image stored on another server.

The example refers to an image that's located in the same directory as the web page that's calling it, but if the image was stored in a directory that was one level higher than the referencing document, the syntax would be as follows:

```
<img src="../giant-prawn.jpg" alt="The Giant Prawn at Ballina"/>
```

Here, ../ equates to "move up one directory in the hierarchy."

You can also reference an image relative to the web site's root (that is, any file or folder after the domain name):

```
<img src="/giant-prawn.jpg" alt="The Giant Prawn at Ballina"/>
```

This basically means "display the image **giant-prawn.jpg** that can be found in **www.example.com**/." This is a very handy way of referencing the file, as you could move the document that referenced the image to any location on the file system without breaking the link.

If you're referencing an image that's held on another server, you'd express the src using a complete URI, as follows:

```
<img src="http://www.example.com/giant-prawn.jpg"
    alt="The Giant Prawn at Ballina"/>
```

Value

This attribute takes as its value the location of the image relative to the referencing document, relative to the server root, or as a complete URI containing the http:// protocol, the server name, and the path to the document on that server.

Compatibility

Internet Explorer			Firefox			Safari			Opera
5.5	6.0	7.0	1.0	1.5	2.0	1.3	2.0	3.0	9.2
Full	Full	Full	Full	Full	Full	Full	Full	Full	Full

It causes no compatibility issues, and has excellent support across all tested browsers.

 **usemap** *for <img>*

```
usemap="#map name"
```

SPEC		
deprecated	required	version
NO	NO	HTML 2
BROWSER SUPPORT		
IE5.5+	FF1+	Saf1.3+	Op9.2+
FULL	FULL	FULL	FULL

Example

Here, the usemap attribute references a map named "bigthings":

```
<map name="bigthings" id="bigthings">
  <area shape="rect" coords="35,4,205,108"
      href="http://en.wikipedia.org/wiki/Australia's_Big_Things"
      alt="Australia's Big Things (on Wikipedia)"/>
  <area shape="rect" coords="136,163,255,230"
      href="http://vwkombi.com/"
      alt="The VW Kombi, another Aussie icon"/>
</map>
  ⋮
<p><img src="giant-prawn.jpg" alt="The Giant Prawn at Ballina"
usemap="#bigthings"/></p>
```

The usemap attribute tells the browser which map (p. 354) element in the document it should refer to. Then one or more hotspots (specified in the area (p. 320) element) are defined, to act as overlays on the image. These areas are similar to links (the a (p. 146) element) in that they allow the user to click to go to the page identified in the area's href attribute (they're also keyboard-navigable).

When an image map is defined in this way, the image displays no hint that the area is actionable. The image must, in itself, hint at the clickable areas, perhaps by containing button-like features, or by the presence of instructional text near to the image. The clickable areas are visible at design time in some web authoring applications, such as Dreamweaver, which shows the clickable areas as depicted in Figure 7.10.

Figure 7.10: Dreamweaver shows the clickable areas on the image in Design View

Value

This attribute takes as its value a reference to the map's name attribute in the form of a hash character ("#") plus the "name", like so:

```
usemap="#bigthings"
```

Compatibility

Internet Explorer			Firefox			Safari			Opera
5.5	6.0	7.0	1.0	1.5	2.0	1.3	2.0	3.0	9.2
Full	Full	Full	Full	Full	Full	Full	Full	Full	Full

It causes no compatibility issues, and has excellent support across all tested browsers.

 **vspace** *for <img>*

`vspace="number"`

SPEC		
deprecated	required	version
YES	NO	HTML 2
BROWSER SUPPORT			
IE5.5+	FF1+	Saf1.3+	Op9.2+
FULL	FULL	FULL	FULL

Example

This vspace attribute is set to "10" pixels around a left-aligned image:

```
<p><img src="giant-prawn.jpg" alt="The Giant Prawn at Ballina"
    align="left" vspace="10"/>Driving along, we spotted a giant prawn,
    so we had to stop and take a closer look.</p>
```

The vspace attribute is similar to hspace (p. 343) and provides a bit of breathing space above and below an image, although it's not exactly a precision design tool. Figure 7.11 shows the problem that occurs when an image is placed between paragraphs (the spacing appears to be unequal because the p (p. 71) element already has a bottom margin of its own, which exists in addition to the vspace of "10").

Lorem ipsum dolor sit amet, consectetuer adipiscing elit. Nulla sapien neque, vulputate a, cursus consequat, ultricies eu, mi. Etiam est nibh, interdum ut, dapibus at, adipiscing eu, quam.

Driving along, we spotted a giant prawn, so we had to stop and take a closer look.

Quisque in eros ultrices risus gravida vestibulum. Maecenas adipiscing, lacus vel laoreet hendrerit, tortor diam viverra velit, id consectetuer orci purus id tortor.

Figure 7.11: Image to which a vspace of 10 is applied (note the space above and below image)

Value

This attribute takes as its value a number representing the amount of space to appear above and below the image in pixels.

Compatibility

Internet Explorer			Firefox			Safari			Opera
5.5	6.0	7.0	1.0	1.5	2.0	1.3	2.0	3.0	9.2
Full	Full	Full	Full	Full	Full	Full	Full	Full	Full

Although support for this attribute is good, it's now deprecated, and is highly presentational in its nature. The desired visual effects can all be achieved with CSS and, as such, this attribute shouldn't be used—it's presented here for informational purposes only.

 # width for <img>

SPEC		
deprecated	required	version
YES	NO	HTML 2
BROWSER SUPPORT		
IE5.5+	FF1+	Saf1.3+	Op9.2+
FULL	FULL	FULL	FULL

```
width=" { number | percentage } "
```

Example

Here, the width attribute is set to "300":

```
<img src="giant-prawn.jpg" alt="The Giant Prawn at Ballina"
    width="300"/>
```

An image doesn't require a width attribute but, like the height (p. 341) attribute, width has its uses (refer to the advantages set out in the height attribute reference).

If the width attribute is set by itself, but no height attribute is set, the image will be rescaled proportionally. In every other respect, the width attribute is identical in usage and behavior to the height attribute.

Value

This attribute takes as its value a number representing the width of the image in pixels, or a percentage of the containing element.

Compatibility

Internet Explorer			Firefox			Safari			Opera
5.5	6.0	7.0	1.0	1.5	2.0	1.3	2.0	3.0	9.2
Full	Full	Full	Full	Full	Full	Full	Full	Full	Full

It causes no compatibility issues, and has excellent support across all tested browsers.

map

```
<map name="string">
</map>
```

SPEC		
deprecated	empty	version
NO	NO	HTML 3.2
BROWSER SUPPORT			
IE5.5+	FF1+	Saf1.3+	Op9.2+
FULL	FULL	FULL	FULL

Example

This code defines an image map named "bigthings":

```
<map name="bigthings">
  <area shape="rect" coords="35,4,205,108"
      href="http://en.wikipedia.org/wiki/Australia's_Big_Things"
      alt="Australia's Big Things (on Wikipedia)"/>
  <area shape="rect" coords="136,163,255,230"
      href="http://vwkombi.com/" alt="The VW Kombi,
      another Aussie icon"/>
</map>
```

The map element is a container for a number of area (p. 320) elements that define specific areas within an image. The map has one required attribute, the name attribute (p. 356), which is associated with the image's usemap attribute (p. 350) to create a relationship between the image and the map.

Note that not every area needs to be actionable. It's perfectly acceptable to use area *without* an href attribute for the purposes of outlining a given area, and for providing additional help in the form of a tooltip created using the title (p. 506) attribute.

map   355

However, this technique is inaccessible to people who use anything other than a mouse to navigate the web page, since there will be no mouse hover event for those users—the usual trigger for the tooltip display.

Use This For ...

This element is used to create specific clickable hotspots within a single larger image, and provides an alternative to the process whereby a larger image is sliced into smaller images, and numerous links are created using the a (p. 146) element.

In the past, the map and area elements have often been used to create navigation bars and the like. However, that approach is used with decreasing frequency, as CSS support is excellent, and in most cases provides a more suitable mechanism for creating navigation blocks.

Other examples for the usage of the map element include:

- identifying regions on a map, be they countries on a world map or areas on regional maps
- outlining locations in a floor plan—for example, a shopping mall or theme park
- creating an overlay for a photo whose different components or features need identification—for example, highlighting the parts of the inside of a laptop computer for the purposes of repair

Compatibility

Internet Explorer			Firefox			Safari			Opera
5.5	6.0	7.0	1.0	1.5	2.0	1.3	2.0	3.0	9.2
Full	Full	Full	Full	Full	Full	Full	Full	Full	Full

It causes no compatibility issues, and has excellent support across all tested browsers.

Other Relevant Stuff

 area (p. 320)

defines a hotspot within a client-side image map

name *for <map>*

```
name="string"
```

SPEC		
deprecated	required	version
NO	YES	HTML 3.2
BROWSER SUPPORT			
IE5.5+	FF1+	Saf1.3+	Op9.2+
FULL	FULL	FULL	FULL

Example

The name attribute provides a means for referencing the map:

```
<map name="bigthings">
  <area shape="rect" coords="35,4,205,108"
      href="http://en.wikipedia.org/wiki/Australia's_Big_Things"
      alt="Australia's Big Things (on Wikipedia)"/>
  <area shape="rect" coords="136,163,255,230"
      href="http://vwkombi.com/" alt="The VW Kombi,
      another Aussie icon"/>
</map>
⋮
<p><img src="giant-prawn.jpg" alt="The Giant Prawn at Ballina"
border="0" usemap="#bigthings"/></p>
```

The name attribute is required to provide a reference for the map element. The image element refers to this attribute (through its usemap attribute (p. 350)) using a combination of the "#" character and the map's name attribute, as the example HTML shows.

Value

This attribute can take as its value any name that the developer chooses, so long as it doesn't contain spaces or special characters.

Compatibility

Internet Explorer			Firefox			Safari			Opera
5.5	6.0	7.0	1.0	1.5	2.0	1.3	2.0	3.0	9.2
Full	Full	Full	Full	Full	Full	Full	Full	Full	Full

It causes no compatibility issues, and has excellent support across all tested browsers.

noembed

```
<embed>
</embed>
```

SPEC		
deprecated	empty	version
YES	NO	N/A
BROWSER SUPPORT			
IE5.5+	FF1+	Saf1.3+	Op9.2+
FULL	FULL	FULL	FULL

The `noembed` element is used to provide alternative content for browsers that do not support the `embed` (p. 332) element. It is not defined by any standard (it was introduced by early Netscape browsers), and as such there are no hard guidelines as to what it may or may not contain.

For more information, visit http://reference.sitepoint.com/html/noembed/.

Other Relevant Stuff

 embed (p. 332)

specifies a generic container for a media object

object

```
<object archive="uri" border=" { number |
percentage } " classid="class ID" codebase="uri"
codetype="MIME type" data="uri" height=" { number |
percentage } " type="MIME type" width=" { number |
percentage } ">
</object>
```

SPEC		
deprecated	empty	version
NO	NO	HTML 4
BROWSER SUPPORT			
IE5.5+	FF1+	Saf1.3+	Op9.2+
PARTIAL	PARTIAL	PARTIAL	PARTIAL

Example

In this example, a super-simple `object` element is used to display an image:

```
<object data="giant-dog.jpg">
</object>
```

The `object` element's purpose is to embed into a document a variety of different kinds of media files. Historically, it was used primarily for placing ActiveX controls onto a page, but it can also be used to embed images (**.gif**, **.jpg**, and so on), movie files and applets, video files, PDF documents, Flash, and even HTML.

While this element is specified in the HTML 4 recommendation, and thus constitutes valid markup, it's often shunned in favor of the better supported, but nonstandard `embed` (p. 332) element.

To embed Flash using `object`, rather than going down the nonstandard `embed` route, use the following markup:

```
<object data="movie.swf"
    type="application/x-shockwave-flash"
    width="200" height="100">
  <param name="movie" value="movie.swf">
  <param name="wmode" value="opaque">
</object>
```

The `param` (p. 378) element with the `name` of `"movie"` helps Internet Explorer to load the Flash file. The `"wmode"` encourages IE to play nicely with the `z-index` property, allowing other elements to be placed on top of the Flash movie.

Use This For ...

This element is used for media files, applets, and ActiveX objects. For images, it's currently better practice to use the completely supported `img` (p. 333) element, rather than take a risk using `object`; `img` is also far less clunky to use.

Compatibility

Internet Explorer			Firefox			Safari			Opera
5.5	6.0	7.0	1.0	1.5	2.0	1.3	2.0	3.0	9.2
Partial	Partial	Partial	Partial	Partial	Partial	Partial	Partial	Partial	Partial

This element is not completely supported, although it has to be said that the support that is available very much depends on the type of object that's being embedded. Internet Explorer displays simple images poorly, with horizontal and vertical scrollbars, but is able to display an embedded Word document, albeit with a warning in the form of an ActiveX alert. Safari and Firefox, on the other hand, behaves impeccably with images, yet no amount of coaxing or installing of third-party plugins will allow the Word document to display—even with Microsoft Office installed on the host machine. For this reason, before you apply it, you should consider the purpose for which you need to use the `object` element. If it's to display images, you'll likely be better off to use the `img` element.

Other Relevant Stuff

 embed (p. 332)

specifies a generic container for a media object

 img (p. 333)

specifies an inline image element

 # align *for <object>*

SPEC		
deprecated	required	version
YES	NO	HTML 4
BROWSER SUPPORT		
IE5.5+ FF1+ Saf1.3+ Op9.2+		
FULL FULL FULL FULL		

```
align=" { bottom | left | middle | right | top } "
```

Example

The `align` attribute for this `object` is set to `"right"`:

```
<object classid="clsid:D27CDB6E-AE6D-11cf-96B8-444553540000"
    codebase="http://download.macromedia.com/pub/shockwave/cabs/flash/
➥swflash.cab#version=9,0,28,0" align="right" width="320"
    height="285" title="Flash tester">
  <param name="movie" value="flash-test.swf"/>
  <param name="quality" value="high"/>
</object>
```

The `align` attribute is used to specify how the object sits on the page in relation to surrounding text and other elements. It is a fairly rudimentary attribute—and a very presentational one—that allows you to move an object to the right or left, with text wrapping around the object accordingly (although generally, whitespace isn't included, which tends to result in quite an ugly result). You can also change the way that adjacent text aligns with the object so that the first line of the text aligns with the top, middle, or bottom of the object.

The example markup shown would render as illustrated in Figure 7.12.

Lorem ipsum dolor sit amet, consectetuer adipiscing elit. Nulla sapien neque, vulputate a, cursus consequat, ultricies eu, mi. Etiam est nibh, interdum ut, dapibus at, adipiscing eu, quam.

Lorem ipsum dolor sit amet, consectetuer adipiscing elit. Nulla sapien neque, vulputate a, cursus consequat, ultricies eu, mi. Etiam est nibh, interdum ut, dapibus at, adipiscing eu, quam.

Figure 7.12: A right-aligned object containing a Flash video

Aside from aligning `"left"` or `"right"`, the `align` attribute isn't very flexible when it's applied to an `object`.

If an `object` is aligned `"left"` or `"right"`, text will continue to wrap around it until either:

- a `br` (p. 40) element with a `clear` (p. 42) attribute is encountered
- any other element whose CSS `clear` property is set to `"left"`, `"right"`, or `"both"` is encountered

Value

Possible values for this attribute include `"bottom"`, `"left"`, `"middle"`, `"right"`, and `"top"`.

Compatibility

Internet Explorer			Firefox			Safari			Opera
5.5	6.0	7.0	1.0	1.5	2.0	1.3	2.0	3.0	9.2
Full	Full	Full	Full	Full	Full	Full	Full	Full	Full

This attribute is now deprecated, and is highly presentational in its nature. The desired visual effects can all be achieved with CSS and, as such, this attribute shouldn't be used—it's presented here for informational purposes only.

archive *for <object>*

```
archive="uri"
```

SPEC		
deprecated	required	version
NO	NO	HTML 4
BROWSER SUPPORT		
IE5.5+	FF1+	Saf1.3+	Op9.2+
PARTIAL	PARTIAL	PARTIAL	PARTIAL

Image and Media Elements

Example

In this code, the archive attribute obtains supporting classes from **giant-dog.jar**:

```
<object classid="java:giant-dog.class" archive="giant-dog.jar">
</object>
```

The archive attribute allows the author to define a number of files that are required for the object content to render or run correctly, effectively preloading the necessary resources.

Value
This attribute takes as its value a space-separated list of URLs of the files required.

Compatibility

Internet Explorer			Firefox			Safari			Opera
5.5	6.0	7.0	1.0	1.5	2.0	1.3	2.0	3.0	9.2
Partial	Partial	Partial	Partial	Partial	Partial	Partial	Partial	Partial	Partial

This attribute's compatibility is dependent on the type of object with which it's used.

border for <object>

```
border="number"
```

	SPEC	
deprecated	required	version
YES	NO	HTML 4
BROWSER SUPPORT			
IE5.5+	FF1+	Saf1.3+	Op9.2+
FULL	FULL	FULL	FULL

Example

This border attribute is set to "10":

```
<object data="giant-dog.jpg" border="10"></object>
```

By default, an object will not have a border around it. The border attribute rectifies this, allowing you to set a border with a width specified in pixels. Depending on the browser, the border will either be black, or will match the color of the text attribute of the body (p. 37) element. An example is shown in Figure 7.13.

Figure 7.13: An object displaying with a border thickness of ten pixels

Value

This attribute takes a number representing the width of the border in pixels.

Compatibility

Internet Explorer			Firefox			Safari			Opera
5.5	6.0	7.0	1.0	1.5	2.0	1.3	2.0	3.0	9.2
Full	Full	Full	Full	Full	Full	Full	Full	Full	Full

This attribute is poorly supported and highly presentational. CSS should be used to control appearance instead.

classid *for <object>*

```
classid="class ID"
```

SPEC		
deprecated	required	version
NO	NO	HTML 4
BROWSER SUPPORT		
IE5.5+	FF1+	Saf1.3+	Op9.2+
FULL	FULL	FULL	FULL

Example

This example shows the definition of a classid attribute for a Flash movie:

```
<object classid="clsid:D27CDB6E-AE6D-11cf-96B8-444553540000"
    codebase="http://download.macromedia.com/pub/shockwave/cabs/flash/
➥swflash.cab#version=9,0,28,0" width="320" height="285" title="Flash
    tester">
  <param name="movie" value="flash-test.swf"/>
  <param name="quality" value="high"/>
    ⋮
</object>
```

The classid attribute provides a reference that the browser can use to understand how the object should be implemented. It's usually used to ensure that the browser has the correct version of the control.

Value

This attribute takes as its value the URI of a document on the Web, or an internal reference in the form of "classid:object-id", as shown in the example above ("classid:D27CDB6E-AE6D-11cf-96B8-444553540000").

Compatibility

Internet Explorer			Firefox			Safari			Opera
5.5	6.0	7.0	1.0	1.5	2.0	1.3	2.0	3.0	9.2
Full	Full	Full	Full	Full	Full	Full	Full	Full	Full

The compatibility of this attribute depends upon the type of object with which it is used.

codebase _for <object>_

```
codebase="uri"
```

SPEC		
deprecated	required	version
NO	NO	HTML 2
BROWSER SUPPORT			
IE5.5+	FF1+	Saf1.3+	Op9.2+
FULL	FULL	FULL	FULL

Example

Here, codebase defines the base URL of `"http://bestjavaappsever.com/classes/"`:

```
<object classid="calendar.class"
    codebase="http://bestjavaappsever.com/classes/"></object>
```

The codebase attribute is used to set the base URL for the value specified in the classid attribute, overriding any base URL set in the head (p. 62) of the document.

In the example shown, the codebase is identified as `"http://bestjavaappsever.com/classes/"` (the complete path suggests that the resources are held on another server), while the classid refers to a file entitled `"calendar.class"`. The full address for the calendar code would therefore be interpreted as **http://bestjavaappsever.com/classes/calendar.class**.

Value

This attribute takes a URI, which may be a complete path on another server (for example, `"http://bestjavaappsever.com/classes/"`, or could be a different folder on the same server, as follows:

```
<object classid="calendar.class"
    codebase="/code/java-classes/"></object>
```

Compatibility

Internet Explorer			Firefox			Safari			Opera
5.5	6.0	7.0	1.0	1.5	2.0	1.3	2.0	3.0	9.2
Full	Full	Full	Full	Full	Full	Full	Full	Full	Full

Every browser listed supports this attribute.

codetype _for <object>_

```
codetype="MIME type"
```

SPEC		
deprecated	required	version
NO	NO	HTML 4
BROWSER SUPPORT			
IE5.5+	FF1+	Saf1.3+	Op9.2+
FULL	FULL	FULL	FULL

Example

This `codetype` attribute identifies an embedded Word document:

```
<object data="Hello.doc" codetype="application/msword"></object>
```

The `codetype` attribute defines the MIME type[5] of the embedded `object`, as specified in the `data` (p. 366) attribute. This shouldn't be confused with the `type` (p. 374) attribute, which is used to specify the MIME type of data that the `object` consumes.

Value

This attribute takes as its value a MIME type in the format type/subtype; for example, `"text/html"`, `"image/x-rgb"`, or `"application/java"`.

Compatibility

Internet Explorer			Firefox			Safari			Opera
5.5	6.0	7.0	1.0	1.5	2.0	1.3	2.0	3.0	9.2
Full	Full	Full	Full	Full	Full	Full	Full	Full	Full

Every browser listed supports this attribute.

---

[5] http://reference.sitepoint.com/html/mime-types/

 **data** *for <object>*

```
data="uri"
```

SPEC		
deprecated	required	version
NO	NO	HTML 4
BROWSER SUPPORT		
IE5.5+	FF1+	Saf1.3+ Op9.2+
FULL	FULL	FULL FULL

Example

The data attribute for this object refers to a **.jpg** file:

```
<object data="giant-dog.jpg"
    type="image/jpeg" height="225"></object>
```

The data attribute tells the browser where it can find the necessary data or file for the object. In the case of images, it's roughly equivalent to src (p. 348), but may point to any number of different file or data types (for example, video files, audio files, or Microsoft Office documents).

Value

This attribute takes as its value the location of the data—the image, video, or audio file, and so on—relative to the referencing document, relative to the server root, or as a complete URI containing the http:// protocol, the server name, and the path to the document on that server.

Compatibility

Internet Explorer			Firefox			Safari			Opera
5.5	6.0	7.0	1.0	1.5	2.0	1.3	2.0	3.0	9.2
Full	Full	Full	Full	Full	Full	Full	Full	Full	Full

It causes no compatibility issues, and has excellent support across all tested browsers.

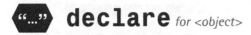

declare *for <object>*

`declare="declare"`

SPEC		
deprecated	required	version
NO	NO	HTML 4
BROWSER SUPPORT		
IE5.5+	FF2	Saf3	Op9.2+
FULL	NONE	NONE	FULL

Image and Media Elements

Example

Here's the `declare` attribute, specified in XHTML-compliant markup:

```
<object data="giant-dog.jpg" declare="declare"
    type="image/jpeg" height="225"></object>
```

The `declare` attribute declares an object, but doesn't instantiate it, which may be useful for the purposes of deferring the object's download until it's actually needed. In HTML, it's not necessary to include the attribute and value pairing—all we need is the attribute on its own, as shown here:

```
<object data="giant-dog.jpg" declare
    type="image/jpeg" height="225"></object>
```

Value

`"declare"` is the only value this attribute can take.

Compatibility

Internet Explorer			Firefox			Safari			Opera
5.5	6.0	7.0	1.0	1.5	2.0	1.3	2.0	3.0	9.2
Full	Full	Full	None	None	None	None	None	None	Full

This element type isn't particularly well supported and has limited practical value.

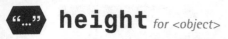

height *for <object>*

```
height=" { number | percentage } "
```

SPEC		
deprecated	required	version
NO	NO	HTML 4
BROWSER SUPPORT			
IE5.5+	FF1+	Saf1.3+	Op9.2+
FULL	FULL	FULL	FULL

Example

Here, the `height` attribute is set to `"100"`:

```
<object data="giant-dog.jpg" height="100">
</object>
```

An `object` doesn't require a `height` attribute, but it has its uses. The main reason for specifying the `height` (and `width` (p. 377)) is to improve the user experience while a page is loading. If the dimensions are specified in the markup, the space required for the object is reserved by the browser as the page loads. Without this information, the browser doesn't know how big the object is, and can't allocate the necessary space to it. On a slow-loading page, the effect can be quite unsightly, as content is constantly reflowed as each new object appears on the page.

The downside of specifying a `height` (and `width`) is that if you later decide to update an object that's used site-wide, you'll need to change the dimension attributes for each page of the site. Depending on how your web site's managed (manually, in a template-driven way, via a CMS, or through server-side includes), this may either be a minor niggle, or a real issue for you. It's a case of weighing up the pros and cons in each situation.

If the `height` attribute is set by itself, but no `width` attribute is set, the image will be rescaled proportionally. The results of this approach vary depending on the type of the object in question, and the browser rendering it. If nonproportional dimensions are specified (for instance, a 200x200-pixel object is set to take a `height` of 100 and a `width` of 300 pixels), the results vary: image objects can be stretched or squashed just as they can when different `width` and `height`s are applied using the `img` (p. 333)id element, but not all multimedia objects distort in the same way.

Image and Media Elements

Value

This attribute takes as its value a number that represents the height of the object in pixels, or a percentage of the containing element.

Compatibility

Internet Explorer			Firefox			Safari			Opera
5.5	6.0	7.0	1.0	1.5	2.0	1.3	2.0	3.0	9.2
Full	Full	Full	Full	Full	Full	Full	Full	Full	Full

The compatibility of this attribute is dependent on the type of the object. For objects of `type` image, there is excellent cross-browser support for the `height` attribute.

hspace *for <object>*

`hspace="number"`

SPEC		
deprecated	required	version
YES	NO	HTML 4
BROWSER SUPPORT		
IE5.5+	FF1+	Saf1.3+ Op9.2+
FULL	FULL	FULL FULL

Example

This `hspace` attribute is set to 30 pixels around a left-aligned image object:

```
<object data="giant-dog.jpg" height="225" width="300" align="left"
    hspace="30"></object>
```

When an object is aligned (p. 359) left or right, text will flow around the image, but no space will appear between it and the image. The `hspace` (and related `vspace` (p. 376)) attribute provides a little breathing space, but it will apply space on both sides of the object, which isn't entirely flexible, as Figure 7.14 reveals.

Lorem ipsum dolor sit amet, consectetuer adipiscing elit. Nulla sapien neque, vulputate a, cursus consequat, ultricies eu, mi. Etiam est nibh, interdum ut, dapibus at, adipiscing eu, quam.

Lorem ipsum dolor sit amet, consectetuer adipiscing elit. Nulla sapien neque, vulputate a, cursus consequat, ultricies eu, mi. Etiam est nibh, interdum ut, dapibus at, adipiscing eu, quam.

Figure 7.14: An image object to which an hspace of "30" is applied

Value

This attribute takes a number representing the pixel width of the spacing to be applied on either side of the image.

Compatibility

Internet Explorer			Firefox			Safari			Opera
5.5	6.0	7.0	1.0	1.5	2.0	1.3	2.0	3.0	9.2
Full	Full	Full	Full	Full	Full	Full	Full	Full	Full

Although support for this attribute is good, it's now deprecated, and is highly presentational in its nature. The desired visual effects can all be achieved with CSS and, as such, this attribute shouldn't be used—it's presented here for informational purposes only.

 **name** *for <object>*

```
name="string"
```

SPEC		
deprecated	required	version
YES	NO	HTML 4
BROWSER SUPPORT		
IE5.5+	FF1+	Saf1.3+	Op9.2+
FULL	FULL	FULL	FULL

Example

The name attribute provides a means for referencing the object:

```
<object data="giant-dog.jpg" height="225" width="300"
    align="left" vspace="30" name="dog-information-kiosk">
</object>
```

The name attribute is one method for referencing an object element in JavaScript (the alternative, forward-thinking method is to reference it by its id (p. 501) attribute). This attribute has historically been used for techniques such as image swaps for rollovers, which have since largely been replaced using CSS techniques.

Value

This attribute takes as its value any name that the developer chooses, so long as it doesn't contain spaces or special characters.

Compatibility

Internet Explorer			Firefox			Safari			Opera
5.5	6.0	7.0	1.0	1.5	2.0	1.3	2.0	3.0	9.2
Full	Full	Full	Full	Full	Full	Full	Full	Full	Full

It causes no compatibility issues, and has excellent support across all tested browsers.

Image and Media Elements

"..." **standby** *for <object>*

`standby="string"`

SPEC		
deprecated	required	version
NO	NO	HTML 4
BROWSER SUPPORT		
IE7	FF2	Saf3	Op9.2
NONE	NONE	NONE	NONE

Example

Here, the standby attribute is used to warn users of a download delay:

```
<object data="Kuata-Joinup.jpg" width="4466" height="535"
    standby="This may take a while. Go put the kettle on.">
</object>
```

For large media files that are pulled into a page using the object element, it's preferable not to have what appears to be a large space where the content should be, making the page appear, to all intents and purposes to, be broken. The standby attribute allows the author to display a message that will remain on screen only while the object's content is being loaded.

Value

This attribute takes as its value a suitable warning message, as shown in the example.

Compatibility

Internet Explorer			Firefox			Safari			Opera
5.5	6.0	7.0	1.0	1.5	2.0	1.3	2.0	3.0	9.2
None	None	None	None	None	None	None	None	None	None

Poor support is provided for this attribute. It's probably better to use a JavaScript technique to create a custom content-is-loading message in the style of your web page or site, which can subsequently be replaced or removed once the object's content has loaded.

"..." **tabindex** *for <object>*

`tabindex="number"`

SPEC		
deprecated	required	version
NO	NO	HTML 4
BROWSER SUPPORT			
IE5.5+	FF1+	Saf1.3+	Op9.2+
FULL	FULL	FULL	FULL

Example

This code sets the `tabindex` for both form controls:

```
<object data="giant-dog.jpg" height="225" tabindex="1"></object>
```

The `tabindex` is used to define a sequence that users follow when they use the Tab key to navigate through a page. By default, the natural tabbing order will match the source order in the markup. In certain circumstances it may be necessary to override the default tabbing order, but it's strongly recommended that you craft a page in a logical flow and let the browser work through it in the default order—an approach that negates the need for the `tabindex` attribute.

A `tabindex` can start at 0 and increment in any value. As such, the sequence 1, 2, 3, 4, 5 would be fine, as would 10, 20, 30, 40, 50. If you need to introduce a `tabindex`, it's advisable to use a sequence that contains intervals (like the second example provided), as this will give you the opportunity to inject other controls later if need be (for example, 10, 15, 20) without having to reindex all the `tabindex` values on the page. Should a given `tabindex` value be applied to more than one element in error, the tabbing order of those affected elements will be as per the source markup order.

If a `tabindex` is set anywhere on a page—even if it's the hundredth link or the fiftieth form control—the tab order will start at the element with the lowest `tabindex` value, and work through the increments. Only *then* will the tab order take in the remaining elements for which no `tabindex` has been set. As such, great care must be taken to ensure that adding a `tabindex` doesn't harm the usability of the page as a whole.

Value

This attribute takes a number value.

Compatibility

Internet Explorer			Firefox			Safari			Opera
5.5	6.0	7.0	1.0	1.5	2.0	1.3	2.0	3.0	9.2
Full	Full	Full	Full	Full	Full	Full	Full	Full	Full

It causes no compatibility issues, and has excellent support across all tested browsers.

type *for <object>*

```
type="MIME type"
```

SPEC		
deprecated	required	version
NO	NO	HTML 4
BROWSER SUPPORT			
IE5.5+	FF1+	Saf1.3+	Op9.2+
FULL	FULL	FULL	FULL

Example

This type attribute is set to "image/gif" to display a **.gif** image:

```
<object data="logo.gif" type="image/gif"></object>
```

The type attribute lets the author define the MIME type[6] of the data used in the object—the file that's specified in the data (p. 366) attribute. This is slightly different from the codetype (p. 365) attribute, which is used to specify the MIME type of the object itself. If the server sends data with the appropriate MIME type, this attribute may be omitted.

Value

This attribute takes a MIME type in the format type/subtype, for example, "text/html", "image/x-rgb", or "application/java".

Compatibility

Internet Explorer			Firefox			Safari			Opera
5.5	6.0	7.0	1.0	1.5	2.0	1.3	2.0	3.0	9.2
Full	Full	Full	Full	Full	Full	Full	Full	Full	Full

Every browser listed supports this attribute.

---

[6] http://reference.sitepoint.com/html/mime-types/

"..." **usemap** *for <object>*

`usemap="#map name"`

SPEC		
deprecated	required	version
NO	NO	HTML 4
BROWSER SUPPORT		
IE5.5+	FF1+	Saf1.3+ Op9.2+
FULL	FULL	FULL FULL

Example

This `usemap` attribute references a map named `"dogmap"`:

```
<p>
  <object data="giant-dog.jpg" usemap="#dogmap"
      height="225" width="300" border="0"></object>
  <map name="dogmap" id="dogmap">
    <area shape="circle" coords="216,120,24"
        href="http://tirauinfo.homestead.com/TheBigDog.html"
        alt="Click on the nose for more info about this big dog!"/>
  </map>
</p>
```

The `usemap` attribute tells the browser which of the `map` (p. 354) elements in the document it should refer to. The hotspots defined (using the `area` (p. 320) element) act as overlays on the object. These areas are similar to links (created with the `a` (p. 146) element), and allow the user to click to go to the page identified in the respective `area`'s `href` attribute. They're also keyboard-navigable.

The `usemap` attribute is only used in the `object` element when the type of object is an image (**.gif**, **.jpg**, or **.png**).

Value

This attribute takes as its value a reference to the map's `name` attribute in form of an `"#"` character plus the `"name"`, like so:

`usemap="#dogmap"`

Compatibility

Internet Explorer			Firefox			Safari			Opera
5.5	6.0	7.0	1.0	1.5	2.0	1.3	2.0	3.0	9.2
Full	Full	Full	Full	Full	Full	Full	Full	Full	Full

It causes no compatibility issues, and has excellent support across all tested browsers.

 **vspace** *for <object>*

`vspace="number"`

SPEC		
deprecated	required	version
YES	NO	HTML 4
BROWSER SUPPORT		
IE5.5+	FF1+	Saf1.3+	Op9.2+
FULL	FULL	FULL	FULL

Example

The `vspace` attribute is set to `"30"` pixels around a left-aligned image object:

```
<object data="giant-dog.jpg" height="225" width="300" align="left"
    vspace="30"></object>
```

The `vspace` attribute is similar to the `hspace` (p. 369) and provides a bit of breathing space above and below an object, although it's not exactly a precision design tool, as Figure 7.15 shows.

Lorem ipsum dolor sit amet, consectetuer adipiscing elit. Nulla sapien neque, vulputate a, cursus consequat, ultricies eu, mi. Etiam est nibh, interdum ut, dapibus at, adipiscing eu, quam.

 Lorem ipsum dolor sit amet, consectetuer adipiscing elit. Nulla sapien neque, vulputate a, cursus consequat, ultricies eu, mi. Etiam est nibh, interdum ut, dapibus at, adipiscing eu, quam.

Figure 7.15: Image object to which `vspace` of `"30"` is applied

Value

This attribute takes a number representing the amount of spacing to appear above and below the image in pixels.

Image and Media Elements

Compatibility

Internet Explorer			Firefox			Safari			Opera
5.5	6.0	7.0	1.0	1.5	2.0	1.3	2.0	3.0	9.2
Full	Full	Full	Full	Full	Full	Full	Full	Full	Full

Although support for this attribute is good, it's now deprecated, and is highly presentational in its nature. The desired visual effects can all be achieved with CSS and, as such, this attribute shouldn't be used—it's presented here for informational purposes only.

width *for <object>*

```
width=" { number | percentage } "
```

SPEC		
deprecated	required	version
NO	NO	HTML 4
BROWSER SUPPORT		
IE5.5+	FF1+	Saf1.3+	Op9.2+
FULL	FULL	FULL	FULL

Example

Here, the width attribute is set to "200":

```
<object data="giant-dog.jpg" height="100" width="200">
</object>
```

An object doesn't require a width attribute but, like the height (p. 368) attribute, it has its uses (refer to the advantages set out in the height attribute reference).

If the width attribute is set by itself, but no height attribute is set, the object will be rescaled proportionally (assuming that object is a simple image).

In every other respect, the width attribute is identical in usage and behavior to the height attribute.

Value

This attribute takes as its value a number representing the width of the object in pixels.

Compatibility

Internet Explorer			Firefox			Safari			Opera
5.5	6.0	7.0	1.0	1.5	2.0	1.3	2.0	3.0	9.2
Full	Full	Full	Full	Full	Full	Full	Full	Full	Full

This attribute's compatibility is dependent on the type of object to which it's applied. For objects of `type` image, excellent cross-browser support is provided for the `height` attribute.

param

```
<param name="string" type="MIME type"
value="value"valuetype=" { data | object | ref } ">
```

SPEC		
deprecated	empty	version
NO	YES	HTML 3.2
BROWSER SUPPORT			
IE5.5+	FF1+	Saf1.3+	Op9.2+
FULL	FULL	FULL	FULL

Example

Here's an example of an `object` (p. 357) element that contains two `param` elements:

```
<object classid="clsid:D27CDB6E-AE6D-11cf-96B8-444553540000"
    codebase="http://download.macromedia.com/pub/shockwave/cabs/flash/
➥swflash.cab#version=9,0,28,0"
    width="320" height="285" title="Flash tester">
  <param name="movie" value="flash-test.swf"/>
  <param name="quality" value="high"/>
</object>
```

The `param` element is used in conjunction with the `applet` (p. 320) and `object` (p. 357) elements to provide parameters or variables to the parent element.

Use This For ...

A typical use for the `param` element is demonstrated in the example above, where it's used to pass to the object information regarding an embedded movie clip's quality and filename. When it's used with an `applet`, the `param` might be used to pass variables to a function that the applet uses, for example, instructing the applet to draw five polygons on the page, and to make them purple:

Image and Media Elements

```
<applet code="draw.class">
  <param name="shape" value="triangle"/>
  <param name="amount" value="5"/>
  <param name="color" value="purple"/>
</applet>
```

Compatibility

Internet Explorer			Firefox			Safari			Opera
5.5	6.0	7.0	1.0	1.5	2.0	1.3	2.0	3.0	9.2
Full	Full	Full	Full	Full	Full	Full	Full	Full	Full

Every browser listed supports this element type.

Other Relevant Stuff

 applet (p. 320)

specifies a Java applet (a mini application) for insertion into the document

 object (p. 357)

specifies a generic, multipurpose container for a media object

 name *for <param>*

	SPEC	
deprecated	required	version
NO	YES	HTML 3.2
BROWSER SUPPORT		
IE5.5+ FF1+ Saf1.3+ Op9.2+		
FULL FULL FULL FULL		

```
name="string"
```

Example

The name of the parameter here is "shape":

```
<param name="shape" value="triangle"/>
```

This required attribute defines the data that's being passed to the `object` or `applet` in the parameter.

Value

The value of the param's name attribute very much depends on the type of object that's being embedded into the web page. Whatever parameter name is being used, it's understood that the object is able to make sense of the information being passed to it. In the example above, the param is named "shape", so the Java applet would presumably have an interface with a function that accepts various values, one of which is a "shape" variable. Therefore, it should understand that a shape is being passed in, and that it will need to act on the value passed to it in the value attribute.

Compatibility

Internet Explorer			Firefox			Safari			Opera
5.5	6.0	7.0	1.0	1.5	2.0	1.3	2.0	3.0	9.2
Full	Full	Full	Full	Full	Full	Full	Full	Full	Full

Every browser listed supports this attribute.

type *for <param>*

```
type="MIME type"
```

	SPEC	
deprecated	required	version
NO	NO	3.2

Example

This code shows a param element whose type is set to "video/mp4":

```
<param type="video/mp4"/>
```

The type attribute lets the author define the MIME type[7] of the applet or object content. In many cases, though, this attribute is not required, as the browser can determine the MIME type on the basis of the URL or the header sent by the server for the embedded content.

---

[7] http://reference.sitepoint.com/html/mime-types/

Value

This attribute takes a MIME type in the format type/subtype, for instance, `"text/html"`, or `"application/x-shockwave-flash"`, or `"video/mp4"`.

 value *for <param>*

`value="value"`

SPEC		
deprecated	required	version
NO	NO	HTML 3.2
BROWSER SUPPORT		
IE5.5+	FF1+	Saf1.3+	Op9.2+
FULL	FULL	FULL	FULL

Example

The value of this `"shape"` parameter is `"triangle"`:

```
<param name="shape" value="triangle"/>
```

The `value` attribute works in conjunction with the `name` attribute (p. 379) to pass the necessary parameter or variable information to the parent `object` or `applet` element. According to the HTML specifications, the `value` attribute isn't a required attribute (only `name` is required), but it's rare to see the `name` attribute specified on its own.

Value

The value of the `value` attribute very much depends on the `name` of the parameter, so there's no fixed list of possible values.

Compatibility

Internet Explorer			Firefox			Safari			Opera
5.5	6.0	7.0	1.0	1.5	2.0	1.3	2.0	3.0	9.2
Full	Full	Full	Full	Full	Full	Full	Full	Full	Full

Every browser listed supports this attribute.

Image and Media Elements

valuetype *for <param>*

`valuetype=" { data | object | ref } "`

SPEC		
deprecated	required	version
NO	NO	HTML 3.2
BROWSER SUPPORT			
IE5.5+	FF1+	Saf1.3+	Op9.2+
FULL	FULL	FULL	FULL

Example

The `valuetype` of the `"shape"` parameter here is `"ref"`, as the `value` is a *ref*erence to a URL:

```
<param name="shape" value="poly.txt" valuetype="ref"/>
```

The `valuetype` provides a mechanism for defining exactly what *type* of data is being passed to the parent object. If a `valuetype` isn't specified, the browser assumes the default value of `"data"`. You only really need to bring the `valuetype` attribute into play if the content inside the value is a URL which points to a file that contains the necessary information. In the example above, the reference is to a text file `poly.txt` which would, presumably, contain the set of rules or coordinates required to draw a polygonal shape, for which you'd specify a `valuetype` of `"ref"`. If `"object"` is specified as the `valuetype`, the `value` attribute should correlate to another object on the page, which is referenced by that object's `id`:

```
<param name="handler" value="mplayer" valuetype="object"/>
   ⋮
<object id="mplayer">
   ⋮
</object>
```

Value

`"data"`, `"ref"`, and `"object"` are the only possible values for `valuetype`.

8

Table Elements

Table markup is used for presenting data in a grid-like fashion, *not* for the purposes of laying out a web page, or the sections within a web page. The elements and attributes listed in this section will provide you with all the tools you need to ensure that your table markup is valid, logically presented, and accessible.

caption

```
<caption>
</caption>
```

SPEC		
deprecated	empty	version
NO	NO	HTML 3.2

BROWSER SUPPORT			
IE5.5+	FF1+	Saf1.3+	Op9.2+
PARTIAL	FULL	PARTIAL	PARTIAL

Example

Here's a table `caption` that provides a visual summary and heading all in one:

```
<table border="1">
  <caption>Interest Rates for Young Saver Accounts</caption>
  <tr>
    <th>Account Type</th>
    <th>Interest Rate</th>
  </tr>
  <tr>
    <td>Smart</td>
    <td>From 2%</td>
  </tr>
  <tr>
    <td>Young Saver</td>
    <td>From 1.6%</td>
  </tr>
</table>
```

The `caption` element provides a means for labeling the following table's content in a visual manner (unlike the `table`'s `summary` attribute, (p. 419) which is non-visible). It has one element-specific attribute, `align` (p. 385), which is very rudimentary and not entirely supported (it's also deprecated, so it should generally be avoided).

The `caption` element can only be used once per `table` and must immediately follow the `table` start tag.

While the `caption` element seems like the most appropriate markup for labeling a `table`, many people instead choose to precede tables with heading elements 1-6 (for example, an `h3` (p. 53) element). This makes it easier for people using assistive technology, such as screen readers, to jump from heading to heading in the document, and arguably offers more semantic information than the `caption`, which doesn't provide any indication of importance or hierarchy within the document.

Use This For ...

This element should be used for providing a short heading for the table; it should not be used to provide a description of the table's structure, as you might do with the `table summary` attribute.

Compatibility

Internet Explorer			Firefox			Safari			Opera
5.5	6.0	7.0	1.0	1.5	2.0	1.3	2.0	3.0	9.2
Partial	Partial	Partial	Full	Full	Full	Partial	Partial	Partial	Partial

As long as you steer clear of the `align` attribute, browser support for `caption` is generally good. It can be problematic to style this element with CSS, though, unlike headings 1-6, which is another reason why the `caption` element isn't used very frequently.

align *for <caption>*

`align=" { bottom | left | right | top } "`

SPEC		
deprecated	required	version
YES	NO	HTML 3.2
BROWSER SUPPORT		
IE5.5+	FF1+	Saf1.3+ Op9.2+
PARTIAL	FULL	PARTIAL PARTIAL

Table Elements

Example

The `align` for this `caption` is set to `"right"`:

```
<table>
  <caption align="right">Interest Rates</caption>
  <tr>
    <th>Account Type</th>
    <th>Interest Rate</th>
  </tr>
  <tr>
    <td>Smart</td>
    <td>From 2%</td>
  </tr>
  <tr>
    <td>Young Saver</td>
    <td>From 1.6%</td>
  </tr>
</table>
```

The `align` attribute should, in theory, align the `caption` as a block element to the left or right of, or above or below, the table, in the same way in which this attribute would work when applied to a table or an image. However, browser support for the attribute is poor, and it's inconsistently interpreted and presented.

Value

Possible values for this attribute include `"bottom"`, `"left"`, `"right"`, and `"top"`.

Compatibility

Internet Explorer			Firefox			Safari			Opera
5.5	6.0	7.0	1.0	1.5	2.0	1.3	2.0	3.0	9.2
Partial	Partial	Partial	Full	Full	Full	Partial	Partial	Partial	Partial

This attribute is now deprecated, and is highly presentational in its nature. The desired visual effects can all be achieved with CSS and, as such, this attribute shouldn't be used—it's presented here for informational purposes only.

Browser support for this attribute is mixed. Firefox honors all the alignment settings, while Safari honors only the `"bottom"` attribute value, ignoring `"left"` and `"right"`. Opera doesn't align the `caption` left or right as a block-level element, but does align the text contained *inside* the caption left or right, as does Internet Explorer. In short, don't count on being able to style a table `caption`.

col

```
<col align=" { center | char | justify | left |
right } "span="number" valign=" { baseline | bottom
| middle | top } " width=" { number | percentage } ">
</col>
```

	SPEC	
deprecated	empty	version
NO	YES	HTML 4
	BROWSER SUPPORT		
IE5.5+	FF1+	Saf1.3+	Op9.2+
FULL	FULL	FULL	FULL

Example

Below, the col element is used to set different class (p. 498) attributes on the first three columns in the table (which can then be styled with CSS):

```
<table border="1">
  <col class="col1"/>
  <col class="col2"/>
  <col class="col3"/>
  <col/>
  <tr>
    <th colspan="4" scope="col">Work Contact Points</th>
  </tr>
    ⋮
</table>
```

Tables are primarily constructed by defining rows, but it's often useful to define their structure as columns as well. Unlike rows, columns don't directly contain any cells; rather, they implicitly group adjacent cells between rows. This may not seem important, but it means that there isn't an easy way to select a column for styling purposes (the best you could do was to set a width attribute on the top-most table cells, be they th or td elements).

The col element aims to solve the problem by providing a mechanism for selecting columns and applying the necessary attributes. The idea is that you can use the col element to define all of your columns' attributes—alignment, colors, and so on, up-front, before you begin the process of writing out each row.

The col element can appear on its own (as shown in the HTML example above, there's one col for each of the subsequent rows' cells, with alignments set only for the first three columns), but it can also appear inside a colgroup (p. 396) element.

Use This For ...

This element is used for identifying individual table columns and applying styles to them (either using HTML attributes or CSS), rather than repeating the styles for each cell, row after row.

Compatibility

Internet Explorer			Firefox			Safari			Opera
5.5	6.0	7.0	1.0	1.5	2.0	1.3	2.0	3.0	9.2
Full	Full	Full	Full	Full	Full	Full	Full	Full	Full

This element has reasonable support, though the breadth of support depends heavily on which attributes are applied. Attribute support varies between browsers (it would be so much easier if all browsers tested, supported, and ignored the same set of attributes, but unfortunately, this is not the case).

A better approach is to apply `class` names to the respective `col` elements, then let CSS styling take care of alignment, colors, widths, and so on.

Other Relevant Stuff

 colgroup (p. 396)

defines a group of columns within a table

align *for <col>*

	SPEC	
deprecated	required	version
NO	NO	HTML 4

`align=" { center | char | justify | left | right } "`

	BROWSER SUPPORT		
IE5.5+	FF2	Saf3	Op9.2+
FULL	NONE	NONE	FULL

Example

This example shows text alignments set on `col` elements:

```
<table border="1">
  <col align="left"/>
  <col align="center"/>
  <col align="right"/>
  <col/>
  <tr>
    <th colspan="4" scope="col">Work Contact Points</th>
  </tr>
  <tr>
    <th>Name sfdg sfg sdfg  sdfg sdfg sfsgsdf gs</th>
    <th>Email</th>
    <th>Phone</th>
    <th>Floor/Block</th>
  </tr>
    ⋮
</table>
```

While it's possible to set the alignment of text at `th` and `td` level—and alignment is well supported for those elements—it does mean repeating the `align` attribute for *every* row. Applying `align` to a `col` element avoids this overhead (or rather, it should).

Value

The recognized attribute values are as shown in the syntax section.

Compatibility

Internet Explorer			Firefox			Safari			Opera
5.5	6.0	7.0	1.0	1.5	2.0	1.3	2.0	3.0	9.2
Full	Full	Full	None	None	None	None	None	None	Full

Table Elements

Compatibility for col's align attribute is very poor, as the support chart shows (this time, it's IE and Opera who are the good guys!). As such, this attribute can't be relied upon, nice as the idea is.

char *for <col>*

```
char="character"
```

SPEC		
deprecated	required	version
NO	NO	HTML 4
BROWSER SUPPORT			
IE7	FF2	Saf3	Op9.2
NONE	NONE	NONE	NONE

Example

This column data is set to align to the ":" character:

```
<table border="1">
  <col align="char" char=":"/>
  <col align="char" char=":"/>
  <col align="char" char=":"/>
  <col align="char" char=":"/>
  <tr>
    <th colspan="4" scope="col">Work Contact Points</th>
  </tr>
  <tr>
    <th>Name sfdg sfg sdfg  sdfg sdfg sfsgsdf gs</th>
    <th>Email</th>
    <th>Phone</th>
    <th>Floor/Block</th>
  </tr>
    ⋮
</table>
```

It may be useful in tables that contain financial information to align contents beyond the simple "left", "right", and "center" determinations. For example, you might align numerical data to a decimal point, or some other symbol. The char attribute allows you to define the character against which the data is aligned, but this only works if the align (p. 389) attribute has also been set to "char".

Value

This attribute takes as its value a single character that appears in the table; for example, a decimal point character.

Compatibility

Internet Explorer			Firefox			Safari			Opera
5.5	6.0	7.0	1.0	1.5	2.0	1.3	2.0	3.0	9.2
None	None	None	None	None	None	None	None	None	None

This attribute is poorly supported and should not be relied upon.

charoff *for <col>*

`charoff="number"`

SPEC		
deprecated	required	version
NO	NO	HTML 4
BROWSER SUPPORT		
IE7	FF2	Saf3	Op9.2
NONE	NONE	NONE	NONE

Example

In this example, the `charoff` is set to align four characters to the right of "`:`" (in columns 1, 2, 4) and two characters to the left of "`.`" (in column 3):

```
<table border="1">
  <col align="char" char=":" charoff="4"/>
  <col align="char" char=":" charoff="4"/>
  <col align="char" char="." charoff="-2"/>
  <col align="char" char=":" charoff="4"/>
  ⋮
</table>
```

If the `align` attribute is set to "`char`", and the `char` attribute has been set to a character—thus telling the browser that cell contents should be aligned to a given character—the `charoff` attribute is used to set a *char*acter *off*set. If a `charoff` figure of "`4`" is chosen, the browser should align the cell contents four characters to the right or the specified character. If `charoff` were a negative value, for example "`-4`", the alignment should be offset four characters to the left of the specified character. Note that there are a few uses of the word "should" in this description, which *should* (there we go again) give you a hint about what to expect in the Compatibility section for this attribute!

Value

The `charoff` attribute takes an integer value, which can be positive or negative.

Compatibility

Internet Explorer			Firefox			Safari			Opera
5.5	6.0	7.0	1.0	1.5	2.0	1.3	2.0	3.0	9.2
None	None	None	None	None	None	None	None	None	None

This element is poorly supported and should not be relied upon.

span *for* <col>

```
span="number (of columns spanned)"
```

SPEC		
deprecated	required	version
NO	NO	HTML 4
BROWSER SUPPORT		
IE5.5+	FF1+	Saf1.3+ Op9.2+
FULL	FULL	FULL FULL

Example

Here, the span is used to group the first two columns separately from the second two columns, and each group is given a different class for styling purposes:

```
<table border="1" cellpadding="5">
  <col class="st1" span="2"/>
  <col class="st2" span="2"/>
  <tr>
    <th colspan="4" scope="col">Work Contact Points</th>
  </tr>
  <tr>
    <th>Name</th>
    <th>Email</th>
    <th>Phone</th>
    <th>Floor/Block</th>
  </tr>
    ⋮
</table>
```

Just as you can set th and td elements to span multiple columns using the colspan attribute, a similar result can be achieved with the col element using the span attribute (*not* colspan —after all, it's obvious that it's a col that's being spanned!). However, using this attribute doesn't cause any cells to be merged (as does colspan). Rather, it tells the browser how many columns or cells the attributes set in the col should apply to (including the first col). So, in the HTML example we have a table with four cells in each row—and, therefore, four columns. But only two col elements are defined, with span attributes of "2".

Value

This attribute takes as its value a number that represents the number of consecutive cells to which the col attributes should apply.

Compatibility

Internet Explorer			Firefox			Safari			Opera
5.5	6.0	7.0	1.0	1.5	2.0	1.3	2.0	3.0	9.2
Full	Full	Full	Full	Full	Full	Full	Full	Full	Full

Support for this attribute has been marked as full, but be aware that this support depends on whether the other attributes are supported. For instance, Safari ignores the align attribute, so asking it to span that attribute across two columns will have no effect. In short, the successful rendering of span depends on the support for the attributes with which it's associated.

valign _for <col>_

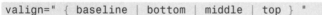

	SPEC	
deprecated	required	version
NO	NO	HTML 4
BROWSER SUPPORT		
IE5.5+	FF1+	Saf1.3+	Op9.2+
PARTIAL	PARTIAL	PARTIAL	PARTIAL

`valign=" { baseline | bottom | middle | top } "`

Example

Here, the valign is set to "bottom" for cells that appear in the first column of the table:

```
<table border="1" cellpadding="5">
  <col valign="bottom"/>
  <col/>
  <col/>
  <col/>
  <tr>
    <th colspan="4">Work Contact Points</th>
  </tr>
  <tr>
    <th>Name</th>
    <th>Email</th>
    <th>Phone</th>
    <th>Floor/Block</th>
  </tr>
    ⋮
<table>
```

Table Elements

In a very similar manner to this element's `align` attribute (p. 389), the `valign` attribute allows you to override the default vertical alignment for content within table cells related to the `col` in question.

Value

The recognized attribute values are as shown in the syntax section.

Compatibility

Internet Explorer			Firefox			Safari			Opera
5.5	6.0	7.0	1.0	1.5	2.0	1.3	2.0	3.0	9.2
Partial	Partial	Partial	Partial	Partial	Partial	Partial	Partial	Partial	Partial

In the browsers tested, `"bottom"`, `"middle"`, and `"top"` alignments were honored, but the `"baseline"` value was ignored by all.

 **width** *for* *<col>*

SPEC		
deprecated	required	version
NO	NO	HTML 4
BROWSER SUPPORT		
IE5.5+	FF1+	Saf1.3+ Op9.2+
FULL	FULL	FULL FULL

```
width=" { number | percentage } "
```

Example

The `width` attribute for each column is set to a larger value than that of the column to its left:

```
<table border="1" cellpadding="5">
  <col width="100"/>
  <col width="150"/>
  <col width="200"/>
  <col width="250"/>
  <tr>
    <th colspan="4" scope="col">Work Contact Points</th>
  </tr>
  <tr>
    <th>Name</th>
    <th>Email</th>
    <th>Phone</th>
    <th>Floor/Block</th>
  </tr>
  ⋮
</table>
```

Unless a `width` is set, a `td` (and the `th` (p. 454)) will take up only the width it requires (obviously this will depend on the amount of content in each table cell). You can use the `width` attribute in the context of the `col` element to fix the column's width to a value of your choosing, regardless of the content of the table cell.

Value

This attribute takes as its value a number representing the width of the column element in pixels, or a percentage.

Compatibility

Internet Explorer			Firefox			Safari			Opera
5.5	6.0	7.0	1.0	1.5	2.0	1.3	2.0	3.0	9.2
Full	Full	Full	Full	Full	Full	Full	Full	Full	Full

It causes no compatibility issues, and has excellent support across all tested browsers.

Table Elements

colgroup

```
<colgroup align=" { center | char | justify | left
| right } "span="number" valign=" { baseline | bottom
| middle | top } " width=" { number | percentage } ">
</colgroup>
```

SPEC		
deprecated	empty	version
NO	NO	HTML 4
BROWSER SUPPORT		
IE5.5+	FF1+	Saf1.3+	Op9.2+
FULL	FULL	FULL	FULL

Example

This colgroup element is used to set a class for first three columns (which can then be styled with CSS):

```
<table border="1">
  <colgroup class="vivid">
    <col/>
    <col/>
    <col/>
  </colgroup>
  <col/>
  <tr>
    <th colspan="4">Work Contact Points</th>
  </tr>
    ⋮
</table>
```

The colgroup is a container for a number of col elements, and allows you to set attributes that you might otherwise set at col level on a number of col elements simultaneously—the attributes defined at this higher level apply to all of the child columns.

Use This For ...

This element is used to apply styles (either using HTML attributes or via CSS) to a number of columns simultaneously.

Compatibility

Internet Explorer			Firefox			Safari			Opera
5.5	6.0	7.0	1.0	1.5	2.0	1.3	2.0	3.0	9.2
Full	Full	Full	Full	Full	Full	Full	Full	Full	Full

This element has reasonable support, though the breadth of support depends heavily on which attributes are applied. Attribute support varies between browsers (it would be so much easier if all browsers tested, supported, and ignored the same set of attributes, but unfortunately, this is not the case).

A better approach is to apply `class` names to the respective `colgroup` elements, then let CSS styling take care of alignment, colors, widths, and so on.

Other Relevant Stuff

 col (p. 387)

defines a column within a table

 align *for <colgroup>*

```
align=" { center | char | justify | left | right } "
```

SPEC		
deprecated	required	version
NO	NO	HTML 4
BROWSER SUPPORT		
IE5.5+	FF2	Saf3	Op9.2+
FULL	NONE	NONE	FULL

Example

This example shows the setting of alignment in `colgroup` elements to `"center"`:

```
<table border="1">
  <colgroup align="center">
    <col/>
    <col/>
    <col/>
    <col/>
  </colgroup>
  <tr>
    <th colspan="4" scope="col">Work Contact Points</th>
  </tr>
  <tr>
    <th>Name</th>
    <th>Email</th>
    <th>Phone</th>
    <th>Floor/Block</th>
  </tr>
  ⋮
</table>
```

Table Elements

While it's possible to set the alignment of text at `th` and `td` level—and alignment is well-supported for those elements—it does mean repeating that `align` attribute for *every* row. Applying the `align` to a `colgroup` element avoids this overhead (or rather, it should).

Value

The recognized attribute values are as shown in the syntax section.

Compatibility

Internet Explorer			Firefox			Safari			Opera
5.5	6.0	7.0	1.0	1.5	2.0	1.3	2.0	3.0	9.2
Full	Full	Full	None	None	None	None	None	None	Full

Compatibility for `align`, when it's set to `colgroup`, is very poor, as the support chart shows (this time it's IE and Opera who are the good guys!). As such, it cannot be relied upon, nice as the idea is.

 char *for <colgroup>*

SPEC		
deprecated	required	version
NO	NO	HTML 4
BROWSER SUPPORT			
IE7	FF2	Saf3	Op9.2
NONE	NONE	NONE	NONE

```
char="character"
```

Example

The column data below is set to align to the ":" and "%" characters in different `colgroup`s:

```
<table border="1">
  <colgroup align="char" char=":">
    <col/>
    <col/>
  </colgroup>
  <colgroup align="char" char="%">
    <col/>
    <col/>
  </colgroup>
    ⋮
</table>
```

It may be useful in tables that contain financial information to align contents beyond the simple `"left"`, `"right"`, and `"center"` determinations. For example, you might align numerical data to a decimal point, or some other symbol. The `char` attribute allows you to define the character against which data is aligned, but this only works if the `align` (p. 397) attribute has also been set to `"char"`.

Value

This attribute takes as its value a single character that appears in the table; for example, a decimal point character.

Compatibility

Internet Explorer			Firefox			Safari			Opera
5.5	6.0	7.0	1.0	1.5	2.0	1.3	2.0	3.0	9.2
None	None	None	None	None	None	None	None	None	None

This attribute is poorly supported and should not be relied upon.

charoff *for <colgroup>*

`charoff="number"`

SPEC		
deprecated	required	version
NO	NO	HTML 4
BROWSER SUPPORT			
IE7	FF2	Saf3	Op9.2
NONE	NONE	NONE	NONE

Example

In the example the `charoff` is set to `"2"`:

```
<table border="1">
  <colgroup align="char" char=":" charoff="2">
    <col/>
    <col/>
  </colgroup>
  <colgroup align="char" char="%" charoff="2">
    <col/>
    <col/>
  </colgroup>
  ⋮
</table>
```

If the `align` attribute is set to `"char"`, and the `char` attribute has been set to a character—thus telling the browser that cell contents should be aligned to a given character—the `charoff` attribute is used to set a *char*acter *off*set. If a `charoff` figure of `"2"` is chosen, as shown in the example HTML, the browser should align the cell contents two characters to the right of the specified character. If `charoff` were a negative value, `"-2"` for example, the alignment should be offset two characters to the left of the specified character. Note that there are a few uses of the word "should" in this paragraph, which *should* (there we go again) give you a hint about what to expect in the compatibility section for this attribute!

Value

This attribute takes an integer value, which can be positive or negative.

Compatibility

Internet Explorer			Firefox			Safari			Opera
5.5	6.0	7.0	1.0	1.5	2.0	1.3	2.0	3.0	9.2
None	None	None	None	None	None	None	None	None	None

This attribute is poorly supported and should not be relied upon.

span *for <colgroup>*

`span="number"`

SPEC		
deprecated	required	version
NO	NO	HTML 4
BROWSER SUPPORT		
IE5.5+	FF1+	Saf1.3+	Op9.2+
FULL	FULL	FULL	FULL

Example

Here, two groups of columns are defined using the span attribute:

```
<table border="1">
  <colgroup width="60%" span="2"/></colgroup>
  <colgroup width="40%" span="2"/></colgroup>
  <tr>
    <th colspan="4" scope="col">Work Contact Points</th>
  </tr>
  <tr>
    <th>Name</th>
    <th>Email</th>
    <th>Phone</th>
    <th>Floor/Block</th>
  </tr>
    ⋮
</table>
```

If you wanted to set attributes for individual columns, you could use the col element and apply the relevant attributes to each as you saw fit. However, if a group of a columns shared the same attribute, this approach would necessitate the following repetition of seven columns:

```
<colgroup align="left">
  <col/>
  <col/>
  <col/>
  <col/>
  <col/>
  <col/>
  <col/>
</colgroup>
```

Instead, you could simply omit the nested col elements, and state how many columns were required with the span attribute, like so:

```
<colgroup align="left" span="7">
</colgroup>
```

If the `colgroup` contains a `span` attribute as well as nested `col` elements, the value in the `span` is ignored, and the number of `col` elements is counted instead.

Value

This attribute takes as its value a number that reflects the number of consecutive cells the `colgroup` represents.

Compatibility

Internet Explorer			Firefox			Safari			Opera
5.5	6.0	7.0	1.0	1.5	2.0	1.3	2.0	3.0	9.2
Full	Full	Full	Full	Full	Full	Full	Full	Full	Full

Support for this attribute has been marked as full, but be aware that this support still depends on whether the other attributes are supported. Safari, for instance, ignores the `align` attribute, so asking it to span that attribute across two columns has no effect. In short, the successful rendering of `span` depends on the support for the attributes with which it's associated.

valign *for <colgroup>*

```
valign=" { baseline | bottom | middle | top } "
```

SPEC		
deprecated	required	version
NO	NO	HTML 4
BROWSER SUPPORT		
IE5.5+	FF1+	Saf1.3+	Op9.2+
PARTIAL	PARTIAL	PARTIAL	PARTIAL

Example

Here, the `valign` is set to "bottom" for cells that appear in the first two columns of the table:

```
<table border="1">
  <colgroup width="60%" span="2" valign="bottom"/></colgroup>
  <colgroup width="40%" span="2"/></colgroup>
  <tr>
    <th colspan="4" scope="col">Work Contact Points</th>
  </tr>
  <tr>
    <th>Name</th>
    <th>Email</th>
    <th>Phone</th>
    <th>Floor/Block</th>
  </tr>
    ⋮
</table>
```

In a very similar manner to this element's `align` attribute (p. 397), the `valign` attribute allows you to override the default vertical alignment for content inside table cells related to the `colgroup` in question.

Value

The recognized attribute values are as shown in the syntax section.

Compatibility

Internet Explorer			Firefox			Safari			Opera
5.5	6.0	7.0	1.0	1.5	2.0	1.3	2.0	3.0	9.2
Partial	Partial	Partial	Partial	Partial	Partial	Partial	Partial	Partial	Partial

In the browsers tested, the "bottom", "middle", and "top" alignments are honored, but the "baseline" value is ignored by all.

Table Elements

width *for <colgroup>*

```
width=" { number | percentage } "
```

SPEC		
deprecated	required	version
NO	NO	HTML 4
BROWSER SUPPORT			
IE5.5+	FF1+	Saf1.3+	Op9.2+
FULL	FULL	FULL	FULL

Example

Here, the width attribute for two column groups is split on a percentage basis—the first column group receives 60% of the available width, while the second receives 40% of the available width:

```
<table border="1">
  <colgroup width="60%" span="2"/></colgroup>
  <colgroup width="40%" span="2"/></colgroup>
  <tr>
    <th colspan="4" scope="col">Work Contact Points</th>
  </tr>
  <tr>
    <th>Name</th>
    <th>Email</th>
    <th>Phone</th>
    <th>Floor/Block</th>
  </tr>
  ⋮
</table>
```

Unless a width is set, a td (and the th (p. 454)) will take up only the width as it requires (obviously this will depend on the amount of content in each table cell). You can use the width attribute in the context of the colgroup element to fix the width to a value of your choosing, regardless of the content of the table cell.

Value

This attribute takes a number representing the width of the column group in pixels, or a percentage.

Compatibility

Internet Explorer			Firefox			Safari			Opera
5.5	6.0	7.0	1.0	1.5	2.0	1.3	2.0	3.0	9.2
Full	Full	Full	Full	Full	Full	Full	Full	Full	Full

It causes no compatibility issues, and has excellent support across all tested browsers.

table   405

table

```
<table summary="string">
</table>
```

SPEC		
deprecated	empty	version
NO	NO	HTML 2

BROWSER SUPPORT			
IE5.5+	FF1+	Saf1.3+	Op9.2+
FULL	FULL	FULL	FULL

Example

Here's a very simple two-column, two-row `table`:

```
<table>
  <tr>
    <th>Account Type</th>
    <th>Interest Rate</th>
  </tr>
  <tr>
    <td>Smart</td>
    <td>From 2%</td>
  </tr>
  <tr>
    <td>Young Saver</td>
    <td>From 1.6%</td>
  </tr>
</table>
```

The `table` element is used to present data in a grid-like fashion (in rows and columns), with appropriate headers to identify the data contained in each column and row.

At its most basic, a table is built using the `table`, `tr` (p. 484), and `td` (p. 428) elements (with `th` (p. 454) elements used for marking up the column or row headings), as shown in the example HTML, which renders as shown in Figure 8.1.

Account Type Interest Rate
Smart   From 2%
Young Saver   From 1.6%

Figure 8.1: A simple table with no formatting

A more complex `table` may also include a `caption` (p. 384); `col` (p. 387) and `colgroup` (p. 396) elements; and the structural `thead` (p. 476), `tfoot` (p. 446), and `tbody` (p. 421) elements, which are used to identify the different regions in the `table`.

Table Elements

Use This For ...

A table should only be used for tabular data. It should *not* be used (or, rather, misused) as a layout mechanism, whether for the layout of an entire web page, or for specific sections of a page. CSS should be used for laying out a page, as it ensures that the content is adaptable to different devices, and doesn't cause problems when it's linearized.

Compatibility

Internet Explorer			Firefox			Safari			Opera
5.5	6.0	7.0	1.0	1.5	2.0	1.3	2.0	3.0	9.2
Full	Full	Full	Full	Full	Full	Full	Full	Full	Full

It causes no compatibility issues, and has excellent support across all tested browsers.

align *for <table>*

```
align=" { center | left | right } "
```

SPEC		
deprecated	required	version
YES	NO	HTML 2
BROWSER SUPPORT		
IE5.5+	FF1+	Saf1.3+	Op9.2+
FULL	FULL	FULL	FULL

Example

The `align` attribute for this `table` is set to `"right"`:

```
<table align="right">
  <tr>
    <th>Account Type</th>
    <th>Interest Rate</th>
  </tr>
  <tr>
    <td>Smart</td>
    <td>From 2%</td>
  </tr>
  <tr>
    <td>Young Saver</td>
    <td>From 1.6%</td>
  </tr>
</table>
```

As a block-level element, a `table` will have a break before and after it (with some margin), regardless of the table's width. The `align` attribute gives us the ability to

table   407

allow text and other HTML elements to wrap around the table, rather than beginning after the table, as Figure 8.2 demonstrates. This layout may be preferable for smaller tables that may look a little lost on the page.

Efficiently empower team driven schemas vis-a-vis interdependent scenarios. Energistically redefine excellent human capital vis-a-vis backward-compatible action items.

Account Type Interest Rate

Smart   From 2%

Young Saver   From 1.6%

Authoritatively productivate dynamic supply chains vis-a-vis just in time infrastructures.

Figure 8.2: A right-aligned table

If a `table` is aligned `"left"` or `"right"`, text will continue to wrap around it until either of the following elements is encountered:

- a `br` (p. 40) element on which a `clear` (p. 42) attribute is set
- any other element whose CSS property `clear` is set to `"left"`, `"right"`, or `"both"`

Value

Possible values for this attribute include `"center"`, `"left"`, and `"right"`.

Compatibility

Internet Explorer			Firefox			Safari			Opera
5.5	6.0	7.0	1.0	1.5	2.0	1.3	2.0	3.0	9.2
Full	Full	Full	Full	Full	Full	Full	Full	Full	Full

This attribute is now deprecated, and is highly presentational in its nature. The desired visual effects can all be achieved with CSS and, as such, this attribute shouldn't be used—it's presented here for informational purposes only.

Table Elements

 **bgcolor** *for <table>*

`bgcolor="color"`

	SPEC	
deprecated	required	version
YES	NO	HTML 2
BROWSER SUPPORT		
IE5.5+	FF1+	Saf1.3+ Op9.2+
FULL	FULL	FULL FULL

Example

The bgcolor for this `table` is set to `"#99FF66"` (a light green shade):

```
<table bgcolor="#99FF66">
  <tr>
    <th>Account Type</th>
    <th>Interest Rate</th>
  </tr>
  <tr>
    <td>Smart</td>
    <td>From 2%</td>
  </tr>
  <tr>
    <td>Young Saver</td>
    <td>From 1.6%</td>
  </tr>
</table>
```

Unless otherwise specified in CSS, a `table` won't display a background color—whatever background is applied to the page will show through. The presentational (and deprecated) `bgcolor` attribute allows you to set a background for the table using a recognized color name or hexadecimal value, as Figure 8.1 illustrates.

Account Type	Interest Rate
Smart	From 2%
Young Saver	From 1.6%

Figure 8.3: A table to which a background color is applied

Value

This attribute takes as its value a recognized color name (for example, `"blue"` or `"red"`)[1], or a value specified in hexadecimal notation (such as `"#003366"`). Note

---

[1] http://reference.sitepoint.com/html/color-names/

table   409

that it's *not* possible to use shorthand hexadecimal values in HTML as you can in CSS—for example, you can't express "#cceeff" as "#cef".

Compatibility

Internet Explorer			Firefox			Safari			Opera
5.5	6.0	7.0	1.0	1.5	2.0	1.3	2.0	3.0	9.2
Full	Full	Full	Full	Full	Full	Full	Full	Full	Full

This attribute is now deprecated, and is highly presentational in its nature. The desired visual effects can all be achieved with CSS and, as such, this attribute shouldn't be used—it's presented here for informational purposes only.

 **border** *for <table>*

SPEC		
deprecated	required	version
NO	NO	HTML 2
BROWSER SUPPORT		
IE5.5+ FF1+ Saf1.3+ Op9.2+		
FULL FULL FULL FULL		

```
border="number"
```

Example

The border for this table is set to "1" pixel:

```
<table border="1">
  <tr>
    <th>Account Type</th>
    <th>Interest Rate</th>
  </tr>
  <tr>
    <td>Smart</td>
    <td>From 2%</td>
  </tr>
  <tr>
    <td>Young Saver</td>
    <td>From 1.6%</td>
  </tr>
</table>
```

A visible grid doesn't appear around the table cells by default, which has the potential to make the table quite difficult to read and understand (and bear in mind that this is a very simple example). In order to create structure and order around the data that's presented, use the `border` attribute. It applies a border to each cell, and to the table as a whole.

If we change the value of the `border` attribute, from `"1"` to `"5"` for example, the size of the border around the table will change, but the border inside the table—between the table cells—won't change size, as Figure 8.4 reflects.

Account Type	Interest Rate
Smart	From 2%
Young Saver	From 1.6%

Account Type	Interest Rate
Smart	From 2%
Young Saver	From 1.6%

Figure 8.4: Two tables, one with a border of one pixel, another with a border of five pixels

Value

This attribute takes a numerical value, which reflects a pixel measurement.

Compatibility

Internet Explorer			Firefox			Safari			Opera
5.5	6.0	7.0	1.0	1.5	2.0	1.3	2.0	3.0	9.2
Full	Full	Full	Full	Full	Full	Full	Full	Full	Full

The `border` attribute isn't deprecated—it can be used in a perfectly valid web page. However, although it enjoys full support, it's preferable not to specify a `border`. Instead, use CSS to apply the border style and color.

table   411

cellpadding _for <table>_

```
cellpadding="number"
```

SPEC		
deprecated	required	version
NO	NO	HTML 2
BROWSER SUPPORT			
IE5.5+	FF1+	Saf1.3+	Op9.2+
FULL	FULL	FULL	FULL

Example

The `cellpadding` for this `table` is set to "5" pixels:

```
<table border="1" cellpadding="5">
  <tr>
    <th>Account Type</th>
    <th>Interest Rate</th>
  </tr>
  <tr>
    <td>Smart</td>
    <td>From 2%</td>
  </tr>
  <tr>
    <td>Young Saver</td>
    <td>From 1.6%</td>
  </tr>
</table>
```

Use the `cellpadding` attribute to create some space around the contents of table cells (in `th` (p. 454) and `td` (p. 428) elements). The effect of this attribute's application won't be immediately obvious unless you've also set a `border` attribute for the table (p. 409), as Figure 8.5 reveals.

The `cellpadding` attribute is similar to the `cellspacing` (p. 413) attribute, which is used to create space between and outside of the table cells.

Account Type	Interest Rate
Smart	From 2%
Young Saver	From 1.6%

Account Type	Interest Rate
Smart	From 2%
Young Saver	From 1.6%

Figure 8.5: Two tables, with `cellpadding` values of five and ten pixels, respectively

Value

This attribute takes a numerical value, which reflects a pixel measurement.

Compatibility

Internet Explorer			Firefox			Safari			Opera
5.5	6.0	7.0	1.0	1.5	2.0	1.3	2.0	3.0	9.2
Full	Full	Full	Full	Full	Full	Full	Full	Full	Full

This attribute suffers no compatibility problems—excellent browser support is provided for it. However, you're advised to use the CSS `padding` property to set padding on `th` and `td` elements, as it's easy to do, is also well supported, and offers greater flexibility than does `cellpadding`.

table   413

cellspacing *for <table>*

```
cellspacing="number"
```

SPEC		
deprecated	required	version
NO	NO	HTML 2
BROWSER SUPPORT			
IE5.5+	FF1+	Saf1.3+	Op9.2+
FULL	FULL	FULL	FULL

Example

The `cellspacing` for this `table` is set to `"5"` pixels:

```
<table border="1" cellspacing="5">
  <tr>
    <th>Account Type</th>
    <th>Interest Rate</th>
  </tr>
  <tr>
    <td>Smart</td>
    <td>From 2%</td>
  </tr>
  <tr>
    <td>Young Saver</td>
    <td>From 1.6%</td>
  </tr>
</table>
```

The `cellspacing` attribute is used to create space around (that is, outside of) table cells. Think of table cells as bricks, and the `cellspacing` as the mortar in between. You can change the thickness of that mortar by altering the `cellspacing` value, as Figure 8.6 shows.

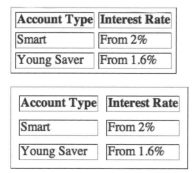

Figure 8.6: Two tables, with `cellspacing` values of five and ten pixels, respectively

There is a CSS-based alternative to the HTML `cellspacing` attribute, called `border-spacing`,[2] but it is not supported by Internet Explorer versions 7 and earlier. So while it's usually better to use the CSS approach, that's not possible for this particular attribute without ignoring what is currently the most commonly used browser.

The `cellspacing` attribute is similar to the `cellpadding` (p. 411) attribute, which is used to create space around the content inside table cells.

Value

This attribute takes a numerical value, which reflects a pixel measurement.

Compatibility

Internet Explorer			Firefox			Safari			Opera
5.5	6.0	7.0	1.0	1.5	2.0	1.3	2.0	3.0	9.2
Full	Full	Full	Full	Full	Full	Full	Full	Full	Full

It causes no compatibility issues, and has excellent support across all tested browsers.

---

[2] http://reference.sitepoint.com/css/border-spacing/

table   415

 frame *for <table>*

SPEC		
deprecated	required	version
NO	NO	HTML 2
BROWSER SUPPORT		
IE5.5+	FF1+	Saf3+	Op9.2+
BUGGY	FULL	FULL	FULL

```
frame=" { above | below | border | box | hsides |
lhs | rhs | void | vsides } "
```

Example

The frame for this table is set to "hsides":

```html
<table frame="hsides">
  <tr>
    <th>Account Type</th>
    <th>Interest Rate</th>
  </tr>
  <tr>
    <td>Smart</td>
    <td>From 2%</td>
  </tr>
  <tr>
    <td>Young Saver</td>
    <td>From 1.6%</td>
  </tr>
</table>
```

The frame attribute allows you to set a border on given edges of a table, as Figure 8.7 shows, or to a combination of edges. For example, you can use it to set a border on just the right-hand side ("rhs"), or on just the horizontal edges of the table. As such, this attribute is slightly more powerful than the humble border (p. 409). However, all of the effects that this attribute makes achievable can be achieved with CSS (using the border-top, border-bottom, border-left, and border-right properties)—and this would be the better option.

Table Elements

frame - above

Account Type	Interest Rate
Smart	From 2%
Young Saver	From 1.6%

frame - below

Account Type	Interest Rate
Smart	From 2%
Young Saver	From 1.6%

frame - border

Account Type	Interest Rate
Smart	From 2%
Young Saver	From 1.6%

frame - box

Account Type	Interest Rate
Smart	From 2%
Young Saver	From 1.6%

frame - hsides

Account Type	Interest Rate
Smart	From 2%
Young Saver	From 1.6%

frame - lhs

Account Type	Interest Rate
Smart	From 2%
Young Saver	From 1.6%

frame - rhs

Account Type	Interest Rate
Smart	From 2%
Young Saver	From 1.6%

frame - void

Account Type	Interest Rate
Smart	From 2%
Young Saver	From 1.6%

frame - vsides

Account Type	Interest Rate
Smart	From 2%
Young Saver	From 1.6%

Figure 8.7: Comparison of different frame values (viewed in Firefox)

Value

The recognized attribute values are as shown in the syntax section.

Compatibility

Internet Explorer			Firefox			Safari			Opera
5.5	6.0	7.0	1.0	1.5	2.0	1.3	2.0	3.0	9.2
Buggy	Buggy	Buggy	Full	Full	Full	None	None	Full	Full

table   417

Most browsers tested do *something* with this attribute's values (with the exception of Safari versions 1 and 2, which ignore them completely), but Internet Explorer interprets `frame` very differently from the other browsers. Firefox, Opera, and Safari 3 all render the borders on the `table`'s edges only, while IE renders the borders on the cells within the table.

 # rules *for <table>*

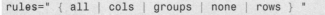
`rules=" { all | cols | groups | none | rows } "`

SPEC		
deprecated	required	version
NO	NO	HTML 2
BROWSER SUPPORT		
IE5.5+	FF1+	Saf3+	Op9.2+
BUGGY	FULL	BUGGY	FULL

Example

The `rules` attribute for this `table` is set to `"rows"`:

```
<table rules="rows">
  <tr>
    <th>Account Type</th>
    <th>Interest Rate</th>
  </tr>
  <tr>
    <td>Smart</td>
    <td>From 2%</td>
  </tr>
  <tr>
    <td>Young Saver</td>
    <td>From 1.6%</td>
  </tr>
</table>
```

The `rules` attribute allows you to set borders (also called rules, surprise, surprise!) inside the `table` at the boundaries between cells. For example, you can set the `rules` to `"rows"`, as you can see in Figure 8.8. This practice creates the dividing lines, but doesn't affect the table's border (for that, you'd use the `frame` (p. 415) attribute—the `rules` attribute's partner in crime—or the `border` (p. 409) attribute).

Account Type	Interest Rate
Smart	From 2%
Young Saver	From 1.6%

Account Type	Interest Rate
Smart	From 2%
Young Saver	From 1.6%

Account Type	Interest Rate
Smart	From 2%
Young Saver	From 1.6%

Figure 8.8: Three tables whose `rules` attributes are set to `"rows"`, `"cols"`, and `"all"`

Table Elements

Value

The recognized attribute values are as shown in the syntax section.

Compatibility

Internet Explorer			Firefox			Safari			Opera
5.5	6.0	7.0	1.0	1.5	2.0	1.3	2.0	3.0	9.2
Buggy	Buggy	Buggy	Full	Full	Full	None	None	Buggy	Full

Most browsers tested do *something* with this attribute's values (with the exception of Safari 1 and 2, which ignore them completely), but there were still some problems. Internet Explorer insists on adding a border around the table, not just to the boundaries between table cells; Safari 3 doesn't apply a border around the table, but adds a border on the outside edges of the affected cells, unlike Firefox, which adds the correct border. The differences are demonstrated in Figure 8.9, which shows the rendering of the table markup in the example HTML above (`rules="rows"`) compared in the three browsers mentioned.

Account Type	Interest Rate
Smart	From 2%
Young Saver	From 1.6%

Account Type	Interest Rate
Smart	From 2%
Young Saver	From 1.6%

Account Type	Interest Rate
Smart	From 2%
Young Saver	From 1.6%

Figure 8.9: The `rules` attribute in action, as viewed in Firefox, Safari, and Internet Explorer

table   419

 **summary** *for <table>*

```
summary="string"
```

	SPEC	
deprecated	required	version
NO	NO	HTML 2
BROWSER SUPPORT		
IE5.5+	FF1+	Saf1.3+	Op9.2+
FULL	FULL	FULL	FULL

Example

The summary for this table provides more information about its contents:

```
<table summary="Interest Rates of accounts for young savers,
    correct as at 12 January 2008">
  <tr>
    <th>Account Type</th>
    <th>Interest Rate</th>
  </tr>
  <tr>
    <td>Smart</td>
    <td>From 2%</td>
  </tr>
  <tr>
    <td>Young Saver</td>
    <td>From 1.6%</td>
  </tr>
</table>
```

The optional summary attribute isn't intended to be displayed on the screen (for that, you should probably use a caption (p. 384) element), but it may be used to provide extra information about the table's contents for non-visual web browsers. For example, a user accessing the web page with a screen reader may find a summary useful—it lets the user decide at that point whether or not the table is of any use or interest. He or she can skip straight to the following content if the answer to that question is "no." Of course, for sighted users, a quick glance at the table as a whole provides an adequate summary.

Value

The value for summary is a brief summary of the table's structure or purpose.

Table Elements

Compatibility

Internet Explorer			Firefox			Safari			Opera
5.5	6.0	7.0	1.0	1.5	2.0	1.3	2.0	3.0	9.2
Full	Full	Full	Full	Full	Full	Full	Full	Full	Full

This attribute's compatibility is debatable. No browser renders it on the page, so it's difficult to say whether or not any browsers have difficulties with it. The biggest question regarding its compatibility is really centered on assistive technology—for example, screen readers—and whether they are capable of retrieving that useful summary information.

width *for <table>*

```
width=" { number | percentage } "
```

SPEC		
deprecated	required	version
NO	NO	HTML 2
BROWSER SUPPORT		
IE5.5+	FF1+	Saf1.3+	Op9.2+
FULL	FULL	FULL	FULL

Example

This width attribute is set to "400" pixels:

```
<table width="400">
  <tr>
    <th>Account Type</th>
    <th>Interest Rate</th>
  </tr>
  <tr>
    <td>Smart</td>
    <td>From 2%</td>
  </tr>
  <tr>
    <td>Young Saver</td>
    <td>From 1.6%</td>
  </tr>
</table>
```

Unless a width is set, a table will take up only the width it requires (obviously this width will depend on the amount of content in each of the table cells). Browser support for this attribute is excellent—whether the dimension is set in pixels or as a percentage—but, like many of the table element's attributes, it's better to use CSS to set its width.

Value

This attribute takes a number representing the width of the `table` in pixels, or a percentage.

Compatibility

Internet Explorer			Firefox			Safari			Opera
5.5	6.0	7.0	1.0	1.5	2.0	1.3	2.0	3.0	9.2
Full	Full	Full	Full	Full	Full	Full	Full	Full	Full

It causes no compatibility issues, and has excellent support across all tested browsers.

tbody

```
<tbody>
</tbody>
```

SPEC		
deprecated	empty	version
NO	NO	HTML 4
BROWSER SUPPORT			
IE5.5+	FF1+	Saf1.3+	Op9.2+
PARTIAL	PARTIAL	PARTIAL	PARTIAL

Example

This tbody element wraps around the two rows containing the table data:

```
<table summary="Interest Rates">
  <caption>Interest Rates</caption>
  <thead>
    <tr>
      <th>Account Type</th>
      <th>Interest Rate</th>
    </tr>
  </thead>
  <tbody>
    <tr>
      <td>Smart</td>
      <td>From 2%</td>
    </tr>
    <tr>
      <td>Young Saver</td>
      <td>From 1.6%</td>
    </tr>
  </tbody>
</table>
```

Table Elements

Just as you can logically group all the header content in a table using thead (p. 476), you can do the same for the main body of the table data using tbody (tbody is a shortening of *table body*). By default, a tbody will not affect the display of the table in any way. However, you may use this element to affect the table's display via CSS (for example, you may choose to set the height of the tbody area to a fixed amount, and let the content in that area scroll, so that the table's header and footer sections remain visible on screen even when the main bulk of the table content is quite lengthy).

Use This For ...

This element is used to group the bulk of the table's content (that is, anything other than the headers, which are contained in the thead (p. 476), and the footer area, which is contained by tfoot (p. 446)).

Compatibility

Internet Explorer			Firefox			Safari			Opera
5.5	6.0	7.0	1.0	1.5	2.0	1.3	2.0	3.0	9.2
Partial	Partial	Partial	Partial	Partial	Partial	Partial	Partial	Partial	Partial

By itself—with none of the element-specific attributes detailed below applied—the presence of a tbody makes no visual difference to the table. For a true indication of compatibility issues, refer to each individual attribute to see what works and what fails.

Other Relevant Stuff

 thead (p. 476)

logically groups header elements in a table

 tfoot (p. 446)

logically groups elements that comprise the footer area of a table's content

align *for <tbody>*

`align=" { center | char | justify | left | right } "`

	SPEC	
deprecated	required	version
NO	NO	HTML 4

BROWSER SUPPORT			
IE5.5+	FF1+	Saf1.3+	Op9.2+
PARTIAL	PARTIAL	PARTIAL	PARTIAL

Example

This `tbody` will set all text inside the nested `td` elements to align to the right:

```
<table summary="Interest Rates" width="400" border="1">
  <caption>Interest Rates</caption>
  <thead>
    <tr>
      <th>Account Type</th>
      <th>Interest Rate</th>
    </tr>
  </thead>
  <tbody align="right">
    <tr>
      <td>Smart</td>
      <td>From 2%</td>
    </tr>
    <tr>
      <td>Young Saver</td>
      <td>From 1.6%</td>
    </tr>
  </tbody>
</table>
```

The `align` attribute can be used to override the default horizontal alignment of text inside table cells contained inside the `tbody`. On the assumption that `th` (table headers) have been used inside the `thead` area, and `td` elements have been used for table body data, the default alignment ranges the text to the left. By applying the `align` attribute to the `tbody`, you could change that alignment, for example, to `"center"` or `"right"` (as shown in the example HTML).

Value

The recognized attribute values are as shown in the syntax section.

Table Elements

Compatibility

Internet Explorer			Firefox			Safari			Opera
5.5	6.0	7.0	1.0	1.5	2.0	1.3	2.0	3.0	9.2
Partial	Partial	Partial	Partial	Partial	Partial	Partial	Partial	Partial	Partial

In the browsers tested, `"left"`, `"right"`, `"center"`, and `"justify"` alignments are all honored, but the `"char"` value, which is used alongside the char (p. 424) and charoff (p. 426) attributes, is ignored by all (or incorrectly deciphered as `"center"`).

char *for <tbody>*

```
char="character"
```

SPEC		
deprecated	required	version
NO	NO	HTML 4
BROWSER SUPPORT			
IE7	FF2	Saf3	Op9.2
NONE	NONE	NONE	NONE

Example

This align attribute is set to match the position of the % character:

```
<table summary="Interest Rates" width="400" border="1">
  <caption>Interest Rates</caption>
  <thead>
    <tr>
      <th>Account Type</th>
      <th>Interest Rate (%)</th>
    </tr>
  </thead>
  <tbody align="char" char="%">
    <tr>
      <td>Smart</td>
      <td>From 2%</td>
    </tr>
    <tr>
      <td>Young Saver</td>
      <td>From 1.6%</td>
    </tr>
  </tbody>
</table>
```

It may be useful in tables that contain financial information to align contents beyond the simple `"left"`, `"right"`, and `"center"` determinations. For example, you might align numerical data to a decimal point, or some other symbol. The char attribute allows you to define the character against which data is aligned, but this only works if the align (p. 423) attribute has also been set to "char".

Value

This attribute takes as its value a single character that appears in the table, such as a decimal point character.

Compatibility

Internet Explorer			Firefox			Safari			Opera
5.5	6.0	7.0	1.0	1.5	2.0	1.3	2.0	3.0	9.2
None	None	None	None	None	None	None	None	Nonc	None

This attribute is poorly supported and should not be relied upon.

Table Elements

 **charoff** *for <tbody>*

`charoff="number"`

SPEC		
deprecated	required	version
NO	NO	HTML 4
BROWSER SUPPORT			
IE7	FF2	Saf3	Op9.2
NONE	NONE	NONE	NONE

Example

Here, the character alignment offset is set to "2" characters:

```
<table summary="Interest Rates" width="400" border="1">
  <caption>Interest Rates</caption>
  <thead>
    <tr>
      <th>Account Type</th>
      <th>Interest Rate (%)</th>
    </tr>
  </thead>
  <tbody align="char" char="%" charoff="2">
    <tr>
      <td>Smart</td>
      <td>From 2%</td>
    </tr>
    <tr>
      <td>Young Saver</td>
      <td>From 1.6%</td>
    </tr>
  </tbody>
</table>
```

If the `align` attribute is set to `"char"`, and the `char` attribute has been set to a character—thus telling the browser that cell contents should be aligned to a given character—the `charoff` attribute is used to set a *char*acter *off*set. If a `charoff` figure of `"2"` is chosen, as shown in the example HTML, the browser should align the cell contents two characters to the right of the specified character. If `charoff` were a negative value, for example `"-2"`, the alignment should be offset two characters to the left of the specified character. Note that there are a few uses of the word "should" in this paragraph, which *should* (there we go again) give you a hint about what to expect in the Compatibility section for this attribute!

Value

This attribute takes an integer value, which can be positive or negative.

Compatibility

Internet Explorer			Firefox			Safari			Opera
5.5	6.0	7.0	1.0	1.5	2.0	1.3	2.0	3.0	9.2
None	None	None	None	None	None	None	None	None	None

This attribute is poorly supported and should not be relied upon.

 **valign** *for <tbody>*

SPEC		
deprecated	required	version
NO	NO	HTML 4
BROWSER SUPPORT		
IE5.5+	FF1+	Saf1.3+	Op9.2+
PARTIAL	PARTIAL	PARTIAL	PARTIAL

```
valign=" { baseline | bottom | middle | top } "
```

Example

The valign attribute is set to "bottom" on this narrow table:

```
<table summary="Interest Rates" width="200" border="1">
  <caption>Interest Rates</caption>
  <thead>
    <tr>
      <th>Account Type (Name titles as per Spring 2006 range)</th>
      <th>Interest Rate</th>
    </tr>
  </thead>
  <tbody valign="bottom">
    <tr>
      <td>Smart</td>
      <td>From 2%</td>
    </tr>
    <tr>
      <td>Young Saver</td>
      <td>From 1.6%</td>
    </tr>
  </tbody>
</table>
```

In a very similar manner to the align attribute (p. 423) for this element, valign allows you to override the default alignment for table cells inside the body of the table.

Value

The recognized attribute values are as shown in the syntax section.

Table Elements

Compatibility

Internet Explorer			Firefox			Safari			Opera
5.5	6.0	7.0	1.0	1.5	2.0	1.3	2.0	3.0	9.2
Partial	Partial	Partial	Partial	Partial	Partial	Partial	Partial	Partial	Partial

In the browsers tested, "bottom", "middle", and "top" alignments are all honored, but the "baseline" value is ignored by all.

---

td

```
<td abbr="string" axis="string" colspan="number"
headers="cell ID …" rowspan="number">
</td>
```

SPEC		
deprecated	empty	version
NO	NO	HTML 2
BROWSER SUPPORT		
IE5.5+	FF1+	Saf1.3+ Op9.2+
FULL	FULL	FULL FULL

Example

These td elements are used in a two-column row:

```
<tr>
  <td>Smart</td>
  <td>From 2%</td>
</tr>
```

You can use two kinds of cells in a table: the th (p. 454) element is reserved for cells that contain header information, but the td can be used for any kind of data. Aside from that difference of usage and meaning (and the default presentational differences—th text is bold and centered while td text is non-bold and left-aligned), in almost every other way, the td element behaves, and has the same attributes, as the th element.

The axis (p. 432) and scope (p. 443) attributes can also be used in td elements, and this is a perfectly valid use of HTML, but you're advised to reserve your usage of these attributes to table headers only. However, the headers (p. 438) and id (p. 501) are almost certainly going to be used in td elements for the purpose of creating relationships between the td content and the header cells.

Finally, this element uses the colspan (p. 436) and rowspan (p. 441) attributes when the content of the cell needs to run across multiple columns or rows.

Use This For ...

The td is used for content in a table that represents standard data (that's to say, it's not a header cell, and most likely falls under a column or row header).

Compatibility

Internet Explorer			Firefox			Safari			Opera
5.5	6.0	7.0	1.0	1.5	2.0	1.3	2.0	3.0	9.2
Full	Full	Full	Full	Full	Full	Full	Full	Full	Full

It causes no compatibility issues, and has excellent support across all tested browsers.

Other Relevant Stuff

 th (p. 454)

defines a header cell in a table

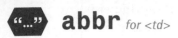 **abbr** *for <td>*

`abbr="string"`

	SPEC	
deprecated	required	version
NO	NO	HTML 4
BROWSER SUPPORT		
IE5.5+ FF1+	Saf1.3+	Op9.2+
FULL FULL	FULL	FULL

Example

This table, which lists vehicle details, shows the `abbr` attribute at `th` and `td` level:

```
<table border="1">
  <tr>
    <th abbr="Make">Car manufacturer (make)</th>
    <th abbr="Model">Vehicle model (name/spec)</th>
    <th abbr="Revised">Date of last revision </th>
  </tr>
  <tr>
    <td abbr="VW">Volkswagen</td>
    <td abbr="Golf">Golf 2.8 GTi</td>
    <td abbr="2007">June 2007</td>
  </tr>
</table>
```

The `abbr` attribute is another one that makes no visual difference to the `table` and its contents but, like the table's `summary` attribute (p. 419), provides additional information that may be useful for people accessing the content using assistive technology such as screen readers. It's normally put to use in the context of the `abbr` (p. 456) element, but it's valid to use `abbr` with `td` elements as well.

Value

This element takes an abbreviated (but still meaningful) form of the `td` content.

Compatibility

Internet Explorer			Firefox			Safari			Opera
5.5	6.0	7.0	1.0	1.5	2.0	1.3	2.0	3.0	9.2
Full	Full	Full	Full	Full	Full	Full	Full	Full	Full

This attribute's compatibility is debatable. No browser renders it on the page, so it's difficult to say whether or not any browsers have difficulties with it. The biggest question regarding its compatibility is really centered on assistive technology—for example, screen readers—and whether they are capable of retrieving that useful summary information.

 **align** *for <td>*

```
align=" { center | justify | left | right } "
```

	SPEC	
deprecated	required	version
NO	NO	HTML 4
	BROWSER SUPPORT	
IE5.5+	FF1+	Saf1.3+	Op9.2+
FULL	FULL	FULL	FULL

Example

Here, the browser default alignment of `"left"` in the `td` is overridden to align the content `"right"`:

```
<tr>
  <td align="right">Fred</td>
  <td align="right">fred@megacorp.com</td>
  <td align="right">123456</td>
  <td rowspan="2" align="right">1/A</td>
</tr>
```

The usual alignment that browsers apply to content inside `td` elements is `"left"`, but you can override that using the `align` attribute. You're better off to use CSS to set the text alignment (you could also apply the `align` attribute to the parent `tr` element (p. 486), rather than repeating it for each cell in the row, but CSS is still the best option).

Value

The recognized attribute values are as shown in the syntax section.

Compatibility

Internet Explorer			Firefox			Safari			Opera
5.5	6.0	7.0	1.0	1.5	2.0	1.3	2.0	3.0	9.2
Full	Full	Full	Full	Full	Full	Full	Full	Full	Full

It causes no compatibility issues, and has excellent support across all tested browsers.

Table Elements

axis *for <td>*

`axis="string"`

SPEC		
deprecated	required	version
NO	NO	HTML 4
BROWSER SUPPORT			
IE7	FF2	Saf3	Op9.2
NONE	NONE	NONE	NONE

Example

In this code, four table headers are grouped into three categories—name, contact, and location—using `axis`:

```
<tr>
  <td axis="name">Fred</td>
  <td axis="contact">fred@megacorp.com</td>
  <td axis="contact">123456</td>
  <td axis="location">1/A</td>
</tr>
```

The `axis` attribute provides a mechanism for grouping related columns or rows of information. In the example above, there are four pieces of information, but the email and phone details could be grouped together as points of contact. You're advised, however, to reserve the use of `axis` for the `th` element (p. 458) (if you feel the urge to use it, which may be unlikely, given its poor support).

Value

This attribute can take as its value any name that the developer chooses, as long as it doesn't contain spaces or special characters.

Compatibility

Internet Explorer			Firefox			Safari			Opera
5.5	6.0	7.0	1.0	1.5	2.0	1.3	2.0	3.0	9.2
None	None	None	None	None	None	None	None	None	None

Very poor support is provided for this attribute. Refer to the compatibility section for this attribute as applied to the `th` element (p. 458) for more information.

bgcolor *for <td>*

```
bgcolor="color"
```

SPEC		
deprecated	required	version
YES	NO	HTML 2
BROWSER SUPPORT			
IE5.5+	FF1+	Saf1.3+	Op9.2+
FULL	FULL	FULL	FULL

Example

A different `bgcolor` is applied to several `td` element in this `table`:

```
<tr>
  <td bgcolor="#99FFFF">Jane</td>
  <td bgcolor="#FFFF99">jane@megacorp.com</td>
  <td bgcolor="#99FFFF">777444</td>
</tr>
<tr>
  <td bgcolor="#FFFF99">Alison</td>
  <td bgcolor="#99FFFF">alison@megacorp</td>
  <td bgcolor="#FFFF99">888652</td>
</tr>
```

Table Elements

Unless otherwise specified in CSS, a `td` will be transparent, and will allow whatever background is on the page (or whatever color has been specified at a higher level in the table) to show through. The presentational (and deprecated) `bgcolor` attribute allows you to set a background for specific `td` elements using a recognized color name or hexadecimal value.

Work Contact Points			
Name	**Email**	**Phone**	**Floor/Block**
Fred	fred@megacorp.com	123456	1/A
Jon	jon@megacorp.com	234567	
Bill	bill@megacorp.com	345678	3/C
Jane	jane@megacorp.com	777444	
Alison	alison@megacorp	888652	

Figure 8.10: A table with far too many background colors set

Value

This attribute takes as its value a recognized color name (for example, `"blue"` or `"red"`)[3], or a value specified in hexadecimal notation (such as `"#003366"`). Note

[3] http://reference.sitepoint.com/html/color-names/

that it's *not* possible to use shorthand hexadecimal values in HTML as you can in CSS—for example, you can't express "#cceeff" as "#cef".

Compatibility

Internet Explorer			Firefox			Safari			Opera
5.5	6.0	7.0	1.0	1.5	2.0	1.3	2.0	3.0	9.2
Full	Full	Full	Full	Full	Full	Full	Full	Full	Full

This attribute is now deprecated, and is highly presentational in its nature. The desired visual effects can all be achieved with CSS and, as such, this attribute shouldn't be used—it's presented here for informational purposes only.

char *for <td>*

```
char="character"
```

SPEC		
deprecated	required	version
NO	NO	HTML 4
BROWSER SUPPORT		
IE7	FF2	Saf3	Op9.2
NONE	NONE	NONE	NONE

Example

In this example the second cell is aligned to the "%" character:

```
<tr>
  <td>Young Saver</td>
  <td align="char" char="%">From 1.6%</td>
</tr>
```

It may be useful in tables that contain financial information to align contents beyond the simple "left", "right", and "center" determinations. For example, you might align numerical data to a decimal point, or some other symbol. The char attribute allows you to define the character against which data is aligned, but this only works if the align (p. 431) attribute has also been set to "char".

Value

This attribute takes as its value a single character that appears in the table; for example, a decimal point character.

Compatibility

Internet Explorer			Firefox			Safari			Opera
5.5	6.0	7.0	1.0	1.5	2.0	1.3	2.0	3.0	9.2
None	None	None	None	None	None	None	None	None	None

This attribute is poorly supported and should not be relied upon.

charoff _for <td>_

SPEC		
deprecated	required	version
NO	NO	HTML 4
BROWSER SUPPORT		
IE7	FF2	Saf3	Op9.2
NONE	NONE	NONE	NONE

```
charoff="number"
```

Example

In this example, the contents of the cell are aligned two characters to the right of the "%" character:

```
<tr>
  <td>Young Saver</td>
  <td align="char" char="%" charoff="2">From 1.6%</td>
</tr>
```

If the `align` attribute is set to `"char"`, and the `char` attribute has been set to a character—thus telling the browser that cell contents should be aligned to a given character—the `charoff` attribute is used to set a _char_acter _off_set. If a `charoff` figure of `"2"` is chosen, as shown in the example HTML, the browser should align the cell contents two characters to the right of the specified character. If `charoff` were a negative value (for example `"-2"`) the alignment should be offset two characters to the left of the specified character. Note that there are a few uses of the word "should" in this paragraph, which _should_ (there we go again) give you a hint about what to expect in the Compatibility section for this attribute!

Value

This attribute takes an integer value, which can be positive or negative.

Compatibility

Internet Explorer			Firefox			Safari			Opera
5.5	6.0	7.0	1.0	1.5	2.0	1.3	2.0	3.0	9.2
None	None	None	None	None	None	None	None	None	None

This attribute is poorly supported and should not be relied upon.

colspan *for <td>*

```
colspan="number"
```

SPEC		
deprecated	required	version
NO	NO	HTML 3.2
BROWSER SUPPORT		
IE5.5+	FF1+	Saf1.3+ Op9.2+
PARTIAL	FULL	PARTIAL PARTIAL

Example

This example shows an extract from a calendar, with a person's availability apparently spanning the whole day, as shown in Figure 8.11:

```
<tr>
  <th scope="row">Tue</th>
  <td colspan="4">Free</td>
</tr>
```

Just as the th element uses colspans, so can the td element to allow data to be shared across numerous columns in a table. The concept is best explained by comparing the example HTML above with Figure 8.11 (where we indicate a person's availability for Tuesday—when that person is free for the whole day—by spanning the cell across four time slots).

	Morning	Afternoon	Evening	Overnight
Mon	Free	Busy	Free	
Tue	Free			
Wed	Busy			
Thur	Free		Busy	
Fri	Free			

Figure 8.11: colspans applied to several cells in a table to show someone's availability for work

When you're introducing a colspan attribute, take care to ensure that each row is equivalent to the number of cells that would ordinary appear in the row. Some tables can become quite complicated with a mixture of colspan and rowspan (p. 441) attributes, and this is not something that you're advised to hand-code—that's just asking for trouble! It's much better to use a WYSIWYG editor, such as Dreamweaver, MS Expression, or something similar, which will allow you to merge and unmerge cells very easily, and takes care of these attributes for you.

Note that when you use the rowspan attribute, you can't span a cell beyond the boundary of its containing rowgroup (namely the thead (p. 476), tfoot (p. 446), or tbody (p. 421) elements). So if the tbody comprises ten rows, the rowspan of a cell that's defined in the first row can't have a value greater than "10".

Value

This attribute takes a number, which should equal the number of cells that this single td should replace. There's also a special value of "0", which should inform the browser to span the cell to the end of the current group of columns.

Compatibility

Internet Explorer			Firefox			Safari			Opera
5.5	6.0	7.0	1.0	1.5	2.0	1.3	2.0	3.0	9.2
Partial	Partial	Partial	Full	Full	Full	Partial	Partial	Partial	Partial

Browser support for colspan is generally good, with one exception: the rendering of colspan="0". Only Firefox successfully spans all the remaining columns properly. The other browsers tested render the cell in the first column only.

Table Elements

headers *for* `<td>`

`headers="cell ID …"`

SPEC		
deprecated	required	version
NO	NO	HTML 4
BROWSER SUPPORT			
IE5.5+	FF1+	Saf1.3+	Op9.2+
FULL	FULL	FULL	FULL

Example

The following example shows how **headers** associates the header cells with the body cell contents:

```
<table border="1">
  <tr>
    <th colspan="4" id="hdr_work">Work Contact Points</th>
  </tr>
  <tr>
    <th id="hdr_n">Name</th>
    <th id="hdr_e">Email</th>
    <th id="hdr_p">Phone</th>
    <th id="hdr_f">Floor/Block</th>
  </tr>
  <tr>
    <td headers="hdr_work hdr_n">Fred</td>
    <td headers="hdr_work hdr_e">fred@megacorp.com</td>
    <td headers="hdr_work hdr_p">123456</td>
    <td headers="hdr_work hdr_f">1/A</td>
  </tr>
</table>
```

This attribute is another one that exists for the purposes of improving the accessibility and understanding of the data table for users who can't see the data—typically users with screen reading software. The **headers** attribute could be translated by the web browser as, "to understand what the data in this cell right here means, you need to be looking at that table header location over there and that other one over there." A user who views the cell in question can very quickly scan up the table from that point to view the table headers above and to the left of it, to get an understanding of what's going on. The **headers** attribute provides explicit instructions to the browser as to which table headers are relevant, by referencing the **id** attributes for the header cells in question.

Look at the example HTML above. Fred's email address is in this row:

```
<td headers="hdr_work hdr_e">fred@megacorp.com</td>
```

The `headers` attribute contains two values: `"hdr_work"` and `"hdr_e"`. If you look at the top of the table markup, you'll notice that those values are contained in the `id` attributes for the respective cells:

```
<th colspan="4" id="hdr_work">Work Contact Points</th>
```

Here's the other one:

```
<th id="hdr_e">Email</th>
```

So, with the correct keyboard combinations, a screen reader user could ascertain that the data is an email address (although that's not too difficult to guess, even without the extra markup!), and that it's a work contact point.

Note that in the example above, the result of the `headers` and `id` approach could also be achieved more simply using the `scope` (p. 443) attribute (even without the accessibility attributes applied, this table is simple enough that a screen reader user might be able to glean the necessary "orientation" information).

For more complex tables—those using `colspan` (p. 436) and `rowspan` (p. 441) attributes—the `scope` attribute will *not* suffice. You will need to use `headers` and `id` attributes to ensure that the table is usable for those operating assistive technology.

Value

This attribute takes a space-separated list of `id`s, which must match exactly (they're case-sensitive) with the `id` attributes for the cells to which they relate.

Compatibility

Internet Explorer			Firefox			Safari			Opera
5.5	6.0	7.0	1.0	1.5	2.0	1.3	2.0	3.0	9.2
Full	Full	Full	Full	Full	Full	Full	Full	Full	Full

It's difficult to state the browser compatibility for this attribute, as the issue depends on how well the assistive technology copes with this information. Regardless, the use of headers is the correct thing to do, so if you have complex tables, make an effort to ensure that you mark them up in a way that ensures that the data is accessible for all.

nowrap *for <td>*

`nowrap="nowrap"`

SPEC		
deprecated	required	version
YES	NO	HTML 3.2
BROWSER SUPPORT			
IE5.5+	FF1+	Saf1.3+	Op9.2+
FULL	FULL	FULL	FULL

Example

Here, the `td` contents are set not to wrap:

```
<td nowrap="nowrap">+44 01793 001100</td>
```

If you need to ensure that the contents of a cell always remains as they are, and don't wrap, use the `nowrap` attribute. You might use `nowrap` in a table cell that contains a telephone number which may contain one or more spaces, but should be output on one line to ensure clarity.

Note that this attribute, which is now deprecated, has a much better alternative in the form of the CSS property `white-space` (which can be set to `"nowrap"`).

The example HTML shows the `nowrap` attribute used in an XHTML-compliant way, but it could equally be expressed in HTML 4.01 as follows:

```
<td nowrap>+44 01793 001100</td>
```

Value

`"nowrap"` is the only value this attribute can take.

Compatibility

Internet Explorer			Firefox			Safari			Opera
5.5	6.0	7.0	1.0	1.5	2.0	1.3	2.0	3.0	9.2
Full	Full	Full	Full	Full	Full	Full	Full	Full	Full

Excellent browser support is provided, but given that this is a deprecated attribute, you should opt for the CSS alternative instead (td {white-space:nowrap}).

rowspan *for <td>*

```
rowspan="number"
```

SPEC		
deprecated	required	version
NO	NO	HTML 3.2
BROWSER SUPPORT		
IE5.5+	FF1+	Saf1.3+ Op9.2+
PARTIAL	FULL	PARTIAL FULL

Example

Here's an extract from a calendar, with a person's availability showing that half the day is free, and half is busy, as shown in Figure 8.12:

```
<tr>
  <th>Evening</th>
  <td rowspan="2">Free</td>
  <td rowspan="2">Busy</td>
</tr>
```

Where information may be relevant to multiple rows in the table, the cell containing that information can be set to span these rows using the rowspan attribute. In the colspan example for this element, which is shown in Figure 8.12, we saw a calendar that showed a person's work availability, with the days running along the *x* axis (horizontally) and time slots running down the *y* axis (vertically). If this table was turned through 90 degrees, it would convey exactly the same information, only the availability would span rows rather than columns. Compare the HTML example above with Figure 8.12.

	Mon	Tue	Wed	Thur	Fri
Morning	Free				
Afternoon	Busy	Free	Busy	Free	Free
Evening	Free			Busy	
Overnight					

Figure 8.12: Rowspans applied to several cells in this table showing someone's availability for work

When you're introducing a rowspan attribute, take care to ensure that every row adds up to same number of cells. Some tables can become quite complicated with

Table Elements

a mixture of `colspan` (p. 436) and `rowspan` attributes, and this is not something that you're advised to hand-code—that's just asking for trouble! It's much better to use a WYSIWYG editor, such as Dreamweaver, MS Expression, or something similar, which will allow you to merge and unmerge cells very easily, and takes care of these attributes for you.

Value

This attribute takes a number, which should equal the number of rows that the spanned `td` cell needs to cover. A special value of `"0"` can also be used to inform the browser to span the cell to the end of all the rows inside the current rowgroup (`thead` (p. 476), `tfoot` (p. 446), or `tbody` (p. 421)).

Compatibility

Internet Explorer			Firefox			Safari			Opera
5.5	6.0	7.0	1.0	1.5	2.0	1.3	2.0	3.0	9.2
Partial	Partial	Partial	Full	Full	Full	Partial	Partial	Partial	Full

Browser support for `rowspan` is generally good, with one exception: the rendering of `rowspan="0"`. Firefox and Opera are the only browsers tested that correctly span the cell to which this attribute is applied across all subsequent rows; the other browsers tested render the cell in the first row only.

scope *for <td>*

`scope=" { col | colgroup | row | rowgroup } "`

SPEC		
deprecated	required	version
NO	NO	HTML 4
BROWSER SUPPORT		
IE5.5+	FF1+	Saf1.3+	Op9.2+
FULL	FULL	FULL	FULL

Example

The information "Acme Industries" is associated with all the cells in its row:

```
<tr>
  <th>Company</th>
  <th>Employees</th>
  <th>Founded</th>
</tr>
<tr>
  <td scope="row">Acme Industries</td>
  <td>1000</td>
  <td>1978</td>
</tr>
```

Table Elements

The scope attribute provides a mechanism for associating the cell to which the attribute is applied with a column or row of data. Normally this attribute is used in the context of a table header—the th (p. 454) element—but it may be used validly with a td element.

Value

The most common attributes you'll use with scope are "col" and "row". However, if you've also marked up your table with colgroup (p. 396) elements, you can make use of the matching "colgroup" value to associate the header with all the columns in that colgroup. One other attribute is available: "rowgroup", which applies to a cell that's spanned using the rowspan (p. 441) attribute.

Compatibility

Internet Explorer			Firefox			Safari			Opera
5.5	6.0	7.0	1.0	1.5	2.0	1.3	2.0	3.0	9.2
Full	Full	Full	Full	Full	Full	Full	Full	Full	Full

It's difficult to state the browser compatibility for this attribute, as the issue depends on how well the assistive technology copes with this information. Regardless, the use of headers is the correct thing to do, so if you have complex tables, make an effort to ensure that you mark them up in a way that ensures that the data is accessible for all.

valign *for <td>*

```
valign=" { baseline | bottom | middle | top } "
```

	SPEC	
deprecated	required	version
NO	NO	HTML 4
BROWSER SUPPORT		
IE5.5+	FF1+	Saf1.3+	Op9.2+
PARTIAL	PARTIAL	PARTIAL	PARTIAL

Example

The valign is set to "bottom" for each of these td elements:

```
<tr>
  <td valign="bottom">Alison</td>
  <td valign="bottom">alison@megacorp</td>
  <td valign="bottom">888652</td>
</tr>
```

In a very similar manner to the align (p. 431) attribute for this element, the valign allows you to override the default vertical alignment for content inside table cells.

Note that there is both a better way, and a much, *much* better way to do this. The better way is *not* to set the valign at the td level, as in a bigger table with more columns, you'll end up with unnecessarily bloated markup. Instead, you could set valign at the parent tr level (p. 491). However, this is still less than ideal. The preferred method would be to set the alignment of text inside the td elements using the CSS vertical-align property.

Value

The recognized attribute values are as shown in the syntax section.

Compatibility

Internet Explorer			Firefox			Safari			Opera
5.5	6.0	7.0	1.0	1.5	2.0	1.3	2.0	3.0	9.2
Partial	Partial	Partial	Partial	Partial	Partial	Partial	Partial	Partial	Partial

In the browsers tested, `"bottom"`, `"middle"`, and `"top"` alignments are all honored, but the `"baseline"` value is ignored by all.

 # width _for <td>_

```
width=" { number | percentage } "
```

SPEC		
deprecated	required	version
YES	NO	HTML 2
BROWSER SUPPORT		
IE5.5+	FF1+	Saf1.3+	Op9.2+
FULL	FULL	FULL	FULL

Example

Here, the `width` attribute is set to `"50%"`:

```
<tr>
  <td width="50%">Smart</td>
  <td width="50%">From 2%</td>
</tr>
```

Unless a `width` is set, a `td` (and also `th` (p. 454)) will take up only the width it requires (obviously this will depend on the amount of content in each of the table cells). You can use the `width` attribute to fix the width to a value of your choosing, regardless of the content of the table cell, but be aware that this is a deprecated attribute. Width should be set using CSS.

If different `width` attributes are applied to several cells within the same column, the browser will render the column with the largest width value specified. It could be understood, therefore, that `width` is really a minimum width value: a table cell will increase in size if the content cannot be wrapped (as may be the case, for example, with a wide image, or a string of text that contains no spaces, such as a web site address).

Value

This attribute takes as its value a number that represents the width of the `td` element in pixels, or a percentage.

Table Elements

Compatibility

Internet Explorer			Firefox			Safari			Opera
5.5	6.0	7.0	1.0	1.5	2.0	1.3	2.0	3.0	9.2
Full	Full	Full	Full	Full	Full	Full	Full	Full	Full

It causes no compatibility issues, and has excellent support across all tested browsers.

tfoot

```
<tfoot>

</tfoot>
```

SPEC		
deprecated	empty	version
NO	NO	HTML 4
BROWSER SUPPORT		
IE5.5+	FF1+	Saf1.3+	Op9.2+
PARTIAL	PARTIAL	PARTIAL	PARTIAL

Example

The tfoot element wraps around the footer area of the table data:

```
<table summary="Interest Rates" width="400" border="1">
  <caption>Interest Rates</caption>
  <thead>
    <tr>
      <th>Account Type</th>
      <th>Interest Rate</th>
    </tr>
  </thead>
  <tfoot>
    <tr>
      <td>Recommended for you: 'Young Saver'</td>
      <td>Interest from: 1.6%</td>
    </tr>
  </tfoot>
  <tbody>
    <tr>
      <td>Smart</td>
      <td>From 2%</td>
    </tr>
    <tr>
      <td>Young Saver</td>
      <td>From 1.6%</td>
    </tr>
  </tbody>
</table>
```

The tfoot is an odd element in that it seems to defy logic. Common sense would suggest that if you have table headers wrapped in the thead (p. 476) element, followed by the body of the table wrapped in a `tbody` (p. 421), the footer content should naturally follow that . But this is not the case. Oddly enough, like a biology experiment gone wrong, the correct order for these elements is head, foot, body (or `thead`, `tfoot`, `tbody`, to use the correct element names).

There are reasons for this apparently illogical approach. By providing the table's header and footer content up-front in the `thead` and `tfoot` elements, respectively, the browser has the opportunity to render that information first, then incrementally fill the body of the table. This approach is often desirable when you're accessing the content over a very slow connection, or when the table runs to a considerable length (or both!).

Despite the `tfoot` content coming before the body of the table, the browsers we tested correctly identify that it's intended as footer content, and place it in the appropriate location—at the end of the table—as Figure 8.13 shows.

Interest Rates

Account Type	Interest Rate
Smart	From 2%
Young Saver	From 1.6%
Recommended for you: 'Young Saver'	Interest from: 1.6%

Figure 8.13: The footer content appears after the body, despite coming before it in the source

Use This For ...

This element is used to group the table's footer area (which may be a summary, an addition of column values, or some call to action based on the preceding content).

Compatibility

Internet Explorer			Firefox			Safari			Opera
5.5	6.0	7.0	1.0	1.5	2.0	1.3	2.0	3.0	9.2
Partial	Partial	Partial	Partial	Partial	Partial	Partial	Partial	Partial	Partial

It causes no compatibility issues, and has excellent support across all tested browsers.

Table Elements

Other Relevant Stuff

 thead (p. 476)

logically groups header elements in a table

 tbody (p. 421)

*logically groups elements that make the body of a **table**'s content*

 align *for <tfoot>*

```
align=" { center | char | justify | left | right } "
```

SPEC		
deprecated	required	version
NO	NO	HTML 4
BROWSER SUPPORT		

IE5.5+	FF1+	Saf1.3+	Op9.2+
PARTIAL	PARTIAL	PARTIAL	PARTIAL

Example

This **tfoot** will set all text inside the nested **td** elements to the right:

```
<table summary="Interest Rates" width="400" border="1">
  <caption>Interest Rates</caption>
  <thead>
    <tr>
      <th>Account Type</th>
      <th>Interest Rate</th>
    </tr>
  </thead>
  <tfoot align="right">
    <tr>
      <td>Recommended for you: 'Young Saver'</td>
      <td>Interest from: 1.6%</td>
    </tr>
  </tfoot>
  <tbody>
    <tr>
      <td>Smart</td>
      <td>From 2%</td>
    </tr>
    <tr>
      <td>Young Saver</td>
      <td>From 1.6%</td>
    </tr>
  </tbody>
</table>
```

The align attribute can be used to override the default horizontal alignment of text inside table cells contained within the tfoot. On the assumption that th (table headers) have been used inside the thead area and td elements are used for normal data, the default alignment is for text to be ranged left. However, by applying the align attribute to the tfoot, you could change that, for example, to "center" or "right" (as shown in the example HTML).

Value

The recognized attribute values are as shown in the syntax section.

Compatibility

Internet Explorer			Firefox			Safari			Opera
5.5	6.0	7.0	1.0	1.5	2.0	1.3	2.0	3.0	9.2
Partial	Partial	Partial	Partial	Partial	Partial	Partial	Partial	Partial	Partial

In the browsers tested, the "left", "right", "center", and "justify" alignments are honored, but the "char" value—used alongside the char (p. 450) and charoff (p. 451) attributes—is ignored by all (or incorrectly interpreted as "center").

Table Elements

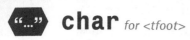

char *for <tfoot>*

```
char="character"
```

SPEC		
deprecated	required	version
NO	NO	HTML 4
BROWSER SUPPORT			
IE7	FF2	Saf3	Op9.2
NONE	NONE	NONE	NONE

Example

This `align` attribute is set to match the position of the "%" character:

```
<table summary="Interest Rates" width="400" border="1">
  <caption>Interest Rates</caption>
  <thead>
    <tr>
      <th>Account Type</th>
      <th>Interest Rate</th>
    </tr>
  </thead>
  <tfoot align="char" char="%">
    <tr>
      <td>Recommended for you: 'Young Saver'</td>
      <td>Interest from: 1.6%</td>
    </tr>
  </tfoot>
  <tbody>
    <tr>
      <td>Smart</td>
      <td>From 2%</td>
    </tr>
    <tr>
      <td>Young Saver</td>
      <td>From 1.6%</td>
    </tr>
  </tbody>
</table>
```

It may be useful in tables that contain financial information to align contents beyond the simple `"left"`, `"right"`, and `"center"` determinations. For example, you might align numerical data to a decimal point, or some other symbol. The `char` attribute allows you to define the character against which data is aligned, but this only works if the `align` (p. 448) attribute has also been set to `"char"`.

Value

This attribute takes as its value a single character that appears in the table, such as a decimal point character.

Compatibility

Internet Explorer			Firefox			Safari			Opera
5.5	6.0	7.0	1.0	1.5	2.0	1.3	2.0	3.0	9.2
None	None	None	None	None	None	None	None	None	None

This attribute is poorly supported and should not be relied upon.

charoff *for <tfoot>*

```
charoff="number"
```

SPEC		
deprecated	required	version
NO	NO	HTML 4
BROWSER SUPPORT			
IE7	FF2	Saf3	Op9.2
NONE	NONE	NONE	NONE

Example

Here, the character alignment offset is set to two characters:

```
<table summary="Interest Rates" width="400" border="1">
  <caption>Interest Rates</caption>
  <thead>
    <tr>
      <th>Account Type</th>
      <th>Interest Rate</th>
    </tr>
  </thead>
  <tfoot align="char" char="%" charoff="2">
    <tr>
      <td>Recommended for you: 'Young Saver'</td>
      <td>Interest from: 1.6%</td>
    </tr>
  </tfoot>
  <tbody>
    <tr>
      <td>Smart</td>
      <td>From 2%</td>
    </tr>
    <tr>
      <td>Young Saver</td>
      <td>From 1.6%</td>
    </tr>
  </tbody>
</table>
```

If the align attribute is set to "char", and the char attribute has been set to a character—thus telling the browser that cell contents should be aligned to a given character—the `charoff` attribute is used to set a *char*acter *off*set. If a `charoff` figure of `"2"` is chosen, as shown in the example HTML, the browser should align the cell contents two characters to the right of the specified character. If `charoff` were a negative value (`"-2"` for example) the alignment should be offset two characters to the left of the specified character. Note that there are a few uses of the word "should" in this paragraph, which *should* (there we go again) give you a hint about what to expect in the Compatibility section for this attribute!

Value

This attribute takes an integer value, which can be positive or negative.

Compatibility

Internet Explorer			Firefox			Safari			Opera
5.5	6.0	7.0	1.0	1.5	2.0	1.3	2.0	3.0	9.2
None	None	None	None	None	None	None	None	None	None

This attribute is poorly supported and should not be relied upon.

valign *for <tfoot>*

`valign=" { baseline | bottom | middle | top } "`

SPEC		
deprecated	required	version
NO	NO	HTML 4
BROWSER SUPPORT		
IE5.5+	FF1+	Saf1.3+	Op9.2+
PARTIAL	PARTIAL	PARTIAL	PARTIAL

Example

The `valign` attribute is set to `"top"` on this narrow table:

```
<table summary="Interest Rates" width="200" border="1">
  <caption>Interest Rates</caption>
  <thead>
    <tr>
      <th>Account Type</th>
      <th>Interest Rate</th>
    </tr>
  </thead>
  <tfoot valign="top">
    <tr>
      <td>Recommended for you: 'Young Saver'</td>
      <td>Interest from: 1.6%</td>
    </tr>
  </tfoot>
  <tbody>
    <tr>
      <td>Smart</td>
      <td>From 2%</td>
    </tr>
    <tr>
      <td>Young Saver</td>
      <td>From 1.6%</td>
    </tr>
  </tbody>
</table>
```

In a very similar manner to the `align` (p. 448) attribute for this element, the `valign` allows you to override the default alignment for table cells inside the foot of the table.

Value

The recognized attribute values are as shown in the syntax section.

Table Elements

Compatibility

Internet Explorer			Firefox			Safari			Opera
5.5	6.0	7.0	1.0	1.5	2.0	1.3	2.0	3.0	9.2
Partial	Partial	Partial	Partial	Partial	Partial	Partial	Partial	Partial	Partial

In the browsers tested, `"bottom"`, `"middle"`, and `"top"` alignments are honored, but the `"baseline"` value is ignored by all.

th

```
<th abbr="string" axis="string" colspan="number"
headers="cell ID …" rowspan="number" scope=" { col
| colgroup | row | rowgroup } " >
</th>
```

SPEC		
deprecated	empty	version
NO	NO	HTML 2
BROWSER SUPPORT			
IE5.5+	FF1+	Saf1.3+	Op9.2+
FULL	FULL	FULL	FULL

Example

This th defines the two cells in the first row as table headers:

```
<table summary="Interest Rates" width="400" border="1">
  <caption>Interest Rates</caption>
  <tr>
    <th>Account Type</th>
    <th>Interest Rate (%)</th>
  </tr>
  <tr>
    <td>Smart</td>
    <td>From 2%</td>
  </tr>
  <tr>
    <td>Young Saver</td>
    <td>From 1.6%</td>
  </tr>
</table>
```

You can use two kinds of table cells: the td (p. 428) can be used for any kind of data, while the th element is reserved for cells that contain header information. Despite the word "head," this element isn't used exclusively for a table heading that appears at the *top* of a table; it can equally be applied to any other cell in a table.

The th element renders the text content it contains slightly differently from the td—in the case of the browsers tested, the rendered style makes the font bold and centered (and this convention is unlikely to change soon). Centered headings are not always desirable, though, and you can use the align (p. 457) attribute to override this (or better still, use CSS to change the alignment).

As a structural element which conveys some orientation information about the data that may follow, the th has some special attributes that reinforce the relationship between header and data cells, namely the axis (p. 458), headers (p. 465), id (p. 501), and scope (p. 471) attributes.

Finally, this element uses the colspan (p. 463) and rowspan (p. 469) attributes when the content of the cell needs to run across multiple columns or rows.

Use This For ...

This element is used to identify a table cell whose content is a header of some kind; for example, you might use it to identify the top-most cell, containing the words "Make of Car," in a column that contains a list of car manufacturers.

Compatibility

Internet Explorer			Firefox			Safari			Opera
5.5	6.0	7.0	1.0	1.5	2.0	1.3	2.0	3.0	9.2
Full	Full	Full	Full	Full	Full	Full	Full	Full	Full

It causes no compatibility issues, and has excellent support across all tested browsers.

Other Relevant Stuff

 td (p. 428)

defines a standard data cell in a table

Table Elements

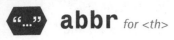

abbr *for <th>*

```
abbr="string"
```

SPEC		
deprecated	required	version
NO	NO	HTML 4
BROWSER SUPPORT		
IE5.5+	FF1+	Saf1.3+	Op9.2+
FULL	FULL	FULL	FULL

Example

This table lists vehicle details using the abbr attribute to contain make, model, and revision information:

```
<table border="1">
  <tr>
    <th abbr="Make">Car manufacturer (make)</th>
    <th abbr="Model">Vehicle model (name/spec)</th>
    <th abbr="Revised">Date of last revision </th>
  </tr>
  <tr>
    <td>Volkswagen</td>
    <td>Golf 2.8 GTi</td>
    <td>June 2007</td>
  </tr>
</table>
```

The abbr attribute is another one that makes no visual difference to the table and its contents but, like the table's summary attribute (p. 419), provides additional information that may be useful for people accessing the content using assistive technology, such as a screen reader. Its purpose is to provide a shorter version of the contents of the th, so that when content further down the table is put into context (for example, when a screen reader announces the table header to which a given cell relates), it's not necessary to have to go through what might be a very long-winded repetition of the header content. So, in this example, a screen reader may announce, "Make: Volkswagen, Model: Golf 2.8 GTi, Revised: June 2007" rather than "Car manufacturer (make): Volkswagen, Vehicle model (name/spec): Golf 2.8 GTi, Date of last revision: June 2007".

Value

This attribute takes as its value an abbreviated (but still meaningful) form of the th content.

Compatibility

Internet Explorer			Firefox			Safari			Opera
5.5	6.0	7.0	1.0	1.5	2.0	1.3	2.0	3.0	9.2
Full	Full	Full	Full	Full	Full	Full	Full	Full	Full

This attribute's compatibility is debatable. No browser renders it on the page, so it's difficult to say whether or not any browsers have difficulties with it. The biggest question regarding its compatibility is really centered on assistive technology—for example, screen readers—and whether they are capable of retrieving that useful summary information.

 align _for <th>_

```
align=" { center | justify | left | right } "
```

SPEC		
deprecated	required	version
NO	NO	HTML 4
BROWSER SUPPORT		
IE5.5+	FF1+	Saf1.3+ Op9.2+
FULL	FULL	FULL FULL

Example

Here, default browser alignment of the th is overridden so the content is aligned to the "right":

```
<tr>
  <th align="right">Account Type</th>
  <th align="right">Interest Rate</th>
</tr>
```

The usual alignment that browsers apply for content inside th elements is "center", but you can override that using the align attribute. However, you'd be better to use CSS to set the text alignment.

Value

The recognized attribute values are as shown in the syntax section.

Table Elements

Compatibility

Internet Explorer			Firefox			Safari			Opera
5.5	6.0	7.0	1.0	1.5	2.0	1.3	2.0	3.0	9.2
Full	Full	Full	Full	Full	Full	Full	Full	Full	Full

It causes no compatibility issues, and has excellent support across all tested browsers.

 axis *for <th>*

```
axis="string"
```

SPEC		
deprecated	required	version
NO	NO	HTML 4
BROWSER SUPPORT		
IE7	FF2	Saf3	Op9.2
NONE	NONE	NONE	NONE

Example

In this example, four table headers are grouped into three categories—name, contact, and location—using axis:

```
<table border="1">
  <tr>
    <th colspan="4">Work Contact Points</th>
  </tr>
  <tr>
    <th axis="name">Name</th>
    <th axis="contact">Email</th>
    <th axis="contact">Phone</th>
    <th axis="location">Floor/Block</th>
  </tr>
  <tr>
    <td>Fred</td>
    <td>fred@megacorp.com</td>
    <td>123456</td>
    <td>1/A</td>
  </tr>
    ⋮
</table>
```

The axis attribute provides a mechanism for grouping related columns or rows of information. In the example above, there are four pieces of information, but the email and phone details could be grouped together as actual points of contact. The intention of the axis attribute's application in a th is that it allows the grouping of sections in tables which contain quite a lot of information, making it possible to extrapolate this information using some kind of query—particularly where assistive technology is concerned. It's very easy for a sighted user to scan down those columns to find what's required, but this may be difficult for non-visual browsers in the context of a larger table.

Value

This attribute takes as its value any name that the developer chooses, provided it doesn't contain any spaces or special characters.

Compatibility

Internet Explorer			Firefox			Safari			Opera
5.5	6.0	7.0	1.0	1.5	2.0	1.3	2.0	3.0	9.2
None	None	None	None	None	None	None	None	None	None

All the talk of intentions and possibilities in this attribute's description should have alerted you to the fact that, despite the good intentions of axis, this is not an attribute that has enjoyed great success to date. It's not supported in any of the current browsers, and questions surround its practical applications. For example, how would one actually query the table data?

To ensure that your table is marked up accessibly and provides the greatest amount of orientation for users of assistive devices, it's best to use the scope (p. 471) attribute (for simple tables that don't make use of colspan (p. 463) and rowspan (p. 469) attributes) or a combination of headers (p. 465) and id (p. 501) attributes for more complex tables. Only apply the axis attribute if it creates minimal overhead (and if you're sure that it won't require maintenance in future—attributes that are invisible on the rendered page are the most likely to suffer from maintenance rot!).

Table Elements

bgcolor *for <th>*

```
bgcolor="color"
```

SPEC		
deprecated	required	version
YES	NO	HTML 2
BROWSER SUPPORT			
IE5.5+	FF1+	Saf1.3+	Op9.2+
FULL	FULL	FULL	FULL

Example

A different `bgcolor` is applied to several `th` elements in this `table`:

```
<table border="1">
  <tr>
    <th colspan="4" bgcolor="#CCFF66">Work Contact Points</th>
  </tr>
  <tr>
    <th bgcolor="#FFbb66">Name</th>
    <th bgcolor="#FFFF33">Email</th>
    <th bgcolor="#FFbb66">Phone</th>
    <th bgcolor="#FFFF33">Floor/Block</th>
  </tr>
  ⋮
</table>
```

Unless otherwise specified in CSS, a `th` will be transparent, and will allow whatever background is on the page (or whatever color was been specified at a higher level in the table) to show through as in Figure 8.14. The presentational (and deprecated) `bgcolor` attribute allows you to set a background for specific `th` elements using a recognized color name or hexadecimal value.

Work Contact Points			
Name	Email	Phone	Floor/Block
Fred	fred@megacorp.com	123456	1/A
Bill	bill@megacorp.com	345678	3/C

Figure 8.14: A table in which a background color is applied to specific `th` elements

Value

This attribute takes as its value a recognized color name (for example, `"blue"` or `"red"`)[4], or a value specified in hexadecimal notation (such as `"#003366"`). Note

---

[4] http://reference.sitepoint.com/html/color-names/

that it's *not* possible to use shorthand hexadecimal values in HTML as you can in CSS—for example, you can't express "#cceeff" as "#cef".

Compatibility

	Internet Explorer			Firefox			Safari			Opera
5.5	6.0	7.0	1.0	1.5	2.0	1.3	2.0	3.0	9.2
Full	Full	Full	Full	Full	Full	Full	Full	Full	Full

This attribute is now deprecated, and is highly presentational in its nature. The desired visual effects can all be achieved with CSS and, as such, this attribute shouldn't be used—it's presented here for informational purposes only.

char *for <th>*

```
char="character"
```

SPEC		
deprecated	required	version
NO	NO	HTML 4
BROWSER SUPPORT			
IE7	FF2	Saf3	Op9.2
NONE	NONE	NONE	NONE

Example

In this example, the second cell is aligned with the "%" character:

```
<tr>
  <th>Account Type</th>
  <th align="char" char="%">Interest Rate (%)</th>
</tr>
```

It may be useful in tables that contain financial information to align contents beyond the simple "left", "right", and "center" determinations. For example, you might align numerical data to a decimal point, or some other symbol. The char attribute allows you to define the character against which data is aligned, but this only works if the align (p. 457) attribute has also been set to "char".

Value

This attribute takes as its value a single character that appears in the table; for example, a decimal point character.

Compatibility

Internet Explorer			Firefox			Safari			Opera
5.5	6.0	7.0	1.0	1.5	2.0	1.3	2.0	3.0	9.2
None	None	None	None	None	None	None	None	None	None

This attribute is poorly supported and should not be relied upon.

charoff *for <th>*

```
charoff="number"
```

	SPEC	
deprecated	required	version
NO	NO	HTML 4
BROWSER SUPPORT		
IE7	FF2	Saf3	Op9.2
NONE	NONE	NONE	NONE

Example

In this example, the cell alignment is offset (charoff) two to the right of the "%" character:

```
<tr>
  <th>Account Type</th>
  <th align="char" char="%" charoff="2">Interest Rate (%)</th>
</tr>
```

If the align attribute is set to "char", and the char attribute has been set to a character—thus telling the browser that cell contents should be aligned to a given character—the charoff attribute is used to set a *char*acter *off*set. If a charoff figure of "2" is chosen, as shown in the example HTML, the browser should align the cell contents two characters to the right of the specified character. If charoff were a negative value ("-2" for example) the alignment should be offset two characters to the left of the specified character. Note that there are a few uses of the word "should" in this paragraph, which should (there we go again) give you a hint about what to expect in the Compatibility section for this attribute!

Value

This attribute takes an integer value, which can be positive or negative.

Compatibility

Internet Explorer			Firefox			Safari			Opera
5.5	6.0	7.0	1.0	1.5	2.0	1.3	2.0	3.0	9.2
None	None	None	None	None	None	None	None	None	None

This attribute is poorly supported and should not be relied upon.

colspan *for <th>*

```
colspan="number"
```

SPEC		
deprecated	required	version
NO	NO	HTML 3.2
BROWSER SUPPORT		
IE5.5+	FF1+	Saf1.3+ Op9.2+
PARTIAL	FULL	PARTIAL PARTIAL

Example

In this example, contact details share a common header, "Work Contact Points," which is spanned across four columns:

```
<table border="1">
  <tr>
    <th colspan="4">Work Contact Points</th>
  </tr>
  <tr>
    <td>Name</td>
    <td>Email</td>
    <td>Phone</td>
    <td>Floor/Block</td>
  </tr>
    ⋮
</table>
```

Where header information may be relevant to multiple columns, the cell can be set to span those columns using the `colspan` attribute. In the HTML example shown, we have four pieces of information for a number of employees—Name, Email, Phone, and Floor/Block—and the `th` is set to span all four of these columns, as shown in Figure 8.15.

Table Elements

Work Contact Points			
Name	Email	Phone	Floor/Block
Fred	fred@megacorp.com	123456	1/A
Jon	jon@megacorp.com	234567	
Bill	bill@megacorp.com	345678	3/C
Jane	jane@megacorp.com	777444	
Alison	alison@megacorp	888652	

Figure 8.15: A th element spanning four columns

When you're introducing a `colspan` attribute, take care to ensure that every row adds up to same number of cells. Some tables can become quite complicated with a mixture of `colspan` and `rowspan` (p. 469) attributes, and this is not something that you're advised to hand-code—that's just asking for trouble! It's much better to use a WYSIWYG editor, such as Dreamweaver, MS Expression, or something similar, which will allow you to merge and unmerge cells very easily, and takes care of these attributes for you. However, if you use such a package, you must pay close attention—unless you're using quite a recent web editor, it may inject some extra unnecessary markup into your table.

Value

This attribute takes a number, which should equal the number of cells that the `th` should replace. There's also a special value of `"0"`, which tells the browser to span the cell to the end of the current group of columns.

Compatibility

Internet Explorer			Firefox			Safari			Opera
5.5	6.0	7.0	1.0	1.5	2.0	1.3	2.0	3.0	9.2
Partial	Partial	Partial	Full	Full	Full	Partial	Partial	Partial	Partial

Browser support for `colspan` is generally good, with one exception—rendering `colspan="0"`. Only Firefox is able to span the cell across all remaining columns; the other browsers tested render the cell in the first column only.

headers *for <th>*

SPEC		
deprecated	required	version
NO	NO	HTML 4
BROWSER SUPPORT		
IE5.5+	FF1+	Saf1.3+	Op9.2+
FULL	FULL	FULL	FULL

```
headers="cell ID …"
```

Example

The example below associates the cell contents using headers with the appropriate header cells:

```
<table border="1">
  <tr>
    <th colspan="4" id="hdr_work">Work Contact Points</th>
  </tr>
  <tr>
    <th id="hdr_n">Name</th>
    <th id="hdr_e">Email</th>
    <th id="hdr_p">Phone</th>
    <th id="hdr_f">Floor/Block</th>
  </tr>
  <tr>
    <td headers="hdr_work hdr_n">Fred</td>
    <td headers="hdr_work hdr_e">fred@megacorp.com</td>
    <td headers="hdr_work hdr_p">123456</td>
    <td headers="hdr_work hdr_f">1/A</td>
  </tr
  <tr>
    <td headers="hdr_work hdr_n">Bill</td>
    <td headers="hdr_work hdr_e">bill@megacorp.com</td>
    <td headers="hdr_work hdr_p">345678</td>
    <th headers="hdr_work hdr_f">3/C</th>
  </tr>
</table>
```

Table Elements

This attribute is another one that exists for the purposes of improving the accessibility and understanding of the data table for users who can't see the data—typically users with screen reading software. The headers attribute could be translated by the web browser as, "to understand what the data in this cell right here means, you need to be looking at that table header location over there and that other one over there." A user who views the cell in question can very quickly scan up the table from that point to view the table headers above and to the left of it, to gain an understanding of what's going on. The headers attribute provides explicit instructions to the browser as to which table headers are relevant, by referencing the id attributes for the header cells in question.

Look at the example HTML above. Fred's email address is in this row:

```
<td headers="hdr_work hdr_e">fred@megacorp.com</td>
```

The headers attribute contains two values, "hdr_work" and "hdr_e". If you look at the top of the table markup, you'll notice that those values are contained within the id attribute for the respective cells:

```
<th colspan="4" id="hdr_work">Work Contact Points</th>
```

Here's the other one:

```
<th id="hdr_e">Email</th>
```

So, with the correct keyboard combinations, a screen reader user could ascertain that the email is an email address (well, that's not too difficult to guess, even without the extra markup!), and that it's a work contact point.

Note that the example shows the headers attribute being applied to a td element, but its application is exactly the same when applied to a th element.

Value

This attribute takes a space-separated list of ids, which must match exactly (they're case-sensitive) with the id attributes for the cells to which they relate.

Compatibility

Internet Explorer			Firefox			Safari			Opera
5.5	6.0	7.0	1.0	1.5	2.0	1.3	2.0	3.0	9.2
Full	Full	Full	Full	Full	Full	Full	Full	Full	Full

It's difficult to state the browser compatibility for this attribute, as the issue depends on how well the assistive technology copes with this information. Regardless, the use of headers is the correct thing to do, so if you have complex tables, make an effort to ensure that you mark them up in a way that ensures that the data is accessible for all.

“...” **nowrap** *for <th>*

SPEC		
deprecated	required	version
YES	NO	HTML 3.2
BROWSER SUPPORT			
IE5.5+	FF1+	Saf1.3+	Op9.2+
FULL	FULL	FULL	FULL

```
nowrap="nowrap"
```

Example

These th contents are set not to wrap:

```
<th nowrap="nowrap">Car manufacturer (make)</th>
```

If you need to ensure that the contents of a cell, in this case a table header, always remain as they are, and don't wrap, use the nowrap attribute. Note that this attribute, which is now deprecated, has a much better alternative in the form of the CSS property white-space (which can be set to "nowrap").

The example HTML shows the nowrap attribute used in an XHTML-compliant way, but it could equally be expressed in HTML 4.01, as follows:

```
<th nowrap>Car manufacturer (make)</th>
```

The effect of using this attribute can be seen in Figure 8.16. Note that it may not always be a wise idea to use nowrap—the image shows a browser window at a reduced size, displaying two versions of the table. In the first version, the nowrap attribute is omitted and the browser reflows the text; in the second version, nowrap forces the text to remain in place, causing the table to disappear off the page, as evidenced by the horizontal scrollbar and missing text.

Table Elements

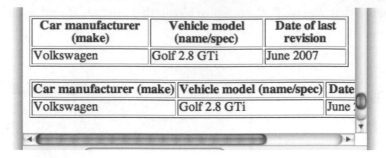

Figure 8.16: Two tables, one without, and one with, the nowrap attribute set on the headers

Value

"nowrap" is the only value this attribute can take.

Compatibility

Internet Explorer			Firefox			Safari			Opera
5.5	6.0	7.0	1.0	1.5	2.0	1.3	2.0	3.0	9.2
Full	Full	Full	Full	Full	Full	Full	Full	Full	Full

Excellent browser support is provided for this attribute, but given that this is a deprecated attribute, you should opt for the CSS alternative instead (th {white-space:nowrap}).

rowspan *for <th>*

```
rowspan="number"
```

SPEC		
deprecated	required	version
NO	NO	HTML 3.2
BROWSER SUPPORT		
IE5.5+	FF1+	Saf1.3+	Op9.2+
PARTIAL	FULL	PARTIAL	FULL

Example

Some of the employees in this example work on the same floor of the building, so this information is shared across the appropriate rows:

```
<table border="1">
  <tr>
    <th colspan="4" scope="col">Work Contact Points</th>
  </tr>
  <tr>
    <th>Name</th>
    <th>Email</th>
    <th>Phone</th>
    <th>Floor/Block</th>
  </tr>
  ⋮
  <tr>
    <td>Bill</td>
    <td>bill@megacorp.com</td>
    <td>345678</td>
    <th rowspan="3">3/C</th>
  </tr>
  <tr>
    <td>Jane</td>
    <td>jane@megacorp.com</td>
    <td>777444</td>
    missing cell taken up by th with rowspan
  </tr>
  <tr>
    <td>Alison</td>
    <td>alison@megacorp</td>
    <td>888652</td>
    missing cell taken up by th with rowspan
  </tr>
</table>
```

Where information may be relevant to multiple rows in the table, the cell containing that information can be set to span those rows using the rowspan attribute. In the HTML example shown, we have three employees who all work on the same floor. Rather than repeat the floor details three times over, that information can be output just once, but made to span the three rows relating to those people, as shown in Figure 8.12.

Work Contact Points			
Name	**Email**	**Phone**	**Floor/Block**
Fred	fred@megacorp.com	123456	1/A
Jon	jon@megacorp.com	234567	
Bill	bill@megacorp.com	345678	
Jane	jane@megacorp.com	777444	3/C
Alison	alison@megacorp	888652	

Figure 8.17: A th element spanning 3 rows

When you're introducing a `rowspan` attribute, take care to ensure that every row adds up to same number of cells. Some tables can become quite complicated, with a mixture of `colspan` (p. 463) and `rowspan` attributes. Tables like this can be quite tricky to hand-code, particularly for newcomers, and if you bungle your calculations, your table may either contain overlapping cells, or gaps where content should appear. Some people may prefer to use a WYSIWYG editor, such as Dreamweaver, MS Expression, or something similar, which will allow you to merge and unmerge cells very easily, and will take care of these attributes for you. However, if you use such a package, pay attention—unless you're using quite a recent web editor, it may inject some extra unnecessary markup into your table.

Note that when you're using the `rowspan` attribute, you can't span a cell beyond the boundary of its containing rowgroup (namely the `thead` (p. 476), `tfoot` (p. 446), or `tbody` (p. 421) elements). So, if the `thead` comprises five rows, the `rowspan` of a cell that's defined in the first row can't have a value that's greater than `"5"`.

Value

This attribute takes as its value a number that should equal the number of rows that the spanned `th` cell needs to cover. There is also a special value of `"0"`, which should tell the browser to span the cell to the end of all rows inside the current rowgroup (that is, the `thead` (p. 476), `tfoot` (p. 446), or `tbody` (p. 421)).

Compatibility

Internet Explorer			Firefox			Safari			Opera
5.5	6.0	7.0	1.0	1.5	2.0	1.3	2.0	3.0	9.2
Partial	Partial	Partial	Full	Full	Full	Partial	Partial	Partial	Full

Browser support for rowspan is generally good, with one exception—rendering rowspan="0". Firefox and Opera are the only browsers tested that correctly span the cell to which this attribute is applied across all subsequent rows; the other browsers tested render the cell in the first row only.

scope *for <th>*

```
scope=" { col | colgroup | row | rowgroup } "
```

SPEC		
deprecated	required	version
NO	NO	HTML 4
BROWSER SUPPORT			
IE5.5+	FF1+	Saf1.3+	Op9.2+
FULL	FULL	FULL	FULL

Example

This scope attribute of "col" identifies the cells as part of the header cell's "colgroup":

```
<table border="1">
  <tr>
    <th colspan="4" scope="colgroup">Work Contact Points</th>
  </tr>
  <tr>
    <th scope="col">Name</th>
    <th scope="col">Email</th>
    <th scope="col">Phone</th>
    <th scope="col">Floor/Block</th>
  </tr>
  <tr>
    <td>Fred</td>
    <td>fred@megacorp.com</td>
    <td>123456</td>
    <td>1/A</td>
  </tr>
  <tr>
    <td>Bill</td>
    <td>bill@megacorp.com</td>
    <td>345678</td>
    <th>3/C</th>
  </tr>
</table>
```

Table Elements

If your simple table displays a single row of header cells—defines by the th element—at the table's top, followed by multiple rows of standard data cells (tds), it should be obvious to the person viewing the table, or using screen reader software to access it, that the headers are column headers. This is also true of a table that has a single column on the left-hand side consisting of th elements, and multiple columns of td elements to its right.

However, it's good practice to make this relationship absolutely clear, which you can do using the scope attribute. In the HTML example, the scope attribute for each of the th elements is set to "col". If your table has table headers along its top *and* down one side, the scope attribute becomes even more important in providing the necessary signposts for people using assistive technology.

Value

The attributes you'll most commonly use with scope are "col" and "row". However, if you've also marked up your table with colgroup (p. 396) elements, you can make use of the matching "colgroup" value to associate the header with all the columns in that colgroup. One other attribute is also available: "rowgroup" applies to a cell that's spanned using the rowspan (p. 469) attribute.

Compatibility

Internet Explorer			Firefox			Safari			Opera
5.5	6.0	7.0	1.0	1.5	2.0	1.3	2.0	3.0	9.2
Full	Full	Full	Full	Full	Full	Full	Full	Full	Full

It's difficult to state the browser compatibility for this attribute, as the issue depends on how well the assistive technology copes with this information. Regardless, the use of headers is the correct thing to do, so if you have complex tables, make an effort to ensure that you mark them up in a way that ensures that the data is accessible for all.

valign *for <th>*

```
valign=" { baseline | bottom | middle | top } "
```

SPEC		
deprecated	required	version
NO	NO	HTML 4
BROWSER SUPPORT			
IE5.5+	FF1+	Saf1.3+	Op9.2+
PARTIAL	PARTIAL	PARTIAL	PARTIAL

Example

The `valign` is set to "bottom" for each of these th elements:

```
<table summary="Interest Rates" width="200" border="1">
  <caption>Interest Rates</caption>
  <thead>
    <tr>
      <th valign="bottom">Account Type (Name titles as per
          Spring 2006 range)</th>
      <th valign="bottom">Interest Rate</th>
    </tr>
  </thead>
  <tbody>
    <tr>
      <td>Smart</td>
      <td>From 2%</td>
    </tr>
    <tr>
      <td>Young Saver</td>
      <td>From 1.6%</td>
    </tr>
  </tbody>
</table>
```

In a very similar manner to this element's `align` (p. 457) attribute, `valign` allows you to override the default alignment for content inside the header cells using a handful of attributes. This approach may not always be necessary, but in the example HTML above, the table is forced into a narrow width, and more content is present in the header cell in the first column than in the second column, which can cause some unsightly rendering effects. The `valign` attribute may be used to address this issue, as Figure 8.18 shows. There, all the content is aligned to the bottom of the header cells.

Table Elements

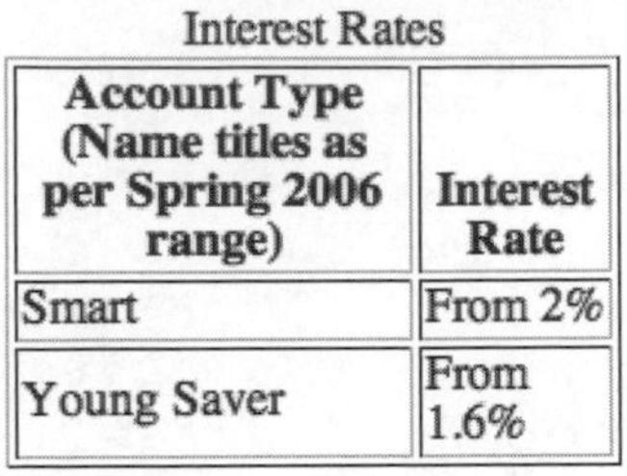

Interest Rates

Account Type (Name titles as per Spring 2006 range)	Interest Rate
Smart	From 2%
Young Saver	From 1.6%

Figure 8.18: The valign attribute applied to each of the th elements

Note that there is both a better way, and a much, *much* better way to do this. The better way is *not* to set the valign at the td level, as in a bigger table with more columns, you'll end up with unnecessarily bloated markup. Instead, you could set valign at the parent tr level (p. 491). However, this is still less than ideal. The preferred method would be to set the alignment of text inside the th elements using the CSS vertical-align property.

Value

The recognized attribute values are as shown in the syntax section.

Compatibility

Internet Explorer			Firefox			Safari			Opera
5.5	6.0	7.0	1.0	1.5	2.0	1.3	2.0	3.0	9.2
Partial	Partial	Partial	Partial	Partial	Partial	Partial	Partial	Partial	Partial

In the browsers tested, "bottom", "middle", and "top" alignments are honored, but the "baseline" value is ignored by all.

width *for <th>*

```
width=" { number | percentage } "
```

SPEC		
deprecated	required	version
YES	NO	HTML 2
BROWSER SUPPORT			
IE5.5+	FF1+	Saf1.3+	Op9.2+
FULL	FULL	FULL	FULL

Example

This width attribute is set to "50%":

```
<table>
  <tr>
    <th width="50%">Account Type</th>
    <th width="50%">Interest Rate</th>
  </tr>
  <tr>
    <td>Smart</td>
    <td>From 2%</td>
  </tr>
  <tr>
    <td>Young Saver</td>
    <td>From 1.6%</td>
  </tr>
</table>
```

Unless a width is set, a th (and also td (p. 428)) will take up only the width it requires (obviously this will depend on the amount of content in each of the table cells). You can use the width attribute to fix the width to a value of your choosing, regardless of the content of the table cell, but be aware that this is a deprecated attribute. Width should be set using CSS.

If different width attributes are applied to several cells within the same column, the browser will render the column with the largest width value specified. It could be understood, therefore, that width is really a minimum width value: a table cell will increase in size if the content cannot be wrapped (as may be the case, for example, with a wide image, or a string of text that contains no spaces, such as a web site address).

Value

This attribute takes as its value a number that represents the width of the th element in pixels, or a percentage.

Compatibility

Internet Explorer			Firefox			Safari			Opera
5.5	6.0	7.0	1.0	1.5	2.0	1.3	2.0	3.0	9.2
Full	Full	Full	Full	Full	Full	Full	Full	Full	Full

It causes no compatibility issues, and has excellent support across all tested browsers.

thead

```
<thead>
</thead>
```

SPEC		
deprecated	empty	version
NO	NO	HTML 4

BROWSER SUPPORT			
IE5.5+	FF1+	Saf1.3+	Op9.2+
PARTIAL	PARTIAL	PARTIAL	PARTIAL

Example

The thead element wraps around the row containing table headers (th elements):

```
<table summary="Interest Rates">
  <caption>Interest Rates</caption>
  <thead>
    <tr>
      <th>Account Type</th>
      <th>Interest Rate</th>
    </tr>
  </thead>
  <tbody>
    <tr>
      <td>Smart</td>
      <td>From 2%</td>
    </tr>
    <tr>
      <td>Young Saver</td>
      <td>From 1.6%</td>
    </tr>
  </tbody>
</table>
```

In a simple table, the first row may contain table headers (th elements), and that may be all you need to do to mark up the table. However, you may find that wrapping a thead around the header row—particularly if you have a table that has multiple header rows at its top—gives you scope for more control via the thead attributes;

you might also make use of this element as a "hook" from which to apply CSS styles to the header area of your table.

By default, a `thead` will not affect the display of the table in any way.

Use This For ...

This element is used for grouping the top layer(s) of header cells.

Compatibility

Internet Explorer			Firefox			Safari			Opera
5.5	6.0	7.0	1.0	1.5	2.0	1.3	2.0	3.0	9.2
Partial	Partial	Partial	Partial	Partial	Partial	Partial	Partial	Partial	Partial

By itself—without the application of any of the element-specific attributes detailed below—the presence of a `thead` makes no visual difference to the `table`. For a true indication of this element's compatibility, you should refer to each individual attribute to see what works and what fails.

Other Relevant Stuff

 tbody (p. 421)

logically groups elements that make the body of a `table`'s content

 tfoot (p. 446)

logically groups elements that comprise the footer area of a `table`'s content

align *for <thead>*

`align=" { center | char | justify | left | right } "`

	SPEC	
deprecated	required	version
NO	NO	HTML 4
BROWSER SUPPORT		
IE5.5+	FF1+	Saf1.3+	Op9.2+
PARTIAL	PARTIAL	PARTIAL	PARTIAL

Example

This thead content is set to align "left":

```
<table summary="Interest Rates" width="400" border="1">
  <caption>Interest Rates</caption>
  <thead align="left">
    <tr>
      <th>Account Type</th>
      <th>Interest Rate</th>
    </tr>
  </thead>
  <tbody>
    <tr>
      <td>Smart</td>
      <td>From 2%</td>
    </tr>
    <tr>
      <td>Young Saver</td>
      <td>From 1.6%</td>
    </tr>
  </tbody>
</table>
```

Assuming that you have used the correct markup for a table header—that is, a th (p. 454) element rather than a styled td (p. 428) element—you'll find that the text in the header cells is centered. If these header cells are contained within a thead, you can use the align attribute at the thead level to override the default alignment. Once again, though, it would be better to use CSS in this instance.

Value

The recognized attribute values are as shown in the syntax section.

Compatibility

Internet Explorer			Firefox			Safari			Opera
5.5	6.0	7.0	1.0	1.5	2.0	1.3	2.0	3.0	9.2
Partial	Partial	Partial	Partial	Partial	Partial	Partial	Partial	Partial	Partial

In the browsers tested, the "left", "right", "center", and "justify" alignments are honored, but the "char" value—used alongside the char (p. 479) and charoff (p. 480) attributes—is ignored by all (or incorrectly interpreted as "center").

char *for <thead>*

```
char="character"
```

SPEC		
deprecated	required	version
NO	NO	HTML 4
BROWSER SUPPORT			

IE7	FF2	Saf3	Op9.2
NONE	NONE	NONE	NONE

Example

Here, the character to which cell contents will be aligned is defined as "%":

```
<table summary="Interest Rates" width="400" border="1">
  <caption>Interest Rates</caption>
  <thead align="char" char="%">
    <tr>
      <th>Account Type</th>
      <th>Interest Rate (%)</th>
    </tr>
  </thead>
  <tbody>
    <tr>
      <td>Smart</td>
      <td>From 2%</td>
    </tr>
    <tr>
      <td>Young Saver</td>
      <td>From 1.6%</td>
    </tr>
  </tbody>
</table>
```

It may be useful in tables that contain financial information to align contents beyond the simple "left", "right", and "center" determinations. For example, you might align numerical data to a decimal point, or some other symbol. The char attribute allows you to define the character against which data is aligned, but this only works if the align (p. 478) attribute has also been set to "char".

Table Elements

Value

This attribute takes as its value a single character that appears in the table, such as a decimal point character.

Compatibility

Internet Explorer			Firefox			Safari			Opera
5.5	6.0	7.0	1.0	1.5	2.0	1.3	2.0	3.0	9.2
None	None	None	None	None	None	None	None	None	None

This attribute is poorly supported and should not be relied upon.

charoff *for <thead>*

```
charoff="number"
```

	SPEC		
deprecated	required		version
NO	NO		HTML 4
BROWSER SUPPORT			
IE7	FF2	Saf3	Op9.2
NONE	NONE	NONE	NONE

Example

Here, the character alignment is offset by two characters:

```
<table summary="Interest Rates" width="400" border="1">
  <caption>Interest Rates</caption>
  <thead align="char" char="%" charoff="2">
    <tr>
      <th>Account Type</th>
      <th>Interest Rate (%)</th>
    </tr>
  </thead>
  <tbody>
    <tr>
      <td>Smart</td>
      <td>From 2%</td>
    </tr>
    <tr>
      <td>Young Saver</td>
      <td>From 1.6%</td>
    </tr>
  </tbody>
</table>
```

If the `align` attribute is set to `"char"`, and the `char` attribute has been set to a character—thus telling the browser that cell contents should be aligned to a given character—the `charoff` attribute is used to set a *char*acter *off*set. If a `charoff` figure of `"2"` is chosen, as shown in the example HTML, the browser should align the cell contents two characters to the right of the specified character. If `charoff` were a negative value (`"-2"`, for example) the alignment should be offset two characters to the left of the specified character. Note that there are a few uses of the word "should" in this paragraph, which *should* (there we go again) give you a hint about what to expect in the Compatibility section for this attribute!

Value

This attribute takes an integer value, which can be positive or negative.

Compatibility

Internet Explorer			Firefox			Safari			Opera
5.5	6.0	7.0	1.0	1.5	2.0	1.3	2.0	3.0	9.2
None	None	None	None	None	None	None	None	None	None

This attribute is poorly supported and should not be relied upon.

Table Elements

valign *for <thead>*

```
valign=" { baseline | bottom | middle | top } "
```

	SPEC	
deprecated	required	version
NO	NO	HTML 4
BROWSER SUPPORT		
IE5.5+	FF1+	Saf1.3+	Op9.2+
PARTIAL	PARTIAL	PARTIAL	PARTIAL

Example

The `valign` is set to `"bottom"` on this narrow table:

```
<table summary="Interest Rates" width="200" border="1">
  <caption>Interest Rates</caption>
  <thead valign="bottom">
    <tr>
      <th>Account Type (Name titles as per Spring 2006 range)</th>
      <th>Interest Rate</th>
    </tr>
  </thead>
  <tbody>
    <tr>
      <td>Smart</td>
      <td>From 2%</td>
    </tr>
    <tr>
      <td>Young Saver</td>
      <td>From 1.6%</td>
    </tr>
  </tbody>
</table>
```

In a very similar manner to this element's `align` (p. 478) attribute, the `valign` allows you to override the default alignment for content inside the header cells using a handful of attributes. This may not always be necessary, but in the example HTML above, the table is forced into a narrow width, and more content is present in the header cell in column one than in column two, which can cause some unsightly effects. The `valign` may be used to address this issue, as Figure 8.19 shows. There, all the content is aligned to the bottom of the header cells.

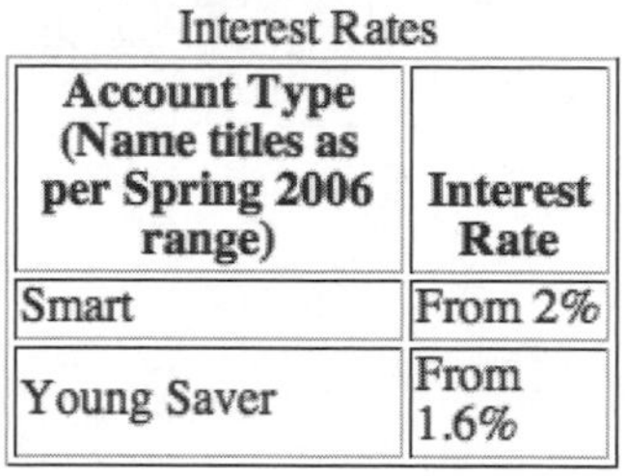

Interest Rates

Account Type (Name titles as per Spring 2006 range)	Interest Rate
Smart	From 2%
Young Saver	From 1.6%

Figure 8.19: The thead's valign attribute vertically aligning the header cells' content to the cells' bottoms

Value

The recognized attribute values are as shown in the syntax section.

Compatibility

Internet Explorer			Firefox			Safari			Opera
5.5	6.0	7.0	1.0	1.5	2.0	1.3	2.0	3.0	9.2
Partial	Partial	Partial	Partial	Partial	Partial	Partial	Partial	Partial	Partial

In the browsers tested, "bottom", "middle", and "top" alignments are honored, but the "baseline" value is ignored by all.

Table Elements

tr

	SPEC	
deprecated	empty	version
NO	NO	HTML 2
BROWSER SUPPORT			
IE5.5+	FF1+	Saf1.3+	Op9.2+
FULL	FULL	FULL	FULL

```
<tr>
</tr>
```

Example

The three rows in this simple `table` are created with the opening and closing `tr` tags:

```
<table summary="Interest Rates">
  <caption>Interest Rates</caption>
  <thead>
    <tr>
      <th>Account Type</th>
      <th>Interest Rate</th>
    </tr>
  </thead>
  <tbody>
    <tr>
      <td>Smart</td>
      <td>From 2%</td>
    </tr>
    <tr>
      <td>Young Saver</td>
      <td>From 1.6%</td>
    </tr>
  </tbody>
</table>
```

The `tr` element is used to create a new row of data in a `table` (p. 405). This element may appear as a child element of the `table` element or, if it has been defined, as a child of a `thead` (p. 476), `tfoot` (p. 446), or `tbody` (p. 421) elements.

The table row contains one or more `th` (p. 454) or `td` (p. 428) elements, but each row should contain the same number of cells (regardless of whether they're `th` or `td` elements), unless cells are set to span multiple columns using the `colspan` attribute (see the section about `colspan` in the `th` reference (p. 463) for more information). If one row has more table cells inside it than do the others (for example, if you accidentally create a header area with 11 `th` elements, but subsequent rows have only ten `td` elements), the web browser will have to fill in the gaps with empty cells. This can have a disastrous effect on the data, so be sure to keep count of your cells!

It's possible to omit the closing `</tr>` tag in HTML 4.01, but I'd advise you to include it, firstly to ensure forwards-compatibility (XHTML requires the closing tag), but also because it can make reading and thus maintaining the markup easier when you revisit it at a later date.

Use This For ...

This element is used to start a new row of data.

Compatibility

Internet Explorer			Firefox			Safari			Opera
5.5	6.0	7.0	1.0	1.5	2.0	1.3	2.0	3.0	9.2
Full	Full	Full	Full	Full	Full	Full	Full	Full	Full

It causes no compatibility issues, and has excellent support across all tested browsers.

Table Elements

align *for <tr>*

```
align=" { center | char | justify | left | right } "
```

SPEC		
deprecated	required	version
NO	NO	HTML 2
BROWSER SUPPORT			
IE5.5+	FF1+	Saf1.3+	Op9.2+
PARTIAL	PARTIAL	PARTIAL	PARTIAL

Example

The th elements' default alignment ("center") is overridden at the tr level, to become "left":

```
<table summary="Interest Rates" width="400" border="1">
  <caption>Interest Rates</caption>
  <thead>
    <tr align="left">
      <th>Account Type</th>
      <th>Interest Rate</th>
    </tr>
  </thead>
  <tbody>
    <tr>
      <td>Smart</td>
      <td>From 2%</td>
    </tr>
    <tr>
      <td>Young Saver</td>
      <td>From 1.6%</td>
    </tr>
  </tbody>
</table>
```

The align attribute can be used in most table elements, and the table row—or tr—is no exception. The value set at the table-row level is then inherited by the th and td elements it contains (unless they, too, are set to a specific alignment).

Once again, it should be noted that setting the alignment using this HTML attribute is not ideal. Use CSS to perform the job.

Value

The recognized attribute values are as shown in the syntax section.

Compatibility

Internet Explorer			Firefox			Safari			Opera
5.5	6.0	7.0	1.0	1.5	2.0	1.3	2.0	3.0	9.2
Partial	Partial	Partial	Partial	Partial	Partial	Partial	Partial	Partial	Partial

In the browsers tested, the "left", "right", "center", and "justify" alignments were honored, but the "char" value—used alongside the char (p. 489) and charoff (p. 490) attributes—was ignored by all (or incorrectly interpreted as "center").

bgcolor *for <tr>*

bgcolor="*color*"

SPEC		
deprecated	required	version
YES	NO	HTML 2
BROWSER SUPPORT		
IE5.5+	FF1+	Saf1.3+	Op9.2+
FULL	FULL	FULL	FULL

Example

A different bgcolor is applied to the first tr element in this table:

```
<table border="1">
  <tr bgcolor="#CCFF66">
    <th colspan="4">Work Contact Points</th>
  </tr>
  <tr>
    <th>Name</th>
    <th>Email</th>
    <th>Phone</th>
    <th>Floor/Block</th>
  </tr>
  ⋮
</table>
```

Unless otherwise specified in CSS, a tr will be transparent, and will allow whatever background is on the page (or whatever color has been specified at a higher level in the table) to show through, as illustrated in Figure 8.20. The presentational, and deprecated bgcolor attribute allows you to set a background for specific tr elements using a recognized color name or hexadecimal value.

Work Contact Points			
Name	Email	Phone	Floor/Block
Fred	fred@megacorp.com	123456	1/A
Jon	jon@megacorp.com	234567	
Bill	bill@megacorp.com	345678	3/C
Jane	jane@megacorp.com	777444	
Alison	alison@megacorp	888652	

Figure 8.20: A table in which a background color is applied to specific th elements

Value

This attribute takes as its value a recognized color name (for example, `"blue"` or `"red"`)[5], or a value specified in hexadecimal notation (such as `"#003366"`). Note that it's *not* possible to use shorthand hexadecimal values in HTML as you can in CSS—for example, you can't express `"#cceeff"` as `"#cef"`.

Compatibility

Internet Explorer			Firefox			Safari			Opera
5.5	6.0	7.0	1.0	1.5	2.0	1.3	2.0	3.0	9.2
Full	Full	Full	Full	Full	Full	Full	Full	Full	Full

This attribute is now deprecated, and is highly presentational in its nature. The desired visual effects can all be achieved with CSS and, as such, this attribute shouldn't be used—it's presented here for informational purposes only.

---

[5] http://reference.sitepoint.com/html/color-names/

char *for <tr>*

```
char="character"
```

SPEC		
deprecated	required	version
NO	NO	HTML 4
BROWSER SUPPORT		
IE7	FF2	Saf3	Op9.2
NONE	NONE	NONE	NONE

Example

In the following example, the rows are aligned to the "%" character:

```
<table summary="Interest Rates" width="400" border="1">
  <caption>Interest Rates</caption>
  <thead align="char">
    <tr>
      <th>Account Type</th>
      <th>Interest Rate (%)</th>
    </tr>
  </thead>
  <tbody>
    <tr align="char" char="%">
      <td>Smart</td>
      <td>From 2%</td>
    </tr>
    <tr align="char" char="%">
      <td>Young Saver</td>
      <td>From 1.6%</td>
    </tr>
  </tbody>
</table>
```

The char attribute allows you to define the character against which data in the th or td elements within this table row are aligned, but this is only works if the align (p. 486) attribute has also been set to "char".

Value

This attribute takes as its value a single character that appears in the table, such as a decimal point character.

Compatibility

Internet Explorer			Firefox			Safari			Opera
5.5	6.0	7.0	1.0	1.5	2.0	1.3	2.0	3.0	9.2
None	None	None	None	None	None	None	None	None	None

Table Elements

This element is poorly supported and should not be relied upon.

charoff *for <tr>*

```
charoff="number"
```

SPEC		
deprecated	required	version
NO	NO	HTML 4
BROWSER SUPPORT			
IE7	FF2	Saf3	Op9.2
NONE	NONE	NONE	NONE

Example

Here, the character alignment is offset by two characters from the "%":

```
<table summary="Interest Rates" width="400" border="1">
  <caption>Interest Rates</caption>
  <thead>
    <tr>
      <th>Account Type</th>
      <th>Interest Rate (%)</th>
    </tr>
  </thead>
  <tbody>
    <tr align="char" char="%" charoff="2">
      <td>Smart</td>
      <td>From 2%</td>
    </tr>
    <tr align="char" char="%" charoff="2">
      <td>Young Saver</td>
      <td>From 1.6%</td>
    </tr>
  </tbody>
</table>
```

If the align attribute is set to "char", and the char attribute has been set to a character—thus telling the browser that cell contents should be aligned to a given character—the charoff attribute is used to set a *char*acter *off*set. If a charoff figure of "2" is chosen, as shown in the example HTML, the browser should align the cell contents two characters to the right of the specified character. If charoff were a negative value ("-2" for example) the alignment should be offset two characters to the left of the specified character. Note that there are a few uses of the word "should" in this paragraph, which should (there we go again) give you a hint about what to expect in the Compatibility section for this attribute!

Value

This attribute takes an integer value, which can be positive or negative.

Compatibility

Internet Explorer			Firefox			Safari			Opera
5.5	6.0	7.0	1.0	1.5	2.0	1.3	2.0	3.0	9.2
None	None	None	None	None	None	None	None	None	None

This element is poorly supported and should not be relied upon.

valign *for <tr>*

```
valign=" { baseline | bottom | middle | top } "
```

SPEC		
deprecated	required	version
NO	NO	HTML 4
BROWSER SUPPORT		
IE5.5+	FF1+	Saf1.3+	Op9.2+
PARTIAL	PARTIAL	PARTIAL	PARTIAL

Example

The valign is set to "bottom" for the first row of this narrow table:

```
<table summary="Interest Rates" width="200" border="1">
  <caption>Interest Rates</caption>
  <thead>
    <tr valign="bottom">
      <th>Account Type (Name titles as per Spring 2006 range)</th>
      <th>Interest Rate</th>
    </tr>
  </thead>
  <tbody>
    <tr>
      <td>Smart</td>
      <td>From 2%</td>
    </tr>
    <tr>
      <td>Young Saver</td>
      <td>From 1.6%</td>
    </tr>
  </tbody>
</table>
```

In a very similar manner to this element's align (p. 486) attribute, the valign allows you to override the default alignment for content inside the header cells using a handful of attributes. This may not always be necessary, but in the example HTML

Table Elements

above, the table is forced into a narrow width, and more content is present in the header cell in column one than column two, which can cause some unsightly effects. The `valign` may be used to address this issue, as Figure 8.21 shows. There, all the content is aligned to the bottom of the header cells.

Interest Rates

Account Type (Name titles as per Spring 2006 range)	Interest Rate
Smart	From 2%
Young Saver	From 1.6%

Figure 8.21: Vertically aligning the content inside the first row to the bottom

Value

The recognized attribute values are as shown in the syntax section.

Compatibility

Internet Explorer			Firefox			Safari			Opera
5.5	6.0	7.0	1.0	1.5	2.0	1.3	2.0	3.0	9.2
Partial	Partial	Partial	Partial	Partial	Partial	Partial	Partial	Partial	Partial

In the browsers tested, `"bottom"`, `"middle"`, and `"top"`, alignments are honored, but the `"baseline"` value is ignored by all.

Frame and Window Elements

This section includes the small collection of HTML elements that deal with windows or, more specifically, frames that allow multi-windowed layouts (using the `frameset` (p. 494) and `frame` (p. 493) elements) or floating window effects (using `iframe` (p. 494)).

While the elements contained in this section are used less and less in modern-day web design, they're still valid, and there are still many web sites that use these elements today as they have for years.

 ## frame

```
<frame frameborder=" { 0 | 1 } " longdesc="string"
marginheight="number" marginwidth="number"
name="string" noresize="noresize" scrolling=" { auto
| no | yes } " src="uri" />
```

SPEC		
deprecated	empty	version
YES	YES	HTML 4.01
BROWSER SUPPORT			
IE5.5+	FF1+	Saf1.3+	Op9.2+
FULL	FULL	FULL	PARTIAL

The `frame` element defines one particular window within a `frameset` (p. 494) collection. In a typical `frameset` construction, one `frame` may be used for the purposes of navigation, with another `frame` used to present content. In this case, the links in the navigation `frame` would be targeted to load content in the other `frame` via a `target` attribute that matched the destination `frame`'s `name` attribute.

For more information, visit http://reference.sitepoint.com/html/frame/.

frameset

```
<frameset cols="{ number | percentage | * } ,…"
rows="{ number | percentage | * } ,…">
</frameset>
```

SPEC		
deprecated	empty	version
YES	NO	HTML 4.01
BROWSER SUPPORT		
IE5.5+	FF1+	Saf1.3+	Op9.2+
FULL	FULL	FULL	FULL

The `frameset` is used to group a collection of windows, sometimes horizontally (using the http://reference.sitepoint.com/html/frameset/rows/ attribute), sometimes vertically (using the http://reference.sitepoint.com/html/frameset/cols/ attribute), or in a combination of horizontal and vertical arrangements. Each child window inside the `frameset` is defined by the `frame` (p. 493) element.

For more information, visit http://reference.sitepoint.com/html/frameset/.

iframe

```
<iframe align=" { bottom | left | middle | right |
top } " frameborder=" { 0 | 1 } " height=" { number
| percentage } " longdesc="string"
marginheight="number" marginwidth="number"
name="string" noresize="noresize" scrolling=" { auto
| no | yes } " src="uri" width=" { number |
percentage } ">
</iframe>
```

SPEC		
deprecated	empty	version
YES	NO	HTML 4
BROWSER SUPPORT		
IE5.5+	FF1+	Saf1.3+	Op9.2+
FULL	FULL	FULL	FULL

The `iframe` provides a window that can be placed anywhere within an existing, non-frame-based page, similarly to the placement of a table or image.

For more information, visit http://reference.sitepoint.com/html/iframe/.

noframes

```
<noframes>
</noframes>
```

	SPEC	
deprecated	empty	version
YES	NO	HTML 4.01
BROWSER SUPPORT		
IE5.5+	FF1+	Saf1.3+	Op9.2+
FULL	FULL	FULL	FULL

This isn't an element that you'll need to use very often. People have generally moved away from using frameset (p. 494)-based web sites, hence the requirement for providing alternative content in the noframes element has similarly declined. Even if you do have to create a frameset-based web site, you'd be hard-pushed to find a mainstream web browser that doesn't support framesets. That said, some people use text browsers that don't support frames, and some mobile devices don't play well with frames, so they shouldn't be dismissed out of hand.

The noframes element can contain all the elements that you would naturally expect to find inside the body (p. 32) of a normal, non-frame-based page—in effect, the noframes element is equivalent to body. However, in the XHTML frameset doctype (p. 6), the noframes element must first contain a body, which can then contain the additional child elements required to create the page content.

For more information, visit http://reference.sitepoint.com/html/noframes/.

Frame and Window Elements

Chapter 10

Common Attributes

In this section, you'll find all the attributes that may be applied to all the HTML elements (unless otherwise stated). These include the core attributes (p. 498) that may be used for the purposes of styling elements with CSS or scripting to specify changes in the language, using `lang` (p. 503); provide extra information about the element, which may appear as a tooltip, using `title` (p. 506); and identify elements uniquely, using `id` (p. 501), or many times over, using the `class` (p. 498) attribute.

In addition to these core attributes, we include event attributes (p. 509) that are used to identify the points at which certain actions take place, such as the instant when a user mouses over an element (p. 523) or presses a key (p. 517). In addition to the W3C-defined event attributes, a raft of Internet Explorer-specific attributes[1] have been defined.

---

[1] http://reference.sitepoint.com/html/extended-event-attributes/

Core Attributes

In addition to element-type-specific attributes (for example, the `cite` attribute used for `blockquotes`), the following core attributes may also be applied to any element, whatever its type.

class

`class="string …"`

SPEC		
deprecated	required	version
NO	NO	HTML 4
BROWSER SUPPORT			
IE5.5+	FF1+	Saf1.3+	Op9.2+
FULL	FULL	FULL	FULL

Example

The `div` (p. 44) element in this example has two classes assigned to it, which identify it both as an `"aside"` and as `"salescopy"`:

```
<div class="aside salescopy">This is a sidebar.</div>
```

While the name of an element specifies its type, the `class` attribute lets you assign to it one or more subtypes. These subtypes may then be used in CSS code for styling purposes, or by JavaScript code (via the Document Object Model, or DOM) to make changes, or add behavior, to elements belonging to a particular subtype.

Value

This attribute takes as its value a space-delimited list of one or more `class` names. Unlike the `id` attribute, the `class` attribute's value may begin with a number; for example, `<div class="3-col-wide">` … `</div>`.

While there have been numerous calls from the developer community to specify a standard set of class names and associated meanings, at the moment you're free to specify whatever `class` names make sense to you. As with all HTML markup, however, it's recommended that you use names that are as semantically meaningful as possible; the class name should indicate to a human who reads it what that element's purpose or meaning is, rather than how it looks. Hence, purely presentational `class` names like `"large"` or `"shiny"` are bad practice, while `class` names such as `"executive-summary"` or `"key-findings"` provide some useful information to those reading the markup.

While it's good to make the markup human-readable, the developer community has made great strides in standardizing the usage of `class` names for certain types of information on the Web, such as contact details or calendar events, so that the markup can also be read, or parsed, by web-based services to great effect. The result of this standardization effort is known as Microformats[2].

Compatibility

Internet Explorer			Firefox			Safari			Opera
5.5	6.0	c7.0	1.0	1.5	2.0	1.3	2.0	3.0	9.2
Full	Full	Full	Full	Full	Full	Full	Full	Full	Full

As with the `id` (p. 501) attribute, compatibility issues with `class` generally depend on the way it's used or accessed by CSS and JavaScript; the presence or lack of a class name on any attribute won't adversely affect its display in HTML when style sheets or JavaScript aren't linked.

It is perfectly valid—indeed, it's extremely useful—to apply multiple values in the `class` attribute; for example, applying both `class="friend colleague"` or `class="spouse muse"`, and have CSS combine different styles depending on the classes in use.

---

[2] http://reference.sitepoint.com/html/microformats/

dir

`dir=" { ltr | rtl } "`

SPEC		
deprecated	required	version
NO	NO	HTML 4
BROWSER SUPPORT		
IE5.5+	FF1+	Saf3+	Op9.2+
FULL	FULL	FULL	FULL

Example

The following example indicates that the direction of the Hebrew text is right-to-left:

```
<p>The bulk of the content is in English and flows left to right,
until this phrase in Hebrew makes an appearance,
<span lang="he" dir="rtl"> שלום</span> (meaning hello), which
needs to be set to read right-to-left.</p>
```

The `dir` attribute tells the browser the direction in which the displayed text is intended to be read. The browser will render text from left to right by default, but as with the `lang` attribute, you'll need to override the intended reading direction if you're including text that runs in the opposite direction (for example, Arabic or Hebrew).

If the bulk of your document is written in English, but it features excerpts in Hebrew, the default rendering will be left to right. However, the Hebrew phrases will need to be marked up as reading right to left, or `"rtl"`. If the page were written primarily in Hebrew, then the reverse is true—the direction should be set on the `body` (p. 32) or `html` (p. 70) element as `"rtl"`, with discrete phrases in English marked up using `"ltr"`.

Using the `dir` attribute doesn't actually reverse the order of the text contained within the element to which the attribute is applied (for that, you'd need to use the bidirectional override element, or `bdo` (p. 175)); it does, however, swap the alignment of text contained in block-level elements so that each new line of text starts at the right of the screen, leaving a ragged left-hand edge.

Note that the `dir` attribute is also used to define the reading order of text or data contained in tables.

Value

"ltr" and "rtl" are the only values this attribute can take.

Compatibility

Internet Explorer			Firefox			Safari			Opera
5.5	6.0	7.0	1.0	1.5	2.0	1.3	2.0	3.0	9.2
Full	Full	Full	Full	Full	Full	Partial	Partial	Full	Full

Browser support for dir is generally good, although Safari 2 and earlier versions don't honor the changed direction of "rtl" when applied to the bdo element as they should, although they do right-align the text in block elements marked as being "rtl".

 # id

id="*identifier*"

SPEC		
deprecated	required	version
NO	NO	HTML 4
BROWSER SUPPORT		
IE5.5+	FF1+	Saf1.3+	Op9.2+
FULL	FULL	FULL	FULL

Example

The span (p. 220) element in this example may be referred to by the unique identifier "thisspan":

```
<span id="thisspan">A uniquely identifiable element.</span>
```

The id attribute provides a unique identifier for an element within the document. It may be used by an a (p. 146) element to create a hyperlink to this particular element.

This identifier may also be used in CSS code as a hook that can be used for styling purposes, or by JavaScript code (via the Document Object Model, or DOM) to make changes or add behavior to the element by referencing its unique id.

Value

The most important aspect of the id attribute is that it must be absolutely unique. Unlike the class (p. 498) attribute, which may apply the same value to many elements in a page, an `id` that's applied to an element must not match an `id` used anywhere else on the same page.

The `id` attribute value must begin with a letter in the roman alphabet (a–z or A–Z); this can be followed by any combination of letters (a–z or A–Z), digits (0–9), hyphens (-), underscores (_), colons (:), and periods (.). The `id` value is case sensitive, thus `<span id="me">This is me</span>` and `<span id="ME">This is me</a>` would be considered to be separate and uniquely identifiable elements on the same web page.

Compatibility

Internet Explorer			Firefox			Safari			Opera
5.5	6.0	7.0	1.0	1.5	2.0	1.3	2.0	3.0	9.2
Full	Full	Full	Full	Full	Full	Full	Full	Full	Full

The `id` attribute can be applied to *almost* anything (although it can't be applied to the `html` (p. 70) element in HTML4), but on its own, it doesn't affect the display of any element on a web page. Compatibility issues relate mostly to the way in which JavaScript is used to access the referenced element (this depends on differences in the ways browsers interpret the Document Object Model) and the support that different browsers provide for CSS, particularly around the topic of specificity.[3]

One notable compatibility problem with the use of the `id` attribute arises when it's used to identify a link destination on the current page:

```
<a href="#section3">Jump to section 3</a>
  ⋮
<h2 id="section3">Section 3</h2>
```

Internet Explorer will not allow the user to activate the link to jump to the section identified on the page; it requires another `a` element as an anchor. What often results is this kind of approach:

---

[3] http://reference.sitepoint.com/css/specificity/

Common Attributes

```
<a href="#section3">Jump to section 3</a>
    ⋮
<h2><a href="#section3" name="section3"
    id="section3"></a>Section 3</h2>
```

As you can see, both the `name` and `id` attributes are used (the `href` is repeated in order to fix a keyboard navigation bug in IE; without it, activating that link with the keyboard won't set the focus at the correct part of the page).

lang

`lang="language code"`

SPEC		
deprecated	required	version
NO	NO	HTML 4
BROWSER SUPPORT			
IE5.5+	FF1+	Saf1.3+	Op9.2+
PARTIAL	PARTIAL	PARTIAL	PARTIAL

Example

This markup specifies the language of a page as English:

```
<html lang="en">
```

The `lang` attribute is used to identify the language of the content on a web page, when it's applied to the `html` element, or within a given section on a web page, when it's applied to a `div`, `span`, `a`, or any other element that may contain content in a language that differs from that used on the rest of the page. Changing the language at a lower level in the document tree overrides the language code that's set higher up, but *only* for the nested element to which the different language code is applied.

The intention of the `lang` attribute is to allow browsers (and other user agents) to adjust their displays. For example, if you use the `q` (p. 204) element, a browser should be able to identify the language in use and present the appropriate style of quotation marks. In practice, though, poor support for the `q` element sees few developers use it—instead, many hard-code quotation marks. This is something of a catch-22 situation.

The `lang` attribute is helpful to users of assistive technology such as screen readers that can adjust the pronunciation depending on the language used. For example, the word *penchant*, meaning "a strong and continued inclination," is French in origin. When the screen reader JAWS encounters the word, it pronounces it similar to "pen-chunt," but when the word is marked up as `<span lang="fr">penchant</span>`, JAWS reads it using the proper French pronunciation, "pon-shont."

It may also be possible that marking up documents or sections of a document in this way benefits search engines that display results to users who have filtered their searches on the basis of language preferences. However, the way in which search engines *actually* deal with content marked up in this way is a secret they tend to keep to themselves. As such, the potential for this attribute to make content more search engine friendly should be considered little more than a lucky bonus.

Value

`lang` takes as its value approved International Standards Organisation (ISO) 2 letter language codes only (refer to the language codes reference for details[4]).

Compatibility

Internet Explorer			Firefox			Safari			Opera
5.5	6.0	7.0	1.0	1.5	2.0	1.3	2.0	3.0	9.2
Partial	Partial	Partial	Partial	Partial	Partial	Partial	Partial	Partial	Partial

As I mentioned in the description above, browsers don't provide great support for the `lang` attribute, but it offers benefits that extend beyond the browser itself (including advantages for search and assistive technology). Language should be indicated for these reasons, as well as for the purpose of forwards compatibility.

---

[4] http://reference.sitepoint.com/html/lang-codes/

style

`style="css-property:css-value;…"`

SPEC		
deprecated	required	version
NO	NO	HTML 4
BROWSER SUPPORT			
IE5.5+	FF1+	Saf1.3+	Op9.2+
FULL	FULL	FULL	FULL

Example

If you want to set a paragraph to display in blue and bold, you could use the following code:

```
<p style="color:blue;font-weight:bold;">This is a very short
    paragraph. No Booker Prize for me.</p>
```

In Cascading Style Sheets (CSS), a key feature is the cascade itself. In the cascade, styles set at different levels take different levels of importance, so a style that's set in a globally linked style sheet can be overridden by a style for the same `class` or `id` that's included in an embedded style sheet. The `style` (p. 505) attribute goes a level further, to override styles set in linked or embedded style sheets.

However, the use of the `style` attribute is generally considered to be a bad practice, as it causes the presentation to become intrinsically mixed with the content of the document—a practice that's almost as bad as using the `font` (p. 190) element to style text. One way in which you might use inline styles is to debug CSS display issues (applying the style at its lowest level in the cascade, and progressively moving higher up the cascade until the problem is isolated). You should, therefore, avoid using inline `style` attributes in your markup.

Value

The `style` attribute includes a series of CSS property and value pairs. Each `"property":"value"` pair is separated by a semicolon, just as it is when it's typed into an embedded or linked style sheet (although there should not be a carriage return after the semicolon when the pair is used inside the `style` attribute.

Compatibility

Internet Explorer			Firefox			Safari			Opera
5.5	6.0	7.0	1.0	1.5	2.0	1.3	2.0	3.0	9.2
Full	Full	Full	Full	Full	Full	Full	Full	Full	Full

Compatibility issues depend heavily on each individual browser's CSS rendering capabilities. All the browsers listed support the `style` attribute, and thus allow the addition of inline styles using the `style` attribute.

title

`title="string"`

SPEC		
deprecated	required	version
NO	NO	HTML 4
BROWSER SUPPORT		
IE5.5+	FF1+	Saf1.3+	Op9.2+
FULL	FULL	FULL	FULL

Example

The `abbr` and `acronym` elements use the `title` attribute to provide the full wording for the abbreviation (it's a required attribute for these elements):

```
<div>The <abbr title="Americans with Disabilities Act">ADA</abbr>
    is there for your protection.</div>
<div>This pub is rated highly by <acronym title="Campaign for Real
    Ale">CAMRA</acronym>.</div>
```

A link may include a `title` attribute, which may offer extra help to a user, and can be enhanced or made more obvious with the use of a JavaScript technique:

```
<a href="minutes.html" title="Minutes cover topics discussed,
    including refuse collection, housing taxes and social care
    policies">June meeting minutes</a>
```

The `title` attribute allows the author to provide extra information about any element on a page. Typically, this attribute's content is rendered as a tooltip that appears when the user hovers the cursor over the element to which the `title` is applied. It's most frequently used for the a (p. 146) element, to provide additional information about the link destination. It also appears within form elements, perhaps to offer tips about the format that data is preferred in (for example, date formats), and it is a required attribute for the `abbr` (p. 164) and `acronym` (p. 168) elements, as it's used to provide the expanded version of the abbreviations contained in those elements.

The way in which browsers have traditionally rendered `title` content—in a tooltip that appears as users mouse over the element in question—has encouraged many developers to use it as a space-saving mechanism. They see it as a way to provide help without cluttering up the page with extra words, and to make content easy to find if a user pauses for thought while mousing over a given element. However, this is not a good technique, for several reasons:

- Not everyone uses a mouse, and few browsers render the tooltip content if the user has tabbed to that element with the keyboard.
- The tooltip content doesn't appear for long in all browsers. It times out after a short while, which can potentially prevent the user from reading it properly (Opera's treatment of the tooltip is the exception to this rule).
- The tooltip content is often truncated, so it may not be possible to convey the desired information in the space provided.
- Users who are having difficulty with a section on a page may not move their cursor over that specific section, so they may not see the tooltip at all.
- The nature of the tooltip means that it's not possible for the user to print out the content contained inside the `title`, nor is there any way of copying and pasting that text anywhere.

As such, the `title` attribute should be considered as one that can be used to offer additional information, but it shouldn't be *relied* upon. If you have key information to present to the user, it should be written directly into the document for all to see—don't rely on the browser to display it on the fly.

Value

Any value can appear within this attribute, but given the problems associated with the ways browsers present this information, it's good practice to keep the information concise. This will increase your chances of having the content read by the user.

Common Attributes

Compatibility

Internet Explorer			Firefox			Safari			Opera
5.5	6.0	7.0	1.0	1.5	2.0	1.3	2.0	3.0	9.2
Full	Full	Full	Full	Full	Full	Full	Full	Full	Full

Every browser listed supports this attribute.

xml:lang

```
xml:lang="language code"
```

SPEC		
deprecated	required	version
NO	NO	XHTML 1.0
BROWSER SUPPORT			
IE5.5+	FF1+	Saf1.3+	Op9.2+
PARTIAL	PARTIAL	PARTIAL	PARTIAL

Example

This example specifies the language of an XHTML Strict document as English:

```
<html xmlns="http://www.w3.org/1999/xhtml" xml:lang="en" lang="en">
```

The `xml:lang` attribute is identical in its usage and purpose to the `lang` attribute (p. 503), but with one difference: it must be applied within documents that use an XHTML doctype (p. 6).

It may be that this attribute is used only once in a document—for example, in the root element `html`—but it may be used to indicate a change of language anywhere within a document:

```
<p>I told the guy in the best French I could muster:
   "<span lang="fr" xml:lang="fr">Mais j'ai oublié
   mes pantalons</span>" and hoped for the best.</p>
```

Value

This attribute takes approved International Standards Organisation (ISO) 2 letter language codes only (refer to the language codes reference for details[5]).

---

[5] http://reference.sitepoint.com/html/lang-codes/

Compatibility

Internet Explorer			Firefox			Safari			Opera
5.5	6.0	7.0	1.0	1.5	2.0	1.3	2.0	3.0	9.2
Partial	Partial	Partial	Partial	Partial	Partial	Partial	Partial	Partial	Partial

As I mentioned in the description above, browsers don't offer great support for the `lang` attribute, but its benefits extend beyond the browser itself (for instance, in terms of search and assistive technology). Language should be indicated for these reasons, as well as for the purposes of forwards compatibility.

Event Attributes

This reference covers event attributes that would be used to capture an event, and trigger an action with a client-side scripting language such as JavaScript.

A note of caution, though. You might intend to apply any of these inline event handlers like so:

```
<span onmouseover="showhoverhelp">view details</span>
```

However, this is *no longer a recommended technique*, as it mixes the document's structure and content (the HTML) with the behavior (JavaScript). The preferred option is to use unobtrusive JavaScript, which negates the need for inline event handlers of this type, and keeps the document structure and content layers separate from its behavior.

onblur

`onblur="script"`

SPEC	
required	version
NO	HTML 4
BROWSER SUPPORT			
IE5.5+	FF1+	Saf1.3+	Op9.2+
FULL	FULL	FULL	FULL

Example

In this example, the `onblur` event calls a function called `validate`:

```
<input type="text" title="Date format = DD/MM/YYYY"
    onfocus="revealTitleHelp();" onblur="validate(this.value);"
    name="dateofbirth"/>
```

As with many of the other event attributes, this is the counterpart of another attribute: `onblur` is the opposite of the `onfocus` (p. 515) attribute. It captures the moment that an element loses focus either because the user has used the **tab** key to move to the next element on the page, or has placed the cursor in another section of the page.

`onblur` is most often used with form validation code. When the user leaves a form field, the `onblur` attribute is used to call a piece of script that performs some sort of validation on the field to make sure that the correct data was entered, rather than leaving all the validation to execute at the form's end.

Value

This attribute has no fixed value. It's up to the author to decide on the scripting that's included here, be that a call to one or more defined functions, or a simple `alert()` statement.

Compatibility

Internet Explorer			Firefox			Safari			Opera
5.5	6.0	7.0	1.0	1.5	2.0	1.3	2.0	3.0	9.2
Full	Full	Full	Full	Full	Full	Full	Full	Full	Full

Every browser listed supports this attribute. However, it should be avoided as it encourages the mixing of content and behavior.

onchange

`onchange="script"`

SPEC		
deprecated	required	version
NO	NO	HTML 4
BROWSER SUPPORT		
IE5.5+	FF1+	Saf1.3+	Op9.2+
FULL	FULL	FULL	FULL

Example

In this example, the `onchange` event calls the `checkStockAvailability` function:

```
<input name="orderAmount" size="2" onchange="checkStockAvailability();"/>
```

The `onchange` attribute is used only within the context of a `form` (p. 243). It can be applied to an `input` (p. 253), a `textarea` (p. 306), or a `select` (p. 296) control to identify when the value of one of those elements is changed either by the user directly, or as a result of some scripting on the page.

Value

This attribute has no fixed value. It's up to the author to decide on the scripting that's included here, be that a call to one or more defined functions, or a simple `alert()` statement.

Compatibility

Internet Explorer			Firefox			Safari			Opera
5.5	6.0	7.0	1.0	1.5	2.0	1.3	2.0	3.0	9.2
Full	Full	Full	Full	Full	Full	Full	Full	Full	Full

Every browser listed supports this attribute. However, it should be avoided as it encourages the mixing of content and behavior.

Common Attributes

onclick

`onclick="script"`

SPEC		
deprecated	required	version
NO	NO	HTML 4
BROWSER SUPPORT			
IE5.5+	FF1+	Saf1.3+	Op9.2+
FULL	FULL	FULL	FULL

Example

Clicking anywhere on the `div` below will call a function, defined elsewhere, called `showStats()`:

```
<div onclick="showStats();">Figures for February's racing.</div>
```

The `onclick` event handler captures a click event from the users' mouse button on the element to which the `onclick` attribute is applied. This action usually results in a call to a script method such as a JavaScript function, like this:

```
onclick="displayHelpInfo();"
```

However, it can also be used to run a script in situ:

```
onclick="alert('You are clicking on me');"
```

Value

This attribute has no fixed value. It's up to the author to decide on the scripting that's included here, be that a call to one or more defined functions, or a simple `alert()` statement.

However, the likely values will be similar to this:

```
onclick="doMyFunction();"
```

You could also specify a value like this:

```
onclick="doThisFunction();thenDoTheOtherFunction();"
```

You may also use a value like this:

Common Attributes

```
onclick="alert('Hello world');window.close();"
```

Note that you can string several functions together, separating them with a semicolon, as shown in the second and third examples above.

Compatibility

Internet Explorer			Firefox			Safari			Opera
5.5	6.0	7.0	1.0	1.5	2.0	1.3	2.0	3.0	9.2
Full	Full	Full	Full	Full	Full	Full	Full	Full	Full

Every browser listed supports this attribute. However, it should be avoided as it encourages the mixing of content and behavior.

ondblclick

```
ondblclick="script"
```

SPEC		
deprecated	required	version
NO	NO	HTML 4
BROWSER SUPPORT		
IE5.5+	FF1+	Saf1.3+	Op9.2+
FULL	FULL	FULL	FULL

Example

Here, the `ondblclick` event handler calls a function called `openFile`:

```
ondblclick="openFile(this.id);"
```

It can also be used to run a script in situ:

```
ondblclick="alert('My, you are a quick clicker');"
```

The `ondblclick` event handler captures a double-click event from the user's mouse button on the element to which the `ondblclick` attribute is applied. This will usually result in a call to a script method such as a JavaScript function. Note that the `onclick` (p. 512) event handler will fire before the `ondblclick` event handler.

Value

This attribute has no fixed value. It's up to the author to decide on the scripting that's included here, be that a call to one or more defined functions, or a simple `alert()` statement.

However, the likely values will be similar to this:

```
ondblclick="doMyFunction();"
```

You could also specify a value like this:

```
ondblclick="doThisFunction();thenDoTheOtherFunction();"
```

You may also use a value like this:

```
ondblclick="alert('Hello, double-clickers of the world. You only
➥needed to click once, you know.');window.close();"
```

Note that you can string several functions together, separating them with a semicolon, as shown in the second and third examples above.

Compatibility

Internet Explorer			Firefox			Safari			Opera
5.5	6.0	7.0	1.0	1.5	2.0	1.3	2.0	3.0	9.2
Full	Full	Full	Full	Full	Full	Full	Full	Full	Full

Every browser listed supports this attribute. However, it should be avoided as it encourages the mixing of content and behavior.

onfocus

`onfocus="script"`

SPEC		
deprecated	required	version
NO	NO	HTML 4
BROWSER SUPPORT			
IE5.5+	FF1+	Saf1.3+	Op9.2+
FULL	FULL	FULL	FULL

Example

The `input` below uses the `onfocus` attribute to trigger a piece of JavaScript. This script performs a little magic with the content found in the `title` attribute when the user tabs to that particular form input, or places the cursor inside the text field:

```
<input type="text" title="Date format = DD/MM/YYYY"
    onfocus="revealTitleHelp();" name="dateofbirth" />
```

The `onfocus` attribute captures the moment when an element receives the focus of the user's attention. This is determined to be the point at which a user clicks inside an element that can be activated or manipulated, such as a form `input` (p. 253) element or `select` (p. 296) element, both of which are used for data entry purposes, or an `a` (p. 146) element, which can be activated with the **Return** key.

Typically, this attribute is used to highlight the section of the page that currently has focus—a useful usability enhancement, particularly for people with low vision—or to provide additional information. For example, when a user's completing a form, additional help text can be made to appear alongside the form `input` that currently has focus.

Value

This attribute has no fixed value. It's up to the author to decide on the scripting that's included here, be that a call to one or more defined functions, or a simple `alert()` statement.

Compatibility

Internet Explorer			Firefox			Safari			Opera
5.5	6.0	7.0	1.0	1.5	2.0	1.3	2.0	3.0	9.2
Full	Full	Full	Full	Full	Full	Full	Full	Full	Full

Every browser listed supports this attribute. However, it should be avoided as it encourages the mixing of content and behavior.

onkeydown

`onkeydown="script"`

SPEC	
required	version
NO	HTML 4
BROWSER SUPPORT			
IE5.5+	FF1+	Saf1.3+	Op9.2+
FULL	FULL	FULL	FULL

Example

This attribute may be used when a key that's being held down continuously has some kind of timer effect—for example, the user presses the space key until an activity on screen is completed (releasing the key may cause the action to pause)—like so:

```
<body onkeydown="increasePower();"/>
```

The `onkeydown` event handler captures the moment that a key is pressed down but has not yet been released. The release of the key is captured by the `onkeyup` (p. 518) and `onkeypress` (p. 517) attributes.

Value

This attribute has no fixed value. It's up to the author to decide on the scripting that's included here, be that a call to one or more defined functions, or a simple `alert()` statement.

Compatibility

Internet Explorer			Firefox			Safari			Opera
5.5	6.0	7.0	1.0	1.5	2.0	1.3	2.0	3.0	9.2
Full	Full	Full	Full	Full	Full	Full	Full	Full	Full

Every browser listed supports this attribute. However, it should be avoided as it encourages the mixing of content and behavior.

onkeypress

`onkeypress="script"`

SPEC		
deprecated	required	version
NO	NO	HTML 4
BROWSER SUPPORT		
IE5.5+ FF1+ Saf1.3+ Op9.2+		
FULL	FULL FULL	FULL

Common Attributes

Example

In the example below, the `onkeypress` attribute triggers a piece of JavaScript that runs some kind of availability check, such as one to ensure that as each letter is typed, the user is provided with feedback.

```
<input type="text" onkeypress="checkAvailability();" name="domain_name"
    id="domain_name"/>
```

The `onkeypress` event handler captures a completed key-press-and-release sequence (equivalent to `onkeydown` (p. 516) followed by `onkeyup` (p. 518)) while the element to which the attribute is applied has focus.

Value

This attribute has no fixed value. It's up to the author to decide on the scripting that's included here, be that a call to one or more defined functions, or a simple `alert()` statement.

Compatibility

Internet Explorer			Firefox			Safari			Opera
5.5	6.0	7.0	1.0	1.5	2.0	1.3	2.0	3.0	9.2
Full	Full	Full	Full	Full	Full	Full	Full	Full	Full

Every browser listed supports this attribute. However, it should be avoided as it encourages the mixing of content and behavior.

onkeyup

onkeyup="*script*"

SPEC		
deprecated	required	version
NO	NO	HTML 4
BROWSER SUPPORT			
IE5.5+	FF1+	Saf1.3+	Op9.2+
FULL	FULL	FULL	FULL

Example

This attribute might be used in a case in which, for example, the user presses the space key until an activity on screen is completed; when the user releases the key, onkeyup may be used to pause the action, like so:

```
<body onkeydown="increasePower();" onkeyup="holdPowerLevel();"/>
```

The onkeyup event handler captures the moment at which a previously pressed key is released while focus is on the element to which the onkeyup attribute is applied. Note that a keydown event followed by a keyup event automatically generates a keypress event, which can be captured using the onkeydown (p. 516), onkeyup, and onkeypress (p. 517) attributes.

Value

This attribute has no fixed value. It's up to the author to decide on the scripting that's included here, be that a call to one or more defined functions, or a simple alert() statement.

Compatibility

Internet Explorer			Firefox			Safari			Opera
5.5	6.0	7.0	1.0	1.5	2.0	1.3	2.0	3.0	9.2
Full	Full	Full	Full	Full	Full	Full	Full	Full	Full

Every browser listed supports this attribute. However, it should be avoided as it encourages the mixing of content and behavior.

onload

`onload="script"`

SPEC		
deprecated	required	version
NO	NO	HTML 4
BROWSER SUPPORT		
IE5.5+	FF1+	Saf1.3+	Op9.2+
FULL	FULL	FULL	FULL

Example

When `onload` is used as an inline attribute, it's most frequently applied to the `body` element, as shown below:

```
<body onload="initialiseHoverEffects();">
```

The `onload` event is used to trigger an action once a web page has completely loaded all content and, importantly, all of the external resources that the page calls in (including images, script files, CSS files, and so on).

It may also be used in the context of `framesets` to indicate that the child `frame` elements have finished loading.

Value

This attribute has no fixed value. It's up to the author to decide on the scripting that's included here, be that a call to one or more defined functions, or a simple `alert()` statement.

Compatibility

Internet Explorer			Firefox			Safari			Opera
5.5	6.0	7.0	1.0	1.5	2.0	1.3	2.0	3.0	9.2
Full	Full	Full	Full	Full	Full	Full	Full	Full	Full

Every browser listed supports this attribute. However, it should be avoided as it encourages the mixing of content and behavior.

onmousedown

`onmousedown="script"`

SPEC		
deprecated	required	version
NO	NO	HTML 4
BROWSER SUPPORT			
IE5.5+	FF1+	Saf1.3+	Op9.2+
FULL	FULL	FULL	FULL

Example

The event handler for the `onmousedown` event calls the function `highlightThis`:

```
<div onmousedown="highlightThis();">Holiday dates for 2008</div>
```

The `onmousedown` attribute is similar to the `onclick` attribute, but differs in that the event is triggered the moment the mouse button is pressed on the element, rather than at the point at which the mouse button is released (`onclick` is effectively a combination of `onmousedown` and `onmouseup` event on the element in question). This event isn't often seen in practice, possibly because it can so easily cause events to be triggered accidentally. If you're using an `onclick` event, the user can move the cursor off the element, release the mouse button, and avoid triggering the action if it was an accidental button press; this is not the case with `onmousedown`.

Value

This attribute has no fixed value. It's up to the author to decide on the scripting that's included here, be that a call to one or more defined functions, or a simple `alert()` statement.

Compatibility

Internet Explorer			Firefox			Safari			Opera
5.5	6.0	7.0	1.0	1.5	2.0	1.3	2.0	3.0	9.2
Full	Full	Full	Full	Full	Full	Full	Full	Full	Full

Every browser listed supports this attribute. However, it should be avoided as it encourages the mixing of content and behavior.

onmousemove

`onmousemove="script"`

SPEC		
deprecated	required	version
NO	NO	HTML 4
BROWSER SUPPORT			
IE5.5+	FF1+	Saf1.3+	Op9.2+
FULL	FULL	FULL	FULL

Example

This example calls the *updatePosition* function:

```
<div onmousedown="grabItem();" onmousemove="updatePosition();">Notepad -
    drag me around the screen, make notes as you go … </div>
```

The `onmousemove` event handler is used to identify any movement of the mouse in any direction, irrespective of any mouse button actions. It's most often used in JavaScript-based drag-and-drop-style interfaces in which an object on the screen is manipulated—the `onmousemove` attribute would be used to identify the cursor's change in position on the screen and move the object accordingly, but as with any of these event handlers, its use is up to the developer.

Value

This attribute has no fixed value. It's up to the author to decide on the scripting that's included here, be that a call to one or more defined functions, or a simple `alert()` statement.

Compatibility

Internet Explorer			Firefox			Safari			Opera
5.5	6.0	7.0	1.0	1.5	2.0	1.3	2.0	3.0	9.2
Full	Full	Full	Full	Full	Full	Full	Full	Full	Full

Every browser listed supports this attribute. However, it should be avoided as it encourages the mixing of content and behavior.

Common Attributes

onmouseout

`onmouseout="`*`script`*`"`

	SPEC	
deprecated	required	version
NO	NO	HTML 4
BROWSER SUPPORT		
IE5.5+ FF1+	Saf1.3+	Op9.2+
FULL FULL	FULL	FULL

Example

The example below shows a simple image swap technique, whereby moving the mouse away from the image causes the original image to be reinstated:

```
<div>
  <img src="map.gif" alt="Hover to reveal the location on the map"
      onmouseover="this.src='map_location_revealed.gif';"
      onmouseout="this.src='map.gif';"/>Figures for February's racing.
</div>
```

The `onmouseout` attribute is the "partner" attribute to the commonly used `onmouseover` (p. 523) attribute. It captures the moment that a mouse pointer crosses the boundary of an element, moving from the inside to the outside of the element to which the attribute is applied.

`onmouseout` is mostly used for resetting a visual effect that was previously applied by the `onmouseover` attribute—for example, reinstating the default state of an image that was swapped for a new image.

Value

This attribute has no fixed value. It's up to the author to decide on the scripting that's included here, be that a call to one or more defined functions, or a simple `alert()` statement.

Compatibility

Internet Explorer			Firefox			Safari			Opera
5.5	6.0	7.0	1.0	1.5	2.0	1.3	2.0	3.0	9.2
Full	Full	Full	Full	Full	Full	Full	Full	Full	Full

Every browser listed supports this attribute. However, it should be avoided as it encourages the mixing of content and behavior.

onmouseover

`onmouseover="`*`script`*`"`

	SPEC		
deprecated	required		version
NO	NO		HTML 4
BROWSER SUPPORT			
IE5.5+	FF1+	Saf1.3+	Op9.2+
FULL	FULL	FULL	FULL

Example

The example below shows a simple image swap technique, whereby mousing over the image causes the image to change to one that reveals a location on a map:

```
<div>
   <img src="map.gif" alt="Hover to reveal the location on the map"
      onmouseover="this.src='map_location_revealed.gif';"
      onmouseout="this.src='map.gif';"/>Figures for February's racing.
</div>
```

The `onmouseover` attribute is one of the most commonly used event attributes. It captures the moment that a cursor crosses the boundary of an element, moving from outside to inside the element to which the attribute is applied. It differs from the `onmousemove` (p. 521) attribute, which is used to detect movement within the element's boundaries. Once the cursor is positioned over the element, the `onmouseover` event remains active until the cursor is moved beyond the element's boundaries—an event that the `onmouseout` (p. 522) attribute would capture.

The `onmouseover` attribute is mostly used to render visual effects such as image swapping or color changes, and has been used in this way for almost as long as JavaScript has been around.

Value

This attribute has no fixed value. It's up to the author to decide on the scripting that's included here, be that a call to one or more defined functions, or a simple `alert()` statement.

Compatibility

Internet Explorer			Firefox			Safari			Opera
5.5	6.0	7.0	1.0	1.5	2.0	1.3	2.0	3.0	9.2
Full	Full	Full	Full	Full	Full	Full	Full	Full	Full

Every browser listed supports this attribute. However, it should be avoided as it encourages the mixing of content and behavior.

onmouseup

`onmouseup="script"`

SPEC		
deprecated	required	version
NO	NO	HTML 4
BROWSER SUPPORT			
IE5.5+	FF1+	Saf1.3+	Op9.2+
FULL	FULL	FULL	FULL

Example

The event handler for `onmouseup` event calls the function `unHighlightThis`:

```
<div onmouseup="highlightThis();" onmouseup="unHighlightThis();">Holiday
    dates for 2008</div>
```

The `onmouseup` attribute is the counterpart to the `onmousedown` attribute. It triggers an event when the user releases the mouse button while the cursor is positioned over the element to which the attribute is applied. Just as `onmousedown` is not greatly used, its partner `onmouseup` isn't common.

Value

This attribute has no fixed value. It's up to the author to decide on the scripting that's included here, be that a call to one or more defined functions, or a simple `alert()` statement.

Compatibility

Internet Explorer			Firefox			Safari			Opera
5.5	6.0	7.0	1.0	1.5	2.0	1.3	2.0	3.0	9.2
Full	Full	Full	Full	Full	Full	Full	Full	Full	Full

Every browser listed supports this attribute. However, it should be avoided as it encourages the mixing of content and behavior.

onreset

`onreset="script"`

SPEC		
deprecated	required	version
NO	NO	HTML 4
BROWSER SUPPORT		
IE5.5+	FF1+	Saf1.3+	Op9.2+
FULL	FULL	FULL	FULL

Example

If the `form` must have a **Reset** button, a good use of the `onreset` attribute would be to check whether the user *really* wanted to clear the form details:

```
<form name="frmPersonalDetails" action="/personal.php"
    onsubmit="checkPersonalDetails();"
    onreset="checkIfReallyWantToReset();"> : </form>
```

The `onreset` attribute is used only within the context of forms, and is applied directly to the `form` (p. 243) element. When the user activates the form's **Reset** button (if indeed it has one), the event is captured by this attribute, and can be used for whatever purpose the developer chooses.

Note that this attribute is used less commonly these days. **Reset** buttons on forms themselves have become increasingly rare, since they make it all too easy to accidentally wipe out all the details the user has spent time entering.

Value

This attribute has no fixed value. It's up to the author to decide on the scripting that's included here, be that a call to one or more defined functions, or a simple `alert()` statement.

Compatibility

Internet Explorer			Firefox			Safari			Opera
5.5	6.0	7.0	1.0	1.5	2.0	1.3	2.0	3.0	9.2
Full	Full	Full	Full	Full	Full	Full	Full	Full	Full

Every browser listed supports this attribute. However, it should be avoided as it encourages the mixing of content and behavior.

Common Attributes

onselect

`onselect="script"`

SPEC		
deprecated	required	version
NO	NO	HTML 4
BROWSER SUPPORT			
IE5.5+	FF1+	Saf1.3+	Op9.2+
FULL	FULL	FULL	FULL

Example

This attribute might be used when the users have submitted a `form` (p. 243) and are presented with something that they then need to copy in order to use—for example, some code to paste into their web page. The form control (`input` or `textarea`) could use the `onselect` attribute to trigger some kind of JavaScript function that would automatically copy the text and notify the user that it was saved to the clipboard, ready for them to paste:

```
<textarea rows="10" name="generatedCode"
    onselect="copyToClipBoard();">Text content inside the
    textarea</textarea>
```

The `onselect` attribute is used in forms, specifically on the text `input` (p. 253) and `textarea` (p. 306) form controls. When the user selects any text inside these elements, either by clicking and dragging the cursor, or using keyboard text selection commands (such as pressing Shift + Right arrow key), the `onselect` attribute captures this event.

Value

This attribute has no fixed value. It's up to the author to decide on the scripting that's included here, be that a call to one or more defined functions, or a simple `alert()` statement.

Compatibility

Internet Explorer			Firefox			Safari			Opera
5.5	6.0	7.0	1.0	1.5	2.0	1.3	2.0	3.0	9.2
Full	Full	Full	Full	Full	Full	Full	Full	Full	Full

Every browser listed supports this attribute. However, it should be avoided as it encourages the mixing of content and behavior.

onsubmit

`onsubmit="script"`

SPEC		
deprecated	required	version
NO	NO	HTML 4
BROWSER SUPPORT		
IE5.5+	FF1+	Saf1.3+	Op9.2+
FULL	FULL	FULL	FULL

Common Attributes

Example

This attribute is used almost exclusively for the purpose of running form validation scripts. In such scenarios, the user fills in the form and clicks submit, at which point the `onsubmit` attribute triggers the form validation routine, and the form is either submitted, or cancelled because of an error of which the user is alerted:

```
<form name="frmPersonalDetails" action="/personal.php"
    onsubmit="checkPersonalDetails();"> ⋮ </form>
```

The `onsubmit` attribute is used on the `form` (p. 243) element only. Its purpose is to capture the moment when the form is submitted, following the moment when the user activates the form's **Submit** button.

Value

This attribute has no fixed value. It's up to the author to decide on the scripting that's included here, be that a call to one or more defined functions, or a simple `alert()` statement.

Compatibility

Internet Explorer			Firefox			Safari			Opera
5.5	6.0	7.0	1.0	1.5	2.0	1.3	2.0	3.0	9.2
Full	Full	Full	Full	Full	Full	Full	Full	Full	Full

Every browser listed supports this attribute. However, it should be avoided as it encourages the mixing of content and behavior.

 # onunload

`onunload="script"`

	SPEC	
deprecated	required	version
NO	NO	HTML 4
BROWSER SUPPORT			
IE5.5+	FF1+	Saf1.3+	Op9.2+
FULL	FULL	FULL	FULL

Example

When used as an inline attribute, `onunload` is most frequently applied to the `body` element, as shown below:

```
<body onunload="sayGoodbye();">
```

The `onunload` event is used to trigger an action once a web page has unloaded (or the browser window has been closed)—effectively, the point at which the visitor to that page has navigated away by following a link, submitting a form, or using some other mechanism that causes a new page to be loaded in its place.

It may also be used in the context of `frameset`s to indicate that the child `frame` elements have unloaded or been replaced with new documents.

Value

This attribute has no fixed value. It's up to the author to decide on the scripting that's included here, be that a call to one or more defined functions, or a simple `alert()` statement.

Compatibility

Internet Explorer			Firefox			Safari			Opera
5.5	6.0	7.0	1.0	1.5	2.0	1.3	2.0	3.0	9.2
Full	Full	Full	Full	Full	Full	Full	Full	Full	Full

Every browser listed supports this attribute. However, it should be avoided as it encourages the mixing of content and behavior.

Deprecated Elements

The following elements are all deprecated, which means that they've been removed from later revisions of the HTML standards. Their use should now be avoided, but these elements are still well supported:

Appendix B

Proprietary & Nonstandard Elements

The following elements aren't deprecated (p. 529)—they haven't been removed from the HTML standards. In fact, none of the elements below have ever been defined by any standards. Their use should be avoided, wherever practically possible:

Appendix

C

Alphabetic Element Index

This is a complete, alphabetical list of the HTML elements contained in this reference:

THE ULTIMATE

CSS

REFERENCE

Tommy Olsson & Paul O'Brien

THE PRINCIPLES OF
BEAUTIFUL
WEB DESIGN

BY **JASON BEAIRD**

DESIGN BEAUTIFUL WEB SITES USING THIS SIMPLE STEP-BY-STEP GUIDE

SIMPLY
JAVASCRIPT

BY **KEVIN YANK**
& CAMERON ADAMS

THE CSS
ANTHOLOGY
101 ESSENTIAL TIPS, TRICKS & HACKS

BY **RACHEL ANDREW**

2ND EDITION